Dr. Sun has developed her innovative ACQS model of addiction treatment into a comprehensive text that will be a valuable resource for potential and current clinicians. A thorough and well-researched presentation on a complex subject.

—Gary L. Fisher, Professor, Center for the Application of Substance Abuse Technologies, University of Nevada, Reno

Treating Addictions: The Four Components by Dr. An-Pyng Sun provides a comprehensive approach to understanding and treating people with addictions. It provides a conceptual framework focusing on four essential components: the fundamentals of addiction, co-occurring disorders, quality of life, and macro factors. In addition to providing a critical, easy-to-read description of each of these components, each chapter offers concrete strategies of helping individuals impacted by the above issues. It is a valuable addition to the libraries of students and clinicians new to the field of addictions. I recommend it highly.

—S. Lala A. Straussner, LCSW, Professor and Director, Post-Master's Program in the Clinical Approaches to the Addictions, New York University, and Founding Editor, *Journal of Social Work Practice in the Addictions*

Dr. Sun has written a book that is well-researched and comprehensive in its approach to educating the reader about addiction. As a co-founder of a residential treatment program for Internet addicts, I can confirm that her holistic ACQS model is excellent. I love that she captures, with compassion, the struggles of addicts and leads the reader to see, as she does, what is needed to effectively address treatment. Thankfully, she understands that behaviors can be just as addictive as substances. Her writing is easy to read and eloquent.

—Hilarie Cash, PhD, LMHC, CSAT, Chief Clinical Officer and Education Director, reSTART Life, LLC

Treating Addictions: The Four Components is a timely and masterfully organized book. It is an ideal introductory textbook to those interested in addiction while offering much needed advanced content through its "four components." It integrates theory, practice, research, and policy into a comprehensive and intellectually stimulating approach to addiction.

—Flavio F. Marsiglia, Regents' Professor, Social Work, and Director, Global Center for Applied Health Research, Arizona State University

Treating Addictions

Treating Addictions: The Four Components offers a unique and coherent understanding of addiction. The book begins with a chapter discussing the framework of addiction and the four essential components of treatments—the fundamentals of addiction, co-occurring disorders, quality of life, and macro factors—and subsequent chapters elaborate on each component. Most currently available addiction treatment books present knowledge and skills in separate chapters and fail to integrate all chapters within a single framework that can weave all concepts into a meaningful tapestry. Using a unified framework, this book offers students a comprehensive skill set for treating addictions.

An-Pyng Sun, PhD, is a licensed clinical social worker (LCSW) and a licensed clinical alcohol and drug counselor (LCADC). She is Professor of Social Work at University of Nevada Las Vegas (UNLV). Dr. Sun specializes in addiction treatments; her research and teaching at UNLV focus on addiction treatments, multicultural practice, and research methods.

Treating Addictions

The Four Components

An-Pyng Sun

NEW YORK AND LONDON

First published 2018
by Routledge
711 Third Avenue, New York, NY 10017

and by Routledge
2 Park Square, Milton Park, Abingdon, Oxon, OX14 4RN

Routledge is an imprint of the Taylor & Francis Group, an informa business

© 2018 Taylor & Francis

The right of An-Pyng Sun to be identified as author of this work has been
asserted by her in accordance with sections 77 and 78 of the Copyright,
Designs and Patents Act 1988.

All rights reserved. No part of this book may be reprinted or reproduced or
utilised in any form or by any electronic, mechanical, or other means, now
known or hereafter invented, including photocopying and recording, or in any
information storage or retrieval system, without permission in writing from
the publishers.

Trademark notice: Product or corporate names may be trademarks or registered
trademarks, and are used only for identification and explanation without intent
to infringe.

Library of Congress Cataloging-in-Publication Data
Names: Sun, An-Pyng, author.
Title: Treating addictions : the four components / An-Pyng Sun.
Description: New York, NY : Routledge, 2018. | Includes bibliographical
   references and index.
Identifiers: LCCN 2018005210 (print) | LCCN 2018010581 (ebook) | ISBN
   9781315679228 (Master Ebook) | ISBN 9781317393542 (Web pdf) |
   ISBN 9781317393535 (ePub) | ISBN 9781317393528 (Mobipocket) |
   ISBN 9781138932487 (hbk.) | ISBN 9781138932500 (pbk.) | ISBN
   9781315679228 (ebk.)
Subjects: LCSH: Substance abuse—Treatment. | Substance abuse—
   Relapse—Prevention.
Classification: LCC RC564 (ebook) | LCC RC564 .S86 2018 (print) | DDC
   616.86/06—dc23
LC record available at https://lccn.loc.gov/2018005210

ISBN: 978-1-138-93248-7 (hbk)
ISBN: 978-1-138-93250-0 (pbk)
ISBN: 978-1-315-67922-8 (ebk)

Typeset in Adobe Caslon and Copperplate
by Apex CoVantage, LLC

To my mother, Kwei-In Chang Sun, with love and gratitude.

CONTENTS

PREFACE   XIII

CHAPTER 1   INTRODUCTION: THE ACQS MODEL: CONSIDERING ADDICTION, CO-OCCURRING DISORDERS, QUALITY OF LIFE, AND SOCIAL FACTORS   1

PART I   **25**

CHAPTER 2   THE FUNDAMENTALS OF ADDICTION   27

The Phenomenological/Clinical Features   27
The Genetic Factor   29
The Neurobiological Processes   30
    Substance Use Disorder Involves a Spectrum   31
    The Severe Cases' Smaller Percentage Should Not
        Negate the Study of Brain Disease Model   34
    A Brain Disease Model Does Not Necessarily Dismiss
        the Importance of the Quality-of-Life Factor   35

CHAPTER 3   ADDICTION AND THE CO-OCCURRING DISORDERS   53

Chronic Pain and Addiction   58
Schizophrenia and Addiction   60
Mood Disorders and Addiction   68
Posttraumatic Stress Disorder (PTSD) and Addiction   73
    Prolonged Exposure Therapy and COPE   75
    Non-Exposure-Based Treatments   76

CONTENTS

	Attention Deficit/Hyperactivity Disorder (ADHD) / Autism Spectrum Disorder (ASD) and Addiction	80
	Personality Disorder and Addiction	88
CHAPTER 4	ADDICTION AND QUALITY OF LIFE	102
	Addiction and Material Poverty	107
	The Linkage Between Addiction and Poverty/SES/ Housing/Employment	107
	Strategies Targeting the Issue of Poverty-Addiction Linkage	110
	Addiction and Spiritual Poverty / Lack of Psychological Well-Being	111
	Interpersonal Relationships	112
	Trauma	120
	Purpose and Meaning in Life	134
CHAPTER 5	ADDICTION AND SOCIAL FACTORS	144
	Social Factors May Precipitate or Curb the Occurrence of Addiction	145
	The Current Prescription Opioid and Heroin Epidemic in the US	146
	The Trend of Gender Convergence in Substance Use	156
	Social and Technological Change and the Emergence of Behavioral Addiction	165
	The Legalization of Medicinal and Recreational Marijuana	173
	Social Factors Affect Quality of Addiction Treatment Service Delivery	188
	Drug Courts	189
	Methadone Clinics	191
	Subsidized Housing	193
	The Five Clocks	194
PART II		207
CHAPTER 6	SPIRITUALITY, CONNECTEDNESS, AND HOPE: THE HIGHER POWER CONCEPT, SOCIAL NETWORKS, AND INNER STRENGTHS	209
	The Higher Power Approach	212
	The Twelve Steps	213
	Spiritual Well-Being	215

The Social Network Approach — 217
Alliance Between Patients
and Clinicians — 218
Families and Other Social Support — 220
The Self-Help Groups (Twelve Step or
Non-Twelve Step) — 227
The Inner Strengths Approach — 230
Exploring and Establishing Meaning in Life — 230
Employing a Developmental Model of Recovery — 231
Teaching Patients Emotion Regulation Skills/
Dialectical Behavior Therapy — 232
Motivational Interviewing — 236
Acceptance and Commitment Therapy — 239

CHAPTER 7 WITHDRAWAL MANAGEMENT AND RELAPSE
PREVENTION: PHARMACOTHERAPY — **245**

Withdrawal Management — 247
Pharmacotherapy for Alcohol Detox — 252
Pharmacotherapy for Opioid Detox — 253
Relapse Prevention — 253
Pharmacotherapy for Relapse Prevention — 254
Issues Related to Pharmacotherapy for
Relapse Prevention — 254
Pharmacotherapy for Relapse Prevention of
Alcohol Use — 256
Pharmacotherapy for Relapse Prevention of
Opioid Use — 262

CHAPTER 8 WITHDRAWAL MANAGEMENT AND RELAPSE
PREVENTION: BEHAVIORAL THERAPY AND
PSYCHOSOCIAL TREATMENT — **287**

Withdrawal Management — 287
Relapse Prevention — 291
Functional Analysis and Skills Training — 292
Avoid Triggers and Manage Them if Unavoidable:
Classical Conditioning — 295
Engage in Cognitive Restructuring, Positive
Reappraisal, and Schema Healing — 297
Cognitive Restructuring — 298
Positive Reappraisal — 300
Schema Healing — 301

Practice Mindfulness	304
A Third Wave Behavioral Therapy	304
Definition of Mindfulness	305
Break Automatic Pilot and Habituation	306
Enhance Bottom-Up Emotion Regulation	307
Enhance Top-Down Emotion Regulation	308
Mindfulness Skills, Training, Exercises, and Practice	309
Risks of Mindfulness	310
Make Recovery More Rewarding: The Operant Conditioning	311
Why It Is Necessary and Important to Make Recovery More Rewarding	311
Barriers to Make Recovery More Rewarding	311
How to Make Recovery More Rewarding	313
Established/Evidence-Based Treatment Methods	317
Cognitive Behavioral Therapy and Schema-Focused Therapy	318
Mindfulness-Based Relapse Prevention	319
Mindfulness-Oriented Recovery Enhancement	320
Community Reinforcement Approach	321
Contingency Management/Motivational Incentives	323
APPENDIX A1 THE CRAFFT QUESTIONNAIRE—SELF ADMINISTERED	333
APPENDIX A2 THE CRAFFT QUESTIONNAIRE—CLINICIAN INTERVIEW	335
APPENDIX B THE ALCOHOL USE DISORDERS IDENTIFICATION TEST (AUDIT)—(INTERVIEW VERSION)	339
APPENDIX C THE CANNABIS USE DISORDERS IDENTIFICATION TEST—REVISED (CUDIT-R) (SELF ADMINISTRATION)	341
APPENDIX D CLINICAL INSTITUTE WITHDRAWAL ASSESSMENT FOR ALCOHOL, REVISED (CIWA-AR)	343
INDEX	347

PREFACE

Addiction is an insidious disease that causes much pain and despair in the lives of many people. No one likes addiction and no one wants to live a life afflicted with addiction, including the addicted person him- or herself. Addicted individuals are keenly aware of this when they are sober; however, when they are not sober, they can hardly see or rationally tell why addiction is destructive, or how addiction creates tremendously negative consequences and tragedies in their lives. The challenging part that creates difficulty in the context for everyone—including the addicted patients, their families and significant others, and even the clinicians—is that many addicted people's sober status is often short-lived and their sober times occur only sporadically and infrequently; during most of their addiction career, they are not sober.

The "not sober" periods can extend from intoxication, acute withdrawal, and protracted withdrawal to a lifelong struggle. Craving tends to exist even after a person stops using for a long time; relapse is always a risk. This is why addiction is considered a chronic disease. It takes repeated and prolonged exposures of alcohol, drugs, or addictive behaviors to cause neuroadaptation and neuropathway changes to the brain. Likewise, it takes time for those affected brain structures, processes, and functions to reverse to mostly, if not totally, healthy operation. In general, recovery seldom happens overnight.

Along the journey of treatment and recovery, many people are disappointed and frustrated, then give up. The family of the addicted individual is heartbroken and resents the fact that the person has taken so much from the family—materially, physically, emotionally, and spiritually—and considers the person beyond rescue. When unable to see obvious and concrete progress in the client undergoing treatment, clinicians may not only have doubts about their own efficacy in helping the client, but also come to the conclusion that the client should not "blame" others, should not be so "entitled," and should take more responsibility. The addicted person is likely to be the one most in pain. This person is in limbo, caught in a dilemma between staying in and staying out of addiction—either or both paths bring hurt, pain, and despair. Addicted individuals may subjugate themselves to remaining in addiction as an "easy way out." "This life is no life, so maybe the next life," they often say.

To help addicted individuals recover, we must facilitate opportunities for the moments and days when they are sober—as well as identify, reinforce, and prolong such time periods. We must also be patient and understanding, and never give up when they "fall off the wagon." Every individual is unique, with or without addiction. With addiction, the situation becomes even more complicated. Some addicted people may have suffered from childhood or adult trauma, psychiatric disorders, or physical ailments and pain; some may be prone to genetic susceptibility for addiction; and others may have grown up in poverty and an addiction-loaded environment. No matter how subtly hidden in the overall presentation and background of the client, his or her strengths and resiliencies can be found and should be highlighted. A client's progress should not be measured by "an absolute level of achievement but rather by the incremental choice to embrace the present and to step forward toward a life worth living" (Hayes et al., 2012, p. 985). Affirmation increases self-efficacy/self-confidence, which is critical for enhancing addicted clients' motivation to change. To help clients abandon their occupation of addictions, they also need new skills and resources that allow them to recognize, access, and maintain those more positive, productive, and enjoyable new occupations. In order to behave and act responsibly, a person needs first to have a sober mind, a nurtured heart, and a supportive environment. It is the person's task to be responsible; it is society's task to cultivate in a person a sober mind and a nurtured heart, as well as offer him or her an environment that is conducive to growth.

Addiction is a difficult but treatable chronic disease. Although more research is still needed, the field has developed evidence-based pharmacotherapy and behavioral therapy as well as psychosocial interventions that are useful to counteract addiction. Twelve Step and non-Twelve Step self-help groups have also played a unique and significant role in contributing to addicted individuals' long-term recovery. Although some clients are able to maintain abstinence for years post-treatment discharge, many will experience multiple treatments and relapses before establishing a stable recovery; still others may relapse even after prolonged sobriety but strive to become sober again—they should all be considered successes. As long as there is a wish to get well, hope exists. Equally important, the clinicians must honor the cardinal value that all human beings have a desire to pursue well-being.

I want to thank all my clients and research participants, as well as all researchers and clinicians in the field. Without them, this book would be impossible. I hope my book provides a framework to help people understand more about addiction and the possible ways and strategies of treating it.

Reference

Hayes, S.C., Pitorello, J., & Levin, M.E. (2012). Acceptance and commitment therapy as a unified model of behavior change. *The Counseling Psychologist, 40*(7), 976–1002.

1

INTRODUCTION

THE ACQS MODEL: CONSIDERING ADDICTION, CO-OCCURRING DISORDERS, QUALITY OF LIFE, AND SOCIAL FACTORS

The phenomenon of addiction has been recognized since ancient times; however, it is still a controversial disorder today regarding its etiology and treatment. There were various historical landmarks that address, define, and explain addiction—for example, Nicolaes Tulp, a Dutch 17th-century physician, replaced sin with a medical disorder to account for addiction; Benjamin Rush, an early American physician, suggested in the 18th century that compulsive drinking is a disease wherein a person loses self-control; in the 19th century, professional journals in addiction medicine first appeared, including the *Journal of Inebriety* in the US and the *British Journal of Addiction*; and addiction-related diagnostic classifications and neurobiological research were first developed in the 20th century (Crocq, 2007). Nevertheless, today in the 21st century, we are still exploring and debating the nature of addiction and its treatment strategies and we are still unable to come to a consensus regarding policies related to addiction treatment and prevention. One example is the recent response, "Brain Disease Model of Addiction: Why Is It So Controversial?" by Volkow and Koob (2015) to the challenges of Hall et al. (2015), who criticized that too much emphasis has been placed on the biological aspect of addiction and not enough on its psychosocial aspect. Crocq stated that "the frequent pendulum swings between opposing attitudes on issues that are still currently being debated"—such as "is addiction a sin or a disease; should treatment be moral or medical; is addiction caused by the substance, the individual's vulnerability and psychology, or social factors; should substance be regulated or freely available,"—questions reflecting the complex causes of addiction (p. 355).

The emergence of the concept of behavioral addiction (e.g., gambling disorder, internet gaming disorder, sex addiction, shopping addiction, and so on) in the past decades has provoked enormous opposition from both lay and professional communities, and further enlarges and intensifies the controversies related to addiction (Sun, 2013). Specifically, the grouping of gambling disorder together with substance use disorder (SUD) under the same umbrella, as well as inclusion of the internet gaming disorder (but not sex addiction) in its Section III by the *Diagnostic Statistical Manual, 5th edition* (*DSM-5*, American Psychiatric Association [APA], 2013), all have generated much disagreement among both sides of the professionals (Sun, 2013). On one hand, we have some scientists who affirm that the advanced technologies, like functional magnetic resonance imaging (fMRI), have enabled us to better understand behavioral addiction and its commonalities to, and close relationship with, substance addiction. On the other hand, others fear that the identification and targeting of behavioral addiction may pathologize everyday life behaviors and create "diagnostic inflation" and "false epidemics" (Sun, 2013).

Regardless, we continuously see patients seeking addiction treatment. It's not uncommon to see mothers, whose cocaine or methamphetamine addiction has led to child neglect, seek treatment to gain back child custody; or husbands with alcoholism request treatment to save their marriage and keep employment; or to see heroin users apply for substitute or other treatments, as heroin has cost all their money and properties, and its satiation can never be achieved. In the past decade, we have also started seeing worried parents give ultimatums to their sons to get treatment, young men who have never abused alcohol or drugs but who have dropped out of college due to internet addiction (Sun & Cash, 2017). Some patients may hide behind the façade of defiance and be labeled as "involuntary" or "resistant" clients; most of them have drained all of their strength and confidence because of addiction and are in total despair. Still others, who are afflicted not only with addiction but also other severe psychiatric disorders and lack resources and social support, may end up on the streets and become chronically homeless (Sun, 2012).

Although some researchers have claimed that people can self-recover or achieve spontaneous remission from addiction, and that addiction is "a disorder of choice" (Heyman, 2009), the research has concurrently shown that it is those who have a lesser or less severe addiction that are likely to succeed in self-recovery (Klingemann et al., 2010). Individuals who end up in treatment programs or on the street are likely to have these factors: they have tried to quit but failed repeatedly; their addiction is moderate to severe rather than mild; they have a comorbid physical ailment or psychiatric disorder that prompts self-medication and exacerbates the addiction; they have low recovery social capital and resources, which weakens their motivation to get well and makes their abstinence unsustainable. These people, therefore, need most the external intervention and help from society and community. Addiction treatment is not only applicable to patients in treatment programs or tertiary prevention, it is critical to the primary and secondary prevention as well. Preventing addiction in the first place, and reducing the odds for a less severe addiction to advance into severe dependency, are equally as important as helping patients already afflicted with severe addiction to reach long-term recovery.

Although far more research is still needed, the clinical and science research communities have accumulated some insights and knowledge to help guide our practice. Based on my many years of research, as well as teaching and practice in the field of addiction, I developed the ACQS model to explain the nature of addiction and its treatments. The ACQS model proposes that a person's addiction and treatment involves four essential components—understanding the fundamentals of addiction, considering the co-occurring disorders, taking account of the quality of life, and awareness of the social factors involved. Among the four components, I consider the "fundamentals of addiction" as the primary and unique feature to understanding addiction, and it is therefore placed first in the ACQS model. The other three components are also crucial to understanding addiction, but they may be relevant to many other phenomena or diseases as well, such as aging or depression, and are not unique to addiction. Nevertheless, to simply rely on the "fundamentals of addiction" without integrating the other three components would be incomplete and ineffective. Many people, when attempting to make sense of the occurrence of addiction and its recovery, focus only on one piece of the puzzle; even if that piece is necessary, it may never be sufficient to complete the puzzle.

Historically the general public, including many addicted people themselves and their families or even scholars, have had difficulty accepting "addiction" as a disease, especially as a brain disease. Volkow and Koob (2015) pondered "whether the difficulty relies in accepting as a bona fide disease one that erodes the neuronal circuits that enable us to exert free-will" (p. 678). This is consistent with society's often loose application of the term "addiction" to any excessively engaged activities or consumed materials, whether or not they've had negative consequences. For example, someone may say jokingly, "I'm addicted to chocolate!" when she has eaten a great many fudge truffles recently. One night as I drove home listening to the radio I heard the DJ say, "I must be addicted to that song," indicating she liked the song so much that she played it frequently. When a concept like "addiction" is used so lightly, it will be defined and perceived carelessly. Laypersons are unaware that real addiction involves a much more complex nature and course. They may see the impulsivity, in that the addicted person focuses only on seeking fun and pleasure, but they do not see compulsivity, in that the person may engage in the addictive behavior against his or her conscious wishes (Chamberlain et al., 2017; Koob, 2009; Koob & Volkow, 2010). They only see the person who gives up his or her job, marriage, and other meaningful life goals and relationships; they do not see his or her pain with regard to withdrawal, tolerance, craving, and multiple failures to quit. This could be the origin of the "moral model," where people judge addicted individuals to be selfish, lazy, irresponsible, and immoral.

Some people—including those with an empathetic heart, general clinicians, and addicted people and their families—have become more receptive of the self-medication theory. This theory suggests that addicted people resort to alcohol and other drugs (AOD) and/or other addictive behaviors such as gambling or internet gaming to help them cope with pain and suffering, loneliness and alienation, dysfunctional interpersonal relationships, feelings of a meaningless and purposeless life, or other frustrations and unfulfilled needs. Knowing that my research area is addiction, some of my lay friends and colleagues will share with me their perspectives that addiction is caused by a lack of social support (a self-medication theory, too). As a matter of fact, Bruce Alexander wrote a book, *The Globalization of Addiction: A Study in Poverty of the Spirit* (2008), suggesting that addiction is "a substitute for an unbearable lack of psychosocial integration" (p. 326). He highlighted an ancient view, stating that "Socrates sees [addicts] as reacting to an impossible social situation in the best way they can" (p. 325). As a social worker and during my own early research career, I indeed felt the same way, and once wanted to title one of my manuscripts, "It's about Life, Not about Drugs." People self-medicate their dissatisfaction about life by abusing alcohol and other drugs, I concluded. However, the self-medication theory is relevant and significant, but insufficient to fully understand addiction. This theory implies that poor quality of life is *the* major factor contributing to addiction, and that addiction is only a by-product of and secondary to the poor quality of life. The rationale then is that once society provides treatment and helps people improve their quality of life, those who rely on alcohol and/or drugs to cope should be rid of addiction once and for all, as there is no reason to self-medicate any more. Society, and the addicted person's significant others, cannot understand nor tolerate why the person relapses after treatment—not only once, but again and again—other than deciding the person to be immoral or weak-willed. Even addicted people may blame themselves and feel self-loathing for their repeated relapses. So, in an unexpected way, the self-medication theory brings people right back to the moral model.

Today, I still think quality of life and psychosocial integration are critical factors (which are covered in Chapter 4) in the occurrence of addiction and its recovery, especially long-term recovery; now, however, I will say, "It's Not Only about the Life, It Is Also about the Drugs." The addictive power and complexity of alcohol and other drugs, gambling, or internet gaming should not be ignored or underestimated. I have had clients or research participants—users of alcohol, heroin, cocaine, methamphetamine, or ketamine, as well as gamblers and gamers—tell me that although they are not using currently, "back in my brain," they said, they are still thinking about the drugs. They missed the enormous pleasure the drugs brought to them; they were also in great fear of relapse (Sun, 2007, 2014; Sun et al., 2016). The craving or urge to use exists even after months and years post detox, and it may be triggered by stress or a cue (places, persons, or things associated with alcohol, other drugs, or gambling). Many addicted individuals wished that they had never used the drugs in the first place, because their addiction has haunted them a lifetime.

In the past several decades, advanced brain imaging technologies and research, such as positron emission tomography (PET) and functional magnetic resonance imaging (fMRI), have identified the addictive features of substance addiction and its effects on the brain's activities and neuro pathways (Grant et al., 2010; Volkow et al., 2004; Volkow et al., 2002). Although more research is still needed, some brain imaging studies have also observed similar effects of addictive behaviors, such as gambling and internet gaming, on the brain's activities and neurobiological mechanisms (de Ruiter et al., 2012; Grant et al., 2010; Ko et al., 2009; Ko et al., 2013; Luijten et al., 2014). Scientific data have suggested that addiction is a brain disease that involves the disturbance and neuro-adaptation of a person's neurobiological systems. Overall, the research has identified three major characteristics of an addicted brain: a combination of impulsivity and compulsivity, neuroadaptation, and a chronic nature. A person's addictive behavior is not only impulsive in nature—the "bottom-up" limbic system is heightened and dominant, whereas the "top-down" prefrontal cortex system is weakened and subdued—but also compulsive during the later stage of addiction, such that the person may engage in the addictive behavior against his or her own conscious wishes (Chamberlain et al., 2017; Koob, 2009; Koob & Volkow, 2010). Impulsivity drives a person to pursue pleasure, and addiction is positively reinforced during the initial stage; in contrast, compulsivity is related to negative reinforcement, in that the person no longer obtains pleasure from using the substances during the late stage of addiction, but rather engages in the addictive behavior in order to reduce anxiety (Koob, 2009). The neuro-adaptation resulting from the brain's prolonged exposure to alcohol and other drugs (AOD) explains the chronic and relapsing nature of addiction. It is inaccurate, biased, and counterproductive to ignore the neurobiological fundamentals of addiction and to assume that once society has helped addicted people—offering detoxification and rehabilitation, healing the traumas, finding them a job, helping them regaining social support, and the like—they ought to be rid of their addiction once for all, and if they are not, they are a moral failure or weak-willed.

In Chapter 2, I discuss in details the fundamentals of addiction and its treatment strategies. Addiction, in and of itself, is a primary disease, not just a by-product from some other major diseases or main problems. To be more specific, drinking or doing drugs may be, initially, only a temporary by-product or secondary to a primary psychiatric disorder (e.g., depression, posttraumatic stress disorder [PTSD]) or other problems in life that the person attempts to self-medicate. But such coping behaviors may turn into a more permanent and difficult primary disorder, or an out-of-control addiction, if the brain is repeatedly exposed to AOD and the neuroadaptation is subsequently formed (Volkow et al., 2009). This could also happen to some people whose initial intention of drug use, gambling, or playing online games is curiosity, fun, or casual entertainment, but who find out later after routine usage that they have become addicted. Addiction is a chronic disease, such that relapse is the norm and relapse prevention should be part of the core treatment. Like other chronic illnesses, there is no cure for addiction so far, but it is treatable. To some people, especially patients with severe addiction, addiction is a lifetime battle and recovery demands a lifetime commitment. It is easier for the general public to accept illnesses such as cancer, diabetes, and hypertension as chronic diseases than addiction, perhaps because the presentation of addiction as a disease is relatively subtle and abstract. Although not all people with substance use disorder (SUD), or gambling or internet gaming disorder, are afflicted with severe addiction, for those who are, the fundamental neurobiological nature of addiction must be taken into consideration when helping the patients and their significant others.

In Chapter 3, I discuss co-occurring disorders (COD)—the second component of the ACQS model—and their treatment guidelines. Two categories of COD are discussed: a) the co-occurring chronic pain and addiction, and b) the comorbid psychiatric disorders and addiction. Studies have found that chronic pain and substance use disorder, especially opioids, tend to co-occur frequently (Boscarino et al., 2010; Rosenblum et al., 2003; Savage et al., 2008), although there also are studies showing low percentages of chronic pain patients who receive opioid analgesic therapy who actually develop opioid addiction (Fishbain et al., 2008). Boscarino et al.'s study (2010, $n = 705$ outpatients in a large health-care system who received four or more physician orders for opioid therapy in the past year) found that 26% of the subjects had current opioid dependence, and 36% of the subjects met the criteria for lifetime opioid dependence. Later, using *DSM-5* diagnostic criteria, Boscarino and colleagues (2015) found that 28.1% of their sample (outpatients with noncancer pain who received 5 or more prescription opioid orders in the previous 12 months) met for a mild opioid use disorder (OUD, 2–3 conditions), 9.7% for a moderate OUD (4–5 conditions), and 3.5% for a severe OUD (6 or more conditions). Many people consider the recent heroin epidemic and soaring opioid addiction to be related to the opioid overprescribing by physicians in the US. Some have hypothesized the heroin epidemic to be caused by the "transition to heroin use among the expanding population of people with nonmedical pain reliever use experience," although the large majority of nonmedical pain reliever (NMPR) users have not advanced to heroin use, and only 3.6% of NMPR initiates had started heroin use in the five year subsequent their initial NMPR use (Muhuri et al., 2013, p. 2). The transition from NMPR to heroin may be because heroin is less expensive and easier to obtain in some areas (Muhuri et al., 2013). Chronic pain patients receiving long-term opioid therapy may be particularly at risk for developing opioid addiction if they have: a history of addiction or substance abuse treatment, existing pain impairment affecting life/work, suicidal thoughts, sleeping problems, illicit drug use, and trauma or other comorbid psychological problems, such as anxiety disorder, and if they are younger than 65 years of age (Boscarino et al., 2015; Salsitz, 2016).

Research has also well established the association between substance use/addiction and other psychiatric disorders. It's not unusual for a client seeking addiction treatment to have additional psychiatric disorder. Likewise, clinicians often find their mental health patients also have addiction problems (Center for Substance Abuse Treatment [CSAT], 2005). Statistics have shown that the substance use disorder rates are higher among individuals with psychiatric conditions such as schizophrenia, mood disorders (e.g., depression, bipolar disorder), anxiety disorders, PTSD, attention deficit/hyperactive disorder (ADHD), antisocial personality disorder, or borderline personality disorder, than among the general populations (Conway et al., 2006; Grant et al., 2016). The co-occurrence between substance use/addiction and other psychiatric disorders and chronic pain has enormous implications to efficacious treatment of substance use disorder and addiction.

While there are various theories explaining why co-occurring disorders (COD) happen and more research is needed in this regard, three areas with great consensus stand out, indicating the critical role COD plays in affecting effective treatments of addiction or substance use disorder. First, although the self-medication theory is not a perfect explanation, its implications and suggestions on identifying and addressing the root problems are meritorious. For example, if a pain patient uses heroin to self-medicate chronic pain, or a schizophrenia patient uses alcohol to self-medicate the positive or negative symptoms (Khantzian & Albanese, 2008), the *root* problems—that is, the chronic pain or schizophrenia—must be screened and treated, in order to treat the secondary problems—i.e., SUD/ addiction—effectively, which will enable relapse prevention and a long-term recovery, as well as prevent the initially a secondary problem (mild SUD/addiction) from transitioning into a primary problem (moderate or severe SUD/addiction).

Second, although research is inconclusive regarding COD theories, it is mostly consistent that treating co-occurring disorders is more difficult than treating each single disorder alone. For example, the clinical course can be more complex, treatment compliance lower, and treatment outcomes less promising when a patient has comorbid PTSD and SUD/addiction versus one who has only PTSD or only SUD/addiction. In order to effectively treat SUD/addiction in the co-occurring disorder context, a simultaneous, instead of sequential, treatment approach that considers both or multiple disorders must be in place (McCauley et al., 2012; McGovern et al., 2015; van Emmerik-van Oortmerssen et al., 2015). An ideal way of treating co-occurring disorders should be not only a simultaneous approach but also an integrated approach. In other words, combining whatever approved treatment method for one single disorder with what's an otherwise effective treatment method for the other single disorder to treat the comorbidity of both disorders may or may not work. For example, a study of a treatment package that combines prolonged exposure for PTSD and cognitive behavioral therapy for substance use disorder to treat patients with PTSD-SUD reported that the treatment group did better than the control group with respect to PTSD, but saw no significant difference in SUD outcomes (Mills et al., 2012). Another example: although methylphenidate is the first line medication for ADHD, it may not be effective in patients with ADHD-SUD comorbidity; ADHD-SUD patients may require a higher dose of the medications (Konstenius et al., 2014; van Emmerik-van Oortmerssen et al., 2015). Both examples suggest that some modifications might be required when applying effective treatment methods for single disorders to treat co-occurring problems. Research has traditionally focused on participants with only a single disorder, and most research projects excluded subjects with COD from their pool (Petrakis & Simpson, 2017). More new research that targets individuals with co-occurring disorders is very much needed. It's important for the clinicians to know how to treat not only addiction and other psychiatric disorders individually, but also when they overlap and reinforce each other. Oftentimes, the strategies and treatment methods for a single disorder may need modification for patients with co-occurring addiction and other psychiatric disorders.

Third, research has shown that individuals with comorbid addiction and psychiatric disorders, especially mood disorders such as depression, bipolar disorder, and PTSD, may be at a higher risk for suicidal attempts and suicides (Blanco et al., 2012; McCauley et al., 2012). This demonstrates the ultimate importance for clinicians to address co-occurring disorder issues when treating substance use and addiction, as well as when treating their mental health patients. A timely COD screening, assessment, and treatment can prevent or reduce violence-related risks.

Quality of life is the next component of the ACQS model and is captured in Chapter 4. In addition to appropriate assessment and treatment of co-occurring disorders, effective addiction treatments must include case management and psychosocial intervention that targets the overall well-being of an addicted person. Here again, treatment would be ineffective if its focus were only about quality of life issues without addressing the fundamentals of addiction, just as it would be ineffectual for a clinician to target only the addiction without improving a person's quality of life, be that physical, psychological, or spiritual matters. Just as we see opposition from lay people to the concept that addiction is a brain disease, there is also resistance within the medical community to recognizing the importance of quality of life factors. Newman (2012) has questioned the legitimacy of addiction treatments that address patients' quality of life instead of simply focusing on addiction symptoms reduction, similar to how other chronic diseases are treated. Laudet (2012) responded well, writing that "[substance use disorders] are somewhat unique among chronic conditions in that, for many, they typically present with numerous co-occurring functional impairments (physical- and mental-health problems, of course, but also housing instability, damaged family and social relations, and poor job readiness or employability). These domains are what constitute 'quality of life'" (Author Reply, para. 3). Laudet went on to say that "clinicians in any field are accountable, first and foremost, for facilitating symptom reduction. However, because of the high prevalence of co-occurring functional impairments among SUD patients, and of the emerging evidence that functional improvements prospectively enhance motivation for, and the likelihood of, sustained abstinence, providing SUD-affected persons with the tools and resources to improve functioning is highly desirable" (Author Reply, para. 4).

The addiction treatment field has long recognized the importance of quality of life in helping its clients. For example, the Community Reinforcement Approach (Meyers & Miller, 2001) identified three major elements—family, vocation, and social activities—in facilitating long-term recovery in clients, with the aim to replace the short-lived pleasure provided by alcohol and other drugs with the real pleasure resulted from supportive interpersonal relationships, rewarding employment, and joyful social and recreational activities. The motivational interviewing approach also highlights the issue: If alcohol or the drug is taken away from an individual—i.e., "when we give something up, when you root it out"—"Sometimes we need to put something in to . . . to replace it" (John Northcross' interview with a client in *Stages of Change for Addiction*, video file, 2007). Another example is the emphasis on fellowship, social support, and the spiritual practices and caring inherent in the Twelve Step facilitation approach and self-help groups (Humphreys et al., 2014; Kelly, 2016; Kelly et al., 2016; Magura et al., 2013; Tonigan et al., 2017; White et al., 2012).

Co-occurring disorders of physical or psychiatric illnesses are important factors that negatively affect a person's quality of life, but quality of life includes many more dimensions. Although quality of life is a subjective perception, or may combine objective-subjective experience, its domain may include a person's physical, mental, and spiritual health; social-economic factors; relationships with significant others such as spouse, parents, children, friends, and neighbors; employment; and the living environment, with such needs as safety, housing, finances, and access to care (Laudet, 2011). In Chapter 4, I examine quality of life as it presents in material poverty and spiritual poverty, and discuss their relationship to the occurrence of addiction. Scientific data have shown a high correlation between the addiction rates and the factors of material poverty. For example (although it's not completely clear whether it's a causal relationship and, if so, what the driving mechanism is), statistics in the US have consistently indicated that the prevalence of illicit drug use disorder, alcohol use disorder, cigarette smoking, serious mental illnesses, and serious thoughts of suicide are all higher among lower socioeconomic groups than higher socioeconomic groups (Substance Abuse and Mental Health Services Administration [SAMHSA], 2015). Data of the World Health Organization (WHO) also show that countries with lower economic wealth, although their populations consume less alcohol per capita than wealthier countries, have a higher burden of disease attributable to alcohol for each liter of pure alcohol people consumed (2014). I examine in Chapter 4 socioeconomic factors such as housing and employment. Spiritual poverty may be related, but not limited, to material poverty. Mother Teresa once said, "Loneliness and the feeling of being unwanted is the most terrible poverty." Raphael, an addicted person quoted in Bruce Alexander's (2008) book, said, "We gravitate to whatever strong drug works for us because nothing else does" (p. 227). In my discussion of spiritual poverty and/or lack of psychological well-being, I include psychosocial dislocation, which further addresses trauma, parent-child relationships, relationships with spouse, and purpose and meaning in life.

Chapter 5 focuses on the social factors of the ACQS model. We like to say "it takes a village to raise a child"; likewise, it involves all sectors of society to successfully prevent a person from falling into addiction, or to facilitate the long-term recovery of an addicted individual. I will consider cultural factors; social-political factors, such as national and local policies; demographic variables, such as gender; and environmental factors in relation to addiction. Social factors may appear subtle, abstract, or distant; their impact, nonetheless, is pronounced when intertwined with addiction, hitting close to home for an addicted person, his or her family, and community. Social factors can affect a person via at least two channels: they may directly affect the treatment's quality and effectiveness, or indirectly affect treatment outcomes through affecting a person's quality of life. Secondly, social factors may precipitate the occurrence of addiction.

Four examples—drug courts, methadone programs, subsidized housing for low-income families, and the "five clocks" concept—are included in Chapter 5 to explain how policies, programs, and their implementation may impact, positively or adversely, the well-being of addicted individuals and their chances for subsequent recovery. For example, the federal policy on subsidized housing for low-income families is supposed to help vulnerable populations. However, its application to a substance-abusing single mother in recovery—who has extremely low resources and desperately needs housing in order to gain back child custody—may be denied because of her previous shoplifting criminal record (Sun, 2014). A practitioner's advocacy and ability to work collaboratively and creatively with the various systems, therefore, are critical in helping the client. Young et al. (1998) mentioned the widely cited concept of "four clocks," which demonstrates how an addicted caregiver client in the child welfare system may fall into service delivery cracks because of different philosophies, rules, and timetables held by the various involved agencies, such as the child welfare system, the substance abuse treatment system, and the Temporary Assistance for the Needy Families (TANF) system. This is further complicated by the developmental timetable for young children during their first 18 months—a critical period for cultivating mother-child bond. Young, therefore, proposed the concept of the fifth clock, asking for practitioners' flexibility and creativity to establish a master schedule that coordinates all involved systems.

Social, cultural, and political factors also precipitate the occurrence of addiction in various ways. Social and cultural changes, as well as technological advancement, are constant and never ending—they have tremendous bearing on our values, behaviors, and lifestyles, for better or worse—some of which may subsequently trigger addiction as well as change the landscape and implications of our addictive behaviors. In addition, different societies may be distinct geographically, historically, socioculturally, and politically, all of which have a large impact on a person's behaviors, including addictive behaviors. The effects of societal factors on substance use and abuse may be gauged through time-space (cohort-country) variations. Researchers can focus on temporal differences and examine contrasts across different birth cohorts within one country; they can also examine spatial variation across different countries within one single cohort (Seedat et al., 2009). It's important to research and understand *current* epidemiology regarding the prevalence of substance use and misuse problems, as well as their origins, so that updated and effective interventions can be developed accordingly. Likewise, the prevalence and nature of substance use problems may be different in different societies, countries, and regions, and intervention strategies that emphasize localization and match the special needs of each unique society should be crafted.

Four pertinent phenomena are discussed in Chapter 5 to show how societal factors may influence the occurrence of addiction and how strategies can be shaped to control the problems accordingly. These are: (a) the current heroin epidemic in the US; (b) the convergent trends of alcohol use and alcohol use disorder between men and women in the past decades in the US and some other western countries, as well as the divergent gender-related patterns of substance use and substance use disorder when comparing western and non-western countries; (c) the availability of and easy access to computers and the internet, and their implications for the emergence and heightening of various behavioral addictions, such as internet gaming addiction, gambling disorder, shopping addiction, and sex addiction; and (d) the legalization of medicinal and recreational marijuana. For example, the current heroin epidemic in the US may be related to the overall inadequate practice in medical pain management and the inappropriate prescribing of opioids, leading to some patients' nonmedical use of prescription opioids and the subsequent heroin use. It's important to develop corresponding strategies to curtail the epidemic, such as establishing guidelines regarding appropriate opioid prescribing and providing related training to physicians and medical school students (Centers for Disease Control and Prevention [CDC], 2017).

This book begins with a chapter introducing the ACQS model. Thereafter, there are two parts. Part I covers four chapters, each elaborating on a component of the ACQS model: Chapter 2, The Fundamentals of Addiction; Chapter 3, Addiction and the Co-occurring Disorders; Chapter 4, Addiction and Quality of Life; and Chapter 5, Addiction and Social Factors. Part II contains various approaches and strategies targeting each component of the ACQS model and includes three chapters: Chapter 6, Spirituality, Connectedness, and Hope; Chapter 7, Withdrawal Management and Relapse Prevention: Pharmacotherapy; and Chapter 8, Withdrawal Management and Relapse Prevention: Behavioral Therapy and Psychosocial Treatment. Treatment strategies for each component of the ACQS model are outlined in Table 1.1.

Table 1.1 Treatment Strategies for Each of the Four Components of the ACQS Model

Component / Strategies	The Fundamentals of Addictions	Co-Occurring Disorders	Quality of Life	Social Factors
ASSESSMENT: • *DSM-5* • ASAM 6 Dimensions • Addiction Severity Index (ASI) • COD Screening Tools • Trauma Screening Tools (e.g., Adverse Childhood Experience) • Quality of Life Assessment Tools • Other Assessment Tools	• Assess Substance Use Disorder (SUD): mild, moderate, or severe • Assess ASAM Dimension 1: Acute intoxication and/or withdrawal potential Dimension 4: Readiness to change (SUD) Dimension 5: Relapse, continued use, or continued problem potential (SUD) • Assess patients' AOD use history • Assess family AOD use history	• Screen for and assess other psychiatric disorders (e.g., schizophrenia, mood disorder, PTSD, ADHD) • Assess ASAM Dimension 2: Biomedical conditions and complications Dimension 3: Emotional, behavioral or cognitive conditions and complications Dimension 4: Readiness to change (Mental Disorders) Dimension 5: Relapse, continued use, or continued problem potential (Mental Disorders)	• Assess ASAM Dimension 6: Recovery/Living environment (SUD and Mental Disorders) • Assess patients' social, educational, vocational, and legal history • Assess patients' trauma history • Assess patients' perception of quality of life (e.g., safety, housing, finance, access to care, physical and mental health, relationship with others, purpose in life)	
SPIRITUALITY- SOCIAL NETWORK- AND INNER STRENGTHS-BASED PRACTICE: • Motivational Interviewing • Dialectical Behavior Therapy (DBT)	• Instill hope • Enhance patients' relatedness, autonomy, and competency • Facilitate trust alliance between clinician and the patient	• Instill hope • Enhance motivation to get well • Learn to self-regulate emotion and tolerate distress	• Instill hope • Enhance self-efficacy and self-esteem • Restore the patient's relationship with his/her family	

(Continued)

Table 1.1 (Continued)

Component	The Fundamentals of Addictions	Co-Occurring Disorders	Quality of Life	Social Factors
Strategies				
• Acceptance and Commitment Therapy (ACT) • Family-oriented treatment • Twelve Step Facilitation Approach • Twelve Step Self-Help Groups/ Dual Diagnosis Self-Help Groups • Non-Twelve Step Self-Help Groups (e.g., SMART Recovery, WRAP Groups)	• Help patients move from the stage of pre-contemplation to contemplation, to preparation, to action, and to maintenance • Enhance relatedness and connectedness Restructure definitions of self, others, and learn emotion regulation (via the relationships with the clinician, sponsors from the self-help group, and other group members)	• Spirituality: Learn to accept and let go of less important frustration and unpleasant personal events, as well as focus on the "big picture" and commit self to important and valued goals in life • Promote resilience in patients • Increase universality and decrease stigma • Enhance medical compliance	• Enhance fellowship, relatedness, and connectedness • Decrease patients' psychosocial dislocation, isolation, and loneliness • Help patients find meaning and purpose in life • Provide patients with "practical" help: Employment, housing, and other social services	
PSYCHOSOCIAL EDUCATION:	• Share information with patients and their significant others regarding: the brain disease model of addiction, the impulsivity and compulsivity aspects of addiction, and the chronic and relapsing nature of addiction	• Emphasize the importance of medical compliance • Address the negative consequences of self-medication using AOD or other addictive behaviors	• Provide drug-refusal skills • Enhance patients' communication and problem-solving skills. • Emphasize to the patients traumas are no fault of theirs and clarify common myths linked to traumas	

PHARMACOTHERAPY:
- For Withdrawal Management
- For Relapse Prevention
- For Co-occurring Disorders

- Pharmacotherapy for detoxification (withdrawal management):
  Alcohol: e.g., benzodiazepines
  Heroin: e.g., methadone buprenorphine
- Pharmacotherapy for relapse prevention:
  Alcohol use disorder: e.g., acamprosate, naltrexone, disulfiram (Antabuse)
  Opioid use disorder: e.g., methadone, buprenorphine (Suboxone) naltrexone
- No FDA-approved medications for stimulant addiction (e.g., cocaine and methamphetamine)
- No FDA-approved medications for behavioral addiction

- Medications for schizophrenia, depression, bipolar, ADHD, PTSD, etc.
- Antipsychotics
- Antidepressants
- Stimulants and other medications

- Continue research on innovative treatment: Currently no effective medications to "cure" addiction
- Continue research on innovative treatment: Currently no FDA-approved medications to treat cocaine, cannabis, amphetamine, or behavioral addictions (e.g., gambling disorder)
- More research is needed in *integrated* pharmacotherapy for co-occurring disorders

(Continued)

Table 1.1 (Continued)

	Component	The Fundamentals of Addictions	Co-Occurring Disorders	Quality of Life	Social Factors
Strategies					
BEHAVIORAL THERAPY/ PSYCHOSOCIAL TREATMENT: • Brief Intervention (BI) • Motivational Interviewing • Cognitive Behavioral Therapy (CBT) • Schema-Focused CBT • Mindfulness-Based CBT (MBCT) • Dialectical Behavioral Therapy (DBT) • Acceptance and Commitment Therapy (ACT) • Trauma-Focused Therapy • Community Reinforcement Approach • Contingency Management • Mindfulness-Oriented Recovery Enhancement (MORE)		• Prevent relapse: the A-B-C chain model (antecedent-behavior-consequence) • Identify triggers and deal with the triggers without resorting to AOD via functional analysis and skills training • Cognitive restructure Modify maladaptive schema • Learn to self-regulate emotion and tolerate distress • Spirituality: Learn to accept and let go of less important frustration and unpleasant personal events, as well as focus on the "big picture" and commit self to important and valued goals in life • Enhance the "top-down" prefrontal cortex function of the brain	• Modified CBT to help deal with depression, ADHD, PTSD, schizophrenia, etc. • Basic CBT, mindfulness-based CBT, CBT involving modifying early maladaptive schemas • Promote healing and empower the patient to move forward • Prevent self-medication • Cognitive restructure Modify maladaptive schema • Learn to self-regulate emotion and tolerate distress • Spirituality: Learn to accept and let go of less important frustration and unpleasant personal events, as well as focus on the "big picture" and commit self to important and valued goals in life	• Promote healing and empower the patient to move forward • Prevent self-medication • Cognitive restructure • Modify maladaptive schema • Emotion self-regulation and distress tolerance • Effective interpersonal communication and relationships • Meaning making; find purpose in life • Spirituality: Learn to accept and let go of less important frustration and unpleasant personal events, as well as focusing on the "big picture" and commit self to important and valued goals in life	• More research is needed in *integrated* behavioral therapy/psychosocial treatments for co-occurring disorders

- Reinforcement-Based Treatment
- Family-Oriented Treatment
- Case Management
- Other or Alternative Treatment:

Computerized cognitive enhancement exercise

Exercise/Acupuncture/ Yoga/ Tai chi/Arts/EMDR/ Biofeedback

MACRO LEVEL INTERVENTION:
- Research
- Social Policy
- Primary and Secondary Prevention
- Macro and Mezzo Level Factors
- Social and Cultural Factors

- Habilitation vs. rehabilitation
- Housing, Employment, Family interaction and dynamics, Social and recreational activities
- Make recovery more rewarding

- Conduct research on emerging trends of addictions and develop corresponding efficacious intervention and treatment
- Conduct research on evaluating current policies (e.g., the outcomes of marijuana legalization)
- Implement primary and secondary prevention in addition to tertiary prevention

(Continued)

Table 1.1 (Continued)

Strategies	Component	The Fundamentals of Addictions	Co-Occurring Disorders	Quality of Life	Social Factors
					• Advocacy for policy change: drug court, methadone program, improve pain management and opioids prescribing practice • Reduce bureaucracy and red tape and enhance coordination between and among different systems to prevent patients from falling into cracks • Decrease health disparity • Implement trauma-informed care • Provide culturally sensitive practice and gender-specific care

References

Alexander, B.K. (2008). *The globalization of addiction: A study in poverty of the spirit.* New York: Oxford University Press.

American Psychiatric Association (2013). *Diagnostic and statistical manual of mental disorders,* Fifth Edition. Arlington, VA: American Psychiatric Association.

Blanco, C., Alegria, A.A., Liu, S.M., Secades-Villa, R., Sugaya, L., Davies, C., & Nunes, E.V. (2012). Differences among major depressive disorder with and without co-occurring substance use disorders and substance-induced depressive disorder: Results from the National Epidemiologic Survey on Alcohol and Related Conditions. *Journal of Clinical Psychiatry, 73*(6), 865–873.

Boscarino, J.A., Hoffman, S.N., & Han, J.J. (2015). Opioid-use disorder among patients on long-term opioid therapy: Impact of final DSM-5 diagnostic criteria on prevalence and correlates. *Substance Abuse and Rehabilitation, 6,* 83–91.

Boscarino, J.A., Rukstalis, M., Hoffman, S.N., Han, J.J., Erlich, P.M., Gerhard, G.S., & Stewart, W.F. (2010). Risk factors for drug dependence among out-patients on opioid therapy in a large US health-care system. *Addiction, 105,* 1776–1782.

Centers for Disease Control and Prevention (CDC, 2017). CDC guideline for prescribing opioids for chronic pain. Retrieved on 02/15/2018 from www.cdc.gov/drugoverdose/prescribing/guideline.html.

Center for Substance Abuse Treatment (2005). *Substance abuse treatment for persons with co-occurring disorders.* Treatment Improvement Protocol (TIP) Series 42. DHHS Publication No. (SMA) 08–3992. Rockville, MD: Substance Abuse and Mental Health Services Administration.

Chamberlain, S.R., Stochl, J., Redden, S.A., & Grant, J.E. (2017). Latent traits of impulsivity and compulsivity: Toward dimensional psychiatry. *Psychological Medicine,* 1–12. Retrieved on 08/14/2017 from https://doi.org/10.1017/S0033291717002185.

Conway, K.P., Compton, W., Stinson, F.S., & Grant, B.F. (2006). Lifetime comorbidity of DSM-IV mood and anxiety disorders and specific drug use disorders: Results from the National Epidemiologic Survey on Alcohol and Related Conditions. *Journal of Clinical Psychiatry, 67*(2), 247–257.

Crocq, M. (2007). Historical and cultural aspects of man's relationship with addictive drugs. *Dialogues in Clinical Neuroscience, 9*(4), 355–361.

Department of Health and Human Services (2016). July 1, 2016, HHS opioid research portfolio brief—Translating science into action. Retrieved on 05/10/2017 from www.hhs.gov/sites/default/files/opioid-report-v4-remediated.pdf.

de Ruiter, M.B., Oosterlaan, J., Veltman, D.J., van den Brink, W., & Goudriaan, A.E. (2012). Similar hyporesponsiveness of the dorsomedial prefrontal cortex in problem gamblers and heavy smokers during an inhibitory control task. *Drug and Alcohol Dependence, 121,* 81–89.

Fishbain, D.A., Cole, B., Lewis, J., Rosomoff, H.L., & Rosomoff, R.S. (2008). What percentage of chronic nonmalignant pain patients exposed to chronic opioid analgesic therapy develop abuse/addiction and/or aberrant drug-related behaviors? A structured evidence-based review. *Pain Medicine, 9*(4), 444–459.

Grant, B.F., Saha, T.D., Ruan, W.J., Goldstein, R.B., Chou, S.P., Jung, J., Zhang, H., Smith, S.M., Pickering, R.P., Huang, B., & Hasin, D.S. (2016). Epidemiology of *DSM-5* drug use disorder: Results from the National Epidemiologic Survey on alcohol and related conditions-III. *JAMA Psychiatry, 73*(1), 39–47.

Grant, J.E., Potenza, M.N., Weinstein, A., & Gorelick, D.A. (2010). Introduction to behavioral addictions. *The American Journal of Drug and Alcohol Abuse, 36*(5), 233–241.

Hall, W., Carter, A., & Forlini, C. (2015). The brain disease model of addiction: Is it supported by the evidence and has it delivered on its promises? *The Lancet Psychiatry, 2*(1), 105–110.

Heyman, G.M. (2009). *Addiction: A disorder of choice.* Cambridge, MA: Harvard University Press.

Humphreys, K., Blodgett, J.C., & Wagner, T.H. (2014). Estimating the efficacy of alcoholics anonymous without self-selection bias: An instrumental variables re-analysis of randomized clinical trials. *Alcoholism: Clinical and Experimental Research, 38*(11), 2688–2694.

Kelly, J.F. (2016). Is alcoholics anonymous religious, spiritual, neither? Findings from 25 years of mechanisms of behavior change research. *Addiction, 112,* 929–936.

Kelly, J.F., Greene, M.C., & Bergman, B.G. (2016). Recovery benefits of the "therapeutic alliance" among 12-step mutual-help organization attendees and their sponsors. *Drug and Alcohol Dependence, 162,* 64–71.

Khantzian, E., & Albanese, M.J. (2008). *Understanding addiction as self medication: Finding hope behind the pain.* Lanham, MD: Rowman & Littlefield Publishers.

Klingemann, H., Sobell, M.B., & Sobell, L.C. (2010). Continuities and change in self-change research. *Addiction, 105*(9), 1510–1518.

Ko, C.H., Liu, G.C., Hsiao, S., Yen, J.Y., Yang, M.J., Lin, W.C., Yen, C.F., & Chen, C.S. (2009). Brain activities associated with gaming urge of online gaming addiction. *Jorunal of Psychiatric Research, 43*(7), 739–747.

Ko, C.H., Liu, G.C., Yen, J.Y., Chen, C.Y., Yen, C.F., & Chen, C.S. (2013). Brain correlates of craving for online gaming under cue exposure in subjects with internet gaming addiction and in remitted subjects. *Addiction Biology, 18*(3), 559–569.

Konstenius, M., Jayaram-Lindstrom, N., Guterstam, J., Beck, O., Philips, & Franck, J. (2014). Methylphenidate for attention deficit hyperactivity disorder and drug relapse in criminal offenders with substance dependence: A 24-week randomized placebo-controlled trial. *Addiction, 109*(3), 440–449.

Koob, G.F. (2009). Neurobiological substrates for the dark side of compulsivity in addiction. *Neuropharmacology, 56,* 18–31.

Koob, G.F., & Volkow, N.D. (2010). Neurocircuitry of addiction. *Neuropsychopharmacology, 35,* 217–238.

Laudet, A.B. (2011). The case for considering quality of life in addiction research and clinical practice. *Addiction Science & Clinical Practice, 6*(1), 44–55.

Laudet, A.B. (2012). Author reply to comment on the case for considering quality of life in addiction research and clinical practice. *Addiction Science & Clinical Practice, 7,* 2.

Luijten, M., Machielsen, M.W.J., Veltman, D.J., Hester, R., de Haan, L., & Franken, I.H.A. (2014). Systematic review of ERP and fMRI studies investigating inhibitory control and error processing in people with substance dependence and behavioural addictions. *Journal of Psychiatry & Neuroscience, 39*(3), 149–169.

Magura, S., Cleland, C.M., & Tonigan, J.S. (2013). Evaluating alcoholics anonymous's effect on drinking in project MATCH using cross-lagged regression panel analysis. *Journal of Studies on Alcohol and Drugs, 74*(3), 378–385.

McCauley, J.L., Killeen, T., Gros, D.F., Brady, K.T., & Back, S.E. (2012). Posttraumatic stress disorder and co-occurring substance use disorders: Advances in assessment and treatment. *Clinical Psychology, 19*(3). doi: 10.1111/cpsp.12006.

McGovern, M.P., Lambert-Harris, C., Xie, H., Meier, A., McLeman, B., & Saunders, E. (2015). A randomized controlled trial of treatments for co-occurring substance use disorders and PTSD. *Addiction, 110*(7), 1194–1204.

Meyers, R.J., & Miller, W.R. (Eds.) (2001). *A community reinforcement approach to addiction treatment*. New York: Cambridge University Press.

Mills, K.L., Teesson, M., Back, S.E., Brady, K.T., Baker, A.L., Hopwood, S., Sannibale, C., Barrett, E.L., Merz, S., Rosenfeld, J., & Ewer, P.L. (2012). Integrated exposure-based therapy for co-occurring posttraumatic stress disorder and substance dependence: A randomized controlled trial. *JAMA*, *15*, 308(7), 690–699.

Muhuri, P.K., Gfroerer, J.C., & Davies, M.C. (2013). Associations of nonmedical pain reliever use and initiation of heroin use in the United States. Center for Behavioral Health Statistics and Quality (CBGHSQ) Data Review. Retrieved on 02/15/2018 from www.samhsa.gov/data/sites/default/files/DR006/DR006/nonmedical-pain-reliever-use-2013.htm.

Newman, R.G. (2012). Comment on the case for considering quality of life in addiction research and clinical practice. *Addiction Science & Clinical Practice*, *7*, 2.

Petrakis, I.L., & Simpson, T.L. (2017). Posttraumatic stress disorder and alcohol use disorder: A critical review of pharmacologic treatments. *Alcoholism: Clinical and Experimental Research*, *41*(2), 226–237.

Rosenblum, A., Joseph, H., Fong, C., Kipnis, S., Cleland, C., & Portenoy, R.K. (2003). Prevalence and characteristics of chronic pain among chemically dependent patients in methadone maintenance and residential treatment facilities. *JAMA*, *289*(18), 2370–2378.

Salsitz, E.A. (2016). Chronic pain, chronic opioid addiction: A complex nexus. *Journal of Medical Toxicology*, *12*, 54–57.

Savage, S.R., Kirsh, K.L., & Passik, S.D. (2008). Challenges in using opioids to treat pain in persons with substance use disorders. *Addiction Science & Clinical Practice*, *4*(2), 4–25.

Seedat, S., Scott, K.M., Angermeyer, M.C., Berglund, P., Bromet, E.J., Brugha, T., et al. (2009). Cross-national associations between gender and mental disorders in the WHO World Mental Health Surveys. *Arch Gen Psychiatry*, *66*(7), 785–795.

Stages of Change for Addictions [Video file] (2007). *Psychotherapy.net*. Retrieved on 02/15/2018 from Kanopy.

Substance Abuse and Mental Health Services Administration (SAMHSA, 2015). *Behavioral health barometer: United States, 2015*. HHS Publication No. SMA-16-Baro-2015. Rockville, MD: SAMHSA. Retrieved on 02/15/2018 from www.samhsa.gov/data/sites/default/files/2015_National_Barometer.pdf.

Sun, A.P. (2007). Relapse among substance-abusing women: Components and processes. *Substance Use & Misuse, 42*, 1–21.

Sun, A.P. (2012). Helping homeless individuals with co-occurring disorders: The four components. *Social Work*, *57*(1), 23–37.

Sun, A.P. (2013). Historical background of behavioral addiction and the trend today. In A.P. Sun, L. Ashley, & L. Dickson (Eds.) *Behavioral addiction: Screening, assessment, and treatment* (pp. 9–33). Las Vegas, NV: Central Recovery Press.

Sun, A.P. (2014). Angelina: The story of a substance-abusing woman and its analysis. *Journal of Womens Health Care*, *3*, 171. doi: 10.4172/2167–0420.1000171.

Sun, A.P., & Cash, H. (2017). Factors related to the occurrence and recovery of internet use disorder. Paper presented at the 2017 National Association for Alcoholism and Drug Abuse Counselors Annual Conference, Denver, CO.

Sun, A.P., Chen, Y.C., & Marsiglia, F. (2016). Trauma and Chinese heroin users. *Journal of Ethnicity in Substance Abuse, 15*(2), 144–159.

Tonigan, J.S., McCallion, E.A., Frohe, T., & Pearson, M.R. (2017). Lifetime Alcoholics Anonymous attendance as a predictor of spiritual gains in the Relapse Replication and Extension Project (RREP). *Psychology of Addictive Behaviors, 31*(1), 54–60.

van Emmerik-van Oortmerssen, K., Vedel, E., van den Brink, W., & Schoevers, R.A. (2015). Integrated cognitive behavioral therapy for patients with substance use disorder and comorbid ADHD: Two case presentations. *Addictive Behaviors, 45*, 214–217.

Volkow, N.D., Fowler, J.S., & Wang, G. (2004). The addicted human brain viewed in the light of imaging studies: Brain circuits and treatment strategies. *Neuropharmacology, 47*, 3–13.

Volkow, N.D., Fowler, J.S., Wang, G.J., Baler, R., & Telang, F. (2009). Imaging dopamine's role in drug abuse and addiction. *Neuropharmacology, 56*, 3–8.

Volkow, N.D., Fowler, J.S., Wang, G., & Goldstein, R.Z. (2002). Role of dopamine, the frontal cortex and memory circuits in drug addiction: Insight from imaging studies. *Neurobiology of Learning and Memory, 78*, 610–624.

Volkow, N.D., & Koob, G. (2015). Brain disease model of addiction: Why is it so controversial? *Lancet Psychiatry, 2*(8), 677–679.

White, W.L., Kelly, J.F., & Roth, J.D. (2012). New addiction-recovery support institutions: Mobilizing support beyond professional addiction treatment and recovery mutual aid. *Journal of Groups in Addiction & Recovery, 7*, 297–317.

World Health Organization (2014). Global status report on alcohol and health 2014. Geneva, Switzerland: World Health Organization. Retrieved on 04/13/2018 from www.who.int/substance_abuse/publications/global_alcohol_report/msb_gsr_2014_1.pdf.

Young, N.K., Gardner, S.L., & Dennis, K. (1998). *Responding to alcohol and other drug problems in child welfare: Weaving together practice and policy.* Washington, DC: CWLA Press.

PART I

2

THE FUNDAMENTALS OF ADDICTION

The American Society of Addiction Medicine (ASAM) defines addiction as

A primary, chronic disease of brain reward, motivation, memory and related circuitry. Dysfunction in these circuits leads to characteristic biological, psychological, social and spiritual manifestations. This is reflected in an individual pathologically pursuing reward and/or relief by substance use and other behaviors. Addiction is characterized by inability to consistently abstain, impairment in behavioral control, craving, diminished recognition of significant problems with one's behaviors and interpersonal relationships, and a dysfunctional emotional response. Like other chronic diseases, addiction often involves cycles of relapse and remission. Without treatment or engagement in recovery activities, addiction is progressive and can result in disability or premature death.

(n.d.)

At least three domains characterize addiction: its phenomenological features, family history/genetics, and neurobiological processes.

The Phenomenological/Clinical Features

The phenomenological or clinical features of addiction may include five elements: "engagement in the behavior to achieve appetitive effects," "preoccupation with the behavior," "temporary satiation," "loss of control," "and "suffering negative consequences" (Sussman & Sussman, 2011, p. 4025). The *Diagnostic and Statistical Manual of Mental Disorders* (5th edition, *DSM-5*) (American Psychiatric Association [APA], 2013) clusters its 11 diagnostic criteria (conditions occurred in the past year) for substance use disorder into four groups (APA, 2013, pp. 490–491):

- Impaired control:
  1. Have consumed greater amounts or used for a longer period than intended.
  2. A "persistent desire" or unsuccessful attempts to stop or decrease the use.
  3. Have spent a lot of time obtaining or using the substance, or recovering from its effects.
  4. "Craving, or a strong desire or urge to use."
- Social impairment:
  5. Repeated use resulting in an inability to carry out obligations related to school, work, or home.
  6. "Continued . . . use despite having persistent or recurrent social or interpersonal problems caused or exacerbated by the effects" of the substance.
  7. "Important social, occupational, or recreational activities are given up or reduced because of . . . use."
- Risky use:
  8. "Recurrent . . . use in situations in which it is physically hazardous."
  9. Continued use "despite knowledge of having a persistent or recurrent physical or psychological problem" that may be attributable to the substance.
- Pharmacological criteria:
  10. Tolerance.
  11. Withdrawal.

In general, each different substance adopts the same 11 criteria (mild if 2–3 criteria met, moderate if 4–5 criteria met, and severe if 6 or more criteria met) to determine whether there is a disorder. In other words, these 11 criteria can be applied to assess whether there is an alcohol use disorder, cannabis use disorder, opioid use disorder, sedative/hypnotic/anxiolytic use disorder, stimulant use disorder, tobacco use disorder, and other (or unknown) substance use disorder (e.g., anabolic steroids, betel nut, nitrous oxide [laughing gas], etc.). There are only 10 criteria to diagnose phencyclidine use disorder, other hallucinogen use disorder (e.g., DMT), and inhalant use disorder, as the withdrawal criterion does not apply to most of these disorders (APA, 2013). For gambling disorder, there are 9 criteria (mild if 4–5 criteria met, moderate if 6–7 criteria met, and severe if 8–9 criteria met). Internet gaming disorder is not a formal diagnosis at present, but *DSM-5* includes this disorder in its section III and lists 9 criteria (positive if 5 or more criteria met) (for details, please refer to the *DSM-5* [APA]).

The Genetic Factor

The occurrence of addiction involves factors of genetics, environment, and interactions between the two; the impacts of genetics are moderate to high (Agrawal & Lynskey, 2008; Bevilacqua & Goldman, 2009; Verhulst et al., 2015). Including 12 twin studies and 5 adoption studies, Verhulst and colleagues' meta-analysis revealed that alcohol use disorder (AUD) is about 50% heritable. It is interesting to know that the heritability estimate of AUD is between the heritability estimate of major depression (approximately 37% heritable) and the heritability estimate of schizophrenia (about 81% heritable) (Verhulst et al., 2015). Yates et al.'s study (1996) found that genetic effects are more associated with more severe alcohol dependence cases (e.g., meeting 5 or more conditions for alcohol dependence in *DSM-IIIR*). Yates and colleagues stated that "Easier access to alcohol . . . may explain . . . the lack of any genetic effect for alcohol dependence at lower definitions of severity. Environmental effects play a more predominant role in the etiology of lesser severe forms of alcoholism" (p. 13).

Genetic factors may link to not only alcohol dependence but also drug dependence. Twin research identified the concept of "shared genetic factors." For example, a shared genetic factor may contribute to the overall variance in different externalizing behaviors, such as alcohol dependence, drug dependence, conduct disorder, and antisocial personality disorder (Kendler et al., cited in Dick & Agrawal, 2008). Twin study findings found that monozygotic twins (identical twins who share 100% of the genes) have a higher co-occurring rate between the development of alcohol dependence in twin 1 and drug dependence in twin 2, compared to dizygotic twins (fraternal twins who share an average of 50% of the genes) (Dick & Agrawal). In addition, some studies suggest that addiction liability predicts addiction heritability. For example, opiates and cocaine are very addictive, and are also very heritable (Goldman et al., 2005).

Twin studies have also mostly verified that monozygotic twins have a higher concordant rate of gambling disorders compared to dizygotic twins (APA, 2013; Beaver et al., 2010). Beaver et al.'s analysis of 602 twins (324 monozygotic and 278 same-sex dizygotic) found that approximately 70% of the variation in gambling can be explained by genetic factors, whereas 30% of the variance is attributable to non-shared environmental factors. Adoption studies have shown that offspring of biological parents with alcohol use disorder (AUD) are three to four times more likely to develop AUD, even when they are being adopted at birth by adoptive parents without AUD (APA, 2013). Studies also found that first-degree relatives of people with moderate or severe alcohol use disorder have a higher rate of gambling disorder than the general population (APA, 2013).

The impact of genetics may be confounded by gender. With caution that more research is needed, Beaver and colleagues (2010) reported that males' gambling seems to be more affected by genetic factors, and females' by environmental factors. That is, genetic factors accounted for about 85% and non-shared environmental factors about 15%, of the variance in gambling among men. In contrast, genetic factors played a zero role in explaining the variance in gambling, but non-shared environmental and shared environmental factors accounted for 55% and 45%, respectively, among women. Consistently, Kendler and colleagues' (2016) twin-sibling study showed that heritability explained about 57% of variance in alcohol use disorders among men, whereas 22% among women. On the other hand, some other studies have indicated that genetic factors with regard to alcohol use disorder are considerable among both men and women (e.g., McGue, 1999; Prescott et al., 1999).

Genetics can also influence a person's temperaments of novelty seeking or impulsivity, which are related to the inclination for the development of substance use disorder. In addition, genetics can prompt the occurrence of addiction indirectly. For example, peer factors may facilitate the development of opioid use disorder and genetics influence how people choose their environment (APA, 2013).

The Neurobiological Processes

Neurobiological processes of addiction capture the fundamentals of addiction, and help us understand the nature of addiction and its implications for treatment and recovery. The brain disease model of addiction (BDMA) explains addiction as neuroadaptation resulting from the repeated exposure to substances such as alcohol or drugs, or to certain processes and behaviors such as gambling or internet gaming. BDMA recognizes that addiction comprises impulsivity, compulsivity, and characteristics that display its chronic and relapsing nature (Koob, 2009; Koob & Volkow, 2010).

The brain disease model, with its emphasis on the chronic and loss-of-control nature of addiction, is not without controversy; most of the issues, nonetheless, can be reconciled. Two major objections have emerged. Some scholars assert that addiction is not a compulsive and chronic disease, as a large percentage of people with addiction can self-change and do recover naturally without treatment (Heyman, 2009). Second, some researchers believe that the brain disease model is overly reliant on neurocentrism and downplays the importance of psychological and social elements in explaining addiction's etiology and recovery, and that addiction problems involve more than a "brain disease" (Satel & Lilienfeld, 2014). Clarifications concerning three areas may help resolve the disputes. "Addiction" and "substance use disorder" are not the same; addiction involves a more severe level of substance use disorder (SUD). Alternatively, if "addiction" and "substance use disorder" are being used to represent the same phenomenon, the existence of a spectrum—ranging from mild to moderate to severe—must be acknowledged. The compulsive, chronic, and relapsing attributes are more applicable to the more severe cases. Although the "hard cases" or persons with severe conditions account for only a small portion of the entire pool of persons with SUD, this should not invalidate the brain disease model, as research in this regard may help us understand the underlying mechanism of how a mild SUD transitions to a moderate and severe level of addiction, and how such a transition can be prevented or reversed (Verhulst et al., 2015). Lastly, an insight of the compulsive and chronic nature of addiction is only part of the puzzle, thus should not, and does not, exclude psychological and social factors in explaining the etiology and recovery of addiction.

Substance Use Disorder Involves a Spectrum

The concept of addiction has been used interchangeably with the concept of SUD, although the two may be different. SUD (or behavioral addiction, such as gambling disorder) involves a spectrum. The *DSM-5* (APA, 2013) defines SUD or gambling disorder as having three levels: mild, moderate, and severe. The term *addiction* may best capture the moderate to severe extreme, if not solely the severe grade. One reason the *DSM-5* uses "substance use disorder" and not "addiction" as its diagnostic language is because the word "addiction" has an "uncertain definition" (p. 485). The *DSM-5*, however, does acknowledge that "[addiction] is in common usage in many countries to describe *severe* problems related to *compulsive* and *habitual* use of substances" (p. 485; [italics added]). In other words, the word "addiction" connotes a disorder with a more severe nature. The undifferentiation between the two concepts (or between the severe and less severe degrees of "substance use disorder," or between mild, moderate, and severe "addiction") has unnecessarily confounded the debate over whether addiction is a personal choice or a brain disease, as well as erroneously deemphasized the fundamentals of addiction in conceptualizing and treating addiction problems.

Two examples demonstrate this issue. First, research on self-change (natural recovery or spontaneous remission) has shown that many people afflicted with addiction actually recovered on their own without external intervention or treatment (Klingemann et al., 2009); some theorists, therefore, assert addiction is a choice, not a disease—people do not lose their ability to control themselves and they can stop using if they so choose. On the other hand, the same research also found a higher prevalence rate of successful self-change among individuals with a lesser degree of severity (Klingemann et al., 2009). This example shows that if we differentiate between people with lesser SUD from those with more severe SUD, the "choice" theory would be more applicable to the former and the "disease" theory to the latter group. Lumping the two together and suggesting that addiction is a choice, based merely on the existence of unassisted recovery among less afflicted people, is misleading. The second example examines Heyman's assertion that addiction is "a disorder of choice" and not a chronic disease (2009). Again, Heyman uses the terms "substance use disorder" (substance abuse and/or substance dependence) and "addiction" interchangeably. He cites the high remission rates in the Epidemiologic Catchment Area Study (ECA), stating that "at approximately age 24 more than half of those who ever met the criteria for addiction no longer reported even one symptom, and that by about age 37 approximately 75 percent of those who ever met the criteria for dependence were no longer reporting any symptoms . . . [I]t is likely that the proportion of those

THE FUNDAMENTALS OF ADDICTION   33

in their thirties who were still dependent was actually less than 25 percent. These findings do not support the view that addiction is a chronic disease" (pp. 70, 71). Heyman uses the term "criteria for addiction," which actually does not exist—the *DSM-IV-TR* (APA, 2000), the standard at the time of Heyman's book, only had criteria for "substance abuse" and "substance dependence." In addition, the 25 percent in the ECA study who were still dependent could very well have embodied the most severe group, while the 75 percent who were in remission contained people with less severe dependence problems. Also, a remission status does not necessarily exclude the notion of addiction as a chronic disease, as a person with a chronic disease is possible to reach remission when he or she engages in right lifestyle practices.

Furthermore, as Klingemann et al. (2009) put it, although self-recovery exists, not all who decide to self-change will succeed. One diagnostic criterion in the *DSM-5* for alcohol use disorder states, "There is a persistent desire or unsuccessful efforts to cut down or control alcohol use" (APA, 2013, p. 490); and for gambling disorder, "Has made repeated unsuccessful efforts to control, cut back, or stop gambling" (p. 585). Who would be the most qualified to describe the symptoms of addiction? Individuals with the addiction problems themselves! Self-help organizations and their members have long identified the compulsive, chronic, and loss-of-control nature of addiction. The website for Gamblers Anonymous (GA, 2018) states: "Our intention is to highlight that gambling for certain individuals is an illness called 'compulsive gambling.'" Alcoholics Anonymous (AA) offers a detailed description: "While there is no formal 'A.A. definition' of alcoholism, most of us agree that, for us, it could be described as *a physical compulsion, coupled with a mental obsession* . . . [W]e had a distinct physical desire to consume alcohol *beyond our capacity to control it* [italics added] . . . We not only had an abnormal craving for alcohol, but we frequently yielded to it at the worst possible times" (AA Grapevine, 1984, pp. 8–9). A recently reported case in the Netherlands represents those in the severest of the severe category. Mark Langedijk—a 41-year-old Dutch man who suffered from alcoholism and was in and out of rehab 41 times—ended his life via euthanasia, saying, "I want to die, enough is enough" (Richardson, 2016). He did not consider it an option to leave or stay with the addiction. Over the years, we have also seen heroin-addicted people committing suicides because of the unbearable pain and struggle between using and not using.

These cases epitomize the compulsive and pathological nature of addiction and nullify the choice theory.

The compulsive nature of addiction requires a tremendous effort for the person to initiate a change; it may also take multiple attempts and treatments before the person reaches a stable recovery. Even after a protracted recovery, the potential to relapse can never be completely ruled out because of the involvement of cravings or urges in addiction. A long-term recovery demands alertness to the possible occurrence of cravings and strategies for effectively dealing with it without resorting to the substance. The *DSM-5* committees recognized this issue, and not only added cravings to the list of the options for the diagnosis of the substance use disorder, they also considered the prolonged nature of cravings when defining remission. For example, they define "sustained remission" for alcohol use disorder as: "After full criteria for alcohol use disorder were previously met, none of the criteria for alcohol use disorder have been met at any time during a period of 12 months or longer (with the exception that Criterion A4, 'Craving, or a strong desire or urge to use alcohol,' may be met)" (p. 491). Treating cravings as an exception to remission criteria is an acknowledgment of the addiction's chronic nature.

The Severe Cases' Smaller Percentage Should Not Negate the Study of Brain Disease Model

Satel and Lilienfeld (2014) argue that "quitting is the rule, not the exception" and that the National Institute on Drug Abuse (NIDA)'s official definition for addiction, that it is a chronic and relapsing brain disease, is not representative of "the universe of addicts." Satel and Lilienfeld further state that the chronic and relapsing patients are the "hard cases," and "[yet] these patients often make the biggest impressions on clinicians and shape their views of addiction, if only because clinicians are especially likely to encounter them" (p. 4). Satel and Lilienfeld's argument can be resolved by Volkow and Koob's (2015) observation that although individuals with the most severe conditions only account for a small portion of those who meet the substance use disorder criteria, this fact should not "negate the value of the disease model in addiction" as it may help us understand the underlying mechanism whereby a mild substance use disorder transitions to a moderate and severe level of addiction, and how such a transition can be prevented or reversed (p. 678).

As we will discuss in details in this chapter, addiction involves not only impulsivity but also compulsivity and habituation. It is easier for people who engage in addictive behavior but whose brain has not been severely implicated by neuroadaptation or compulsion to recover without external intervention. Scientific research shows that addiction begins with impulsivity initially—the person seeks pleasure without checking negative consequences and the behavior is more ego-syntonic and voluntary in nature—but that impulsivity may transition to compulsivity during the later stages (Koob & Volkow, 2010). Compulsion is characterized by ingrained inflexibility, and the compulsive behavior is more ego-dystonic, involuntary, and stress-relieving in nature; the person feels compelled to engage in the behavior, despite knowing that the behavior would no longer be pleasurable or beneficial to him- or herself. Although it is not totally impossible, it is much more difficult for a severely addicted person to have a natural recovery. The compulsivity may drive the person to use actively and continuously, and become unable to think clearly or make sound decisions. This explains why it is easier for less severe cases to recover on their own or via treatment, whereas more severe cases often require extensive external treatment. Research regarding how to prevent addiction transitioning from a mild to moderate or severe grade, and how to reverse such a transition if it has already been formed, will be valuable investments that can benefit individuals, families, communities, and society.

A Brain Disease Model Does Not Necessarily Dismiss the Importance of the Quality-of-Life Factor

In addition to the genetic and biological theory—which the brain disease model may be placed under—systematic research has long proposed other theories explaining the etiology of addiction, including, for example, the developmental theory, the attachment theory, the psychological theory, the social theory, and the multivariate theory (Fisher & Harrison, 2018; Lassiter & Culbreth, 2017). These theories complement the brain disease model theory and reconcile the criticism by Satel and Lilienfeld (2014) that the brain disease model of addiction is neuro-centric, because it supposedly downplays "the underlying psychological and social reasons that drive drug use" (p. 5, online publication). Indeed, the insight of "self-medication," as it relates to issues of bio-psycho-social origin, is convincing and valuable as it sheds light on the importance of identifying and treating the *root* problems. For example, substance use disorder or addiction could be the result of self-medication of a physical pain, or a psychiatric disorder such as depression or posttraumatic stress disorder, or a psychosocial isolation or dislocation, or a general discontentment with life. The logic is that if these root problems can be resolved, the substance use problems will disappear. However, to consider substance use problems and addictive behaviors as only symptoms or by-products of a root problem or secondary to that root problem—be it biological, psychological, social, or a combination—underestimates the impact of a chronic exposure to the substances and activities on a person's brain and his or her subsequent behavior. After a brain's prolonged exposure to alcohol or drugs, an initially secondary problem may turn into a primary problem itself because of neuroadaptation. Quality of life (QoL)—covering such factors as physical and mental health, financial stability, access to health care, social support, employment, self-esteem, etc.—is a critical factor facilitating recovery (see Chapter 4), but the component of the chronic nature of addiction and its implication should not be excluded from the recovery formula. Focusing on QoL without emphasizing the nature of addiction is as insufficient as targeting only addiction symptoms without addressing the issue of QoL. Based on individual differences with regard to addiction symptoms, vulnerabilities, resources, and strengths, some people may benefit more with treatment of addiction symptoms, whereas others progress more if their quality of life can also be improved.

In the past two decades, scientific studies have suggested that addiction is a primary and independent disorder, in and of itself; specifically, a brain disease. The brain disease model of addiction has recognized the following three major characteristics of an addicted brain: neuroadaptation that involves a disrupted reward pathway and prefrontal cortex, a combination of impulsivity and compulsivity, and a disease of chronic nature. Let's examine these characteristics.

1. Addiction Implicates Neuroadaptation: Disrupted Limbic Reward Pathway and Prefrontal Cortex

Neuroadaptation is the result of the brain's repeated and chronic exposure to drugs or addictive behavior/process; it is one primary feature of a diseased brain, and is a key factor contributing to addiction. Volkow et al. (2009) state that the repeated perturbation of the dopamine system leads to "neuroadaptations in reward/saliency, motivation/drive, inhibitory control/executive function and memory/conditioning circuits, all of which are modulated by dopaminergic pathways" (p. 4). The two major areas of the brain involved in this process are the reward pathway in the limbic region and the prefrontal cortex; both are closely connected to each other.

The vulnerabilities of the two brain regions can be predisposed or acquired. People with the predisposed vulnerable limbic reward pathway tend to have a lower number of dopamine D_2 receptors and, subsequently, they are more likely to experience a sense of reward through potent drugs than via everyday life activities (Blum, 2000). As a result, they are more susceptible to drug addiction. On the other hand, the acquired vulnerability of the limbic reward pathway is its neuroadaptation, which is the consequence of repeated and chronic exposure of a person's brain to drugs. For the prefrontal cortex region, the predisposed vulnerabilities tend to happen to individuals with a higher level of innate impulsivity and lower self-control ability. As a result, they are particularly at risk for developing substance use disorder, and "[T]he roots of substance use disorder . . . can be seen in behaviors long before the onset of actual substance use itself" (*DSM-5*, 2013, p. 481). In contrast, the acquired vulnerability of the prefrontal cortex is its neuroadaptation, which is the outcome of repeated and chronic exposure of a person's brain to drugs. Following is a more detailed description of the acquired vulnerabilities or neuroadaptation of the limbic reward pathway and the prefrontal cortex.

The Mesolimbic Dopamine System Several reasons explain why drugs are rewarding, reinforcing, and addictive. First, drugs trigger large amounts of dopamine (DA) in our brain's limbic regions, creating the effects of pleasure. Not only do drugs produce pleasure, but they do so in a faster manner and with a larger amount compared to the natural rewards such as food, sex, music, and achievement (NIDA, 2014). Some drugs can create "2 to 10 times the amount of dopamine that natural rewards such as eating and sex do" and this may occur almost instantly in certain cases when the drugs are injected or smoked (NIDA, 2014, p. 18). Also, the effects of drugs can last a longer time than the effects resulting from natural rewards (NIDA, 2014). Second, this faster and larger release of dopamine makes the brain value drugs as salient, which thus motivates the person to want more drugs, regardless of whether he or she consciously perceives drugs as pleasurable or not (Volkow et al., 2009). Third, the brain's repeated and chronic exposure to drugs may deplete its dopamine D_2 receptors and disrupt dopamine release, subsequently decreasing the person's sensitivity to the natural rewards in life such as food, sex, and recreation (Volkow et al., 2009). The person may additionally experience withdrawal and tolerance. Drugs, which are more potent than the natural rewards, still have the ability to activate the depressed reward circuits, but would no longer make the person feel "high" but feel "normal" (Volkow et al., 2009). This explains the occurrence of tolerance (i.e., the person may need a larger amount of drugs to reach the same effect) as well as withdrawal (i.e., the person may experience dysphoria and pain if drug use is discontinued). Fourth, chronic exposure to drugs can prompt neuroadaptations in non-conscious memory systems or habits. Pavlovian classical conditioning explains this phenomenon. Exposure to drug-associated cues (e.g., things, persons, and places), even in the absence of actual drugs, may still trigger uncontrollable urges or cravings in the person, even after he or she has maintained abstinence for many years (Koob, 2009; NIDA, 2014).

In light of the fact that dopamine plays an important role in reinforcing the effects of drugs, Volkow and colleagues suggest several strategies to combat addiction, including: (a) enhance the reward value of non-drug activities and reinforcers, as well as decrease the reward value of substance use and other addictive behaviors; (b) dwindle the conditioned drug behaviors and weaken the motivation to use the drug; and (c) fortify frontal executive control and inhibitory ability (Volkow et al., 2009; Volkow et al., 2011). Several methods help to increase the reward value of non-drug activities and reinforcers. Contingency management (CM), community reinforcement approach (CRA), mindfulness-based intervention (MBI), mindfulness-oriented recovery enhancement (MORE), or even exercises are some examples. (Although methods that enhance prefrontal executive control are discussed later in the subsection of prefrontal cortex, many methods are relevant to both the mesolimbic dopamine system and the prefrontal cortex system as the two systems are related).

CM systematically provides patients with vouchers or prizes if their urine tests negative and takes away those vouchers and prizes if the urine tests positive. Numerous studies have consistently proved the efficacies and effectiveness of CM in facilitating treatment compliance and outcomes

(Petry, 2011; Winger et al., 2005). One major concern for CM, however, is that the treatment effectiveness may not necessarily be carried over for long term, once the contingency reinforcers (e.g., vouchers or prizes) are discontinued. CRA suggests helping addicted patients by replacing their pleasure acquired from alcohol and other drugs with reward feelings obtained from family, occupation, and recreational social activities (Smith et al., 2009). MBI proposes that a short-term practice of mindfulness and meditation may be more likely to enhance a person's top-down neural systems and cognitive function, whereas a longer term of such practice could actually robustly change a person's brain structure, leading to the restoration of the bottom-up neural systems (Chiesa et al., 2013). Chiesa et al. state, "This might explain why long-term meditators frequently report increased mental stability rather than continuous need to regulate their own mental processes" (p. 93). More rigorous research is still needed in this regard.

Eric Garland suggests that the knowledge of the neuroplastic adaptations that support dysregulated circuit-function related to addiction can enlighten treatment advance efforts to steer the next generation of mindfulness-based intervention. Garland subsequently developed the mindfulness-oriented recovery enhancement (MORE) treatment method, which targets changing the drug-usurped dopaminergic salience neuropathways by accentuating skills that heighten savoring of natural rewards rather than drugs (Garland et al., 2014). Natural rewards can come from a beautiful scenery, a warm hug, a family reunion, and many other sources. Robertson and colleagues (2016) randomize methamphetamine users who are attending an inpatient behavioral treatment program to two groups: one receives exercise training and the other receives health education training. Although the two groups were not different in their striatal D_2/D_3 dopamine receptor availability at baseline, Robertson and colleagues found that the exercise group showed a significant increase in their striatal D_2/D_3 receptor availability after 8 weeks, whereas the health education group did not. Haglund and colleagues' study (2014) showed that exercise can effectively reduce depression among abstinent methamphetamine-dependent patients who are in early recovery. In addition, patients who attended the most exercise sessions acquired the most benefits; this treatment with exercise also seems to particularly benefit individuals with co-occurring disorders such as comorbid psychiatric, medical, and addictive disorders.

The Prefrontal Cortex The research has initially focused on the effects of a disrupted reward pathway in the limbic region on the formation of addiction; however, more recent data have extended the emphasis to the prefrontal cortex region of the brain (Feil et al., 2010; Goldstein & Volkow, 2002). The functions of the prefrontal cortex include decision-making, planning, judgment, problem-solving, impulse control, and response inhibition. Volkow and colleagues (2009) report that a chronic exposure to drugs leads to a decrease in dopamine D_2 and dopamine release, which is also related to reduced activity in the brain regions of the orbitofrontal cortex, the cingulate gyrus, and the dorsolateral prefrontal cortex. The orbitofrontal cortex involves salience attribution, and its disruption brings about compulsion; the cingulate gyrus involves inhibitory control, and its disruption results in impulsivity; and the dorsolateral prefrontal cortex involves executive function, and its disruption causes dysfunctional regulation of intentional actions (Volkow et al., 2009). Executive function (EF) may be conceptualized as having two components: the cold EF and the hot EF (Hagen et al., 2016). The cold EF involves the ability to focus on and plan goal-directed tasks and behaviors, which are more linked to the dorsolateral prefrontal cortex; the hot EF, on the other hand, affects processes that have a more marked emotional salience and tends to associate with the orbitofrontal cortex (Hagen et al., 2016). Major symptoms of executive function deficits include decreased sensitivity to future consequences; preference for immediate, albeit smaller, rewards over larger but delayed rewards; decreased ability to inhibit inappropriate responses; and compromised and weakened decision-making ability in daily life situations (Alfonso et al., 2011; Fernández-Serrano et al., 2011; Hagen et al., 2016).

Many preclinical and clinical studies have indicated neuroadaptations in the prefrontal cortex, and shown that drugs and drug cues uniquely activate the prefrontal cortex only in the addicted but not in non-addicted individuals (Volkow et al., 2013). Caracuel et al.'s study (2008) found that both individuals with acquired brain injury and substance abusers had higher total scores than the controls in the Frontal Systems Behavioral Scale (which measures behavioral problems related to frontal-striatal neural damage). For the subscales, the participants with acquired brain injury had higher scores than substance-abusing participants and control subjects regarding executive dysfunction, disinhibition, and apathy, whereas the substance abusers had higher scores than the controls regarding executive dysfunction. Fernández-Serrano et al.'s review (2011) revealed that poly substance-abusing individuals may still experience prefrontal cortex deficits even after six months of abstinence. The prefrontal cortex deficits—including executive dysfunction—often deter treatment compliance and retention and lead to poor treatment outcomes; such deficits also precipitate relapses, as well as negatively affect occupational functioning, quality of life, community integration, and long-term recovery (Alfonso et al., 2011; Hagen et al., 2016).

Hagen et al. (2016) suggest that assessment of a patient's executive function should be part of clinical routine and be integrated to individualized treatment plan. Their study also found the Behavior Rating Inventory of Executive Functions—Adult Version (BRIEF-A) to be a promising inventory to assess executive function among patients with substance use disorder. BRIEF-A includes the behavioral regulations index (including subscales measuring shift, inhibit, emotional-control, and self-monitor) and the metacognition index (including subscales measuring initiate, plan, working memory, etc.) (Roth, Isquith, & Gioia/Roth, Lance, Isquith, Fischer, & Giancola, cited in Hagen et al., 2016).

Various pharmacological treatments targeting prefrontal cortex deficits have been proposed and are currently undergoing research. For example, atomoxetine, a drug used to treat ADHD because of its ability to remediate high levels of impulsivity, is suggested to be, if administered systemically, able to help treatment of some individuals who are addicted to cocaine or heroin (Everitt & Robbins, 2013). An fMRI study showed that oral methylphenidate has cognitive benefits and can decrease impulsivity in cocaine-addicted individuals (Goldstein & Volkow, 2011).

Behavioral treatments have emerged to enhance a person's prefrontal cortex and cognitive function. For example, Goal Management Training (GMT)—which has been effective in helping clients with brain injury and the elderly clinical population—was designed to enhance participants' ability to organize and achieve goals, including improving inadequate forethought, deficient self-control, and poor decision-making skills, with respect to addiction treatment outcomes (Alfonso et al., 2011). Alfonso et al.'s study showed that participants of a GMT + MF (mindfulness) group made significant progress in their neuropsychological performance after treatment, including working memory, response inhibition, and decision-making;

however, participants of the standard treatment group did not make such progress. Other behavioral treatment techniques may include "response-cost procedure," an effective method that adopts operant conditioning principles to improve clients' disinhibition problems. In that, clients are given tokens which can be redeemed for rewards; the tokens, however, can be taken away if the client breaks the rules (Szczepanski & Knight, 2014).

Cognitive behavioral therapy, mindfulness-based intervention, mindfulness-oriented recovery enhancement, mindfulness-based relapse prevention (see Chapter 8), and motivational interviewing (see Chapter 6) may also increase the cognitive function of addicted clients as well as strengthen their top-down neural system in modulating the emotion generative bottom-up neural system (Chiesa, 2013).

2. Addiction Involves Impulsivity, Compulsivity, and Habits

Earlier studies suggested that addiction is mainly the result of a person's impulsive tendency to pursue short-term, ego-syntonic, and appetitive effects, without taking into consideration the possible detrimental, long-term consequences. Those studies emphasized that addiction is a goal-directed behavior seeking rewards. More recent research, however, points out that addiction, particularly during its later stages, involves a more complex process and encompasses not only impulsivity but also compulsivity and habit (Everitt & Robbins, 2013; Koob, 2009). In contrast to impulsivity, compulsivity involves relieving distress and discomfort rather than pursuing pleasure; it entails engaging in a behavior against one's own conscious wishes. Obsessive compulsive disorder (OCD) epitomizes compulsivity, in that the person knows the absurdity of a behavior but cannot help but still perform it, just to relieve discomfort or anxiety (Torregrossa et al., 2008). While impulsivity and compulsivity may appear to act in opposing directions, the more recent data show both may implicate the same one psychiatric disorder, such as OCD, addiction, and other impulse-control disorders (Chamberlain et al., 2018). For addiction, the current data underscore the role of compulsivity in the development of addiction and its chronicity. Specifically, addiction may begin with impulsivity, but end with compulsivity—that is, the person continuously and compulsively engages in the behavior even when the reinforcing and rewarding outcomes of the behavior have gone, which happens in addiction during its later stages (Koob, 2009).

THE FUNDAMENTALS OF ADDICTION

43

Researchers have also recently proposed the concept of habits to explain addiction. Sjoerds and colleagues (2014) said that the literature tends to treat the terms "habits" and "compulsivity" interchangeably, but they see distinctions between the two. To them, compulsivity is more "motivational habits," in that there is an urge to perform the behavior or a purpose of decreasing distress and discomfort; whereas habits can be "motor habits" that are driven directly by motor-schemes and stimulus-response contingencies, involving no thoughts, feelings, or urges. They view both compulsivity and motor habits important in forming addiction. Let's examine in more detail the concepts of impulsivity, compulsivity, and habits.

Impulsivity Impulsivity has traditionally been considered the core of the pathogenesis of substance use disorder (Allen et al., 1998; Goldstein & Volkow, 2002; Koob & Volkow, 2010), and equivalent to the memory impairment problem in Alzheimer's or the motor control problem in Parkinson's disease (Stevens et al., 2014). In general, impulsivity encompasses three dimensions: (a) impulsive action involves response disinhibition, or inhibitory deficits, or low self-control; (b) impulsive choices refer to a person's picking an immediate reward or gratification over a larger delayed reward; and (c) impulsive decision-making concerns making quick decisions without forethought and concern for possible consequences (Dalley et al., 2011; Grant & Chamberlain, 2014; Torregrossa et al., 2008).

Some researchers conceptualized impulsivity as an imbalance between two contending neural systems—the reward-sensitive limbic system, which is an evolutionarily older, impulsive, bottom-up system; versus the prefrontal cortex system, which is a relatively newly developed, reflective, cognitive top-down system (Bechara, 2005; Stevens et al., 2014). When the top-down system overrides the bottom-up system, the person is more able to make sound decisions and function reasonably, including suppressing inappropriate thoughts and prepotent responses, as well as choosing a delayed but larger benefit over a smaller but immediate reward (Stevens et al., 2014). A prolonged exposure to the substances or processes, however, leads to the brain's neuroadaptation, resulting in the impulsive bottom-up system's dominance over the executive top-down system, which subsequently damages a person's ability to exercise his or her "willpower to resist drugs" (Bechara, 2005, p. 1458). Although neuroadaptation may lead to impulsivity (Grant & Chamberlain, 2014), impulsivity could be inherited and thus a risk factor precipitating addiction (APA, 2013). Grant and Chamberlain's literature review found not only that a chronic exposure to addictive substances or processes associates with enhanced impulsivity, but also that such an intensified impulsivity could actually predate addiction. In addition, impulsivity is a complex concept—it is inconclusive whether it is a unitary phenomenon or involves multi-faceted behavioral traits (Dalley & Roiser, 2012). Dalley and Roiser point out the paradox that symptoms of attention deficit and hyperactivity disorder (ADHD) can be improved by dopamine-releasing stimulant medications, whereas medications boosting dopamine transmission (e.g., dopamine agonists) seem to trigger impulsivity among some patients with Parkinson's disease.

Compulsivity Neuroadaptation not only associates with impulsivity but also compulsivity. The insight of the coexistence of impulsivity and compulsivity may reconcile the debate about the nature of addiction: Is addiction a choice or a disease? In the beginning phase, it may be a voluntary action as the person chooses to start the use or the behavior, and therefore "a choice." However, after a repeated engagement—and the subsequent neuroadaptation—the impulsivity component may transition to a compulsivity component or both may coexist (Koob, 2009). Koob and Volkow (2010) stated: "impulsivity often dominates at the early stages and impulsivity combined with compulsivity dominates at the later stages. As an individual moves from impulsivity to compulsivity, a shift occurs from positive reinforcement driving the motivated behavior to negative reinforcement and automaticity driving the motivated behavior" (p. 218).

Compulsivity in this regard may be explained by three approaches: (1) A chronic exposure to the substances (e.g., alcohol) or the processes/behaviors (e.g., gambling) leads to withdrawal, tolerance, and/or craving, all of which may trigger and compel the person to continuously use the substance or engage in the process to combat and counteract the physical and psychological distress brought about by those three symptoms. The person is now pursuing "normal" rather than "high." (2) The neuroadaptation of the brain's reward pathway not only has caused the person to credit the substance or process with great importance, but also instigated cognitive rigidity in the person. Such erroneous salience attribution and a lack of cognitive flexibility result in the person's continuous, or even uncontrollable, seeking of the substance and/or the process in spite of the absence of pleasure and presence of multiple negative consequences. (3) A prolonged exposure to the substance and/or process may create response patterns or operant conditionings, which in turn foster ingrained habits within the person (Everitt & Robbins, 2013; Koob & Volkow, 2010). The exposure to substances or processes gives rise to pleasure and reward during the initial stage of the addiction course—and thus, a positive reinforcement conditioning; the exposure takes away the distress, anxiety, and discomfort during the late stage of the addiction course—hence, a negative reinforcement conditioning (Koob, 2009). These conditionings lead to the formation of habit; the initially voluntary behavior now becomes a habit which compels the person to continue the use or the act even in the absence of pleasure and reward (Everitt & Robbins, 2103; Koob & Volkow, 2010; Schwabe et al., 2011). Schwabe et al. said the "transition from voluntary drug use to involuntary drug addiction may be seen as a transition from prefrontal cortex-dependent goal-directed to dorsolateral striatum-dependent habitual action" (pp. 54–55). Based on this perspective of compulsivity, addiction can be construed as a disease.

3. Addiction Is a Chronic Disease

Just like many other chronic diseases—such as diabetes, asthma, high blood pressure, AIDS, and cancer—addiction is a chronic disease, which can be treated effectively, but has no cure. Subsequently, self-monitoring and relapse prevention are a normal part of the person's long-term recovery. Alcoholics Anonymous (AA) highlights this concept in simple language: "One day at a time, for the rest of your life." AA and other self-help groups also emphasize the importance of humility and safeguarding against complacency with respect to one's perception of and attitude toward substance use and other life issues, along the life-long journey of recovery. To addicted people, working on recovery and maintaining abstinence demand lifetime commitment.

Emerging research indicates that addiction affects neurotransmission and interactions not only within reward structures of the brain but also between the brain's hippocampal circuits and cortical circuits, as well as reward structures, leading to the memory of prior exposure to drug rewards and their associations with places, things, and persons (Volkow et al., 2002). Recognizing the fact that addiction is a chronic disease and cravings may still exist in people even after they have been abstinent for a prolonged time, the *DSM-5* defines remission as essentially the lack of substance use disorder criteria except for craving. For example, the definition for "Alcohol Use Disorder, In Sustained Remission" is "After full criteria for alcohol use disorder were previously met, none of the criteria for alcohol use disorder have been met at any time during a period of 12 months or longer (with the exception that Criterion A4, 'Craving, or a strong desire or urge to use alcohol,' may be met)" (APA, 2013, p. 491). The *DSM-5*'s definition for "in early remission" is the same except the time period is "at least 3 months but for less than 12 months" (p. 491).

Basically, craving can be triggered or induced under at least three conditions: (a) Withdrawal-induced craving: Because of withdrawal symptoms such as insomnia, the individual experiences the urge to use in order to counteract those discomforts. Withdrawal may range from short-term, as in a couple of weeks, to longer-term, as in several months. (b) Stress-induced craving: Studies have shown that stress may also trigger a person's craving (Breese et al., 2011; Fox et al., 2007). (c) Cue-induced craving: Altered brain memory and other circuit mechanisms, as well as the Pavlovian classical conditioning theory, may explain the drug-related cue-induced craving (Everitt & Robbins, 2013, 2016; Fox et al., 2007; Volkow et al., 2002). Ko and colleagues (2009) compared 10 respondents with an online-gaming addiction and 10 respondents without such an addiction (the control group). They found that several regions of the brain (e.g., right orbitofrontal cortex, right nucleus accumbens, etc.) were activated when the addicted respondent viewed the gaming-related pictures, whereas such activation did not occur when the addicted respondent viewed the mosaic pictures or when the control respondent viewed the gaming-related pictures. The activation of those brain areas was also positively related to the respondent's self-reported gaming urge. Many studies reveal that substance-dependent individuals (including, for example, those using heroin, cocaine, and alcohol) show elevated craving when exposed to substance-related videos; they don't show such elevated craving when exposed to neutral-content videos; while non-substance-dependent individuals do not show elevated craving when exposed to substance-related videos (Zhao et al., 2012). One important finding is that such cue-induced craving may

THE FUNDAMENTALS OF ADDICTION

occur both among people who have had only a short abstinence period (e.g., less than one month) and among those with a long abstinence period (e.g., more than one year) (Zhao et al., 2012). This research evidence reinforces our understanding of the chronic nature of addiction.

Although craving does not equal relapse, it often precipitates relapse. Relapse is the "norm" during recovery, meaning not that it should be encouraged but that it may be a typical part of the recovery process. Dennis et al. (2007) studied the data that followed up 1,162 clients for eight years and found that the initial abstinence does not represent changes related to long-term recovery, that relapse risk is especially high in the earliest three years of abstinence, and that the risk of relapse "never completely goes away" (p. 607). Systematic research has suggested eight categories of relapse triggers: unpleasant emotions, physical discomfort, pleasant emotions, testing control over use, urges and temptations, conflict with others, social pressure to use, and pleasant times with others (Annis, 1986; Breslin et al., 2000).

Because of society's lack of understanding of addiction as a chronic disease, addiction is still perceived by many people, even some researchers, as "a disorder of choice" (e.g., Heyman, 2009). Addiction has a great deal of stigma attached to it. Addicted people often are labeled as "lacking a moral character," "lazy," "unproductive," and "destructive." Family members are frustrated by the *repeated* relapses of their addicted significant others. Even the addicted persons may blame themselves, have a sense of self-loathing, lose hope of getting well, and swirl down to despair. The philosophy of treating a *chronic* disease requires spirituality, which can empower the person when addiction has drained all of his or her strengths and confidence. Spirituality and faith can come from within self, significant others, groups, or community. An awareness and acceptance of a higher power that is greater than self can be comforting and relieving. Regardless of the origin of spirituality, it gives an addicted person hope and faith that with the proper pharmacological and behavioral treatments, social support, and case management, long-term recovery can be achieved.

Although currently no medications have been developed to cure addiction, pharmacological therapies have been developed, and development research continues, to help prevent or reduce relapse. Chapter 7 of Part II of this book addresses pharmacotherapy for addiction. Many evidence-based behavioral therapies have also been established, including spiritual development, motivational interviewing, self-help groups, cognitive behavioral therapy, mindfulness-based intervention, dialectical behavioral therapy, acceptance and commitment therapy, contingency management, community reinforcement therapy, and other treatment strategies. Together, they help prevent relapse and empower people to reach a long-term recovery. Chapters 6 and 8 of Part II of this book discuss these behavioral and psychosocial treatment strategies in detail.

Many addicted persons do not perceive their lives as having been rewarding prior to the addiction; they may experience even worse situations after the addiction. Hardships and challenges in life are unavoidable for all human beings; like others, addicted persons may experience or encounter such adversities prior to their addiction. Unlike others, not only such "normal" everyday life problems or issues will escalate into much worse conditions but also the abilities of the addicted persons to manage such conditions will deteriorate after their addiction onset and prolonged addiction career. Addiction has changed the way they think, feel, and behave. Helping an addicted person to manage everyday life issues is more difficult compared to helping a non-addicted person to do the same, let alone the need to handle issues of addiction and relapses. Addiction treatments and recovery thus should target not only eliminating addiction and preventing relapse but also transforming the person's dysfunctional and distorted ways of thinking, feeling, and behaving into those more functional and healthy. Furthermore, some addicted people grew up in a detrimental environment and have never learned functional life skills even before their addiction, and what they need is "habilitation" rather than "rehabilitation."

A common assumption is that once society has attempted to help them—offering detoxification, treating the co-occurring disorders and traumas, finding employment, assisting with social support and other resources, and boosting their self-esteem and self-confidence—they ought to be cured and rid of the addiction *once and for all*. All of these services and treatments are salient for facilitating recovery, except that one major piece of the puzzle is missing: an understanding of addiction as a brain malady, with the complication of being a chronic and relapsing disease. Society and family members often are frustrated by the repeated relapses of addicted persons, and subsequently perceive them as moral failures, weak-willed, out-of-control, unproductive, and destructive. Addicted individuals may internalize the stigma and become loaded with shame and guilt, which

THE FUNDAMENTALS OF ADDICTION 49

further adds barriers to recovery. A treatment that emphasizes quality of life improvement without addressing the neurophysiological nature of addiction is as incomplete as a treatment that accentuates reduction of addiction symptoms without tackling quality of life issues.

References

A.A. Grapevine, Inc. (1984, first printing). This is A.A.: An introduction to the A.A. Recovery Program. Retrieved on 04/11/2018 from www.aa.org/assets/en_US/p-1_thisisaa1.pdf

Agrawal, A., & Lynskey, M.T. (2008). Are there genetic influences on addiction: Evidence from family, adoption and twin studies. *Addiction, 103*, 1069–1081.

Alfonso, J.P., Caracuel, A., Delgado-Pastor, L.C., & Verdejo-Garcia, A. (2011). Combined goal management training and mindfulness meditation improve executive functions and decision-making performance in abstinent polysubstance abusers. *Drug and Alcohol Dependence, 117*, 78–81.

Allen, T.J., Moeller, F.G., Rhoades, H.M., & Cherek, D.R. (1998). Impulsivity and history of drug dependence. *Drug and Alcohol Dependence, 50*, 137–145.

American Psychiatric Association [APA]. (2000). *Diagnostic and statistical manual of mental disorders-text revision (DSM-IV-TR)*, Fourth Edition. Arlington, VA: American Psychiatric Association.

American Psychiatric Association [APA]. (2013). *Diagnostic and statistical manual of mental disorders*, Fifth Edition. Arlington, VA: American Psychiatric Association.

American Society of Addiction Medicine website (n.d.). Definition of Addiction. Retrieved on 05/23/2018 from www.asam.org/resources/definition-of-addiction

Annis, H.M. (1986). *A relapse prevention model for the treatment of alcoholics*. New York: Pergamon Press.

Beaver, K.M., Hoffman, T., Shields, R.T., Vaughn, M.G., DeLisi, M., & Wright, J.P. (2010). Gender differences in genetic and environmental influences on gambling: Results from a sample of twins from the national longitudinal study of adolescent health. *Addiction, 105*, 536–542.

Bechara, A. (2005). Decision making, impulse control and loss of willpower to resist drugs: A neurocognitive perspective. *Nature Neuroscience, 8*(11), 1458–1463.

Bevilacqua, L., & Goldman, D. (2009). Genes and addictions. *Clinical Pharmacology and Therapeutics, 85*(4), 359–361.

Blum, K., Braverman, E.R., Holder, J.M., Lubar, J.F., Monastra, V.J., Miller, D., Lubar, J.O., Chen, T.J., & Comings, D.E. (2000). Reward deficiency syndrome: A biogenetic model for the diagnosis and treatment of impulsive, addictive, and compulsive behaviors. *Journal of Psychoactive Drugs, 32*(Suppl i–iv), 1–112.

Breese, G.R., Sinha, R., & Heilig, M. (2011). Chronic alcohol neuroadaptation and stress contribute to susceptibility for alcohol craving and relapse. *Pharmacology & Therapeutics, 129*(2), 149–171.

Breslin, F.C., Sobell, L.C., Sobell, M.B., & Agrawal, S. (2000). A comparison of a brief and long version of the situational confidence questionnaire. *Behaviour Research and Therapy, 38*, 1211–1220.

Caracuel, A., Verdejo-Garcia, A., Vilar-Lopez, R., Perez-Garcia, M., Salinas, I., Cuberos, G., Coin, M. Santiago-Ramajo, S., & Puente, A. (2008). Fronta.l behavioral and emotional symptoms in Spanish individuals with acquired brain injury and substance use disorders. *Archives of Clinical Neuropsychology, 23*, 447–454.

Chamberlain, S.R., Stochl, J., Redden, S.A., & Grant, J.E. (2018). Latent traits of impulsivity and compulsivity: Toward dimensional psychiatry. *Psychological Medicine, 48*(5), 810–821. doi: 10.1017/S0033291717002185.

Chiesa, A., Serretti, A., & Jakobsen, J.C. (2013). Mindfulness: Top-down or bottom-up emotion regulation strategy? *Clinical Psychology Review, 33*, 82–96.

Dalley, J.W., & Robbins, T.W. (2011). Impulsivity, compulsivity, and top-down cognitive control. *Neuron, 69*, 680–694.

Dalley, J.W., & Roiser, J.P. (2012). Dopamine, serotonin and impulsivity. *Neuroscience, 215*, 42–58.

Dennis, M.L., Foss, M.A., & Scott, C.K. (2007). An eight-year perspective on the relationship between the duration of abstinence and other aspects of recovery. *Evaluation Review, 31*(6), 585–612.

Dick, D.M., & Agrawal, A. (2008). The genetics of alcohol and other drug dependence. *Alcohol Research & Health, 31*(2), 111–118.

Everitt, B.J., & Robbins, T.W. (2013). From the ventral to the dorsal striatum: Devolving views of their roles in drug addiction. *Neuroscience and Biobehavioral Reviews, 37*, 1946–1954.

Everitt, B.J., & Robbins, T.W. (2016). Drug addiction: Updating actions to habits to compulsions ten years on. *Annual Review of Psychology, 67*, 23–50.

Feil, J., Sheppard, D., Fitzgerald, P.B., Yucel, M., Lubman, D.I., & Bradshaw, J.L. (2010). Addiction, compulsive drug seeking, and the role of frontostriatal mechanisms in regulating inhibitory control. *Neuroscience and Biobehavioral Reviews, 35*, 248–275.

Fernández-Serrano, M.J., Pérez-García, M., & Verdejo-García, A. (2011). What are the specific vs. generalized effects of drugs of abuse on neuropsychological performance? *Neuroscience and Biobehavioral Reviews, 35*, 377–406.

Fisher, G.L., & Harrison, T.C. (2018). *Substance abuse: Information for school counselors, social workers, therapists, and counselors.* New York: Pearson.

Fox, H.C., Bergquist, K.L., Hong, K.I., & Sinha, R. (2007). Stress-induced and alcohol cue-induced craving in recently abstinent alcohol-dependent individuals. *Alcoholism: Clinical and Ecperimental Research, 31*(3), 395–403.

Gamblers Anonymous (GA, 2018). Recovery Program (para. 4). Retrieved on 04/10/2018 from www.gamblersanonymous.org/ga/content/recovery-program

Garland, E.L., Froeliger, B., & Howard, M.O. (2014). Mindfulness training targets neurocognitive mechanisms of addiction at the attention-appraisal-emotion interface. *Frontiers in Psychiatry, 4*(173). doi: 10.3389/fpsyt.2013.00173.

Goldman, D., Oroszi, G., & Ducci, F., (2005). The genetics of addictions: Uncovering the genes. *Nature Reviews Genetics, 6*, 521–532.

Goldstein, R., & Volkow, N.D. (2002). Drug addiction and its underlying neurobiological basis: Neuroimaging evidence for the involvement of the frontal cortex. *American Journal of Psychiatry, 159*(10), 1642–1652.

Goldstein, R., & Volkow, N.D. (2011). Oral methylphenidate normalizes cingulate activity and decreases impulsivity in cocaine addiction during an emotionally salient cognitive task. *Neuropsychopharmacology, 36*, 366–367.

Grant, J.E., & Chamberlain, S.R. (2014). Impulsive action and impulsive choice across substance and behavioral addictions: Cause or consequence? *Addictive Behaviors, 39*, 1632–1639.

Hagen, E., Erga, A.H., Hagen, K.P., Nesvag, S.M., McKay, J.R., Lundervold, A.J., & Walderhaug, E. (2016). Assessment of executive function in patients with substance use disorder: A comparison of inventory- and performance-based assessment. *Journal of Substance Abuse Treatment, 66*, 1–8.

Haglund, M., Ang, A., Mooney, L., Gonzales, R., Chudzynski, J., Cooper, C.B., Dolezal, B.A., et al. (2014). Predictors of depression outcomes among abstinent methamphetamine-dependent individuals exposed to an exercise intervention. *The American Journal on Addictions, 24*, 246–251.

Heyman, G.M. (2009). *Addiction: A disorder of choice.* Cambridge, MA: Harvard University Press.

Kendler, K.S., PirouziFard, M., Lonn, S., Edwards, A.C., Maes, H.H., Lichtenstein, P., Sundquist, J., & Sundquist, K. (2016). A national Swedish twin-sibling study of alcohol use disorders. *Twin Research and Human Genetics, 19*(5), 430–437.

Klingemann, H., Sobell, M.B., & Sobell, L.C. (2009). Continuities and changes in self-change research. *Addiction, 105*, 1510–1518.

Ko, C.H., Liu, G.C., Hsiao, S., Yen, J.Y., Yang, M.J., Lin, W.C., Yen, C.F., & Chen, C.S. (2009). Brain activities associated with gaming urge of online gaming addiction. *Journal of Psychiatric Research, 43*(7), 739–747.

Koob, G.F. (2009). Neurobiological substrates for the dark side of compulsivity in addiction. *Neuropharmacology, 56*, 18–31.

Koob, G.F., & Volkow, N.D. (2010). Neurocircuitry of addiction. *Neuropsychopharmacology, 35*, 217–238.

Lassiter, P.S., & Culbreth, J.R. (Eds.) (2017). *Theory and practice of addition counseling.* Thousand Oaks, CA: SAGE.

McGue, M. (1999). The behavioral genetics of alcoholism. *Current Directions in Psychological Science, 8*, 109–115.

National Institute on Drug Abuse (NIDA, 2014). Drugs, brains, and behavior: The science of addiction. NIH Pub. No: 14–5605. Retrieved on 02/17/2018 from https://d14rmgtrwzf5a.cloudfront.net/sites/default/files/soa_2014.pdf.

Petry, N.M. (2011). Contingency management: What it is and why psychiatrists should want to use it. *The Psychiatrist, 35*(5), 161–163.

Prescott, C.A., Aggen, S.H., & Kendler, K.S. (1999). Sex differences in the sources of genetic liability to alcohol abuse and dependence in a population-based sample of U.S. twins. *Alcoholism: Clinical and Experimantal Research, 23*(7), 1136–1144.

Richardson, B. (2016, November 30). Mark Langedijk, Dutch man, euthanized over alcoholism. *Washington Times.* Retrieved on 04/11/2018 from www.washingtontimes.com/news/2016/nov/30/mark-langedijk-dutch-man-euthanized-over-alcoholis/.

Robertson, C., Ishibashi, K., Chudzynski, J., Mooney, L.J., Rawson, R.A., Dolezal, B.A. Cooper, C.B., et al. (2016). Effect of exercise training on striatal dopamine D_2/D_3 receptors in methamphetamine users during behavioral treatment. *Neuropsychopharmacology, 41*, 1629–1636.

Satel, S., & Lilienfeld, S.O. (2014). Addiction and the brain-disease fallacy. *Frontiers in Psychiatry, 4*(141).

Schwabe, L., Dickinson, A., & Wolf, O.T. (2011). Stress, habits, and drug addiction: A psychoneuroendocrinological perspective. *Experimental and Clinical Psychopharmacology, 19*(1), 53–63.

Sjoerds, Z., Luigjes, J., van den Brink, W., Denys, D., & Yucel, M. (2014). The role of habits and motivation in human drug addiction: A reflection. *Frontiers in Psychiatry, 5*(8). doi: 10.3389/fpsyt.2014.00008.

Smith, J.E., Campos-Melady, M., & Meyers, R.J. (2009). CRA and CRAFT. *Journal of Behavior Analysis in Health, Sports, Fitness and Medicine, 2*(1), 4–31.

Stevens, L., Verdejo-Garcia, A., Goudriaan, A.E., Roeyers, H., Dom, G., & Vanderplasschen, W. (2014). Impulsivity as a vulnerability factor for poor addiction treatment outcomes: A review of neurocognitive findings among individuals with substance use disorders. *Journal of Substance Abuse Treatment, 47*, 58–72.

Sussman, S., & Sussman, A.N. (2011). Considering the definition of addiction. *International Journal of Environmental Research and Public Health, 8*, 4025–4038. doi: 10.3390/ijerph8104025.

Szczepanski, S.M., & Knight, R.T. (2014). Insights into human behavior from lesions to the prefrontal cortex. *Neuron, 83*(5), 1002–1018.

Torregrossa, M.M., Quinn, J.J., & Taylor, J.R. (2008). Impulsivity, compulsivity, and habit: The role of orbitofrontal cortex revisited. *Biology Psychiatry, 63*(3), 253–255. doi: 10.1016/j.biopsych.2007.11.014.

Verhulst, B., Neale, M.C., & Kendler, K.S. (2015). The heritability of alcohol use disorders: A meta-analysis of twin and adoption studies. *Psychological Medicine, 45*(5), 1061–1072.

Volkow, N.D., Fowler, J.S., Wang, G.J., Baler, R., & Telang, F. (2009). Imaging dopamine's role in drug abuse and addiction. *Neuropharmacology, 56*, 3–8.

Volkow, N.D., Fowler, J.S., Wang, G., & Goldstein, R.Z. (2002). Role of dopamine, the frontal cortex and memory circuits in drug addiction: Insight from imaging studies. *Neurobiology of Learning and Memory, 78*, 610–624.

Volkow, N.D., & Koob, G. (2015). Brain disease model of addiction: Why is it so controversial? *Lancet Psychiatry, 2*(8), 677–679.

Volkow, N.D., Wang, G.J., Fowler, J.S., Tomasi, D., & Telang, F. (2011). Addiction: Beyond dopamine reward circuitry. *PNAS, 108*(37), 15037–15042.

Volkow, N.D., Wang, G.J., Tomasi, D., & Baler, R.D. (2013). Unbalanced neuronal circuits in addiction. *Current Opinion in Neurobiology, 23*, 639–648.

Winger, G., Woods, J.H., Galuska, C.M., & Wade-Galuska, T. (2005). Behavioral perspectives on the neuroscience of drug addiction. *Journal of the Experimental Analysis of Behavior, 84*(3), 667–681.

Yates, W.R., Cadoret, R.J., Troughton, E., & Stewart, M.A. (1996). An adoption study of DSM-IIIR alcohol and drug dependence severity. *Drug and Alcohol Dependence, 41*, 9–15.

Zhao, M., Fan, C., Du, J., Jiang, H., Chen, H., & Sun, H. (2012). Cue-induced craving and physiological reactions in recently and long-abstinent heroin-dependent patients. *Addictive Behaviors, 37*, 393–398.

3

ADDICTION AND THE CO-OCCURRING DISORDERS

Addiction alone is challenging; when addiction co-occurs with another psychiatric disorder or chronic pain, its clinical course, diagnosis, and treatment become even more difficult as the two interact, synergize, and exacerbate each other. Addicted people with comorbid psychiatric disorders tend to have a more severe addiction problem and higher relapse rates, have interpersonal conflicts, have legal problems, be homeless, be unemployed, not comply with treatment, and be involved with self-harm and violence (Kelly & Daley, 2013; McCauley et al., 2012; Volavka, 2013). There is a high tendency for addiction to co-occur with other psychiatric disorders as both involve the neurobiological systems of human brain. The concept of co-occurring disorders (COD) began to emerge during the 1980s and 1990s, and today the field has accepted COD as expectation rather than exception (Minkoff, cited in Kelly & Daley, 2013). In 2013, the American Society of Addiction Medicine (ASAM) revised and expanded its criteria guide from the previous *ASAM Patient Placement Criteria* to *ASAM Treatment Criteria for Addictive, Substance-Related, and Co-Occurring Conditions* (Mee-Lee et al., 2013).

Statistics on treatment-seeking patients, as well as general populations, show evidence of high prevalence rates of co-occurring disorders. Studies done in substance abuse treatment programs reveal that about 50% to 75% of the clients suffer from some type of co-occurring mental disorder; studies conducted in mental health settings indicate that 20% to 50% of the clients have co-occurring substance use disorder (SUD) (see review of the

Center for Substance Abuse Treatment [CSAT], 2005). Many national population studies have also documented the high comorbidity prevalence rates (National Institute on Drug Abuse [NIDA], n.d.). For example, data have consistently indicated that compared to general respondents, those with a mood or anxiety disorder diagnosis are about two times as likely to also have a drug use disorder (Conway et al., 2006; Grant et al., 2016). This also applied to respondents with an anti-social personality or conduct disorder diagnosis. Consistently, individuals with a drug use disorder diagnosis are about twice as likely to also have a mood or anxiety disorder, compared to general respondents. The National Survey on Drug Use and Health reported that, among people aged 18 or older, the odds for substance-using people to have reported a major depressive episode is doubled (Substance Abuse and Mental Health Services Administration [SAMHSA], 2014, cited in Brook et al., 2016). Some European studies reported consistent findings as well. The results of a German study show that among the individuals with an alcohol use disorder diagnosis, 20% met the diagnostic criteria for one other mental disorder, 7.8% for two other diagnoses, and 14.4% for three or more additional diagnoses. Among people who fulfilled diagnostic criteria for drug use disorder, an even higher fraction were comorbid (total 54.7%) (Lieb, 2015).

Addiction may co-occur with chronic pain, and the co-occurrence rates for chronic pain and opioids use disorder vary. The rates are based on either the percentage of patients with chronic pain who develop addiction or the percentage of patients with opioids addiction who experienced previous or current pain. Boscarino et al.'s study (2010) showed a 35% lifetime prescription opioids use disorder rate among patients with chronic pain. However, Fishbain and colleagues (2008) suggest that chronic opioid analgesic therapy will contribute to addiction only in a very small percentage of patients with chronic pain; for example, only 3.27% of the patients with chronic pain in their study analyses developed addiction. This may be related to different sample characteristics. On the other hand, Rosenblum et al. (2003) indicate that 80% of the methadone patients with opioid addiction in their study reported recent pain, and 37% reported chronic pain.

Identifying and treating co-occurring disorder (COD) issues is critical for at least three reasons. First, it helps prevent relapse and promotes long-term recovery. The self-medication theory suggests that some addiction could be a surface problem accompanied by an underlying physical ailment or a mental disorder, and that addressing the root problem will facilitate a more solid and lasting recovery. Second, COD-specific practices and an integrated treatment approach can improve clients' treatment compliance and outcomes for both the substance use disorder (SUD) and the co-occurring psychiatric disorder. In other words, efficacious treatment methods for a single diagnosis may not necessarily work for the diagnosis when it has a co-occurring disorder. The two comorbid conditions usually interact and unfavorably affect each other, worsening the clinical course and treatment outcomes. For example, patients with comorbid SUD and a mood disorder generally are less responsive to either treatment. Patients with comorbid SUD and posttraumatic stress disorder (PTSD) tend to involve a more complex clinical course—including more chronic physical problems, reduced social functioning, poorer treatment adherence, more legal troubles, and less treatment progress—compared to their counterparts with either SUD or PTSD alone (see review of McCauley et al., 2012). Third, tackling COD issues sensitizes practitioners to detect early risk factors related to violence and suicide, allowing better prevention. Patients with comorbid mental illnesses and SUD present a higher rate of attempted and completed suicide and/or violence than do their counterparts with only one disorder (see review of McCauley et al., 2012; Torrens & Rossi, 2015; Volavka, 2013). For example, more than 50% of the individuals with bipolar disorder have an alcohol use disorder; and individuals with both disorders have a higher likelihood of attempting suicide than those with only one disorder (American Psychiatric Association [APA], 2013). Based on data derived from the National Epidemiologic Survey on Alcohol and Related Conditions (N = 43,093), Blanco et al. (2012) found that people with major depression disorder plus SUD are more vulnerable to additional psychopathology and suicide attempts than people with major depression disorder but without SUD.

Although the field has recognized the existence of the co-occurring disorders of addiction and other mental disorders, knowledge regarding its underling mechanisms and treatment is still very limited. The phenomenon of the comorbidity can be complicated and more research is still needed (National Institute on Drug Abuse [NIDA], 2010). The literature thus far has shown five theories explaining the COD between addiction/SUD and other psychiatric disorders; some of the theories are not necessarily mutually exclusive. (a) The two co-occur not necessarily because one causes the other, but because they both share similar risk factors—such as psychological trauma, stress, genetic vulnerability, and preexistent neurobiological alterations—that result in their co-occurring expression (Torrens & Rossi, 2015). Some externalizing psychopathy—such as alcohol dependence, drug dependence, conduct disorder, and antisocial personality disorder—may share a common genetic factor, albeit they each additionally have its own disorder-specific genes (Dick & Agrawal, 2008). Volkow states that it's not surprising to see a high rate of comorbidity between addiction and other mental illnesses, given the fact that drug abuse may induce change in brain structure and function and the brain areas in which these changes occur overlap with some of the same brain areas that are disrupted in other mental illnesses, including depression, anxiety, or schizophrenia (NIDA, 2010). (b) The two may share similar symptoms and, therefore, are wrongly diagnosed as COD (Torrens & Rossi, 2015). (c) Addiction/SUD is secondary to a psychiatric disorder. The two co-occur because the person uses substance or addictive behaviors to self-medicate a psychiatric disorder. For example, depressed people may self-medicate, using substances to reverse or compensate their diminished dopamine activities; people with mood disorder may use substances to soothe anxiety; schizophrenic patients may abuse drugs to cope with aversive symptoms, such as the positive or negative symptoms (Baskin-Sommers & Foti, 2015; Ross & Peselow, 2012; Torrens & Rossi, 2015). (d) Psychopathology or a psychiatric disorder is secondary to addiction/SUD, in that a psychiatric disorder is induced by the pharmacologic or psychological effects of alcohol or drugs (Ross & Peselow, 2012). For example, SUD induces neurobiological alterations via neuroadaptations that mediate mood disorder (Baskin-Sommers & Foti, 2015; Torrens & Rossi, 2012). A long-term six-time wave study found that chronic concurrent use of cigarette, alcohol, and marijuana was related to a greater likelihood of occurrence of Antisocial Personality Disorder, Major Depressive Disorder, and Generalized Anxiety Disorder later in adulthood (Brook et al., 2016). Another example is Caspi and colleagues' (2005) findings. They found that adolescent-onset cannabis use may trigger adult schizophreniform disorder if the person possesses certain genes. (e) The "hybrid model" suggests that an initially secondary disorder may later become a primary disorder. Ross and Peselow discussed this model in detail: "although the secondary problem only came about because of the

ADDICTION AND THE CO-OCCURRING DISORDERS 57

influence of presenting problem, it now has taken on a separate life of its own and can continue to exist even if the causative problem is treated or remits. This typically occurs after an extended, chronic period of the index condition being active" (p. 237).

One of the above five theories—the self-medication theory—has been consistently emphasized with regard to the comorbid relationship between addiction and another psychiatric disorder (see review of Flanagan et al., 2016; see review of McCauley et al., 2012; Walter, 2015). Individuals use substances (or engage in certain behaviors) repeatedly to help cope with physical or mental pain, traumas, difficult symptoms, and challenging situations. For instance, they may use heroin to numb their severe stomach or back pain, use alcohol to manage insomnia, or use alcohol or drugs to deal with the unfavorable aversive symptoms from schizophrenia, major depression, bipolar, anxiety, PTSD, trauma, or personality disorder (Khantzian & Albanese, 2008). If SUD is only secondary to the primary psychiatric disorder, it would be important to treat the psychiatric disorder—the root problem—in order to treat SUD effectively; once the psychiatric disorder is handled, the SUD symptoms should diminish as the need to self-medicate is lessened. On the other hand, however, according to the hybrid model (Ross & Peselow, 2012), it's also possible that the initially only secondary SUD may have progressed into addiction or a severe SUD (instead of a mild or moderate SUD) after a prolonged exposure. It may, by now, have become a primary disease in and of itself, which requires as much attention and a formal treatment as the other primary psychiatric disorder does. Practitioners should not ignore nor underestimate the insidious and chronic nature of addiction (see Chapter 2).

Regardless of whether addiction causes the other psychiatric disorder, or vice versa, or both are caused by the same risk factors (e.g., genetic or environmental), the two coexisting conditions usually mingle and adversely affect each other, exacerbating the clinical course and treatment outcomes. For example, stimulant medication can effectively treat about 70% of adult patients with attention deficit/hyperactivity disorder (ADHD), but its effect is not clear in treating patients with co-occurring ADHD and substance use disorder (Levin et al., 2007; van Emmerik-van Oortmerssen et al., 2015). The insight that the assessment and treatment of one condition in this context necessitates the screening, assessment, and treatment of the other is, thus, invaluable (CSAT, 2005; Khantzian & Albanese, 2008).

Furthermore, the traditional "sequential model" of treatment—treating one condition first before the other—is considered to be less effective than the "integrated model," where both conditions are treated simultaneously (Garland et al., 2016; McCauley et al., 2012; McGovern et al., 2015).

In addition, treatments that are efficacious for patients with a single diagnosis may not necessarily work for that diagnosis when it involves comorbidity (Petrakis & Simpson, 2017). Many evidence-based treatments are based on clinical trials that systematically exclude participants with comorbidity; as a result, there may be incompatibility between the clinical populations in the "real world"—who are often with dual or multiple diagnosis—and those clinical-trial participants who often have only a single diagnosis (Petrakis & Simpson, 2017). Following are treatment principles and guidelines for the comorbidity between addiction and other disorders. The list is not exhaustive but includes physical pain and major psychiatric disorders—such as schizophrenia, depression, bipolar, PTSD, ADHD, autism spectrum disorder, and personality disorder. Most treatment strategies here are derived from treatment studies that targeted COD patients and emphasize an integrated approach.

Chronic Pain and Addiction

Although pain is subjective, a widely accepted definition is that pain is "whatever the experiencing person says it is, existing whenever s/he says it does" (McCaffery, cited in Morgan & White, 2009). Pain is unpleasant or could even be excruciating; people may self-medicate pain by using opioids or heroin. A developing addiction may arise via at least two routes. First, individuals use these substances to self-medicate insomnia, stomach pain, back pain, toothache, or other pain. They experience heroin as an informal or even folk therapy that "effectively" reduces their pain, at least initially, and word of mouth spreads in their social circles. This onset pattern may happen especially among heroin users in some societies outside the US, such as China and Taiwan. The second route is more iatrogenic in nature and has taken place in the US recently—the person is prescribed opioids for his or her acute or chronic pain, only to end up becoming addicted.

According to the Centers for Disease Control and Prevention (CDC, 2017), although the amount of pain reported by Americans did not change from 1999 to 2014, the prescription opioids sold during that period increased nearly four-fold. Many people attribute the soaring addiction to opioids to overprescribing practices by physicians. Experts have suggested that opioid analgesics may swiftly relieve acute pain but they may not benefit those in chronic pain (Pohl & Smith, 2012; Volkow & McLellan, 2016). Several concerns are identified when prescribing opioids long term (for example, more than eight weeks) for patients (Volkow & McLellan, 2016). First, opioids may cause hyperalgesia, i.e., the person may become more sensitive to pain (Pohl & Smith, 2012; Volkow & McLellan, 2016). Citing Mao, Pohl and Smith state, "Through repeated administration of opioids, the baseline nociceptive thresholds may diminish and cause increased pain sensitivity" (p. 121). Hyperalgesia can result in an inappropriate opioid dose increase. Second, a long-term exposure to opioids inevitably leads to tolerance and physical dependence; tolerance decreases opioid potency. Volkow and McLellan's literature review shows that "prescribing opioids long-term for their analgesic effects will typically require increasingly higher doses in order to maintain the initial level of analgesia— up to 10 times the original dose" (p. 1256). The third concern is that patients may use the prescribed opioids to treat not only the physical pain but also their emotional pain. The combination of physical and emotional pain by patients may exacerbate their perception of their pain (Pohl & Smith, 2012).

Following are strategies for helping individuals with comorbid pain and addiction:

1. Clinicians must address the issues of pain when working with clients with comorbid disorders of addiction and pain. The pain may create multiple problems in a person, such as mood disorder, sleep disturbance, decrease of productivity (Demyttenaere et al., 2006; Smith & Haythornthwaite, 2004). A delay in treating pain can result in opioid addiction and overdose, as well as many other negative consequences (Cheatle, 2013).
2. Be respectful to clients of this comorbid population. Morgan and White (2009) state that, to enhance trust relationship with clients, clinicians should pay attention to clients' pain problems, instead of assuming they are seeking more drugs and dismissing them.
3. Assess high-risk patients and adopt a mitigation strategy. It's important for physicians to assess the addiction risks of a patient—including

the factors of other psychiatric disorder such as depression, substance use disorder history, being adolescent, and so on—before prescribing opiates to avoid medication diversion (Volkow & McLellan, 2016). Other possible risk factors may include a history of substance abuse or addiction treatment, existing pain impairment affecting life/work, suicidal thoughts, sleeping problems, trauma, and being younger than 65 years of age (Boscarino et al., 2015; Salsitz, 2016).

4. When prescribing opioids, choose "the lowest effective dose for the shortest effective duration (for both acute and chronic pain) without compromising effective analgesia" (Volkow & McLellan, 2016, p. 1257). An opioid prescribing practice with higher doses (over 100 MME) and longer duration (for example, more than eight weeks) tends to increase the risk of addiction and overdose, and should be avoided (Volkow & McLellan, 2016).

5. Involve the patient in the treatment team and discuss with him or her an exit strategy prior to starting opioid medications. When opioids are considered for pain treatment, the approach must also include psychological intervention and non-medication modalities, as well as close monitoring for abnormal behavior and side effects, and a well-thought-out plan of discontinuing the drug when it's time (Pohl & Smith, 2012).

6. Consider alternative treatment. For example, nonopioid analgesics; nonpharmacologic approaches such as cognitive behavioral therapy, exercise therapy, physical therapy; complementary medicine such as acupuncture, yoga, meditation; and biofeedback (Volkow & McLellan, 2016).

7. Conduct more research in the areas of (a) differentiation between the distinctive properties of chronic and acute pain and (b) the process of acute pain transitioning into chronic pain (Volkow & McLellan, 2016).

Schizophrenia and Addiction

The occurrence of substance use disorder (SUD) among schizophrenia patients is high—the lifetime rate was close to 50%. The odds of developing an alcohol use disorder were three times higher among schizophrenia patients compared to the general population and, for drug use disorder, the odds were six times higher (Regier et al., 1990). Compared to patients with only psychotic disorders/schizophrenia, patients with co-occurring SUD and psychotic disorders/schizophrenia tend to have a worse clinical course and symptoms, such as more positive symptoms (e.g., hallucinations, delusions), tardive dyskinesia, relapses, and hospitalizations. They also have lower treatment compliance, as well as higher rates of interpersonal conflicts, suicide attempts, aggressive and violent behavior, unemployment, homelessness, and social exclusion (see Gregg et al.'s review, 2007; see Thoma & Daum's review, 2013; Suokas et al., cited in Schmidt et al., 2011; Volavka, 2013).

It is not completely clear what mechanism links schizophrenia with substance use disorder (SUD); several theories are available so far, including the self-medication theory and the schizophrenia-as-secondary-to-SUD theory. The self-medication theory suggests that schizophrenia patients may abuse substances to seek pleasure or to cope with stress (Volkow, 2009). Also, schizophrenia patients may abuse substances to deal with the side effects of typical antipsychotic medications. Typical antipsychotic medications often block a person's dopamine D_2 receptors; schizophrenia patients may abuse substances to compensate, albeit temporarily, for the anhedonia and cognitive deficits caused by a D_2R blockade in brain regions (Samaha, 2014; Volkow, 2009). They may also resort to alcohol or drugs to self-medicate the extrapyramidal side effects and tardive dyskinesia associated with use of typical antipsychotic medications (Koola et al., 2012).

The schizophrenia-as-secondary-to-SUD theory suggests that the onset of marijuana use during adolescence precipitates the development of schizophrenia later on during adulthood among vulnerable individuals with certain genes. Many prospective studies have provided strong evidence showing the connection between adolescent-onset cannabis use and adult schizophrenia development. Those studies also emphasize that only marijuana, not other substances or drugs, is applicable to the connection and that heavy cannabis users show a stronger correlation than lighter cannabis users (Caspi et al., 2005; Gregg et al.'s review, 2007). In addition, drug intoxication from marijuana, methamphetamine, or cocaine may also trigger psychosis, but more of an acute form or time-limited state (Gouzoulis-Mayfrank & Walter, 2015; Volkow, 2009). This could be because the mesolimbic dopamine pathway involves not only the reward mechanisms for all drugs but also the occurrence of schizophrenia positive symptoms (Volkow, 2009).

Traditionally, the substance treatment system is separate from the mental health treatment system, and each network has a low tolerance and acceptance of symptoms from the "other" disorder, with the result that many patients with comorbid schizophrenia and substance use disorder (SUD) "fall between the cracks" (Gouzoulis-Mayfrank & Walter, 2015; Tenhula et al., 2009). Research has suggested that an integrated treatment approach that offers treatments for SUD and schizophrenia simultaneously results in better long-term treatment outcomes (Kelly & Daley, 2013). Under the umbrella of an integrated substance abuse and mental health treatment system, following are strategies for working with clients with schizophrenia-SUD comorbidity:

1. Implement the principles of empathy, harm reduction, small goals, structure, concreteness, and repetitiveness. The factors of cognitive deficit and social impairment need to be taken into account when working with this client population (Sun, 2012; Tenhula et al., 2009). Empathy and a sense of alliance are important for working with any clients, but are essential for patients with severe mental illness, who often are less able than others to tolerate stress, confrontation, and criticism. Reduced use and harm reduction goals rather than total abstinence may be more attainable by individuals with comorbidity, especially those with severe mental illnesses (Carey et al., 2001; DiClemente et al., 2008; Tenhula et al., 2009). Sun's (2012) summary of various studies showed that, theoretically, it would be safer to adopt total abstinence (versus reduced use) for clients with comorbidity, because patients with mental disorders may be more sensitive to the biological effects of alcohol and other drugs, and even moderate amounts may aggravate psychiatric symptoms and worsen problems; in reality, however, comorbid clients may experience more difficulty in achieving total abstinence than do clients with only SUD because of their impaired cognitive functions and other psychiatric symptoms.

Other important principles derived from Sun's (2012) review of literature include: group sessions with a topical focus are better than process groups; in-session role playing and homework can also enhance session

ADDICTION AND THE CO-OCCURRING DISORDERS   63

structure; using written materials, such as written cues for daily activity checklists and written worksheets, may be helpful to patients with schizophrenia as they may have difficulty with auditory materials; information related to CODs and the link between alcohol and other drugs (AOD) and negative consequences should be presented to clients repeatedly, as well as opportunities to practice newly learned skills over and over; and interventions should be adapted according to a patient's level of alertness.

One example that integrates these principles is the Behavioral Treatment for Substance Abuse in Serious and Persistent Mental Illness (BTSAS) developed by Bellack and colleagues (Tenhula et al., 2009). They modified treatment strategies effective for primary substance abusers to better fit the needs of comorbid patients with severe mental illness, and research has shown that BTSAS can increase treatment attendance, reduce drug use, and improve quality of life (Tenhula et al., 2009). To reduce strains on attention, memory, and other cognitive demands, the BTSAS breaks down topics, such as drug refusal skills, into smaller and concrete steps for easy learning. It also emphasizes repeated learning of a few important skills and helps patients acquire skills via role play so that they can automatically apply those skills during high-risk situations. BTSAS also offers psychoeducation on the impact of AOD on individuals with severe mental illnesses, motivational interviewing to discuss negative consequences of drug use, contingency management to reward drug reductions, social skills training to enhance drug refusal ability, and relapse prevention training to help patients more effectively deal with high risk situations (Tenhula et al., 2009).

2.   Provide psychoeducation, motivational interviewing (MI), cognitive behavioral therapy (CBT), contingency management (CM), dual-focus self-help groups, and family involvement. Bennett and colleagues (2017) found that psychosocial interventions—such as MI, CBT, CM, and family education—indicated certain positive findings in 13 of the 16 studies they reviewed that examined substance use disorders in schizophrenia patients. In the 2009 Schizophrenia PORT Psychosocial Treatment Recommendations and Summary Statements, Dixon and colleagues (2010) emphasized that motivational enhancement and cognitive-behavioral interventions are evidence-based practices to help patients with comorbid schizophrenia and SUD, and that

these interventions "have yielded improved outcomes in terms of treatment attendance . . . substance use and relapse . . . symptoms . . . and functioning" among this client population (p. 59).

Psychoeducation is an important component of the treatment package for schizophrenia-SUD comorbid patients and their families (Bennett et al., 2017; Gouzoulis-Mayfrank & Walter, 2015). Psychoeducation contents include an emphasis on illness self-management of both the SUD and schizophrenia, medication compliance, the relationship between substance use and psychosis (for instance, some drug intoxication may trigger acute psychosis), and the negative consequences of substance abuse. Effective psychoeducation may enhance a patient's motivation to reduce or stop substance use (Gouzoulis-Mayfrank & Walter).

Motivational interviewing (MI) and motivation enhancement therapy have shown some evidence of decreasing substance use and psychiatric symptoms among individuals with schizophrenia and SUD comorbidity (Cleary et al., Graeber et al., cited in Sun, 2012). In addition, combining MI with cognitive behavioral therapy (CBT) and family intervention may help such clients with comorbid SUD and schizophrenia, and combining MI, contingency management, and social skills training can result in better treatment outcomes than did the control condition among patients with comorbidity (Barrowclough et al., Bellack et al., cited in Sun, 2012). Individuals with comorbidity, especially those with a severe mental illness, may be less motivated to change because of their positive (e.g., hallucinations) and negative symptoms (e.g., avolition), and other cognitive limitations and deficient social support systems. Research, albeit preliminary, suggests that with proper encouragement, guidance, cues, and structure, comorbid patients can reflect on the pros and the cons of their substance-abusing behaviors and be involved in decisional balance and goal setting (Carey et al., cited in Sun, 2012).

The treatment outcomes of stand-alone CBT on patients with SUD and schizophrenia are not consistent, but some suggestions include: offering CBT only when clients are stabilized both in their SUD and in their mental disorders; starting low and going slow, and refraining from pushing clients too soon to address their ingrained habits of thoughts; helping clients learn specific coping skills to deal with the combined burdens of SUD and mental disorder; accommodating clients' cognitive limitations and refraining from addressing too many specific skills; enhancing clients' self-efficacy by reinforcing their early success (CSAT, Ziedonis et al., cited in Sun, 2012).

Although mainstream Twelve Step group involvement appears to be beneficial to individuals with SUD, it may not be appropriate for individuals with comorbid SUD and schizophrenia. This is because of its emphasis on total abstinence—which may be interpreted by some of its members as even including medications prescribed by a psychiatrist—and its members' possible prejudice toward mental illnesses, which are often highly stigmatized. A specialized Twelve Step group, such as Double Trouble in Recovery, allows for open discussion of not only SUD issues, but also issues related to mental disorders, psychiatric medications, medication side effects, and psychiatric hospitalization (see Sun's review, 2012). Studies have revealed promising effects regarding specialized Twelve Step groups on individuals with comorbidity (e.g., Bogenschutz, Magura et al., cited in Sun, 2012).

3. Provide pharmacotherapy and accentuate adherence to antipsychotic medications. Adherence to antipsychotic medications is essential to effective treatments of schizophrenia (Gouzoulis-Mayfrank & Walter, 2015; Marcus et al.'s review, 2015); however, medication noncompliance is a major problem among schizophrenia patients (Haddad et al., 2014; Marcus et al., 2015). Patients with schizophrenia plus SUD further showed a lower medication compliance than schizophrenia patients without SUD (see Koola et al.'s summary, 2012; see Marcus et al.'s summary, 2015; Pedersen et al., 2018). Multiple factors may explain the medication noncompliance. The patients may dislike the side effects of the antipsychotic medications, distrust the effectiveness of a medication, or be in denial of their illnesses and the need to take medications (Weiss et al., cited in Weiss, 2004). They may discontinue the antipsychotic medications while engaging in substance abuse for fear of the medication-substance interaction (Weiss, 2004; Ziedonis et al., 2005). They may be so disorganized that it becomes too difficult for them to get anything done, including taking medications (Ziedonis et al., 2005). In addition, prescribers may hesitate to prescribe certain antipsychotic medications, such as clozapine, as those medications require regular blood monitoring for agranulocytosis, but the patients may not show up routinely for the procedure (Kavanagh et al., cited in Koola et al., 2012).

Although the 2009 schizophrenia PORT (Dixon et al., 2010) found insufficient evidence at the time of its development to recommend any particular intervention that promotes adherence to antipsychotic medications, some promising approaches have been suggested by researchers. There are two major strategies to counteract medication noncompliance among patients with comorbid schizophrenia and SUD. First, use atypical or second-generation antipsychotic medications instead of typical or first-generation antipsychotic medications. Patients with comorbid schizophrenia and SUD are more vulnerable to the tardive dyskinesia and extrapyramidal side effects associated with use of typical antipsychotic medications (Koola et al., 2012). Typical antipsychotics can generate a strong D_2 receptor blockade, which may prompt a patient to self-medicate using alcohol or other drugs. The second generation or atypical antipsychotic medications, on the other hand, have more extensive receptor profiles and are more effective against side effects and negative symptoms (Samaha, 2014). Studies have shown promising results regarding atypical antipsychotic medications, such as clozapine and risperidone, in reducing patients' alcohol and drug craving/use (Awad & Voruganti, 2015; Gouzoulis-Mayfrank & Walter, 2015). The second major strategy is to use long-acting depot injections. Empirical studies have shown the effectiveness of depot injections over the oral antipsychotics for medication adherence and the benefit of second-generation depot injections in the decrease of re-hospitalization. Researchers have therefore suggested that the second-generation depot injections should be the first line of treatment (Khan et al., 2016; Marcus et al., 2015). A long-acting injectable approach has many advantages. It gets rid of covert nonadherence; it detects and intervenes in noncompliance early by reaching out to the patient and assertive community program; and it has slow clearance, which allows a steady level of antipsychotic serum that does not drop swiftly when noncompliance occurs (Koola et al., 2012).

Other strategies to decrease medication noncompliance may include: discontinuing medications with side effects that lead to nonadherence; using all appointments to discuss the medications, including purpose, the expected time course and results, side effects, and AOD-psychiatric medication interaction effects to promote hope and realistic expectations; encouraging patients to continue taking antipsychotic medications despite their AOD use, as discontinuing the former may be more risky than the concurrent use of both; and involving significant others in medication

ADDICTION AND THE CO-OCCURRING DISORDERS 67

psychoeducation and treatment monitoring (Sun, 2012; Ziedonis et al., 2005). Reducing patients' perceived trauma (e.g., feeling coerced at treatment admission) via psychoeducation and enhancing transparency, increasing patients' insights concerning their illness and their awareness of the function of the medications, as well as enhancing the trust relationship and alliance between patients and clinicians/physicians, can also improve medication adherence (Tessier et al., 2017).

Bennett and colleagues' review (2017) examined antipsychotic medications to see if any of these agents can also affect substance use, in addition to reducing psychiatric symptoms; they found insufficient evidence to make recommendation in this regard. Bennett and colleagues' review also investigated whether medications approved by the US Food and Drug Administration (FDA) to treat substance use disorder are effective to treat substance use disorders in patients with schizophrenia. Although emphasizing the need for more research for verification, these researchers found that naltrexone can decrease heavy drinking and drinking in people with comorbid alcohol use disorder and schizophrenia. They also advocate that more research should be done to assess whether medications for opioid use disorders (OUD) can be as efficacious for patients with comorbid OUD and schizophrenia.

4. Link individuals who have comorbid substance use disorder (SUD) and schizophrenia to resources and services. People with comorbid SUD and schizophrenia not only suffer a more adverse illness course and treatment outcomes than individuals with only schizophrenia, they may also be less likely to seek services, which often worsens their quality of life leading to, for example, homelessness. Pedersen and colleagues (2018) studied 801 veteran patients with schizophrenia; they found that those who use or misuse alcohol were less likely to use general health and mental health services, as well as housing and occupational services, at the Veterans Health Administration, compared to their counterparts who do not use alcohol. Pedersen and colleagues stated that "It is clear that efforts need to be made to engage veterans with alcohol use into services. Particularly . . . in housing services" and that substance use disorders, severe mental illnesses, and "comorbid disorders are common among homeless veterans" (p. 8, online publication).

Mood Disorders and Addiction

Mood disorders (major depression, bipolar, and dysthymia) are the most common co-occurring psychiatric disorders among substance-abusing patients (Quello et al., 2005; Torrens & Rossi, 2015). Analyzing the data from the 2012–13 National Epidemiologic Survey on Alcohol and Related Conditions-III (N = 36,309), Grant and colleagues (2016) found that people with any mood disorder are 1.9 times more likely to have a comorbid drug use disorder than others. An earlier epidemiologic study by Grant and colleagues (2004) found that the prevalence rate of substance use disorder was about 30% among individuals with mania.

Two major theories explain the high co-occurrence between major depressive disorder (MDD) and substance use disorder (SUD). One theory proposes that SUD induces MDD, in that taking substances may induce neuro-adaptation, leading to decreased dopamine output in the nucleus accumbens and degradation of neuronal integrity in the region of the frontal cortex, especially during the withdrawal phase; these neurobiological changes overlap with those of a seriously depressed person's reduced ability to sense salient events (Baskin-Sommers & Foti, 2015). The second theory is the self-medication theory, which suggests that the psychotropic effects of many substances can reverse or subdue the distressful psychological symptoms related to MDD through stimulating dopamine activity in the brain's limbic regions (Baskin-Sommers & Foti). As mentioned previously, the co-existence of both the SUD and MDD conditions exacerbates each. Warden and colleagues' research (2012) showed that depressed adolescents with ADHD and SUD tend to have a more severe level of substance use both at baseline and during the course of treatment than their non-depressed counterparts. The influence of comorbid SUD and MDD on treatment outcomes appears to be complex and more research is needed. Here are some insights and strategies developed so far when working with individuals with comorbid mood disorder and SUD:

1. Implement screening and assessment of possible co-occurrence of mood disorders and SUD when working with SUD or mood disorder clients. As mentioned earlier, mood disorders and SUD are the most common co-occurring disorders in the substance use field; when one condition presents, clinicians should screen and assess for the other condition. Findings of a 2008–14 national study in the US (N = 25,500) reveal

that only 14.9% of the individuals with comorbid depression and SUD received both substance use treatment and depression care (Han et al., 2017). Han and colleagues further found that the depressed adults with comorbid SUD were modestly yet significantly less likely to receive depression care compared to depressed adults without comorbid SUD. Barriers for people to receive treatment for both disorders may include: the intoxication or withdrawal symptoms from substances mirror the symptoms of depression, leading to a delay of depression treatment; SUD impairs a person's executive function, resulting in his or her poor illness insight; and a person uses substances to self-medicate depression (Crum et al., 2013; Han et al., 2017). A timely identification of the co-occurring depression and SUD is critical in effective treatment of each.

2. Apply a cognitive behavioral therapy (CBT) approach. Three relevant variations of CBT are a regular CBT approach, a mindfulness-based CBT, and CBT with an emphasis on modification of clients' early maladaptive schemas (EMS).

(a) CBT has long been used to treat depression, as well as substance use disorder. Cognitive behavioral therapy is largely based on the A–B–C model of functional analysis and skills training. A represents antecedents (triggers); B, behaviors (e.g., depressive episodes or substance use, or their relapse); C, consequences resulting from B, including the short-term positive consequences and the long-term negative consequences. Clients also learn skills to help them more effectively deal with the triggers (see Chapter 8 for details about CBT).

Many studies have also shown that CBT, within the format of individual or group counseling, can be adapted to effectively treat the depression–SUD comorbidity of various severities (Brown et al., 1997; Watkins et al., 2012). CBT can also be applied to adolescents. A manual-based CBT/motivation enhancement therapy (MET) approach showed effectiveness in helping adolescents with comorbid major depressive disorder and alcohol use disorder (AUD) (Cornelius et al., 2011). The CBT focuses on AUD and depression, whereas the MET enhances the adolescent participants' motivations to get treatment.

(b) Add the component of mindfulness to CBT and relapse prevention. The mindfulness approach to relapse prevention is considered as part of the third wave of CBT; it additionally emphasizes self-awareness, observing and investigating one's own thoughts and emotions without judgment, and accepting affective and psychological discomforts. By doing so, a person becomes more able to "pause" before his or her automatic immediate response—which is usually habitual and dysfunctional—to a crisis or challenging situation. Witkiewitz and Bowen (2010) suggest that mindfulness-based cognitive therapy (MBCT) helps a client deal with depression relapse by recognizing "depressive thoughts, sensations and feelings that can be risk factors" and by learning "to accept these experiences as separate from themselves and as transient or subject to change, thereby interrupting the cognitive processes that may contribute to depressive relapse" (p. 364). The component of mindfulness can be added to the CBT substance relapse prevention program (see Chapter 8 for details about mindfulness-based CBT).

(c) Modify clients' early maladaptive schemas (EMS). EMS are a person's dysfunctional core beliefs about oneself and one's relationship with others. Such dysfunctional core beliefs are established based on traumatic or negative early experiences, which are elaborated and reinforced throughout life development, and they are extremely stable and enduring themes (Young, et al., 2003). Research has indicated the relationship between EMS and the occurrence of various psychopathologies, such as depression, substance use, and anxiety. Shorey et al.'s (2015) research on 122 patients from a substance abuse treatment residential program found an association between major depressive disorder and the EMS areas of "disconnection and rejection" (for example, believing oneself to be defective and worrying about being abandoned by others) and "impaired limits," as well as an association between generalized anxiety disorder and the EMS areas of "impaired autonomy and performance" (for example, believing oneself to be unable to function independently and perform successfully). Shorey and colleagues suggest that clinicians may want to include early maladaptive schemas in their assessment when working with substance-abusing clients with comorbid mental disorders, and that cognitive behavioral techniques, including cognitive restructuring and problem solving, could be used to target individual client's specific EMS.

3. Provide interpersonal psychotherapy. As with cognitive behavioral therapy, interpersonal psychotherapy (IPT) is a major psychotherapeutic intervention with efficacious evidence for treating mood disorders (Markowitz & Weissman, 2004). IPT focuses on helping patients to deal more successfully with situations and crises in their relationships with others. This might include, for example, "someone important may have died . . . there may be a struggle with a significant other . . . or the patient may have gone through some other important life change . . . or interpersonal deficits. . . [or] the absence of a current life event" (pp. 136–37). The goal is for the therapist to strengthen a patient's interpersonal skills—in that if the outcomes to a situation are negative, the therapist will be supportive and empathetic to the patient, helping him or her explore what went wrong in the situation, brainstorm new options, and role-play and rehearse with the patient. IPT is efficacious for major depression, and may add benefit to pharmacological treatment for treating dysthymic disorder (Markowitz & Weissman, 2012).

Johnson and Zlotnick (2012) applied interpersonal psychotherapy to 38 incarcerated women with major depression who were attending substance-use treatment in prison. Their randomized study results showed that compared to the control group, women receiving IPT had a significantly lower score on depressive symptoms after an 8-week treatment period. Although the control group also improved later, Johnson and Zlotnick believe the swifter improvement resulting from IPT show that this form of therapy may help lessen the serious consequences of major depression in prison. Different clients will have different interpersonal situations and crises, and treatment sessions need to be tailored to the client's needs. For example, the specific interpersonal situations and needs of the incarcerated women focused on: disturbed family and friend relationships that were related to the women's drug use and criminal lifestyles, communication problems and substance-related social support, issues involved with a loss or potential loss of child custody, and interpersonal relationship problems related to childhood or adulthood abuse trauma (such as distrust, isolation, and boundary issues) (Johnson & Zlotnick).

One relevant strategy under the same umbrella of interpersonal psychotherapy to help patients with comorbid substance use disorder (SUD) and major depressive disorder (MDD) is to enhance their *engagement* coping skills. For example, Adan et al. (2017) found that male patients with SUD and those with SUD–MDD tend to adopt disengagement coping strategies, and patients with SUD–MDD are especially more detached than patients with only SUD. The maladaptive coping strategies included "wishful thinking" ("the desire that the stressful event would not ever happen"); "social withdrawal" ("avoid any contact with those persons related to the stressful situation"); and "self-criticism" ("self-blame for the stressful event that happened") (p. 330). Adan and colleagues suggest that clinicians should help their clients substitute the maladaptive strategies with more adaptive and engaging ones, such as cognitive restructuring and problem solving.

4. Incorporate pharmacotherapy. Although some clinicians and researchers suggest that "maximum use of behavioral approaches is the first principle of treatment for patients with SUD and a concurrent mood disorder" because "learning and gaining self-confidence in one's ability to self-regulate subjective states can be extremely helpful in recovery from both disorders" and that "to self-regulate mood symptoms may help patients to break out of the mindset of using external agents to combat intolerable subjective states" (Quello et al., 2005, p. 17), pharmacotherapy may be beneficial or necessary for some patients. For example, studies have shown that while the interpersonal psychotherapy may be efficacious for major depression, it alone did not generate much success in treating dysthymic disorder but may add advantage to pharmacotherapy (Markowitz & Weissman, 2012).

The selective serotonin reuptake inhibitors (SSRIs) are the most often used antidepressants because of their safety, fewer side effects, and broad effectiveness (Center of Substance Abuse Treatment [CSAT], 2005). Bupropion is another type of antidepressant, which is unrelated to other antidepressants and causes more effect on dopamine and norepinephrine levels than on the brain's serotonin levels (CSAT). Quello and colleagues (2005) listed medications used for treating mood disorders in patients with substance use disorder, including certain serotonin reuptake inhibitors (e.g., sertraline [Zoloft], fluoxetine [Prozac], Paroxetine [Paxil], etc.), and tricyclic antidepressants (e.g., imipramine [Tofranil]), and bupropion (Wellbutrin) for depression. For bipolar disorder, listed are certain mood stabilizers (e.g., lithium, valproate), atypical antipsychotics (e.g., olanzapine [Zyprexa], risperidone [Risperdal]), typical antipsychotics (e.g., haloperidol [Haldol]), and benzodiazepines (e.g., clonazepam [should avoid long-term use]). These authors also listed medications to avoid, including avoiding certain monoamine oxidase inhibitors (e.g., tranylcypromine [Parnate]) for depression; and certain benzodiazepines (e.g., diazepam [Valium] and alprazolam [Xanax]) and stimulants (e.g., methylphenidate [Ritalin]) for bipolar disorder.

Research found some evidence on a combination of sertraline (for depression) and naltrexone (for alcohol dependence) for treating patients with comorbidity of major depression and alcohol use disorders. Pettinati and colleagues' (2010) double-blind placebo-controlled study of four groups revealed that a combination of sertraline, naltrexone, and cognitive behavioral therapy (CBT) generates better drinking and depressive symptom outcomes—that is, patients are more likely to be abstinent from alcohol, to have a longer time before heavy-drinking relapse, and less likely to be depressed at the end of treatment—than the groups who took sertraline alone plus CBT, naltrexone alone plus CBT, and a placebo plus CBT. These authors did emphasize that replication of the study is necessary and future research should also target how long the medications are still needed after symptoms remitted.

Posttraumatic Stress Disorder (PTSD) and Addiction

PTSD and substance use disorder (SUD) often co-occur. Up to 90% of some SUD groups reported experiences of traumatic events, and the rates of PTSD ranged from 20% to 38% among individuals with SUD (see Torchalla et al.'s review, 2014). The PTSD–SUD comorbidity is noticeable, especially among military populations and those who seek treatment. Veterans are at a higher risk for PTSD–SUD comorbidity than the general population, and there is a direct link between the risk for the chronicity of symptoms and the severity of combat exposure (McCauley, et al., 2012). Treatment-seeking populations have high PTSD–SUD comorbid rates: PTSD patients are up to 14 times more likely to have an SUD than patients without PTSD; the lifetime PTSD rates among SUD patients range from 30% to 60% or higher (McCauley et al.'s review, 2012). Homeless populations may also have a high PTSD–SUD comorbidity. Torchalla and colleagues' study (2014) indicated that 18.8% of their homeless participants (N = 489) had co-occurring PTSD and SUD; 73% of the sample reported having experienced traumatic events; and 20.5% met PTSD diagnosis criteria. The study also revealed that 22.8% of their subsample with SUD had PTSD, and 92% of their subsample with PTSD had a SUD. Criminal justice detainees and adolescents are two other populations that may have high PTSD–SUD comorbidity rates.

Theories explaining the co-occurrence of PTSD and SUD include the self-medication theory, the high risk theory, the high susceptibility theory, and the common factor theory. The self-medication theory—which suggests that individuals may abuse substances to alleviate the highly distressing symptoms of PTSD—receives the most empirical support among all the theories (Flanagan et al., 2016; McCauley et al., 2012; Schafer & Langeland, 2015). In the self-medication theory SUD plays a secondary role to PTSD, a situation that is reversed in both the high risk and the high susceptibility theories where PTSD is the secondary condition and SUD the primary.

The high risk theory suggests that the SUD lifestyle usually involves dangerous environments and behaviors, such as intoxication and illegal activities, and therefore increases the risk to traumatic events exposure and its subsequent PTSD development (McCauley et al.'s review, 2012; Torchalla et al.'s review, 2014). Researchers have validated the linkage between the risk-loaded, substance-abusing lifestyle and the proneness to traumas and other stress-related disorders (Schafer & Langeland, 2015; Sun, 2000; Sun et al., 2016). Many SUD patients may experience not merely a single incident, such as a traffic accident or a criminal assault, but rather repeated traumatic stressors, and may still be exposed to continuing victimization (Schafer & Langeland, 2015).

The high susceptibility theory proposes that individuals with substance use disorder (SUD) are more vulnerable, biologically, to develop PTSD after exposure to traumatic events, because their poor coping skills combine with their augmented arousal, anxiety, and neurobiological stress sensitization, all of which are caused by chronic SUD (McCauley et al.'s review, 2012; Torchalla et al.'s review, 2014). The common factor theory proposes that some common factors such as genetics, history of traumatic events exposure, and common neurophysiological systems may precipitate the occurrence of PTSD–SUD comorbidity (McCauley et al., 2012).

A comorbid PTSD and SUD indicate a more difficult clinical course than each disorder alone, including worse or more frequent conditions in the areas of chronic physical problems, hospital admissions, suicide attempts, severity of addiction, social functioning, legal problems, risk of violence, and treatment adherence and improvement (McCauley et al., 2012; Norman et al.'s review, 2012). Treatment options emphasizing the co-occurrence of PTSD and SUD, rather than each disorder alone, have increased substantially in the area of psychosocial therapy, but are scarce, albeit growing, in the area of pharmacotherapy (McCauley et al., 2012; Petrakis & Simpson, 2017; Schafer & Langeland, 2015). Let's discuss some treatment strategies for helping individuals with co-occurring PTSD and addiction:

1. Apply approaches that are exposure-based (past-focused treatments) and non-exposure-based (present-focused treatments).

Prolonged Exposure Therapy and COPE

Prolonged exposure therapy (PE) is a highly effective and evidence-based treatment that has long been considered the gold standard for PTSD (Foa et al., 2007; Mills et al., 2012). However, not much research has been done regarding whether PE is efficacious for treating PTSD patients with comorbid SUD until recently (Flanagan et al., 2016; Mills et al.). One such method is called concurrent treatment of PTSD and substance use disorders using prolonged exposure (COPE), which integrates PE with cognitive behavioral therapy for SUD (Back et al., 2015; Mills et al., 2012). Mills and colleagues' study showed that PTSD–SUD individuals who received COPE plus the usual treatment achieved a significantly higher reduction in the severity of their PTSD symptoms at the 9-month follow-up compared to their counterparts who received only the usual treatment, although both groups made progress. Both groups also made progress in decreasing their substance dependence rates and severity of depression; however, there were no significant differences between the two groups. In Mills and colleagues' study, COPE included six components: motivational enhancement and CBT for substance use; psychoeducation related to both disorders and their interaction; in vivo exposure; imaginal exposure;

cognitive therapy for PTSD; and a review of the treatment, after-care plan formulation, and termination of therapy (Mills et al., 2012, p. 692).

Killeen et al. (2015) stated that although exposure-based therapy has been well implemented and adopted in mental health care systems, and that although studies have shown that exposure-based therapy is safe and generally improves PTSD symptoms among patients with comorbid PTSD and substance use disorders, the "majority of community substance abuse treatment programs that utilize integrated interventions focus on non-exposure-based integrated therapies, despite the limited evidence based and the need for improved treatment models" (p. 235). Killeen and colleagues commented that this could be because clinicians in those treatment programs are not trained with exposure-based therapy techniques and that "Addiction clinicians with less experience in PTSD and other mental health problems may be more comfortable with an integrated model that focuses on current coping skills rather than exploring past trauma memories" (p. 238).

Non-Exposure-Based Treatments

Treatment that focuses on the present and provides clients with skills training and psychoeducation can also be beneficial and has been accepted and practiced in the substance abuse treatment community. Examples include Seeking Safety (SS), integrated cognitive behavioral therapy (ICBT), the Trauma Recovery and Empowerment Model (TREM), the Trauma Affect Regulation: Guide for Education and Therapy (TARGET), and the Addictions and Trauma Recovery Integrated Model (ATRIUM) (Flanagan et al., 2016; SAMHSA, 2014)—all of which were included and described under the section "Integrated Models for Trauma" in SAMHSA's Treatment Improvement Protocol (TIP) 57.

SS is the most adopted and evaluated non-exposure-based treatment (Flanagan et al., 2016). Seeking Safety considers personal safety as the highest priority—which can be achieved through substance abstinence, decrease of self-destructive behaviors, protection of self from related dangers (for instance, domestic violence, HIV-risk), and building a supportive social network (Najavits, 2002). However, the outcomes of SS appear to be not significantly different compared to other approaches related to addiction treatment. For example, Hien et al.'s (2004) study found that both the group of SUD–PTSD comorbid women who received SS and the group who received relapse prevention made progress over time on the PTSD outcomes and some substance use measures; but there was no significant difference between the two groups regarding those outcomes. Similarly, Myers et al. (2015) compared a group of SUD–PTSD comorbid women who received SS and a group of their counterparts who received facilitated Twelve-Step group treatment, finding no between-group differences in PTSD severity and drinking outcomes at follow-up.

2. Consider the stage-based framework. Following Judy Herman's stages of trauma recovery, Najavits and Johnson (2014) crafted and evaluated the "Creating Change" behavioral therapy for patients with PTSD–SUD comorbidity. Najavits (2002) developed the Seeking Safety model—a model that has been widely and well accepted in the substance abuse treatment community to treat patients with co-occurring PTSD and substance use disorders. In the Creating Change therapy, Najavits and Johnson added the component of past-focused exploration to Najavits' present-focused Seeking Safety model. Creating Change therapy includes three stages. Stage 1: safety, which is present-focused and emphasizes psychoeducation and coping skills training. Stage 2: grieving and remembrance, which is past-focused and encourages processing painful emotions and memories related to trauma or others. Stage 3: reconnection, which is future-focused and accentuates establishing a healthy and functional work and social life ahead. Najavits and Johnson's study found that the participants made significant improvements in the areas of PTSD and other trauma-related symptoms (such as depression, anxiety, and dissociation), psychopathology (such as psychotic symptoms, interpersonal sensitivity, and obsessive symptoms), daily functioning, and suicidal ideation. Although the improvement on substance use was not significant, the Addiction Severity Index showed a large effects size on alcohol and medium effects size on drugs. These authors, however, also pointed out that their study is just a pilot study and more rigorous randomized controlled trials (RCT) with larger sample sizes are needed to confirm the efficacy of Creating Change.

Regardless, Najavits and Johnson (2014) consider that some recent RCT did not show superior treatment outcomes yielded by the past-oriented

PTSD treatment in contrast to other "less intensive" treatments when treating comorbid PTSD–SUD patients; they suggest that the stage-oriented treatment—a gentle approach that begins first with the present-focused seeking-safety coping skills and then follows that with the past-focused probe skills—may provide a new alternative for helping people with comorbid PTSD–SUD disorders. Najavits and Johnson emphasized the fact that the stage-based conceptual framework in understanding trauma recovery has been identified consistently for a century by many people and can be described as a "consensus model."

3. Addiction-focused interventions may still be beneficial for SUD–PTSD comorbid individuals (Simpson et al., 2017). One study that compared a group that received chronic care management (such as motivational enhancement therapy, relapse prevention) with a group that received an appointment with a primary care provider (Park et al., 2015) indicated that both groups improved in reduced substance use over time and found no between-group differences. Another study showed that SUD–PTSD comorbid combat veterans who received motivational interviewing had a better reduction in the number of drinks per week at the 6th week follow up compared to counterparts who received written personalized feedback (McDevitt-Murphy et al., 2014). Neither study assessed PTSD outcomes.

Overall, Simpson and colleagues' 2017 review suggests: (a) Encourage patients to get their PTSD assessed and treated when they are in a readily available substance abuse treatment. (b) When available, integrate behavioral SUD treatment and exposure-based PTSD treatment, as these generate better PTSD outcomes than SUD care alone. (c) SUD treatments can be beneficial and practical, when coping-based and exposure-based therapies are difficult to implement, especially because SUD treatments contribute to treatment retention, which is associated with positive treatment outcomes. (d) More research is needed to identify patient characteristics and facilitate patient matching with regards to who may make great improvements from treatments that integrate coping skills or exposure therapy, and who may benefit more from addiction-focused treatments.

ADDICTION AND THE CO-OCCURRING DISORDERS   79

4. Incorporate pharmacological treatments. Although medications such as naltrexone have been developed to treat alcohol use disorder (AUD), more research is still needed to confirm their efficacies on treating AUD when a person has AUD–PTSD comorbidity. Likewise, some antidepressants such as sertraline have been used to treat PTSD, but their efficacies on treating PTSD among patients with PTSD–AUD comorbidity await more systematic investigation. In addition, medications that can treat both SUD and PTSD are also needed. So far, few randomized trials have been conducted in this regard, but such studies are growing. With those caveats in mind, preliminary evidence points to the following directions:

(a) Naltrexone and disulfiram may be safe and efficacious to treat alcohol-dependent clients with PTSD. For example, Foa and colleagues' randomized study (2013) compared four groups categorized by treatments (prolonged exposure therapy + naltrexone, prolonged exposure therapy + placebo, supportive counseling + naltrexone, and supportive counseling + placebo) and found that participants treated with naltrexone had significantly lower percentages for days drinking compared to participants with placebo treatment ($p = .008$). Petrakis et al.'s randomized study (2006) found that veterans who received disulfiram, naltrexone, or both had better treatment outcomes than the placebo groups regarding consecutive days of abstinence and heavy drinking days. On the other hand, Petrakis and colleagues' more recent randomized study (2012) showed that although naltrexone reduces alcohol craving more so than a placebo, there is no significant difference in terms of alcohol use outcomes between the two.

(b) The serotonergic reuptake inhibitor (SRI) sertraline—an FDA-approved pharmacotherapy for PTSD—is somewhat promising in treating PTSD individuals with alcohol use disorder (Petrakis & Simpson, 2017). For example, Hien et al.'s study (2015) compared a group using "seeking safety + sertraline" with a group using "seeking safety + placebo," revealing that the sertraline group had a significant decrease of PTSD symptoms than the placebo group at the end of treatment, and at the 6-month and 12-month follow-ups.

5. Combine psychosocial therapy and pharmacotherapy. At least two studies combining psychosocial therapy and pharmacotherapy demonstrated some advantageous treatment results among the PTSD–SUD comorbid populations. Foa et al. (2013) integrated prolonged exposure therapy and naltrexone, showing at the 6-month follow-up that this group had the least increases in percentage of days drinking than all other groups, including the prolonged exposure + placebo group, the supportive counseling + naltrexone group, and the supportive counseling + placebo group. Hien et al.'s (2015) study, noted above, showed good results with combined therapies. More studies need to be done to disentangle the individual contributions and interactions of these psychosocial and pharmacotherapies.

Attention Deficit/Hyperactivity Disorder (ADHD) / Autism Spectrum Disorder (ASD) and Addiction

Extensive research has consistently suggested that children and adolescents with attention deficit/hyperactivity disorder (ADHD) have a higher rate of substance use disorder (SUD)—including nicotine use disorder, alcohol use disorder, cocaine use disorder, and marijuana use disorder—than their peers without ADHD, and that a diagnosis of ADHD during adolescence associates with a person's developing SUD later during young adulthood (see Harstad et al.'s review, 2014). Recent National Survey of Children's Health data show that ADHD is the most prevalent behavioral disorder among youth—about 14% of minors (11–17 years of age) were given a diagnosis of ADHD at certain point in life; in addition, about 25% to 66% of adolescents who attended substance use treatment have ADHD comorbidity (Hogue et al., 2017). The International ADHD in Substance Use Disorders Prevalence Study (IASP study, van Emmerik-van Oortmerssen et al., 2013) reported that 13.9% of treatment-seeking patients with substance use disorder had a comorbid adult ADHD. ADHD tends to co-occur with not only substance addiction but also behavioral addiction. Karaca et al.'s (2017) review showed a high comorbidity between ADHD and behavioral addictions, such as gambling disorder, binge-eating disorder, internet addiction, and sex addiction. They found that the rates of co-occurring ADHD among people with behavioral addictions were from 5.8% to 88.3%, and the rates of co-occurring behavioral addictions among people with ADHD were 5.9% to 71.8%.

ADDICTION AND THE CO-OCCURRING DISORDERS 81

Although it is not completely clear why ADHD and addiction tend to co-occur, theories have been proposed. The self-medication theory suggests that because of their higher levels of dopamine transporter density and the subsequent rapid clearance and lower synaptic dopamine, individuals with ADHD may be more likely to abuse various drugs—such as cocaine, amphetamine, methamphetamine, nicotine, opiates, alcohol, marijuana, and ecstasy—to increase synaptic dopamine concentrations in the brain's reward center (see Harstad et al.'s review, 2014). In addition, adolescents and children with ADHD are more likely to experience academic failures, leading to substance abuse to self-medicate anxiety and depression related to academic difficulties (Erskine et al., 2016). Academic failures may further push the individuals to associate with substance-abusing peers and thus facilitate substance-abusing behaviors (see Harstad et al.). The common factor model is another theory, which suggests that impulsivity is not only one major characteristic of ADHD but also a precursor for SUD (Harstad et al.). In addition, some researchers believe that individuals with ADHD may be biologically more vulnerable to addiction than those without ADHD (Harstad et al.).

Furthermore, individuals with substance use disorder (SUD) and ADHD are more likely to have additional comorbid disorders compared to SUD individuals without ADHD. The IASP study (van Emmerik-van Oortmerssen et al., 2013; $N = 1,205$ treatment-seeking SUD patients) indicated that among their participants, 37% of those without ADHD had as a minimum one additional comorbid disorder, whereas it was 75% for those with ADHD. Specifically, about 51.8% of their ADHD[+] SUD patients had a comorbid antisocial personality disorder while only 17% of their ADHD[-] SUD patients did ($p. < .001$); about 34.5% of their ADHD[+] SUD patients (alcohol as primary substance) versus 8.2% of their ADHD[-] SUD patients (alcohol as primary substance) had a borderline personality disorder. About 29% of their ADHD[+] SUD patients (drugs as primary substance) versus 16.7% of their ADHD[-] SUD patients (drugs as primary substance) had a borderline personality disorder ($p. < .001$).

More research has been conducted on ADHD–SUD comorbidity than on autism spectrum disorder (ASD) that presents along with substance use (De Alwis et al., 2014; Rengit et al., 2016), but many researchers and clinicians have started to pay attention to issues related to ASD and addiction, including substances (e.g., alcohol) and behavioral addictions (such as video games) (van Wijngaarden-Cremers & van der Gaag, 2015). Unlike the well-established linkage between ADHD and SUD, research findings on the co-occurrence between ASD and SUD are limited and inconsistent. On the one hand, some studies found that substance-related problems are rare among the ASD population; they suggest this is because individuals with ASD lack social skills and have a lower novelty-seeking tendency, both of which lead to less access to substances or substance-abusing peers (see De Alwis et al.'s review, 2014). On the other hand, some researchers suggested that high functioning ASD individuals may use substances to enhance social interaction or self-medicate anxiety and depression related to social frustrations and the like. They further suggested that once substance use is initiated, individuals with ASD tend to progress to SUD faster than individuals without ASD (De Alwis et al., 2014; Rengit et al.'s review, 2016). Butwicka and colleagues' (2017) recent Swedish population-based cohort study found that individuals with ASD but without ADHD or intellectual disability were at a doubled risk to substance use problems. In addition, they also found that individuals with both ASD and ADHD had the highest risk of developing substance use-related problems, and that there may be a genetic and/or shared environment liability, as the substance use-related problems tended to also occur among full siblings, half-siblings, and parents of ASD probands.

Although the link between ASD and SUD is vague, the link between ASD and behavioral addiction—primarily internet addiction or video game addiction—has been substantiated with greater evidence. Compared to non-ASD children, the research indicated that ASD children spent a longer amount of time playing video games per day and had a higher level of problematic video game use (MacMullin et al., 2016; Mazurek & Wenstrup, 2013). The measurements of "problematic video game use" involve components of compulsivity and behavioral addiction.

Theories explaining the co-occurrence of ASD and addiction include the self-medication theory, the common factor model, and others. Self-medication theory suggests that individuals with ASD—who are characterized as hypersensitive to external stimuli—may use substances or activities to cope with anxiety and stress resulting from a stimulus-overloaded environment (Sizoo et al., cited in Rengit et al., 2016; van Wijngaarden-Caremers & van der Gaag, 2015). Also, although some studies have shown a lower or similar rate of SUD among individuals with ASD compared

ADDICTION AND THE CO-OCCURRING DISORDERS   83

to psychiatric control groups or the general population (Hofvander et al., 2009; Santosh & Mijovic, 2006), among high functioning ASD individuals, a desire for social relationship may emerge during adolescence and may prompt them to use alcohol and drugs to overcome social incompetency (van Wijngaarden-Caremers & van der Gaag, 2015), and/or to lessen anxiety and depression resulting from social or other difficulties (Rengit et al.'s review, 2016). Furthermore, the progression from alcohol use to alcohol use disorder may be accelerated among this population (De Alwis et al., 2014; see Rengit et al.'s review, 2016).

The common factor model suggests that ASD and addiction may both involve dysregulation of the brain's limbic pathways, and that impulse control deficits are associated both with an ASD diagnosis and with a diagnosis of problematic video gaming, which is also precipitated by the core social competency deficiency (review of MacMullin et al., 2016; Mazurek & Wenstrup, 2013; Rengit et al., 2016). Recent research also suggests that there may be a neurobiological overlap in autism and addiction, in that both disorders involve deregulated dopamine of the cortico-striatal-limbic loop, resulting in compulsive and distorted behaviors. Van Wijngaarden-Cremers and van der Gaag (2015) suggest that dopaminergic deregulation places ASD together with ADHD on one segment, with addiction on the other together with obsessive-compulsive disorder; they, however, emphasized that far more research is needed in this regard.

With that qualification, insights so far for strategies to help clients with co-occurring ADHD/ASD and substance use disorder (SUD) may include the following:

1. Consider medications. Pharmacological treatment has been well established for ADHD, but less so for ADHD–SUD comorbidity (Hogue et al., 2017; Levin et al., 2007; van Emmerik-van Oortmerssen et al., 2015). First line of pharmacological therapy for ADHD usually includes stimulants—i.e., methylphenidate (e.g., Ritalin and Concerta) or amphetamines (e.g., Adderall). Depending on the factors of side effects, effectiveness and medication abuse/diversion risk, non-stimulants—which often take a longer time to act but can last for about 24 hours—may be prescribed alone or combined with stimulants. Non-stimulants include atomoxetine (e.g., Strattera); some antidepressants such as bupropion (e.g., Wellbutrin) may also be prescribed (Zaso et al., 2015).

Medications usually work for about 70% of ADHD patients, but it's not clear how effective they are for patients with comorbid ADHD and SUD. Van Emmerik-van Oortmerssen et al. (2015) said that although methylphenidate is the first line medication for ADHD, it may not be effective in patients with ADHD–SUD comorbidity. ADHD–SUD patients may require a higher dose of the medications (Konstenius et al., 2014; Levin et al., 2007). This may be because ADHD patients who are also chronic substance abusers may have developed tolerance to stimulants and thus, may need a higher dose to effectively treat their ADHD symptoms than ADHD patients who are stimulant-naïve previously (Konstenius et al.). It's also recommended that a patient stop using substances before taking the medications, as the medications may be disturbed by withdrawal and/or intoxication from substances (van Emmerik-van Oortmerssen et al.). In addition, because of the possible overlap of symptoms between ADHD and SUD, an initial stabilization of SUD (i.e., total abstinence or reduction in use) can enable a more accurate diagnosis of ADHD (Harstad et al., 2014).

Medication can be important for ADHD–SUD patients, in that it "allows them to put the thoughts and emotions in their heads on hold and then contemplate what they could and would like to do in life. They report being able to start work towards new goals more or less on their own . . . they gain faith in their capabilities, gain hope, and gain pride" (Kronenberg, Verkerk-Tamminga et al., 2015, p. 246). Karaca et al.'s review (2016) additionally showed that—although more research is needed to secure an evidence-based clinical approach for working with patients with co-occurring ADHD and behavioral addictions—stimulant medications that have successfully treated ADHD symptoms also help to decrease the symptoms of comorbid internet addiction, sex addiction, or binge-eating disorder.

Hogue and colleagues (2017) considered it important to promote and integrate ADHD medication uptake into behavioral treatment of adolescents with comorbid ADHD and substance use problems. They recommended two evidence-based and family-centered strategies. "Family ADHD psychoeducation" provides families with consumer-friendly knowledge regarding ADHD symptoms and course of the disorder, prevalence, etiology, its impact on various life areas and functioning, co-occurring disorders, and so on among teens. "Family-based medication decision making" strategy actively involves adolescents and caregivers and targets

ADHD medication receptivity, systematically processes family attitudes concerning medications, and facilitates patient-centered decision-making about medication use (Hogue et al.).

One legitimate question is whether early treatment of ADHD will influence the risk for later development of substance use disorder (SUD). In other words, there has been concern regarding a potential abuse of the medication, especially stimulants. Many existing studies and meta-analyses have shown either that there is no link between ADHD stimulant medication and the increase or decrease of risks for later development of SUD (Humphreys et al., 2013) or that ADHD medication actually improves later SUD and other related outcomes (Zulauf et al., 2014). Nevertheless, the potential misuse and abuse of stimulant medications among individuals with comorbid ADHD and SUD are possible and represent a challenge for treatment. To counteract stimulant medication diversion and misuse among at-risk patients, long-acting stimulants—which can be prescribed once or twice a day rather than four or five times a day (the immediate release medications)—or nonstimulant medications may be prescribed (van Emmerik-van Oortmerssen et al., 2015; Zaso et al., 2015). The American Academy of Pediatrics has also developed recommendations for safe prescribing of ADHD medications for teens, such as delivering substance use psychoeducation and preventive guidance concerning prescription misuse, tracking pharmaceutical database records, and making an agreement with teens and caregivers to keep a responsible medication-monitoring system (Hogue et al., 2017).

2. Apply cognitive behavioral therapy (CBT) and integrated CBT (ICBT). Individuals with ADHD or ASD and a comorbid substance use disorder (SUD) will suffer *cumulative* cognitive or executive functioning (EF) impairment (Kronenberg et al., 2014). On one hand, ADHD patients show EF dysfunction, including impaired inhibition and meta-cognition, such as planning, problem solving, and emotion self-regulation. On the other hand, the executive functioning of many SUD patients is also greatly impaired. To fully restore and maximize a person's cognitive functioning, both SUD and ADHD need to be treated. Only reducing substance use may not solve the cognitive impairment caused by ADHD; likewise, ADHD medication treatment only does not seem to be effective in treating the SUD in individuals with comorbid ADHD–SUD (Kronenberg

et al., 2014; Zulauf et al., 2014). Furthermore, medication may improve ADHD patients' attention, but many of them have never learned organization and planning skills (van Emmerik-van Oortmerssen et al., 2015). These authors, therefore, believe that treatment of ADHD–SUD comorbidity should concentrate on enhancing a client's cognitive domain or EF.

Randomized trials have suggested noteworthy effects of cognitive behavioral therapy in treating ADHD patients, but CBT's efficacy has not been systematically studied in individuals with co-occurring ADHD and SUD (van Emmerik-van Oortmerssen et al., 2015; Zulauf et al., 2014). More recently, by combining two evidence-based CBT programs—one for ADHD and one for SUD—van Emmerik-van Oortmerssen et al. (2015) developed an integrated cognitive behavioral therapy (ICBT). They published treatment outcomes of two cases, showing ICBT as a promising approach helping ADHD–SUD comorbid patients. The ICBT includes two phases: the first phase focuses on stabilizing a person's SUD—the goal is to reduce or stop substance use, which will enable the clinician to reconfirm the person's ADHD diagnosis, as there are overlaps between substance withdrawal and/or intoxication and ADHD symptoms. The second phase begins only after the ADHD diagnosis is reconfirmed. In each session during the second phase, both SUD and ADHD issues are addressed. For SUD, the ICBT aims at functional analysis, training the person to identify and better deal with craving and triggers, and thus prevent relapse. For ADHD, the ICBT enhances the person's planning and organizing skills, including prioritizing tasks based on their urgency and breaking down into parts overwhelming tasks; the program also teaches distraction reduction techniques and mood problem coping. Despite ICBT's promising results, van Emmerik-van Oortmerssen and colleagues point out the high dropout rates among this dual diagnosis client population, suggesting more research is needed to enhance treatment retention and to compare the ICBT treatment outcomes with regular addiction treatment outcomes.

3. Develop a more adaptive and active coping style. Clinicians should help ADHD–SUD and ASD–SUD patients, especially the latter, develop a more adaptive and active coping style. Kronenberg, Goossens, et al.'s study (2015) compared an SUD-only group, an ADHD–SUD group, and an ASD–SUD group with a non-SUD group, using the Utrecht

Coping List. They found that all three SUD groups had a higher mean score than the non-SUD group in the areas of palliative reaction ("try to feel better by smoking, drinking, distraction of problems, relaxing"), avoidance (to "avoid situation, waiting, keeping clear of the problem"), and passive reaction ("rumination, drawing back, retreat, pondering, incapacity to do something about the situation") (p. 3).

Furthermore, the Kronenberg, Goossens, et al.'s study (2015) showed that the SUD-only group and the ADHD–SUD group were similar in the measurements of coping skills. In contrast, the ASD–SUD group received a higher score on passive reaction, and a lower score on reassuring thoughts ("calms oneself by thinking that worse things can happen, self-encouragement") than the ADHD–SUD and SUD only groups. The ASD–SUD group also scored lower than the ADHD–SUD group on expression of emotions ("expression of annoyance or anger, letting off of stream"). A coping style characterized with palliative reaction, avoidance, and passive reaction may only work in the short term; ADHD–SUD patients and especially ASD–SUD patients should be guided towards a more problem-focused and adaptive coping style (Kronenberg, Goossens, et al., p. 3, online publication).

4. Provide social skills training and foster a supportive family and social environment for clients with ASD–SUD. Core symptoms of ASD include an inadequate ability to cope with an overstimulated environment and a lack of social skills and social competency, which may result in anxiety, isolation, frustration, and depression, which in turn may lead to self-medication with substance use and misuse. Social skills training and a supportive family and social environment can soothe the emotional demands and help reduce the risk of resorting to substance misuse to self-medicate among this population (Rengit et al., 2016). Kronenberg, Verkerk-Tamminga, and colleagues' study (2015) also found that along the journey of recovery, it appears easier for the SUD with ADHD clients to "become more active agents of change within their own lives" than the SUD with ASD clients, whose difficulties with communication and social interaction may impose more challenges as they try to deal with their problems (p. 247).

5. Take into consideration both positive and negative effects when applying electronics to help ASD populations. Some studies indicate ASD populations' attraction to electronics use and suggest that clinicians integrate those tools into their teaching or treatment devices (Burton & Anderson 2013; Cihak et al., 2010). Many other studies, however, reveal consistent data showing a strong connection between ASD and internet gaming addiction (Engelhardt et al., 2017; Mazurek & Engelhardt, 2013; Moore, 2017). It's important to take both insights into consideration when conducting assessment and developing treatment plans for ASD clients to meet their individual needs (MacMullin et al., 2016).

6. Have patience. Hogue and colleagues (2017) consider patience the most important feature of treatment planning for adolescents with comorbid ADHD and SUD. They said reliable improvements in academic and social functioning are long-term goals and may take months or years to achieve. For immediate impacts and results, they think the clinicians can instead focus on growth in a client's confidence ("I feel like I have a better handle on things now"), symptom moderation ("I can pay attention longer"; "I get much more work done at night"), and hopefulness ("I think this could really help"), all of which can lead to future developmental successes (p. 288).

7. Conduct more research and develop more effective integrated treatment for patients with ADHD–SUD comorbidity. As mentioned previously, although pharmacotherapy has been well established for ADHD, its treatment of ADHD among SUD patients has "been less effective than expected" (van Emmerik-van Oortmerssen et al., 2013, p. 269). It is also important to investigate how to enhance treatment compliance and effectiveness among patients with ADHD–SUD comorbidity plus other additional comorbid psychiatric disorders such as major depression, borderline personality disorder, etc. (van Emmerik-van Oortmerssen et al.).

Personality Disorder and Addiction

Personality disorders—especially antisocial personality disorder (ASPD) and borderline personality disorder (BPD)—may co-occur with substance use disorder (SUD) (Bowden-Jones et al., 2004; Haase, 2009). The prevalence rate of ASPD is about 3–4% in the overall population;

in contrast, the rate is approximately 40–50% among the drug treatment study samples (Daughters et al., 2008). Furthermore, literature has indicated that about 90% of people with a diagnosis of ASPD have coexistent substance use disorders (Daughters et al.). The rate of BPD in general population is about 1–3%, whereas about 15% of people with alcohol use disorder meet BPD diagnostic criteria; in addition, about 50% of BPD individuals are affected by alcohol use disorder (Carpenter et al., 2017). Drawing data from the National Epidemiologic Survey on Alcohol and Related Conditions, Hasin et al. (2011) found that, among individuals who had nicotine dependence, alcohol dependence, or cannabis use disorder at baseline and who were interviewed again at the 3-year-post baseline, Axis I disorders did not play a strong role regarding *persistent* SUD; rather, ASPD, BPD, and schizotypal personality disorder are strongly and consistently associated with persistent SUD. Lauritzen and Nordfjærn's (2018) 10-year prospective study (481 patients, Norway) found that ASPD is one major predictor for sustained opiate use and stimulant use.

At least two theories explain the personality disorder-SUD comorbidity: one is the self-medication theory, which suggests that the personality disorder is the primary problem and SUD is secondary; the other is the common factor theory, which proposes that the personality disorder and SUD share common biological vulnerability factors and both disorders present difficulties in impulse control (Walter, 2015). The self-medication or self-regulation of emotion theory is the most common model explaining the co-occurrence of SUD and personality disorder—especially cluster B personality disorders, such as ASPD, BPD, and narcissistic personality disorder (Walter, 2015). Research has shown that cluster B personality disorders, which often includes characteristics like being dramatic, erratic, and impulsive, have the highest rates of substance use disorder or gambling disorder when compared to cluster A or cluster C personality disorders (Brown et al., 2016; Ekleberry, 2009). Addressing internet use addiction, Wu et al. (2016) suggest that both cluster B and cluster C personality disorders may be relevant to the development of internet addiction. Individuals with cluster B personality disorders are characterized with dramatic features such as impulsivity and affect dysregulation, and may engage with the internet to seek sensation and disinhibition. For people with cluster C personality disorders, who usually show traits of anxiety, interpersonal problems, and high harm avoidance, the internet may be used to achieve interpersonal interactions.

Following are strategies for helping ASPD–SUD and BPD–SUD patients:

1. Encourage patients' treatment adherence. A co-occurring personality disorder may unfavorably affect a patient's treatment motivation and compliance. Clinicians should be alerted to potential difficulties involved in treatment, and therefore should set behavioral limits, be more tolerant of patients' poor compliance, and anticipate longer terms of treatment (Brown et al., 2015). Although some studies have indicated—when treated under a sound behavioral therapy/psychosocial treatment protocol—no significant difference between substance-abusing patients with and without comorbid ASPD concerning their substance use treatment retention and outcomes (e.g., Easton et al., 2012), some other studies suggest that ASPD tends to associate with inadequate emotional regulation and cognitive deficit such as impulsivity and is usually a major risk factor for treatment drop-out (Brorson et al., 2013; Lauritzen & Nordfjærn, 2018).

2. Apply motivational interviewing (MI) and contingency management (CM). MI and CM that emphasize personal benefit may enhance the motivation of ASPD-SUD clients to comply with treatment and seek recovery (Daughters et al., 2008; Ekleberry, 2009; Messina et al., 2003). To ASPD–SUD clients, freedom and autonomy are high priorities in life; however, they often lose both because of their involvement with the criminal justice system and those in the addiction treatment field. Recovery can be conceptualized as a road to freedom and autonomy as it fulfills the requirements of both the legal and treatment systems. Ekleberry (2009) said that "[I]t is a candid validation of these individuals to suggest that the strengths inherent in their personality will make recovery possible and give them what they need to achieve their goals" and that "It is important to go for pro-recovery behavior without worrying about whether the motivations behind the behavior has anything to do with compliance to social norms. It may be that willingness to seek recovery as a way to stay out of jail or a hospital is enough" (p. 77). Daughters et al.'s study (n = 236 inner-city males receiving substance abuse residential treatment, US) found that ASPD patients

voluntarily attending treatment had a significantly higher drop-out rate compared to court-mandated ASPD patients, court-mandated non-ASPD patients, and non-ASPD patients voluntarily receiving treatment; in addition, no differences existed in the drop-out rates across the groups of court-mandated ASPD patients, court-mandated non-ASPD patients, and voluntary non-ASPD patients. Both Ekleberry's points and Daughters et al.'s findings demonstrate the function of negative reinforcement, in that although ASPD patients may not yet be ready to become intrinsically motivated, they may still comply with treatment as long as they sense a personal gain or benefit—in this case, avoidance of legal consequences/restriction of freedom (Daughters et al.).

3. Apply CBT to alter cognitive distortions among ASPD–SUD clients. Some of the distorted thoughts of individuals with ASPD may include "believing that wanting something justifies any action to get it," "thinking that if they feel right about what they do, it must be the right thing to do," "experiencing other people as irrelevant," and "believing that negative consequences will not happen or will not matter" (Ekleberry, 2009, p. 76).

4. Foster participation of the Twelve Step programs among ASPD–SUD clients. The Twelve Step programs and their communities (detailed in Chapter 6) can be especially meaningful and powerful to facilitate recovery among ASPD–SUD individuals. The Twelve Steps enable a person to honestly face one's distorted thoughts and wrong-doing, as well as to genuinely alter and improve one's character defects and dysfunctional behaviors, leading to a more functional and healthy life philosophy and lifestyle. The cultivation of the Twelve Steps can not only change a person's substance addiction but also his or her antisocial cognition and behaviors. Step 1—which states that "we admitted we were powerless over alcohol [or drugs, or other behavioral addiction such as gambling], that our lives had become unmanageable"—is critical to ASPD–SUD clients, who often are characterized as being self-centered, arrogant, strongly opinioned, and disregarding right and wrong. Step 1 facilitates humility and honesty in the person, propels the person to admit that there's a crisis in life that is beyond control, and paves the beginning for a recovery journey. Likewise, steps 4 to 9—which focus on admitting "the exact nature of our wrongs," humbly

asking the higher power to "remove our shortcomings," and making "a list of all persons we had harmed, and became willing to make amends to them all"—are a concrete structure that guides the person to live a more functional life. These steps have the potential to benefit ASPD–SUD patients enormously, in that they enhance a person's sensitivity to the feelings and needs of others, acceptance of responsibility in various life areas, and abilities to tolerate stress and inhibit impulsive actions (Ekleberry, 2009). Having presented all the positive impact of a Twelve Step program, it is important to also discuss "appropriate behaviors" with individuals with an ASPD diagnosis when attending self-help groups, including, for example, not borrowing money from or engaging in inappropriate sex with other vulnerable members, or engaging in other exploitive behaviors (Carruth, cited in Ekleberry).

5. Impulsivity and emotion dysregulation are features of both ASPD and BPD; however, ASPD is associated with both positive urgency (e.g., sensation seeking) and negative urgency (e.g., alleviating negative emotion) whereas BPD is more so with negative urgency (Hahn et al., 2016). Substance abuse treatment for each client population may be more likely to find success when targeting its corresponding aspect (Hahn et al., 2016). Studies have found that ASPD is linked to both alcohol consumption and alcohol problems, but BPD is linked only to alcohol problems ((Hahn et al., 2016; Lane et al., 2016). Lane and colleagues' study reported that individuals with BPD tend to crave alcohol under stressful situations and environments such as work and study (to reduce negative affect and emotion), compared to the community comparison group, who are more apt to have craving under normative contexts such as restaurants and bars (to enhance positive emotion and affect).

6. Prevent borderline personality disorder (BPD) patients from transferring substance addiction to other addictive behaviors. BPD clients may be vulnerable to switch or transfer their substance addiction to eating, gambling, shopping, and impulsive sexual behavior, once they become abstinent from their drug(s) (Ekleberry, 2009). To counteract the risk, recovery activities must address the entire scope of self-destructive behaviors. Clinicians need to equip the patients with skills to effectively manage their strong affect and emotions. Many BPD clients are likely to have physical and sexual abuse histories and trauma therapies are necessary.

7. Connect BPD patients with groups and meaningful interpersonal relationships. BPD patients can be linked with a mutual support group or a recovery community. Preparing BPD patients with pre-Twelve Step practice sessions, helping them to organize thoughts, and practicing a strategy of saying "pass" if feeling unsafe can facilitate more success in their participation in the self-help groups (Ekleberry, 2009). Ekleberry recommends the Wellness Recovery Action Plan (WRAP) groups for people afflicted with comorbid BPD and addiction. Established by Mary Ellen Copeland, WRAP Plan helps individuals develop daily or weekly tools and lists to (a) support their recovery and maintain equilibrium and stability, (b) deal with cravings, (c) and handle crises. The patients can design their own WRAP toolkit by borrowing from any therapy skills (for instance, dialectic behavioral therapy), the skills of AA/NA/peer group members, and the toolkit plans of other members in the WRAP groups.

References

Adan, A., Antunez, J.M., & Navarro, J.F., (2017). Coping strategies related to treatment in substance use disorder patients with and without comorbid depression. *Psychiatry Research, 251*, 325–332.

American Psychiatric Association [APA]. (2013). *Diagnostic and statistical manual of mental disorders*, Fifth Edition. Arlington, VA: American Psychiatric Association.

Awad, A.G., & Voruganti, L.L.N.P. (2015). Revisiting the 'self-medication' hypothesis in light of the new data linking low striatal dopamine to comorbid addictive behavior. *Therapeutic Advances in Psychopharmacology, 5*(3), 172–178.

Back, S.E., Foa, E.B., Mills, K., Teesson, M., & Carroll, K. (2015). *Concurrent treatment of PTSD and substance use disorders using prolonged exposure (COPE)*. Therapist manual. Treatments that work. New York: Oxford University Press.

Baskin-Sommers, A.R., & Foti, D. (2015). Abnormal reward functioning across substance use disorders and major depressive disorder: Considering reward as a transdiagnostic mechanism. *International Journal of Psychophysiology, 98*, 227–239.

Bennett, M.E., Bradshaw, K.R., & Catalano, L.T. (2017). Treatment of substance use disorders in schizophrenia. *The American Journal of Drug and Alcohol Abuse, 43*(4), 377–390.

Blanco, C., Alegria, A.A., Liu, S.M., Secades-Villa, R., Sugaya, L., Davies, C., & Nunes, E.V. (2012). Differences among major depressive disorder with and without co-occurring substance use disorders and substance-induced depressive disorder: Results from the national epidemiologic survey on alcohol and related conditions. *Journal of Clinical Psychiatry, 73*(6), 865–873.

Boscarino, J.A., Hoffman, S.N., & Han, J.J. (2015). Opioid-use disorder among patients on long-term opioid therapy: Impact of final DSM-5 diagnostic criteria on prevalence and correlates. *Substance Abuse and Rehabilitation, 6*, 83–91.

Boscarino, J.A., Rukstalis, M., Hoffman, S.N., Han, J.J., Erlich, P.M., Gerhard, G.S., & Stewart, W.F. (2010). Risk factors for drug dependence among out-patients on opioid therapy in a large US health-care system. *Addiction, 105*, 1776–1782.

Bowden-Jones, O., Iqbal, M.Z., Tyrer, P., Seivewright, N., Cooper, S., Judd, A., et al. (2004). Prevalence of personality disorder in alcohol and drug services and associated comorbidity. *Addiction, 99*(10), 1306–1314.

Brook, J.S., Zhang, C., Rubenstone, E., Primack, B.A., & Brook, D.W. (2016). Comorbid trajectories of substance use as predictors of antisocial personality disorder, major depressive episode, and generalized anxiety disorder. *Addictive Behaviors, 62*, 114–121.

Brorson, H.H., Arnevik, E.A., Rand-Hendriksen, K., & Duckert, F. (2013). Drop-out from addiction treatment: A systematic review of risk factors. *Clinical Psychology Review, 33*, 1010–1024.

Brown, M., Allen, J.S., Dowling, N.A. (2015). The application of an etiological model of personality disorders to problem gambling. *Jounal of Gambling Studies, 31*, 1179–1199.

Brown, M., Oldenhof, E., Allen, J.S., & Dowling, N.A. (2016). An empirical study of personality disorders among treatment-seeking problem gamblers. *Journal of Gambling Studies, 32*, 1079–1100.

Brown, R.A., Evans, D.M., Miller, I.W., Burgess, E.S., & Mueller, T.I. (1997). Cognitive-behavioral treatment for depression in alcoholism. *Journal of Consulting and Clinical Psychology, 65*(5), 715–726.

Burton, C.E., & Anderson, D. (2013). Video self-modeling on an iPad to teach functional math skills to adolescents with autism and intellectual disability. *Focus on Autism and Other Developmental Disabilities, 28*(2), 67–77.

Butwicka, A., Langstrom, N., Larsson, H., Lundstrom, S., Serlachius, E., Almqvist, C., Frisen, L., & Lichtenstein, P. (2017). Increased risk for substance use-related problems in autism spectrum disorders: A population-based cohort study. *Journal of Autism and Development Disorder, 47*, 80–89.

Carey, K.B., Purnine, D.M., Maisto, S.A., & Carey, M.P. (2001). Enhancing readiness-to-change substance abuse in persons with schizophrenia: A four-session motivation-based intervention. *Behavior Modification, 25*(3), 331–384.

Carpenter, R.W., Trela, C.J., Lane, S.P., Wood, P.K., Piasecki, T.M., & Trull, T.J. (2017). Elevated rate of alcohol consumption in borderline personality disorder patients in daily life. *Psychopharmacology, 234*, 3395–3406.

Caspi, A., Moffitt, T.E., Cannon, M., McClay, J., Murray, R., et al. (2005). Moderation of the effect of adolescent-onset cannabis use on adult psychosis by a functional polymorphism in the catechol-o-methyltransferase gene: Longitudinal evidence of a gene x environment interaction. *Biological Psychiatry, 57*, 1117–1127.

Centers for Disease Control and Prevention (2017). Prescribing data. Retrieved on 02/03/2018www.cdc.gov/drugoverdose/data/prescribing.html.

Center for Substance Abuse Treatment (2005). *Substance abuse treatment for persons with co-occurring disorders.* Treatment Improvement Protocol (TIP) Series 42. DHHS Publication No. (SMA) 08–3992. Rockville, MD: Substance Abuse and Mental Health Services Administration.

Cheatle, M.D. (2013). Pain and addiction. *Interventions for Addiction, 3*, 503–515 (D/C).

Cihak, D., Fahrenkrog, C., Ayres, K.M., & Smith, C. (2010). The use of video modeling via a video iPod and a system of least prompts to improve transitional behaviors for students with autism spectrum disorders in the general education classroom. *Journal of Positive Behavior Interventions, 12*(2), 103–115.

Conway, K.P., Compton, W., Stinson, F.S., & Grant, B.F. (2006). Lifetime comorbidity of DSM-IV mood and anxiety disorders and specific drug use disorders: Results from the National Epidemiologic Survey on Alcohol and Related Conditions. *Journal of Clinical Psychiatry, 67*(2), 247–257.

Cornelius, J.R., Douaihy, A., Bukstein, O.G., Daley, D.C., Wood, D.S., et al. (2011). Evaluation of cognitive behavioral therapy/motivational enhancement therapy (CBT/MET) in a treatment trial of comorbid MDD/AUD adolescents. *Addictive Behaviors, 36*(8), 843–848.

Daughters, S.B., Stipelman, B.A., Sargeant, M.N., Schuster, R., Bornovalova, M.A., & Lejuez, C.W. (2008). The interactive effects of antisocial personality disorder and court-mandated status on substance abuse treatment dropout. *Journal of Substance Abuse Treatment, 34*(2), 157–164.

De Alwis, D., Agrawal, A., Reiersen, A.M., Constantino, J.N., Henders, A., Martin, N.G., & Lynskey, M.T. (2014). ADHD symptoms, autistic traits, and substance use and misuse in adult Australian twins. *Journal of Studies on Alcohol and Drugs*, March, 211–221.

Demyttenaere, K., Bonnewyn, A., Bruffaerts, R., Brugha, T., de Graaf, R., & Alonso, J. (2006). Comorbid painful physical symptoms and depression: Prevalence, work loss, and help seeking. *Journal of Affective Disorders, 92*, 185–193.

Dick, D.M., & Agrawal, A. (2008). The genetics of alcohol and other drug dependence. *Alcohol Research & Health, 31*(2), 111–118.

DiClemente, C.C., Nidecker, M., & Bellack, A.S. (2008). Motivation and the stages of change among individuals with severe mental illness and substance abuse disorders. *Journal of Substance Abuse Treatment, 34*, 25–35.

Dixon, L.B., Dickerson, F., Bellack, A.S., Bennett, M., Dickinson, D., Goldberg, R.W., et al. (2010). The 2009 schizophrenia PORT psychosocial treatment recommendations and summary statements. *Schizophrenia Bulletin, 36*(1), 48–70.

Easton, C.J., Oberleitner, L.M., Scott, M.C., Crowley, M.J., Babuscio, T.A., & Carroll, K.M. (2012). Differences in treatment outcome among marijuana-dependent young adults with and without antisocial personality disorder. *The American Journal of Drug and Alcohol Abuse, 38*(4), 305–313.

Ekleberry, S.C. (2009). *Integrated treatment for co-occurring disorders: Personality disorders and addiction*. New York: Routledge.

Engelhardt, C.R., Mazurek, M.O., & Hilgard, J. (2017). Pathological game use in adults with and without autism spectrum disorder. *PeerJ 5*: e3393; doi 10.7717/peerj.3393.

Erskine, H.E., Norman, R.E., Ferrari, A.J., Chan, G.C.K., Copeland, W.E., Whiteford, H.A., et al. (2016). Long-term outcomes of attention-deficit/hyperactivity disorder and conduct disorder: A systematic review and meta-analysis. *Journal of the American Academy of Child & Adolescent Psychiatry, 55*(10), 841–850.

Fishbain, D.A., Cole, B., Lewis, J., Rosomoff, H.L., & Rosomoff, R.S. (2008). What percentage of chronic nonmalignant pain patients exposed to chronic opioid analgesic therapy develop abuse/addiction and/or aberrant drug-related behaviors? A structured evidence-based review. *Pain Medicine, 9*(4), 444–459.

Flanagan, J.C., Korte, K.J., Killeen, T.K., & Back, S.E. (2016). Concurrent treatment of substance use and PTSD. *Current Psychiatry Report, 18*(8), 70. doi: 10.1007/s11920-016-0709-y.

Foa, E.B., Hembree, E.A., Rothbaum, B.O. (2007). *Prolonged exposure therapy for PTSD: Emotional processing of traumatic experiences therapist guide*. New York: Oxford University Press.

Foa, E.B., Yusko, D.A., McLean, C.P., Suvak, M.K., Bux, D.A., Oslin, D., O'Brien, C.P., Imms, P., Riggs, D.S., & Volpicelli, J. (2013). Concurrent naltrexone and prolonged exposure therapy for patients with comorbid alcohol dependence and PTSD: A randomized clinical trial. *JAMA, 310*(5), 488–495. doi: 10.1001/jama.2013.8268.

Garland, E.L., Roberts-Lewis, A., Tronnier, C.D., Graves, R., & Kelley, K. (2016). Mindfulness-oriented recovery enhancement versus CBT for co-occurring substance dependence, traumatic stress, and psychiatric disorders: Proximal outcomes from a pragmatic randomized trial. *Behaviour Research and Therapy*, 77, 7–16. doi: 10.1016/j.brat.2015.11.012.

Gouzoulis-Mayfrank, E., & Walter, M. (2015). Schizophrenia and addiction. In G. Dom & F. Moggi (Eds.) *Co-occurring addictive and psychiatric disorders* (pp. 75–86). Berlin Heidelberg: Springer-Verlag.

Grant, B.F., Saha, T.D., Ruan, W.J., Goldstein, R.B., Chou, S.P., Jung, J., Zhang, H., Smith, S.M., Pickering, R.P., Huang, B., & Hasin, D.S. (2016). Epidemiology of *DSM-5* drug use disorder: Results from the National Epidemiologic Survey on alcohol and related conditions-III. *JAMA Psychiatry*, 73(1), 39–47.

Gregg, L., Barrowclough, C., & Haddock, G. (2007). Reasons for increased substance use in psychosis. *Clinical Psychology Review*, 27, 494–510.

Haase, J.M. (2009). Co-occurring antisocial personality disorder and substance use disorder: Treatment interventions. *Graduate Journal of Counseling Psychology*, 1(2), 57–64.

Haddad, P.M., Brain, C., & Scott, J. (2014). Nonadherence with antipsychotic medication in schizophrenia: Challenges and management strategies. *Patient Related Outcome Measures*, 5, 43–62.

Hahn, A.M., Simons, R.M., & Hahn, C.K. (2016). Five factors of impulsivity: Unique pathways to borderline and antisocial personality features and subsequent *alcohol* problems. *Personality and Individual Differences*, 99, 313-319.

Han, B., Olfson, M., & Mojtabai, R. (2017). Depression care among depressed adults with and without comorbid substance use disorders in the United States. *Depression and Anxiety*, 34, 291–300.

Harstad, E., Levy, S., & Committee on Substance Abuse (2014). Attention-deficit/hyperactivity disorder and substance abuse. *Pediatrics*, 134(1), e293–e301.

Hasin, D., Fenton, M.C., Skodol, A., Krueger, R., Keyes, K., Geier, T., Greenstein, E., Blanco, C., & Grant, B. (2011). Personality disorders and the 3-year course of alcohol, drug, and nicotine use disorders. *Archieves of General Psychiatry*, 68(11), 1158–1167.

Hien, D.A., Cohen, L.R., Miele, G.M., Litt, L.C., & Capstick, C. (2004). Promising treatments for women with comorbid PTSD and substance use disorders. *American Journal of Psychiatry*, 161(8), 1426–1432.

Hien, D., Levin, F.R., Ruglass, L., Lopez-Castro, T., Papini, S., Hu, M.C., Cohen, L., & Herron, A. (2015). Combining seeking safety with sertraline for PTSD and alcohol use disorders: A randomized controlled trial. *Journal of Consulting and Clinical Psychology*, 83(2), 359–369. doi: 10.1037/a0038719.

Hofvander, B., Delorme, R., Chaste, P., Nydén, A., Wentz, E., Ståhlberg, O., et al. (2009). Psychiatric and psychosocial problems in adults with normal-intelligence autism spectrum disorders. *BMC Psychiatry*, 9(35). doi:10.1186/1471-244X-9-35.

Hogue, A., Evans, S.W., & Levin, F.R. (2017). A clinician's guide to co-occurring ADHD among adolescent substance users: Comorbidity, neurodevelopmental risk, and evidence-based treatment options. *Journal of Child & Adolescent Substance Abuse*, 26(4), 277–292.

Humphreys, K.L., Eng, T., & Lee, S.S. (2013). Stimulant medication and substance use outcomes: A meta-analysis. *JAMA Psychiatry*, 70(7), 740–749.

Johnson, J.E., & Zlotnick, C. (2012). Pilot study of treatment for major depression among women prisoners with substance use disorder. *Journal of Psychiatric Research*, 46, 1174–1183.

Karaca, S., Saleh, A., Canan, F., & Potenza, M.N. (2017). Comorbidity between behavioral addictions and attention deficit/hyperactivity disorder: A systematic review. *International Journal of Mental Health Addiction, 15*, 701–724. doi: 10.1007/s11469-016-9660-8.

Kelly, T.M., & Daley, D.C. (2013). Integrated treatment of substance use and psychiatric disorders. *Social Work in Public Health, 28*(0), 388–406.

Khan, A.Y., Salaria, S., Ovais, M., & Ide, G.D. (2016). Depot antipsychotics: Where do we stand? *Annals of Clinical Psychiatry, 28*(4), 289–298.

Khantzian, E., & Albanese, M.J. (2008). *Understanding addiction as self medication: Finding hope behind the pain.* Lanham, MD: Rowman & Littlefield Publishers.

Killeen, T.K., Back, S.E., & Brady, K.T. (2015). Implementation of integrated therapies for comorbid post-traumatic stress disorder and substance use disorders in community substance abuse treatment programs. *Drug and Alcohol Review, 34*(3), 234–241.

Konstenius, M., Jayaram-Lindstrom, N., Guterstam, J., Beck, O., Philips, & Franck, J. (2014). Methylphenidate for attention deficit hyperactivity disorder and drug relapse in criminal offenders with substance dependence: A 24-week randomized placebo-controlled trial. *Addiction, 109*(3), 440–449.

Koola, M.M., Wehring, H.J., & Kelly, D.L. (2012). The potential role of long-acting injectable antipsychotics in people with schizophrenia and comorbid substance use. *Journal of Dual Diagnosis, 8*(1), 50–61.

Kronenberg, L., Slager-Visscher, K., Goossens, P., van den Brink, W., & van Achterberg, T. (2014). Everyday life consequences of substance use in adult patients with a substance use disorder (SUD) and co-occurring attention deficit/hyperactivity disorder (ADHD) or autism spectrum disorder (ASD): A patient's perspective. *BMC Psychiatry, 14*, 264. doi: 10.1186/s12888-014-0264-1.

Kronenberg, L.M., Goossens, P., van Busschbach, J., van Achterberg, T., & van den Brink, W. (2015). Coping styles in substance use disorder (SUD) patients with and without co-occurring attention deficit/hyperactivity disorder (ADHD) or autism spectrum disorder (ASD). *BMC Psychiatry, 15*, 159. doi: 10.1186/s12888-015-0530-x.

Kronenberg, L.M., Verkerk-Tamminga, R., Goossens, P., van den Brink, W., & van Achterberg, T. (2015). Personal recovery in individuals diagnosed with substance use disorder (SUD) and co-occurring attention deficit/hyperactivity disorder (ADHD) or autism spectrum disorder (ASD). *Archives of Psychiatric Nursing, 29*, 242–248.

Lane, S.P., Carpenter, R.W., Sher, K.J., & Trull, T.J. (2016). Alcohol craving and consumption in borderline personality disorder: When, where, and with whom. *Clinical Psychological Science, 4*(5), 775–792.

Levin, F.R., Evans, S.M., Brooks, D.J., & Garawi, F. (2007). Treatment of cocaine dependent treatment seekers with adult ADHD: Double-blind comparison of methylphenidate and placebo. *Drug and Alcohol Dependence, 87*, 20–29.

Lieb, R. (2015). Epidemiological perspectives on comorbidity between substance use disorders and other mental disorders. In G. Dom & F. Moggi (Eds.) *Co-occurring addictive and psychiatric disorders* (pp. 3–12). Berlin Heidelberg: Springer-Verlag.

Lauritzen, G., & Nordfjærn, T. (2018). Changes in opiate and stimulant use through 10 years: The role of contextual factors, mental health disorders and psychosocial factors in a prospective SUD treatment cohort study. *PLoS ONE, 13*(1): e0190381. doi.org/10.1371/journal.pone.0190381.

MacMullin, J.A., Lunsky, Y., & Weiss, J.A. (2016). Plugged in: Electronics use in youth and young adults with autism spectrum disorder. *Autism, 20*(1), 45–54.

Marcus, S.C., Zummo, J., Pettit, A.R., Stoddard, J., & Doshi, J.A. (2015). Antipsychotic adherence and rehospitalization in schizophrenia patients receiving oral versus long-acting injectable antipsychotics following hospital discharge. *Journal of Managed Care & Specialty Pharmacy, 21*(9), 754–768.

Markowitz, J.C., & Weissman, M.M. (2004). Interpersonal psychotherapy: Principles and applications. *World Psychiatry, 3*(3), 136–139.

Markowitz, J.C., & Weissman, M.M. (2012). Interpersonal psychotherapy: Past, present and future. *Clinical Psychology & Psychotherapy, 19*(2), 99–105.

Mazurek, M.O., & Engelhardt, C.R. (2013). Video game use in boys with autism spectrum disorder, ADHD, or typical development. *Pediatrics, 132*(2), 260–266.

Mazurek, M.O., & Wenstrup, C. (2013). Television, video game and social media use among children with ASD and typically developing siblings. *Journal of Autism and Development Disorders, 43*, 1258–1271.

McCauley, J.L., Killeen, T., Gros, D.F., Brady, K.T., & Back, S.E. (2012). Posttraumatic stress disorder and co-occurring substance use disorders: Advances in assessment and treatment. *Clinical Pshychology, 19*(3), doi: 10.1111/cpsp.12006.

McDevitt-Murphy, M.E., Murphy, J.G., Williams, J.L., Monahan, C.J., Bracken-Minor, K.L., & Fields, J.A. (2014). Randomized controlled trial of two brief alcohol interventions for OEF/OIF veterans. *Journal of Consulting and Clinical Psychology, 82*, 562–568.

McGovern, M.P., Lambert-Harris, C., Xie, H., Meier, A., McLeman, B., & Saunders, E. (2015). A randomized controlled trial of treatments for co-occurring substance use disorders and post-traumatic stress disorder. *Addiction, 110*, 1194–1204.

Mee-Lee, D., Shulman, G.D., Fishman, M.J., Gastfriend, D.R., & Miller, M.M. (Eds.) (2013). *The ASAM criteria: Treatment criteria for addictive, substance-related, and co-occurring conditions*, Third Edition. Carson City, NV: The Change Companies.

Messina, N., Farabee, D., & Rawson, R. (2003). Treatment responsivity of cocaine-dependent patients with antisocial personality disorder to cognitive-behavioral and contingency management interventions. *Journal of Counseling and Clinical Psychology, 71*(2), 320–329.

Mills, K.L., Teesson, M., Back, S.E., Brady, K.T., Baker, A.L., Hopwood, S., Sannibale, C., Barrett, E.L., Merz, S., Rosenfeld, J., & Ewer, P.L. (2012). Integrated exposure-based therapy for co-occurring posttraumatic stress disorder and substance dependence: A randomized controlled trial. *JAMA, 15*, 308(7), 690–699.

Moore, D. (2017). Internet and gaming addiction in youth on the autism spectrum: A particularly vulnerable population. In K.S. Young (Ed.) and C.N. de Abreu (Ed.) *Internet addiction in children and adolescents: Risk factors, assessment, and treatment* (pp. 83–100). New York: Springer.

Morgan, B.D., & White, D.M. (2009). Managing pain in patients with co-occurring addictive disorders. *Journal of Addictive Nursing, 20*, 41–48.

Myers, U.S., Browne, K.C., Norman, S.B. (2015). Treatment engagement: Female survivors of intimate partner violence in treatment for PTSD and alcohol use disorder. *Journal of Dual Diagnosis, 11*, 238–247.

Najavits, L.M. (2002). *Seek safety: A treatment manual for PTSD and substance abuse.* New York: Guilford.

Najavits, L.M., & Johnson, K.M. (2014). Pilot study of creating change, a new past-focused model for PTSD and substance abuse. *The American Journal on Addictions, 23*, 415–422.

National Institute on Drug Abuse (2010). Comorbidity: Addiction and other mental illnesses. *Research Report Series.* NIH Publication Number 10-5771.

Norman, S.B., Myers, U.S., Wilkins, K.C., Goldsmith, A.A., Hristova, V., Huang, Z., et al. (2012). Review of biological mechanisms and pharmacological treatments of comorbid PTSD and substance use disorder. *Neuropharmacology, 62*(2), 542–551.

Park, T.W., Cheng, D.M., Samet, J., Winter, M., & Saitz, R. (2015). Chronic care management for substance dependence in primary care among patients with co-occurring mental disorders. *Psychiatry Service, 66*, 72–79.

Pedersen, E.R., Huang, W., Cohen, A.N., & Young, A.S. (2018). Alcohol use and service utilization among veterans in treatment for schizophrenia. *Psychological Services, 15*(1), 21–30.

Petrakis, I.L., Poling, J., Levinson, C., Nich, C, Carroll, K., Ralevski, E., et al. (2006). Naltrexone and disulfiram in patients with alcohol dependence and comorbid posttraumatic stress disorder. *Biological Psychiatry, 60*, 777–783.

Petrakis, I.L., Ralevski, E., Desai, N., Trevisan, L., Gueorguieva, R., Rounsaville, B., et al. (2012). Noradrenergic vs Serotonergic antidepressant with or without naltrexone for veterans with PTSD and comorbid alcohol dependence. *Neuropsychopharmacology, 37*, 996–1004.

Petrakis, I.L., & Simpson, T.L. (2017). Posttraumatic stress disorder and alcohol use disorder: A critical review of pharmacologic treatments. *Alcoholism: Clinical and Experimental Research, 41*(2), 226–237.

Pettinati, H.M., Oslin, D.W., Kampman, K.M., Dundon, W.D., Xie, H., Gallis, T.L., et al. (2010). A double-blind, placebo-controlled trial combining sertraline and naltrexone for treating co-occurring depression and alcohol dependence. *American Journal of Psychiatry, 167*(6), 668–675.

Pohl, M., & Smith, L. (2012). Chronic pain and addiction: Challenging co-occurring disorders. *Journal of Psychoactive Drugs, 44*(2), 119–124.

Quello, S.B., Brady, K.T., & Sonne, S.C. (2005). Mood disorders and substance use disorder: A complex comorbidity. *Science & Practice Perspectives, 3*(1), 13–21.

Regier, D.A., Farmer, M.E., Rae, D.S., Locke, B.Z., Keith, S.J., Judd, L.L., & Goodwin, F.K. (1990). Comorbidity of mental disorders with alcohol and other drug abuse. Results from the Epidemiologic Catchment Area (ECA) study. *The Journal of the American Medical Association, 264*(19), 2511–2518.

Rengit, A.C., McKowen, J.W., O'Brien, J., Howe, Y.J., & McDougle, C.J. (2016). Brief report: Autism spectrum disorder and substance use disorder: A review and case study. *Journal of Autism and Development Disorders, 46*, 2514–2519.

Rosenblum, A., Joseph, H., Fong, C., Kipnis, S., Cleland, C., & Portenoy, R.K. (2003). Prevalence and characteristics of chronic pain among chemically dependent patients in methadone maintenance and residential treatment facilities. *JAMA, 289*(18), 2370–2378.

Ross, S., & Peselow, E. (2012). Co-occurring psychotic and addictive disorders: Neurobiology and diagnosis. *Clinical Neuropharmacology, 35*(5), 235–243.

Salsitz, E.A. (2016). Chronic pain, chronic opioid addiction: A complex nexus. *Journal of Medicla Toxicology, 12*, 54–57.

Samaha, A. (2014). Can antipsychotic treatment contribute to drug addiction in schizophrenia? *Progress in Neuro-Psychopharmacology & Biological Psychiatry, 52*, 9–16.

Santosh, P.J., & Mijovic, A. (2006). Does pervasive developmental disorder protect children and adolescents against drug and alcohol use? *European Child & Adolescent Psychiatry, 15*, 183–188.

Schafer, I., & Langeland, W. (2015). Posttraumatic stress disorders and addiction. In G. Dom & F. Moggi (Eds.) *Co-occurring addictive and psychiatric disorders* (pp. 161–177). Berlin Heidelberg: Springer-Verlag.

Schmidt, L.M., Hesse, M., & Lykke, J. (2011). The impact of substance use disorders on the course of schizophrenia—A 15-year follow-up study: Dual diagnosis over 15 years. *Schizophrenia Research, 130*, 228–233.

Shorey, R.C., Elmquist, J., Anderson, S., & Stuart, G.L. (2015). The relationship between early maladaptive schemas, depression, and generalized anxiety among adults seeking residential treatment for substance use disorders. *Journal of Psychoactive Drugs, 47*(3), 230–238.

Simpson, T.L., Lehavot, K., & Petrakis, I. (2017). No wrong doors: Findings from a critical review of behavioral randomized clinical trials for individuals with co-occurring alcohol/drug problems and posttraumatic stress disorder. *Alcoholism: Clinical and Experimental Research, 41*(4), 681–702. doi: 10.1111/acer.13325.

Smith, M.T., & Haythornthwaite, J.A. (2004). How do sleep disturbance and chronic pain inter-relate? Insights from the longitudinal and cognitive-behavioral clinical trials literature. *Sleep Medicine Reviews, 8*, 119–132.

Substance Abuse and Mental Health Services Administration (SAMHSA, 2014). *Trauma-informed care in behavioral health services*. Tretment Improvement Protocol (TIP) Series 57. HHS Publication No. (SMA) 13-4801. Rockville, MD: SAMHSA.

Sun, A.P. (2000). Helping substance-abusing mothers in the child-welfare system: Turning crisis into opportunity. *Families in Society: The Journal of Contemporary Social Services, 81*(2), 142–151.

Sun, A.P. (2012). Helping homeless individuals with co-occurring disorders: The four components. *Social Work, 57*(1), 23–37.

Sun, A.P., Chen, Y.C., & Marsiglia, F. (2016). Trauma and Chinese heroin users. *Journal of Ethnicity in Substance Abuse, 15*(2), 144–159.

Tenhula, W.N., Bennett, M.E., Kinnaman, J.E.S. (2009). Behavioral treatment of substance abuse in schizophrenia. *Journal of Clinical Psychology: In Session, 65*(8), 831–841.

Tessier, A., Boyer, L., Husky, M., Baylé, F., Llorca, P.M. & Misdrahi, D. (2017). Medication adherence in schizophrenia: The role of insight, therapeutic alliance and perceived trauma associated with psychiatric care. *Psychiatry Research, 257*, 315–321.

Thoma, P., & Daum, I. (2013). Comorbid substance use disorder in schizophrenia: A selective overview of neurobiological and cognitive underpinnings. *Psychiatry and Clinical Neurosciences, 67*, 367–383.

Torchalla, I., Strehlau, V., Li, K., Linden, I.A., Noel, F., & Krausz, M. (2014). Posttraumatic stress disorder and substance use disorder comorbidity in homeless adults: Prevalence, correlates, and sex differences. *Psychology of Addictive Behaviors, 28*(2), 443–452.

Torrens, M., & Rossi, P. (2015). Mood disorders and addiction. In G. Dom & F. Moggi (Eds.) *Co-occurring addictive and psychiatric disorders* (pp. 103–117). Berlin Heidelberg: Springer-Verlag.

Van Emmerik-van Oortmerssen, K., van de Glind, G., Koeter, M.W.J., Allsop, S., Auriacombe, M., Barta, C., Bu, E.T.H., Burren, Y., et al. (2013). Psychiatric comorbidity in treatment-seeking substance use disorder patients with and without attention deficit hyperactivity disorder: Results of the IASP study. *Addiction, 109*, 262–272.

Van Emmerik-van Oortmerssen, K., Vedel, E., van den Brink, W., & Schoevers, R.A. (2015). Integrated cognitive behavioral therapy for patients with substance used disorder and comorbid ADHD: Two case presentations. *Addictive Behaviors, 45*, 214–217.

Van Wijngaarden-Cremers, P.J.M., & van der Gaag, R.J. (2015). Addiction and autism spectrum disorder. In G. Dom & F. Moggi (Eds.). *Co-occurring addictive and psychiatric disorders* (pp. 193–204). Berlin Heidelberg: Springer-Verlag.

Volavka, J. (2013). Violence in schizophrenia and bipolar disorder. *Psychiatria Danubina, 25*(1), 24–33.

Volkow, N.D. (2009). Substance use disorders in schizophrenia—Clinical implications of comorbidity. *Schizophrenia Bulletin, 35*(3), 469–472.

Volkow, N.D., & McLellan, A.T. (2016). Opioid abuse in chronic pain—Misconceptions and mitigation strategies. *The New England Journal of Medicine, 374* (13), 1253–1263.

Walter, M. (2015). Personality disorder and addiction. In G. Dom & F. Moggi (Eds.) *Co-occurring addictive and psychiatric disorders* (pp. 137–148). Berlin Heidelberg: Springer-Verlag.

Warden, D., Riggs, P.D., Min, S., Mikulich-Gilbertson, S.K., Tamm, L., Trello-Rishel, K., & Winhusen, T. (2012). Major depression and treatment response in adolescents with ADHD and substance use disorder. *Drug and Alcohol Dependence, 120*, 214–219.

Watkins, K.E., Hunter, S.B., Hepner, K., Paddock, S.M., Zhou, A., & de la Cruz, E. (2012). Group cognitive-behavioral therapy for clients with major depression in residential substance abuse treatment. *Psychiatric Services, 63*(6), 608–611.

Weiss, R. D. (2004). Treating patients with bipolar disorder and substance dependence: Lessons learned. *Journal of Substance Abuse Treatment, 27*, 307–312.

Witkiewitz, K., & Bowen, S. (2010). Depression, craving and substance use following a randomized trial of mindfulness-based relapse prevention. *Journal of Consulting and Clinical Psychology, 78*(3), 362–374.

Wu, J.Y.-W., Ko, H.-C., & Lane, H.-Y. (2016). Personality disorders in female and male college students with Internet addiction. *The Journal of Nervous and Mental Disease, 204*(3), 221–225.

Young, J.E., Klosko, J.S., & Weishaar, M.E. (2003). *Schema therapy: A pratitioner's guide.* New York: Guilford.

Zaso, M.J., Park, A., & Antshel, K.M. (2015). Treatments for adolescents with comorbid ADHD and substance use disorder: A systematic review. *Journal of Attention Disorders*, 1–12. doi: 10.1177/1087054715569280.

Ziedonis, D.M., Smelson, D., Rosenthal, R.N., Batki, S.L., Green, A.I., Henry, R.J., et al. (2005). Improving the care of individuals with schizophrenia and substance use disorders: Consensus recommendations. *Journal of Psychiatric Practice, 11*, 315–339.

Zulauf, C.A., Sprich, S.E., Safren, S.A., & Wilens, T.E. (2014). The complicated relationship between attention deficit/hyperactivity disorder and substance use disorders. *Current Psychiatry Report, 16*(3), 436. doi: 10.1007/s11920-013-0436-6.

4
ADDICTION AND QUALITY OF LIFE

"[T]here is more to living than just staying alive"; human beings crave happiness such as pleasure, the gratification of being loved and loving, fulfillment, recognition, a sense of self-worth, and personal value (Glasser, 1976, p. 3). A life without happiness is unbearable; for individuals who have given up hope on pursuing life happiness, then suicide, mercy killing, or addiction provides a solution, despite it being a poor one (Glasser, 1976). The significant relationship between addiction and quality of life was recognized thousands of years ago. Alexander (2008) states that "Because [addicts] are unable to achieve or even understand dikaiosune [i.e., psychosocial integration] in their bizarre society, they seek satisfaction elsewhere, and achieve a shred of satisfaction in their total subjugation to a few, base appetites" (p. 325). Psychosocial dislocation is an addiction theory proposed by Bruce Alexander (2008), who suggests that "the success story of the human species" requires that "all citizens recognize all other citizens as essential to the whole, and each is respected for his or her unique function" (p. 319). The psychosocial dislocation theory believes that most people are aware of the destructive consequences of addiction to drugs or certain behaviors, but they still do drugs or engage in those behaviors because "it is the lesser evil" and "it provides a substitute for an *unbearable* lack of psychosocial integration" (Alexander, p. 326 [italics added]).

Consistently, William Glasser, in his book *Positive Addiction* (1976), suggests that people who give up, or do not fight for, their dreams or life goals—which often provide rewards and a sense of well-being and life contentment—may experience devastating symptoms and pain, and may subsequently choose addiction to substances or some dysfunctional behavior to get by the despair. A well-known and widely cited experiment conducted by Morgan and colleagues (2002) showed the beneficial impact of the environmental resources on monkeys' brain dopamine D_2 receptors. The team found that monkeys demonstrate no difference concerning their dopamine receptors or cocaine use when being individually housed. However, when socially housed, those who climb to the top of the social rank—and, therefore, enjoy more natural rewards and less stress—indicate more dopamine D_2 receptors and use less cocaine than do those more subordinate monkeys. The philosophers and scientists have identified the connection between addiction and the aspects of psychosocial integration, a sense of well-being, and life contentment, all of which can actually be more concretely operationalized by the concept of *quality of life*.

One way to define quality of life (QoL) is Maslow's (1943) hierarchy of human needs. Maslow ranks human needs from the lower but more prepotent needs (such as the physiological needs of respiration, hunger, sleep) to needs like safety, belongingness, love, esteem, and, ultimately, self-actualization. Addressing the issues of clients' perceptions of QoL and enriching their QoL accordingly can facilitate a sense of well-being, life content, and psychosocial integration, and thus promote long-term recovery in clients. Specifically, although QoL is a subjective perception, its domain may include a person's living environment with such needs as safety, housing, finance, and access to care; social-economic factors; physical and mental health; relationships with significant others such as a spouse, parent, children, friends, and neighbors; employment; and spirituality (Laudet, 2011; Luty & Arokiadass, 2008; World Health Organization [WHO], 1997).

Despite the development of insight and knowledge regarding the connection between addiction and psychosocial integration and quality of life (QoL), the inclusion of QoL improvement in addiction treatments is not without challenges. Two issues emerged in this regard. The first issue was raised by Newman (2012), in that he questioned the legitimacy for the addiction treatment field to address patients' quality of life instead of simply focusing on symptom reduction (e.g., addiction symptoms per se) as other chronic diseases are treated. In response, Laudet (2012) states that although addiction is a chronic disease, it is somewhat unique compared to many other conventional chronic diseases—in that it usually co-occurs with other problems in life, such as impaired physical and mental health, unemployment, housing instability, dysfunctional family relationships, poor social support, and so on. Laudet concludes that although the intensive treatment model delivered by specialist professionals can help patients achieve their initial remission—i.e., symptom reduction—such short-term treatment is insufficient to help these patients maintain their acquired initial remission and reach long-term recovery. Recovery involves a long-term process and draws in multiple areas in life as it unfolds; scientific research has shown that a recovery orientation with an emphasis on post-treatment services is valuable (Laudet, 2012).

The second issue is related to the temporal ordering of the association between quality of life (QoL) and abstinence. Some studies found that abstinence contributes to improved QoL (e.g., Hagen et al., 2017; Picci et al., 2014), whereas other studies indicated that a better QoL stabilizes and extends abstinence (e.g., Laudet et al., 2009; Moos & Moos, 2007). For example, Hagen et al.'s prospective study revealed that substance use disordered (SUD) patients have a significant recovery of executive functions, psychological distress, and life contentment subsequent to one year of abstinence. On the other hand, both the qualitative and quantitative research evidence points to the positive and prospective impact of QoL on motivating and maintaining abstinence. For example, Moos and Moos (2007) measured participants' level of resources at year one, including their financial resources, the quality of family relationships, as well as relationships with friends and coworkers, work contribution-related recognitions, and so on. They found that a higher level of resources at 1 year was related to a greater likelihood of 3-year remission ($p. < .01$). In addition, 26.4% of the no 1-year resource individuals remitted at 3 years, whereas 74.2% of people who possess 5 or more resources at 1-year remitted. A higher level of 1-year resources also predicted remission at 8-year ($p. < .01$) and 16-year ($p. < .01$). A participant in Sun's (2000) qualitative study of substance-abusing mothers in the child-welfare system stated, "I now have my son back from the court . . . my husband and I no longer fight that much like in those days when we were using [drugs] . . . We bought a house, and we have a car now . . . I will never ever touch drugs again. No way! . . . I know I will lose everything I've got now if I touch the drugs again . . . It's not worth it! It's so stupid!" (p. 144). Consistently, participants in qualitative interviews by Laudet et al. (2009) said, "What worked for me is just the thought that I don't wanna go through that madness no more . . . See, cause if I was to do that, I probably would lose everything" (p. 6, online publication).

Laudet et al.'s quantitative logistic regression results of the same study also support the notion that life satisfaction can prospectively predict remission at 1- and 2-year follow up. One reasoning is that a higher life satisfaction may raise the price of, and thus deter, future use (Laudet et al., 2009).

Aside from concerns related to the research methodological inconsistencies, two explanations may reconcile these two divergent findings. First, a notion of abstinence leading to QoL improvement is not necessarily in conflict with a notion of QoL improvement enhancing abstinence. In fact, both together could constitute a cycle, in that addiction or substance abuse precipitates a worse QoL, which, in turn, adds barriers to maintaining abstinence. For example, Henkel's review (2011) of over 130 studies as well as Walton and Hall's review (2016) of 12 studies showed both that substance use disorders increase the odds of unemployment and reduce the likelihood of securing a job, and that unemployment augments relapse risk after addiction treatment. Consistently, Collard et al.'s review (2014) also revealed the bidirectional relationship, or "a cyclical problem," in that homeless people with substance addiction and/or chronic physical and mental problems encounter major barriers to obtaining affordable housing; their inability to acquire affordable and safe housing also creates a hindrance for them to remain sober (p. 469).

The temporal-ordering issue between QoL and abstinence may be further reconciled by participants' status of original resource level prior to addiction. To some patients who have had a relatively normal and resourceful life prior to being trapped in addiction, it is not surprising to see that their lives improved after abstinence, as sobriety—compared to addiction or intoxication—usually enables more clear thoughts, better judgments, and more logical decisions, and thus is more likely to bring back their prior-to-addiction functioning levels. For many others who are low-income or with a lower level of resources, however, the situations may not be that straightforward because: (1) they were born to and grew up in a dysfunctional family or environment, and have never acquired normal and functional life skills even prior to their onset of addiction, (2) their early onset of substance use and abuse propelled them to drop out of schools early and prevented them from acquiring basic academic education and vocational skills, or (3) they have engaged in a prolonged addiction career and have severely damaged their cognitive and life skills and other resources (Sun, 2006; Tropiano, 2014). Holtyn et al.'s (2015) study (n = 559 drug-addicted and chronically unemployed adults, US) found that although the education of their participants was 11 years on average, most of them were considered "Low Average" or below when compared to the norms of age groups. The academic skill level was actually below or at the 7th grade for 81% of them in math, 61% of them in spelling, and 43% of them in reading. For people with meager resources or low recovery capital to begin with, abstinence alone will not automatically create or bring up in a better life. To many of these patients, it may be that they have nothing to gain if they abstain and nothing to lose if they relapse. This is one reason why many scholars and practitioners advocate "habilitation" instead of "rehabilitation" for clients of vulnerable populations (Tropiano, 2014).

A person may self-medicate the pain associated with mental or physical disorders; similarly, she or he may "self-medicate" the frustration and suffering caused by physical, economic, psychological, social, and spiritual deprivation or deficiency by seeking reward from alcohol or drugs or some addictive behavior (e.g., gambling, internet gaming), which act directly on the reward pathway of the human brain. Enhancing quality of life (QoL) may ameliorate such deprivation or deficiency in life and enable a replacement of the spurious and short-lived reward obtained from drugs or addictive behaviors with the more functional and permanent natural reward obtained from the person's life. A better life or a positive perception of QoL can reinforce abstinence and make abstinence more sustainable, whereas an abstinence that does not have the backup of positive QoL is often tenuous and short-lived. Research has consistently emphasized that recovery is better achieved by a combination of pursuing both abstinence and an improvement of a person's global functioning or quality of life (Laudet, 2011; Laudet et al., 2009; Sun, 2000). Poverty, unemployment, education deprivation, trauma, dysfunctional interpersonal relationships, alienation and isolation, a lack of problem-solving skills, and a lack of life goal or an inability to pursue the goal may all precipitate and aggravate addiction. Proper and effective addiction treatments must include psychosocial intervention and case management that targets QoL or the overall well-being of an addicted person. Following is an elaboration on (a) the relationship between addiction and material poverty, which addresses Maslow's basic human needs, such as physiological needs and safety needs, and (b) the relationship between addiction and spiritual poverty / lack of psychosocial well-being, which tackles both Maslow's safety needs and

Maslow's higher order of human needs, such as love needs, self-esteem needs, and self-actualization needs.

Addiction and Material Poverty

The relationship between addiction and poverty is complex, and at least two hypotheses have been posited (Jones & Sumnall, 2016). The social causation hypothesis suggests that the chronic and acute stress provoked by poverty—such as material deprivation and extreme financial hardships that threaten survival, childhood maltreatment, intimate partner violence, community violence, unemployment, and so on—drives a person to engage in, for example, problem drinking behaviors to reduce stress (Jones & Sumnall, 2016; Mossakowski, 2008). On the other hand, the social drift hypothesis suggests that a person's problem drinking behaviors result in negative economic and social consequences for the person—such as family breakdown, financial problems, unemployment, loss of earnings, and so on—and thus impact his or her economic and social position (Jones & Sumnall, 2016; Schmidt et al., 2010). Although inconclusive, Jones and Sumnall's review seems to tilt to the social causation hypothesis. Regardless, there is strong evidence on the linkage between poverty and addiction.

The Linkage Between Addiction and Poverty/ SES/Housing/Employment

Although addiction happens to people from all walks of life, data have consistently indicated higher prevalence rates of illicit drug use disorder, alcohol use disorder (not just alcohol use), cigarette smoking, serious mental illnesses, and serious thoughts of suicide among people without health insurance and/or whose family income is below federal poverty line, compared to their counterparts otherwise (See Table 4.1, SAMHSA, 2015). According to the Centers for Disease Control and Prevention (CDC, 2015), the 2011–2013 annual average rates of heroin use (per 1,000 people in each group) were 5.5 for families whose annual household income were less than $20,000, followed by 2.3 for the group of $20,000–$49,999, and followed by 1.6 for the group of $50,000 or more. Similarly, the rate was 6.7 for the group without health insurance coverage, 4.7 for the Medicaid group, and 1.3 for the private or other insurance group. Also, as per the CDC (2013), the current cigarette smoking rates among US adults aged 18 years and older were 29.2% for the group with income below the poverty level and 16.2% for their counterparts with income at or above the poverty level. Furthermore, the association between drinking-related liabilities and the financially disadvantaged population appears to exist not only in the US, but also globally as well. The World Health Organization (WHO, 2014) data show that although wealthier countries have higher alcohol consumption, countries with lower economic conditions may have a higher burden concerning alcohol-attributable diseases for every liter of alcohol consumed. In other words, "for a given amount of consumption, poorer populations may experience disproportionately higher levels of alcohol-attributable harm" (Schmidt et al., 2010, p. 12).

Research has indicated strong evidence concerning the impact of the factors of financial resources, housing, employment, and other socioeconomic status (SES)-related resources on relapse. For example, Panebianco and colleagues (2016, N = 80 past clients) found an inverse (negative) association between SES and relapse risk, meaning individuals with higher SES tended to have lower relapse risk. The SES was measured by adding a person's scores of education and occupational status. Response categories for education were: 0 = "never went to school/elementary school"; 1 = "secondary school"; 2 = "low school diploma"; 3= "high school diploma"; 4 = "graduated from college (bachelor degree)"; and 5 = "professional education." Response categories for occupation included: 0 = "unemployed"; 1= "unskilled worker"; 2 = "skilled worker"; 3 = "low-level white collar";

Table 4.1 Past Year Illicit Drug Use Disorder, Alcohol Use Disorder, Serious Mental Illness, and Serious Thoughts of Suicide in the U.S., by Health Insurance Status and Poverty Status (2014)

	Illicit Drug Use Disorder (aged 12 or older)	*Alcohol Use Disorder (aged 12 or older)*	*Serious Mental Illness (aged 18 or older)*	*Serious Thoughts of Suicide (aged 18 or older)*
With Health Insurance	2.4%	5.9%	3.9%	3.7%
Without Health Insurance	5.0% (p. < .05)	10.0% (p. < .05)	5.2% (p. < .05)	5.5% (p. < .05)
Family Income > Federal Poverty Level (FPL)	2.3%	6.2%	3.6%	3.6%
Family Income < FPL	4.8% (p. < .05)	7.5% (p. < .05)	7.0% (p. < .05)	6.0% (p. < .05)

(Source: SAMHSA, 2015)

4 = "high-level white collar"; and 5 = "professional." These researchers found that the mean of the SES for the drug-free group was 3.77, in contrast to 1.6 for the relapsed group ($p.$ < .001). Similarly, Moos and Moos (2007) assessed 461 individuals who sought help for their alcohol-related problems at baseline, 1, 3, 8, and 16 years subsequent. Their findings revealed that more financial resources at the 1-year measurement predicted less alcohol consumption and fewer drinking related problems at the 3-year measurement. More financial resources also predicted a lesser amount of depression. Slopen et al.'s study (2013; N = 4,938 participants) showed that persistent smokers tended to have fewer years of education and smaller annual incomes.

Lack of employment and stable housing was one of the five themes of relapse triggers revealed from the findings of Johnson and colleagues' qualitative study (N = 15 depressed women leaving prison, US). As one participant noted, "First, I'm homeless. I had no place to go. I had no job. So I just was drinking" (2013, p. 176). Johnson and colleagues said that many participants became frustrated and impatient—which triggered relapse—after realizing that their housing and employment were not coming together as they thought they would be post leaving prison. Henkel's (2011) review revealed several important insights concerning unemployment and addiction problems. They found that the unemployed were more likely to use prescription and illegal drugs, to have drug and alcohol use disorders, and to smoke. They also found a bidirectional relationship between unemployment and problematic substance use. On one hand, problem substance use enhances the odds of unemployment and reduces the likelihood of finding and holding a job. On the other hand, unemployment significantly predicts substance use and the development of substance use disorder; unemployment also augments the relapse risk after substance addiction treatment. Similarly, Walton and Hall's (2016) review showed that successful job performance reinforces sobriety. Rollins and colleagues' (2005) study (n = 129 dual-diagnosed patients, US) showed that patients who were employed at initial remission were about 4 times more likely to have upheld substance remission at their 1-year follow-up outcome compared to unemployed patients at initial remission. Lauritzen and Nordfjærn's (2018) 10-year prospective, long-term study found that employment and income earned from work tend to be significant elements in an enduring recovery process.

Strategies Targeting the Issue of Poverty-Addiction Linkage

The pathway and mechanism explaining how poverty and addiction are connected are not clear and more research is needed in this regard (Jones & Sumnall, 2016). Because of the limited understanding of the mechanism between poverty and addiction, corresponding strategies to deal with the poverty-addiction issue are deficient. Based on available literature, the following are three preliminary strategies:

1. Enhance Employment/Housing Among the Clients

A high percentage of individuals who attend substance abuse treatment have employment difficulties. Unemployment affects a person not only in the areas of financial loss, but also prestige and meaning in life (Backhans et al., 2016). Although research has established a strong link between unemployment and alcohol-related diagnosis or relapse, addiction treatment programs have traditionally either paid little attention to the domain of employment or treated employment assistance only an adjunct to core treatment (Walton & Hall, 2016). Walton and Hall suggest that by including employment as a core treatment for substance-abusing clients and linking addiction treatment programs with career counseling and job coaching, agencies could help clients achieve long-term recovery. Sun's (2012) systematic review suggests four strategies to help homeless individuals with co-occurring disorders of severe mental illness and substance use problems: (a) ensure the clients transit effectively from an institution (e.g., prison, residential program) into the community; (b) link the clients with government entitlements or supported employment, (c) connect the clients with supportive housing, considering Housing First options, and being flexible in helping them in housing matters, (d) facilitate addiction and mental health treatment among the clients.

2. Prevent and Reduce Poverty-Associated Stress Among the Clients

Research has suggested that one mechanism linking poverty to addiction is stress reduction, as poverty brings about more stress in people—for example, adverse childhood experiences (ACE), intimate partner violence (IPV), and other stressors. (Strategies targeting ACE and IPV are discussed under the trauma section of this chapter.)

3. Cultivate "Recovery-Oriented Social Spaces"

Although the research findings are not completely consistent, many studies have found a relationship between a disadvantaged socioeconomic neighborhood and a higher substance abuse rate in the area (Jackson et al., 2010; Matto & Cleaveland, 2016). Deprived neighborhoods are likely to offer "a normative context in which hazardous drinking is not sanctioned as strongly as within more affluent neighborhoods" (Jones & Sumnall, 2016, p. 12). People living in a disadvantaged community have to face open-air drug trading and markets, advertisements marketing alcohol and liquor stores, and frequent exposure to violence, all of which create relapse risks (Matto & Cleaveland, 2016). "Those who live in chronically stressful environments often cope with stressors by engaging in unhealthy behaviors that may have protective mental-health effects" (Jackson et al., 2010, p. 1, online publication). Matto and Cleaveland suggest a strategy to help clients in low-income neighborhoods is to cultivate and construct recovery-oriented and visible social spaces, such as recovery houses, to promote sobriety and supportive interpersonal relationships.

Addiction and Spiritual Poverty / Lack of Psychological Well-Being

This section discusses three areas under the umbrella of psychological well-being: interpersonal relationships, trauma, and existential purpose in life, all of which capture Maslow's safety needs, love needs, self-esteem needs, and self-actualization needs and may affect quality of life. Positive interpersonal relationships—such as positive family, spouse, parent-child, peers and other social relationships—are rewarding as they not only make a person feel secure but also loved and, thus, not isolated or lonely. A person may experience pain if feeling unloved and/or alienated. Trauma represents severe degradation and harm. Often taking place in relationships, trauma is an extreme form of maltreatment that "violates our beliefs that the world is a safe place and that people can be trusted" (Brown, Harris, et al., 2013, p. 387). Trauma often diminishes addiction treatment compliance and treatment outcome effectiveness, as well as prevents a person from long-term recovery. Existential purpose in life, on the other hand, helps fulfill a person's needs with respect to self-identity, self-esteem, and self-actualization. All these three areas have implications for addiction development and treatment. Together with the aforementioned material poverty issues (e.g., poverty, housing, and employment), assessing and addressing these psychological well-being topics can help develop a thorough treatment plan, improve the treatment outcomes, and enhance patients' long-term recovery.

Interpersonal Relationships

A positive interpersonal relationship is a critical part of psychological well-being for human beings; a negative, or a lack of, interpersonal relationship often inflicts pain on a person. The concept of "social pain" captures this pain well. Macdonald and Leary define social pain as "a specific emotional reaction to the perception that one is being excluded from desired relationships or being devalued by desired relationship partners or groups" (cited in Leach & Kranzler, 2013, p. 184). The social pain is consistent with, and can be considered as partially overlapping with, the concept of psychosocial dislocation (Alexander, 2008). Social pain—or interpersonal rejection, stress, and conflict—has been an important predictor of substance use disorders or a factor that impedes individuals' recovery from substance dependence (Leach & Kranzler, 2013).

Based on various research and discussions on issues related to social pain—including, for example, Macdonald and Leary's "Why does social exclusion hurt?" Eisenberger and Lieberman's "Why rejection hurts" and "Why it hurts to be left out"—Leach and Kranzler (2013) provide a coherent theory explaining the evolutionary sources of social pain. These authors suggest that "Mammals evolved with a unique need for prolonged maternal care to survive . . . in this process, mammals co-opted the opioid-based physical pain system to ensure maternal proximity and infant survival . . . Because physical pain is aversive, demands attention, and drives behavioral responses to decrease the source of the pain, it is an ideal system, from an evolutionary standpoint, to promote mother-infant proximity . . . Mammals need social proximity throughout their lifespan; in addition to being necessary to the survival of mammalian infants, it enhances the adaptation and survival of adult mammals . . . The endogenous opioid-based pain system of mammals has evolved to prevent social separation and to ensure social connection" (p. 184). In other words, the inclination to connect and affiliate with others has been one fundamental instinct of human beings for more than a million years (Leach & Kranzler, 2013). Because humans linked not only physical pain but also social pain to the endogenous opioid pain system, some researchers consider narcotic addiction is equivalent to social bonds formation (Leach & Kranzler, 2013).

The following covers two areas—the spouse/family/social relationships and the parent-child/family/social relationships—to discuss the relevance of interpersonal relationships to the development and treatment of addiction. Two things should be noted in this context. First, although interpersonal relationships are relevant to the development of addiction, they are not necessarily the "root cause" of addiction, as addiction may involve multiple factors, including both genetic and environmental (Ventura & Bagley, 2017). Second, it is difficult to establish a causal link between interpersonal relationships and addiction and the two may be bidirectional, in that addiction results in poor relationships, which further increase a person's addiction, or in that poor relationships lead to addiction, which subsequently worsens the already strained relationships. Regardless, it is critical to assess and address interpersonal relationships to enhance addiction treatment effectiveness and to enhance patients' long-term recovery. For example, family systems are not static and a family member's addiction problem can exacerbate the family relationships and create a vicious cycle, be the family otherwise healthy or already strained prior to the occurrence of addiction (Ventura & Bagley, 2017). Addressing the family factors and involving family in treatment when appropriate can improve patients' quality of life and enhance treatment outcomes.

Spouse/Family/Social Relationships

Close relationships are critically related to a person's well-being, both physical and psychological, because of the interdependence embedded in these relationships (Rodriguez & Derrick, 2017). Actions and beliefs of each individual of a romantic relationship tend to influence the other member's actions and beliefs (vanDellen et al., 2016). Not only intimate partner relationship quality and functional or not-partner communication and interaction patterns, but also a person's relationships with other family members and social network, as well as whether the family members and social network use substances or not, may all play an important role on the person's substance abuse development, treatment, and recovery.

For example, Derrick, Leonard, and Homish studied newlywed couples with either one or both smoking and they found that those who report, at the time of marriage, their partners' being highly responsive are less likely to be a smoker or are more likely to cut their cigarette quantities in the subsequent 9 years compared to couples who revealed low partner responsiveness at the time of marriage (cited in Rodriguez & Derrick, 2017). VanDellen and colleagues (2016) found that romantic partner relationship quality (measured by questions such as "Our relationship makes me happy" and "I want our relationship to last a very long time" [p. 1843]) predicted a person's support of his or her partner's quitting attempt, including engaging in positive influence (measured by items such as "compliment him or her on not smoking, express confidence in his or her ability to quit/remain quit" [p. 1843]), providing support (measured by assessing the "extent to which they would support instituting a smoking ban in the household, be patient with the partner's mood swings during a quit attempt, be willing to help pay for resources for a quit attempt, be generally supportive, and be willing to take on extra chores to help the partner during a quit attempt" [p. 1844]). Rodriguez and Derrick emphasize the positive influence of close others and suggest that "perceived partner responsiveness" and close others' support provision can be a focus when implementing addiction prevention and treatment.

O'Farrell and colleagues' research indicated that alcoholic clients with high "expressed emotion" spouses have higher likelihood to relapse than their counterparts whose spouses have low expressed emotion (Leach & Kranzler, 2013). Expressed emotion was defined as the degree to which family members relate to the client in critical and hostile ways. In addition to expressed emotion, "perceived criticism" (measured by the question "How critical is your spouse of you?" [p. 8]) is another significant factor predicting substance use relapse among people with alcohol dependence (Leach & Kranzler, 2013). Marital distress is often related to worse treatment outcomes, whereas the support of "reassurance of worth" from family members and friends foresees treatment improvement even among patients with high prior recidivism rates (Leach & Kranzler, 2013). Marital therapy can reduce relapse and facilitate recovery by improving communication and decreasing criticisms among alcoholic patients who have spouses with high degrees of expressed emotion and by enhancing alcoholic patients' perception of self-worth.

The domain of family and significant others may be especially relevant for addicted individuals who are involved with the criminal justice system.

More men are involved with the legal system and among incarcerated men, about half plan to go back to their partners once released from confinement (Calcaterra et al., 2014). A Swedish study of DUI re-offence among 290 DUIs found that family and social relations were among the major risk factors for DUI relapse (Hubicka et al., 2010). That study found that men are more likely to have DUI relapse during a 2-year follow-up and that men who relapsed to DUI tend to have significantly worse scores in the domain of social and family relationships but not in other domains of the Addiction Severity Index measurement. Hubicka et al. suggest that to reduce the DUI relapse risks, the practitioners must increase quality of life of these DUI drivers via addressing their psychosocial problems, including social and family relations. Calcaterra and colleagues' (2014) study revealed that former inmates who perceive having problems with friends, family, and/or other significant others at baseline tended to have a higher likelihoods of engaging in risky drinking behaviors or drug use at follow up. The baseline interviews were conducted between 1 and 3 weeks following prison release; the follow-up interviews were conducted between 2 and 9 months post baseline interviews. Specifically, former inmates who perceive being bothered moderately, considerably, or extremely by family problems at baseline were about 3 times more likely to use drugs at follow up compared to their counterparts who did not perceive being bothered at all or who perceive only being slightly bothered by family problems. Incarceration may disrupt and weaken family relationships and social support because of separation and limited contact, lessened emotional and financial support and resources, and stigma and social marginalization; incarceration may also aggravate the already dysfunctional family relations that existed prior to the patient's imprisonment (Calcaterra et al., 2014). One strategy to help ex-inmates reintegrate to society and prevent relapse is to reestablish his or her relationships with non-using family members and other social networks. These significant others can be included in group therapy and/or patients' meetings with their parole officers. When it is inappropriate or unfeasible to connect a patient with his or her family, other support groups, such as self-help groups, religious organizations, and other community social networks should be arranged (Calcaterra et al., 2014).

It is important to address the issue of family and social support to facilitate recovery among certain groups of men; however, family and social relationships are especially salient for recovery among most women. Women are more relationship-oriented than men and the research has consistently demonstrated that women fare worse than men in the domain of family and social relationships at treatment admission (e.g., Green et al., 2009; Han et al., 2016; Rash & Petry, 2015; see also Chapter 5). For example, Green et al. found that 46.7% of female recent prescription opioid abusers reported serious family conflicts, compared to 35.6% of their male counterparts ($p. < .0001$). In addition, substance-abusing women are more likely to grow up in dysfunctional families and/or families with substance-abusing parents, compared to substance-abusing men. Women are also more likely to be influenced by their families, especially spouses, in substance initiation, cessation of use, and relapse, than vice versa (Sun, 2007, 2009). Brown et al.'s (2015) study indicated that women also perceived children and their relationships with the children as important factors contributing to or preventing recovery. Factors such as children having difficult problems to deal with, including health concerns, behavioral and emotional issues, and learning disabilities, are risk factors for women's relapse; factors like allowing women for more frequent visitations with their kids in foster care and granting women back custody of their kids motivate women's recovery. Risk factors for relapse other than children may include the family's lack of knowledge about addiction, absence of support for women's treatment and women's emotional needs, and family members' own substance use (Brown et al., 2015). Women's interpersonal relationships with service providers may also play a role in women's recovery (Brown et al., 2015; Sun, 2007). Sun's qualitative study revealed that negative and hostile relationships with addiction treatment counselors and the child protective service staff members may precipitate relapse among some women. Brown and colleagues found that women considered treatment providers who are disrespectful and negative toward them to be risk factors for their relapse; in contrast, treatment providers who offer education to family members and provide informational, emotional, and sobriety support to patients are considered by the women to enhance their recovery. Furthermore, the women perceived that their positive relationships with sponsors and Twelve Step groups decrease their isolation, increase their access to information for recovery and association with sober and healthy people, and ultimately enhance their recovery.

Parent-Child/Family/Social Relationships

This subsection targets adolescent and young adult patients, addressing the impact of interpersonal relationships, parent-child relationship quality, parenting quality, and family structure and environment on the development of addiction and its treatment. To take internet gaming as an example, a study in Italy found that teenagers who developed problematic internet use tend to have a lower level of interpersonal relationship quality (Milani et al., 2009). These adolescents scored high on "avoidance coping strategy"—usually a maladaptive coping strategy—and often used the internet for socializing rather than learning or data collecting purposes (Milani et al., 2009). The study showed that a lower level of the interpersonal relationship quality is correlated with a higher level of problematic internet use; also, a higher level of problematic internet use is correlated with more time spent on internet engagement as well as a higher score on avoidance coping measurement (Milani et al., 2009).

Among various interpersonal relationships, the parent-child relationship is among the most important ones for adolescents. Schneider, King, et al.'s (2017) systematic review shows that a poor parent-child relationship was "the most consistent finding" associated with augmented problem gaming (p. 328). The review reveals that problem gamers were less likely to engage in social activities together with their parents and that they also perceived great hostility and less affection from parents. In addition, although both paternal and maternal bonds are influential, paternal bond is especially a protective factor that prevents problem gaming. Schneider, King, et al. cited Liu et al.'s study, reporting the success of a family-oriented treatment for gaming problems that includes decreasing parents' criticism and their unreasonable expectations plus identifying alternative methods to help teenagers to meet their needs for relatedness and competence.

Parenting quality is another important factor related to problem internet gaming. Schneider, King, et al. (2017) reconcile the various research findings, suggesting that effective parental supervision requires parents to monitor and regulate more than just their children's gaming activities. In other words, parents supervising gaming devices per se may not be sufficient; parents need to get involved with their children's world in a broader sense. For example, one item measuring this was "When I am outside, my mother knows where I am" (Kwon et al., cited in Schneider et al., 2017).

Parental modeling is another issue. Intergenerational effects on internet gaming problems may become more prevalent now as more children are likely to be raised by parents who held positive attitudes toward computer, internet systems, and games, and/or who play online gaming (Schneider, King, et al., 2017; Sun & Cash, 2017). Parents who play high levels of internet gaming themselves enlarge the risk of their children's engaging in extreme gaming playing, regardless of their imposing restrictions on their children's gaming (Schneider, King, et al., 2017).

Family structure and environment may also affect the interactions between an adolescent and his or her parents/families, which in turn, may create implications on the initiation of addiction and its treatments. For example, single-parent families or blended families may create stress on adolescents because of possible complex family situations. An adolescent may need to cope with a difficult relationship with a step parent or may not have opportunities to engage in regular leisure activities because of his or her single parent's lack of resources. Not only adolescents who were raised in blended or single-parent families but also adolescents who have a family maltreatment history were reportedly at higher risk for problem gaming (Schneider, King, et al., 2017; Vadlin et al., 2016).

Three Characteristics of an Interpersonal Relationship Conducive to Recovery

Literature has suggested at least three characteristics for a functional relationship conducive to recovery: nonjudgmental, non-using, and reciprocal. Research has consistently suggested that being nonjudgmental is fundamental in helping individuals with addiction problems. Being nonjudgmental has been well established as a cardinal value and guideline for clinicians working with any clients including individuals with addiction. Patients whose family members are critical or hostile toward them or patients who perceive their spouses being critical of them are more likely to relapse (Leach & Kranzler, 2013). Johnson et al.'s study (2013) found that female clients consider a support system that is nonjudgmental as being critical to their recovery. Reducing parents' criticisms and unreasonable expectations can also increase treatment effectiveness of adolescents' problem gaming (Liu et al., 2015).

The relationship or social network needs to be non-using to be conducive to (long term) recovery. Alcoholics Anonymous (AA) is a major example for this. Many studies have demonstrated the function and positive outcomes of AA participation (Humphreys et al., 2014; Kelly et al., 2016; Magura et al., 2013; Moos & Moos, 2007; Tonigan et al., 2017). AA is a social network that welcomes all people afflicted with addiction as long as the person has a desire to stop using. Best and colleagues (2016) identified the "social identity model of recovery," in that they suggest that a recovery-oriented social network is critical as it exposes an addicted person to recovery values and recovery processes. It is in this recovery-oriented environment that the addicted person is nurtured by the values and expectations of the group and subsequently develops a sense of non-using self and identity. Best and colleagues' review shows that the more a person's social network opposes his or her drinking, the more days the person has without drinking. Their review also indicates that cocaine users who were more socially engaged and connected, especially with groups with norms against continued use, tended to have better outcomes. Consistently, studies have revealed that the greater the number of members in a person's network who use drugs, the higher the risk the person will have for relapse; these social supports promote drug use through giving drug purchasing advice, providing money for drugs, and offering places to use (Panebianco et al., 2016). Lauritzen and Nordfjarn's 10-year prospective, longitudinal study (n = 481 patients with substance use disorder, Norway, 2018) also demonstrates such importance. Their multivariate model—after adjusting for factors of mental health disorders, psychosocial factors, and other contextual factors—revealed "living together with a person who abuses drugs" to be one major risk factor for continued stimulant and opiate use. They further stated, "The finding draws attention towards the challenges of establishing and keeping drug free relations for many of these patients. It also points at the needs for material conditions amplifying adequate housing" (p. 12, online publication).

Finally, the relationship needs to be reciprocal. Panebianco and colleagues (2016) found relapsed participants were more likely to have support networks that comprised mainly family members or treatment community—i.e., a pre-existing relationship and an asymmetrical relationship with no reciprocity. On the other hand, a give-and-take drug-free relationship indicates that the relationship is not only need-oriented. Rather, the relationship is relationally equal and mutual, which will promote growth in the addicted person, who subsequently will provide support to others. Such reciprocity may enhance the addicted person's self-esteem and self-efficacy, leading to a lower risk for relapse (Panebianco et al., 2016).

Trauma

Trauma—whether occurring during childhood or adulthood—is devastating. As Brown and colleagues said, "Trauma violates our beliefs that the world is a safe place and that people can be trusted" (2013, p. 387). Under Maslow's hierarchy of human needs, safety needs are considered the basic needs, second only to the physiological needs, such as water and food. Trauma, in many cases, involves interpersonal violence—physical and/or psychological—that deeply erodes a person's sense of safety and quality of life. According to Substance Abuse and Mental Health Services Administration (SAMHSA, 2014), trauma "results from an event, series of events, or set of circumstances that is experienced by an individual as physically or emotionally harmful or threatening and that has lasting adverse effects on the individual's functioning and physical, social, emotional, or spiritual well-being" (2014, p. 7).

Most men and women attending substance abuse treatment have trauma histories (Brown, Harris, et al., 2013; Najavits et al., 1997; Ouimette et al., 2000). Approximately 35–50% of patients who seek addiction treatment have been diagnosed with post-traumatic stress disorder (PTSD) during their lifetime (Brown et al., 2013). Addiction treatment programs traditionally did not tackle trauma or PTSD, because of concerns of possibly aggravating trauma symptoms and jeopardizing early abstinence (Brown et al., 2013). Avoiding addressing trauma may precipitate poorer addiction treatment outcomes, higher treatment dropout rates, and higher relapse rates among patients with co-occurring addiction and trauma problems (Claus & Kindleberger, 2002; Lipsky et al., 2010). Many difficult and challenging behaviors, as well as treatment noncompliance, displayed by addiction patients may be attributable to trauma instead of drug dependence, being aggressive or antisocial, or irresponsibility (Hammersley et al., 2016). It is thus critical to identify and address trauma to effectively treat addiction patients with co-occurring trauma problems.

One way to categorize types of trauma is to view it from an individual or a group level. At an individual level, trauma can at least include individual trauma (e.g., physical injuries), interpersonal trauma (e.g., intimate partner violence), and developmental trauma (e.g., adverse childhood experiences). At group level, trauma can at least cover historical trauma (e.g., genocide), vocational trauma (e.g., military service men and women, first responders such as firemen), community trauma (e.g., Las Vegas strip shooting on October 1, 2017, where more than 50 people were killed), and political war trauma (e.g., refugees who ran from wars or political persecutions). SAMHSA (2014) has detailed descriptions for each specific type of trauma. In addition to individual and group levels of trauma, a third category of trauma is system-oriented traumas, which is defined by SAMHSA as re-traumatization experienced by trauma patients that are caused by clinicians and treatment settings that are insensitive to patients' trauma background. Understanding the scope and the various types of trauma enables us to become more sensitive to a patient's background and its relevance to trauma and addiction, and thus conduct a more thorough and accurate assessment and develop a more effective treatment plan. Among the various categories of trauma, I arbitrarily highlighted four of those that are highly relevant to addiction: individual physical/psychological injuries, intimate partner violence, adverse childhood experiences, and system-oriented traumas.

Individual Physical and Psychological Injuries

Trauma and addiction are closely associated and their relationships can be bidirectional. Substance abuse and its related lifestyle are trauma provoking. Excessive drinking often leads to physical injuries; close to 50% of trauma center patients have injuries related to alcohol dependence and abuse at admission (SAMHSA, 2014). Nunn et al.'s (2016) systematic review reveals a strong relationship between recurrent trauma and alcohol use/abuse, in that about 26.7% to 76.9% (weighted estimate as 41.0%) of trauma recidivisms were alcohol-related. Furthermore, the illegal nature of drug use and chaotic drug-using lifestyle—such as drug buying and selling and the related disputes and conflicts between drug buyers and dealers, prostitution, running away from law enforcement officers, and other crimes that are engaged to obtain drugs or money for drugs—also frequently implicate violence and subsequent trauma (Sun, 2009; Sun et al., 2016). Among heroin users, experiencing severe withdrawal pain and/or witnessing peers' such incidence and/or tragic overdose and death, may also result in trauma (Sun et al., 2016). Substance abuse implicates trauma, which leads to further substance abuse for self-medication, forming a vicious cycle. Furthermore, the stigma attached to drug use, contracting HIV/AIDS because of IV drug use, as well as rejection from significant others and society, may also inflict trauma on addicted individuals (Sun et al., 2016).

Intimate Partner Violence

Research findings regarding the relationship between intimate partner violence (IPV) and substance use disorder are mixed and inconclusive (Rivera et al., 2015), but numerous studies have indicated high rates of IPV victimization reported by women who seek substance abuse treatment and high rates of IPV perpetration reported by men attending substance abuse treatment (Lipsky et al., 2010). Intimate partner violence is not uncommon in the general population—approximately 1 in every 4 women and 1 in every 7 men in the US are affected by intimate partner severe physical violence (lifetime prevalence) (Breiding et al., 2014). Clinical settings, including family medicine, emergency departments, and addiction treatment programs, encounter even more frequent IPV cases. Studies have shown that the IPV rates—perpetration/victimization—among individuals attending substance use disorder treatment are 3 to 5 times higher than rates among the general population. Specifically, about 50% of partnered men who entered substance use disorder treatment have assaulted in the previous year; they are 11 times more likely to assault in a day when they drank. On the other hand, about 67% to 80% of women who attend substance use disorder treatment report IPV victimization. IPV decreases women's likelihood of completing substance abuse treatment and increases men's chances of relapse (Bennett et al., 2016; Lipsky et al., 2010; Mignone et al., 2009).

The contexts that connect substance use with IPV include one or more of the three situations: (a) the acute effects of psychoactive substances, (b) unequal power between men and women, and (c) self-medication. Because of their sharp decrease of inhibition and/or increase of paranoia, alcohol and some other drugs (e.g., cocaine, PCP) may intensify an argument or conflict into a physical confrontation between couples and among significant others, leading to spouse abuse and domestic violence (Crane et al.,

2013; Irons, 1996; SAMHSA, 2014). The second situation is associated with unequally gendered power relationship, which may be especially relevant to drug-using women in inner cities. These women live in an environment where "a male-centered street ideology" is prevalent and they consider violence, including violence from their male partners, as "normal" in their everyday lives (Torchalla et al., 2014). The relationships of these women with their male intimate partners were often exploitative and abusive, in that the women found from the men protection from street violence and sexual harassment, whereas the men treated the women as sexual and income-generating tools (Torchalla et al., 2014). The third situation is self-medication by IPV survivors, who often are subjected to various levels of adverse physical and mental effects resulting from IPV—such as injury, chronic pain, PTSD, and depression—and may use substances to manage the traumatic effects of IPV (Rivera et al., 2015).

Although IPV can have a critical impact on substance abuse treatment outcomes, IPV has traditionally been ignored by addiction treatment programs; the importance of adding IPV brief intervention (including screening and referral) to addiction medicine has gradually been recognized (Bennett et al., 2016). Some research findings have emerged regarding helping IPV survivors, especially female IPV survivors, although more rigorous studies are needed. For example, the integrated Relapse Prevention and Relationship Safety (RPRS) intervention has shown preliminary evidence regarding some treatment effectiveness at 3 months—a decrease in minor physical/sexual IPV, minor and severe psychological IPV, and a decrease in drug use (though $p. = .08$, not significant at .05 level)—compared to the Information Control (IC) condition (Gilbert et al., 2006) among women receiving methadone. The RPRS intervention aims to foster relationship safety and diminish drug use; its strategies include enhancing women's self-worth and cultural pride, building their social cognitive skills (e.g., boundary setting abilities, self-regulatory skills, communication and negotiation skills, and other coping skills), increasing their positive norms regarding relapse prevention and healthy relationships, and enriching their social support so that they can utilize services to reduce drug use and relationship problems (Gilbert et al., 2006).

IPV survivors often face multiple problems in life, including safety issues, ability to manage communal living in shelters, mental illness, substance abuse, economic hardships, parenting, and complex grief related to significant decisions regarding staying or leaving the abusive relationship (Arroyo et al., 2017). To meet their complex needs and reestablish stability, IPV survivors are in need of great support and services; furthermore, individual IPV survivors may have diverse and unique needs and "one size does not fit all" (Arroyo et al., 2017). Arroyo and colleagues' (2017) meta-analysis revealed that most short-term interventions can benefit IPV survivors; interventions that are based on cognitive behavioral therapy and that are designed specifically for IPV survivors achieved especially larger effect sizes. In addition to gender-responsive and trauma-informed treatment and services, some experts also emphasize the insight that substance abuse and violence are not associated in a simple direct causal way but rather multiple structural and social factors are involved. These experts suggested that attention should be given to women's multiple needs, such as housing, employment, and child care; their responsibilities, such as mothering; and their stressors in the areas of financial concerns, relationship issues, legal problems, substance abuse, and other health matters (Poole, 2008). Consistently, Torchalla et al. (2014) suggest that to help poor and marginalized women, clinicians should target the areas of developing innovative housing for women, implementing victim services for homeless women and women who engage in sex trade, and lessening economic inequities to decrease women's dependence on sex trade for survival.

It is important to discuss services for IPV *survivors*, it is also critical to address treatment for IPV *perpetrators*. Although IPV perpetration may involve various factors such as trauma, addiction, mood symptoms, and personality disorders, traditionally most court-involved IPV perpetrators are required to attend "standard" treatment programs that usually conform to a feminist-based model or a cognitive behavioral therapy (CBT) model (Crane & Easton, 2017). A feminist-based model is similar to the Duluth model, in that it focuses on psychoeducation emphasizing gender equality. Under this model, the perpetrators are confronted with, and held accountable for, their aggressive, power-struggling, controlling, and manipulative behavior toward their female victims. A CBT model adopts social learning theory and considers IPV a learned maladaptive behavior. CBT provides skills training to equip clients with more adaptive and functional skills to recognize and cope with or avoid negative situations.

Because of the high prevalence rates of comorbidity between intimate partner violence perpetration and other diagnoses such as addiction, trauma, and personality disorder, some experts believe the "one-size-fits-all" intervention is likely to diminish treatment compliance and outcome effectiveness among clients with multiple and various individual needs. Motivational interviewing has been recommended in this regard (Crane & Easton, 2017). Many experts also proposed integrated treatment models or holistic approaches, such as the "Substance Abuse-Domestic Violence Behavioral Therapy" (SADV), "Fathers for Change," "The Strength at Home Men's Program," and "Psychodynamic/Attachment Therapy" (Crane & Easton, 2017; Murphy & Meis, 2008; Saunders, 2008). SADV is an integrated model, in that both substance abuse and domestic violence treatment are provided at a single site to reduce clients' burden for cross referrals (Crane & Easton, 2017). SADV treatment covers topics such as substance use patterns, drug refusal strategies, communication skills, problem solving skills, craving coping, anger awareness and management, cognitive restructuring, and so on. Perpetrators are required to monitor their substance use / violent urges and their relationship, to identify the triggers and consequences of the urges, and to practice adaptive and functional skills to cope with the urges and triggers. "Fathers for Change" integrates CBT treatment and family systems, targeting fathers who have young children and co-occurring IPV and addiction problems. The focus is on improving parenting skills and family interactions (Crane & Easton, 2017). Targeting servicemen and veterans, the "Strength at Home Men's Program" adopts a client-centered philosophy and trauma-focused CBT and addresses IPV, addiction, and trauma concurrently. This approach helps clients build associations among trauma, military service, and intimate partner violence, enhancing motivation to change their violent behavior (Crane & Easton, 2017). Other trauma-focused IPV interventions aim at resolving a client's childhood trauma. This treatment approach emphasizes the notion that IPV perpetration may be related to the perpetrator's experience of childhood physical abuse and/or witnessing violence between their parents during childhood; as a result, they are less able to empathize with others (Saunders, 2008). Addressing also childhood trauma, the Attachment Therapy model suggests that IPV perpetrators' violence towards their partners may be related to their fearful and insecure attachment styles, which often originate from their exposure to childhood maltreatment involving abuse and/or shame or their borderline personality disorder in adulthood. This approach helps clients explore their controlling and aggressive behaviors—e.g., pathological jealousy—gain insight regarding the linkage between these maladaptive behaviors and the underlying insecurity and fear, and learn constructive strategies and skills to cope (Murphy & Meis, 2008).

Adverse Childhood Experiences

Since their early formulations, theories explaining mental illness or psychopathology have emphasized the lasting impact of early childhood experience, but it is only recently that systematic scientific research on childhood adversity and its impact has emerged (McLaughlin, 2016). Rich literature in the recent decades has documented the strong and graded relationship between adverse childhood experiences (ACEs) and many risk factors for chronic diseases—physical illnesses or psychiatric disorders, including addiction problems—later in life (Dube et al., 2003; Felitti et al., 1998; Gilbert et al., 2015; Herts et al., 2012; Stein et al., 2017; Wade et al., 2017). ACEs may also affect a child's learning (e.g., low academic performance) and/or behavior problems (e.g., violent behavior) (Burke et al., 2011). Furthermore, Metzler and colleagues (2017) found that compared with participants without ACEs, participants who had higher ACE scores had a higher likelihood of unemployment, high school dropout, and living below the poverty level. The ACEs theory suggests that childhood adversities can disrupt a child's neurodevelopment, which in turn impairs the child's later development socially, emotionally, and cognitively, leading to the person's poor decision-making and espousal of health-risk behaviors. The engaging in health-risk behaviors often leads to disease and disability, which ultimately brings about early death (Felitti et al., 1998).

ACEs originally included 7 categories (Felitti et al., 1998) and later extended to 10 categories (Dube et al., 2003) encompassed within three domains: childhood abuse (physical abuse, emotional abuse, and sexual abuse), childhood neglect (physical neglect and emotional neglect), and household dysfunction (household substance abuse, an incarcerated household member, a mentally ill household member, a battered mother or stepmother, and parental divorce or separation). In addition to the original 10 ACEs items, at least three more items were added later to define childhood adversity, including: other types of interpersonal loss, such as parental death and being placed in foster care; life-threatening physical illness during childhood; and extreme childhood poverty (Green et al.,

2010). Consistently, Stevens and colleagues (2015) identified the concept of "intergenerational traumatic family loss," which they suggested a child may experience when his or her family member dies (especially unexpectedly) or through a more ambiguous loss process—e.g., when he or she is taken away from the home by child protective workers. Citing Golonka, Stevens et al. stated that youth in foster care usually have a higher level of mental health issues, become pregnant at a younger age, and have a higher rate of incarceration compared to youth not in foster care. The different types of childhood adversity tend to be interrelated, meaning an exposure to one of the ACE items substantially increases the probability to be exposed to any other item of ACE (Dube et al., 2003; Felitti et al., 1998). In addition, the relationship between ACEs and risks leading to later diseases and disabilities is a strong, dose-responsive, graded relationship—that is, the higher number of the ACE items a person experiences, the more likely he or she engages in health-risk behaviors (Dube et al., 2003; Felitti et al., 1998).

Empirical research has clearly demonstrated the impact of childhood adversity on later development. For example, Felitti et al.'s study (1998) indicated that participants who experienced 1 ACE item were 1.3 times as likely, those who experienced 2 ACE items were 3.8 times as likely, those who experienced 3 ACE items were 7.1 times as likely, and those who experienced 4 ACE items were 10.3 times as likely to have ever engaged in drug injection compared to those who experienced 0 ACE items. Dube et al.'s study (2003) revealed that participants who endorsed childhood emotional abuse were 2.4 times as likely to initiate illicit drug use prior to age 14 compared to others; 1.8 times if physical abuse; 2.8 times if sexual abuse; 2.3 times if a mentally ill household member; 3.7 times if substance abuse in home; 2.5 times if parental separation/divorce; and 3.3 times if incarcerated household member. In addition, participants who experienced 5 or more ACE items were 6.5 times as likely to ever have a drug problem, 7.7 times as likely to ever be addicted to drugs, and 10.1 times as likely to ever have injected drugs compared to those who experienced no ACE items. Stein and colleagues' (2017) study—including 457 persons who sought opioid detox inpatient treatment—showed that almost 50% of their respondents, in contrast to only 15.5% of the participants in Dube et al.'s (2003) community-based study (n = 8613 adults attending a primary care clinic), reported having experienced 4 or more ACE items. Consistently, Burke and colleagues' study (n = 701 urban youth, aged 0–20.9 years, M = 8.13 year old) showed that only 3% of the youth with 0 ACE score had behavioral or learning problems; in contrast, 50% of the youth with a 4 or greater ACE score indicated such problems (2011).

How do we tackle ACE problems? How do we protect children and adolescents from the negative consequences of ACEs, as well as help adults recover from ACEs and their co-occurring disorders? Research has strongly suggested the significant impact of ACEs on later development of health-risk behaviors/psychopathology; it is time for research and practice communities to move forward to explore the underlying mechanisms that link the two, to find the risk factors that precipitate and protective factors that buffer the negative outcomes, and to develop effective intervention and treatments (McLaughlin, 2016). Felitti and colleagues (1998) proposed using a public health model—i.e., primary, secondary, and tertiary prevention—to confront the issue of ACEs. The discussions in the following follow this framework.

At the primary prevention level, the goal is to prevent the occurrence of adverse childhood experiences (ACEs) in the first place and the practice is applicable universally to all families. To reach the goal requires societal efforts to enhance the quality of household and family environment for children (Felitti et al., 1998). One promising program, "Healthy Steps for Young Children," was launched in 1995 through the support of the Commonwealth Fund. The Healthy Steps program relies on specialists with specialty in child development to provide services to families with young children from birth to the age of three. Via home and office visits and telephone advice line, the specialists help the children and the families develop positive relationships. Evaluations of Healthy Steps programs have shown excellent outcomes for participating children and there were more than 60 sites operating in 2006. Unfortunately, some sites had to stop offering services because of discontinued funding. Despite the positive impact, implementations of Healthy Steps programs face difficulty as stable funding from government is lacking (Barth, 2010).

Several strategies can be applied at the secondary prevention level. Identifying at-risk families and intervening early is important; in addition to the 10 or 11 item adverse childhood experiences (ACEs) screening tools, Wade and colleagues (2017) developed a 2-item screener, including emotional and household alcohol abuse. Wade and colleagues suggest this can reduce the clinician's burden of assessment, as patients will be assessed for the remaining 9 items only if they are positive for the 2 items. Communication between and among pediatric care, family medicine, emergency medicine, social work, nursing, and public health should be encouraged (Felitti et al., 1998). The negative impact of ACEs on pathology development can be buffered by various resilience factors at individual, family, and community levels (Brown, Barbarin, et al., 2013). Individuals with higher social competence (including emotion regulation), higher order cognitive abilities, and higher self-esteem are less likely to display psychopathologies as a result of ACEs (Brown, Harris, et al., 2013; Jonzon & Lindblad, 2006). Nolen-Hoeksema and Watkins (cited in McLaughlin, 2016) suggested that proximal risk factors mediate the linkage between ACEs (distal risk factors) and the emergence of psychopathologies. Identifying the proximal factors—which are often within-person factors that are easier to modify compared to distal risk factors—is the key to developing the intervention that prevents or decreases the impact of ACEs on the development of psychopathologies (McLaughlin, 2016). McLaughlin suggests that the proximal risk factor in this context includes two domains: emotional processing and executive functioning. Emotional processing (e.g., attention, memory, and emotional reactivity) affects emotion regulation (e.g., automatic or cognitive reappraisal); executive functions involve cognitive processes, supporting a person's ability to acquire new knowledge, to establish goals, and to execute complex plans, as well as to inhibit behaviors not conducive to the implementation of the plans (McLaughlin, 2016).

Intervention at the family and/or community levels can also facilitate secondary prevention. One is to identify and provide relevant parenting services and training to caregivers who themselves have experienced childhood trauma. Although research findings regarding intergenerational transmission of child maltreatment are contradictory, studies have shown the negative impact of caregivers with childhood trauma themselves on the social-emotional development of their offspring. A 30-year prospective follow-up study found that offspring of caregivers with child maltreatment histories have a higher likelihood to report childhood neglect and sexual abuse, but not necessarily other forms of child maltreatment (Widom et al., 2015). Briggs and colleagues' (2014) quasi-experimental design revealed that appropriate intervention—that emphasizes secure attachment (e.g., helping the caregivers interpret and soothe their children's emotions), helps caregivers reduce stressors, and increases caregivers' positive parenting skills—can moderate the association between caregivers' early traumas and their children's negative social-emotional development. Choi and colleagues' study (2017) found that women who experienced childhood trauma themselves tended to experience more depressive symptoms over the six-month period of postpartum, and that maternal postpartum depression predicted infants' negative outcomes at the first year. Perinatal interventions targeting women with childhood trauma and addressing trauma and depression may help break the intergenerational vicious cycle. Families with children with problems or disabilities often face more stressors. Preparing these families with appropriate knowledge and skills concerning prevention of child adversities and linking them with community resources can also reduce the occurrence of child maltreatment (Larkin et al., 2014).

School and community can play a role as well in buffering the impact of adverse childhood experiences (ACEs) on a child or adolescent's negative developmental outcomes. For example, Forster and colleagues' study (2017, N = 104,332 8th, 9th, and 11th graders) found convincing evidence that a positive student-teacher relationship—i.e., a positive view of teachers by students and a belief by students that teachers are concerned about them—can alleviate the risks brought about by the association between nonmedical use of prescription drugs and ACE. This is especially evident among students with higher ACE levels. The results of this study suggest that to reduce nonmedical use of prescription drugs among adolescents, we should not only focus on fortifying factors at the individual level, improving the family environment, but also enhancing protective factors at the school level and in community contexts (Forster et al., 2017). Forster and colleagues recommended training educators to identify trauma symptomology and nurture strong and positive student-teacher relationships as an essential component for school-based substance abuse prevention programs.

Tertiary care for helping adults with chronic physical or psychiatric disorders and who also suffer a history of adverse childhood experiences (ACEs) can be challenging, as the topics related to childhood abuse and family alcoholism can be sensitive, resulting in physicians' avoidance of discussion about the issues (Felitti et al., 1998). Felitti et al., however, stated that physicians' such fears are mostly unfounded. Another reason why tertiary care of adult ACE survivors is important but challenging is that the time period between exposure to ACEs and adult disease recognition can be lengthy, or many people with ACEs may not access help until adulthood and their problems, by then, may be very deep-rooted (Felitti et al., 1998; Korotana et al., 2016). ACEs affect an adult in various areas, including addictions and other psychiatric disorders, chronic physical illnesses, low life opportunities, intimate partner violence, and so on (Afifi et al., 2017; McMahon et al., 2015).

Although it is inconclusive which treatment or intervention approach is most effective in treating adults with ACEs, cognitive-behavioral therapies seem to be the approach that has the most evidence in reducing mental problems and risky health behaviors (Korotana et al., 2016). Other promising treatment strategies may include mindfulness-based therapies and expressive writing (Korotana et al., 2016). In addition, clinicians can also help adult survivors by strengthening their social support systems and reducing the negative impact of the related systems that are stressful (Schneider, Loveland Cook, et al., 2017). (See also Chapter 3 for treatment for co-occurring PTSD and substance use disorder.)

System-Oriented Traumas

It is critical for clinicians to be nonjudgmental and provide unconditional regard to any client, and it is especially important when working with clients with trauma history. As Judith Herman says, since trauma takes place mostly in relationships, healing and recovery from trauma must also happen within relationships with trustworthy, reliable, and safe helpers (cited in Brown, Harris, et al., 2013). Although we often hear positive feedback from clients about how they were helped by their clinicians and agencies, studies also revealed that some clients perceived being re-traumatized by treatment program staff members. For example, Torchalla and colleagues (2014) identified the concept of "structural violence" that was experienced by marginalized drug-using postpartum/pregnant women who reported psychological violence and stigmatization from health care programs. A woman states,

> I did have a family doctor for some time, until I told her I was escorting for work. And she totally turned her nose up at me. I wanted to get

a pap smear and a blood test, but she basically sent me out. So I went somewhere else and got it done. My safety and my wellbeing is still, huge. I might be a drug addict, but, like, regardless I want to make sure that I'm healthy and get checked. Because, you know, it's a dangerous lifestyle. And you would expect your doctor to help you.

(Torchalla et al., 2014, p. 6)

Sun's (2007) qualitative study showed that a woman became sober for three months and was ready to visit her two children at a foster family but was rejected by the foster family. Her CPS worker further warned her that there would be consequences if she kept bothering the foster family. This woman said:

She [the CPS worker] told me that I can visit my son. I have prepared many presents to give my son . . . clothes . . . toys . . . I missed him so much. It's holiday time . . . but the foster family do not let me visit my child . . . I called my CPS worker, but was only told that I should not intervene in the foster family. She [the CPS worker] did tell me that I can visit my children after three months . . . I had a big fight with my CPS worker, which only made things worse. I felt so outrageous and yet, so helpless. No one could help me. No one would help me. I relapsed.

(Sun, 2007, pp. 7–8)

This type of negative interaction and relationship between the client and the provider not only does not offer an opportunity to help the client heal the trauma, but further reinforces the client's previous or current traumatic experience related to personal relationships and street life (Torchalla et al., 2014). System-oriented trauma takes place when clients feel as if they are experiencing another trauma from their providers. Sometimes, both the providers and the clients may be unaware that a clinical circumstance has in fact caused a traumatic reaction from the clients (SAMHSA, 2014). As mentioned previously, a great proportion of clients who seek addiction treatment have trauma history. These clients may feel upset or fear being betrayed and hurt again upon entering treatment. They may be worried about being labeled as "bad addicts" or "crazy," and may act suspicious or even belligerent (Brown, Harris, et al., 2013). These difficult and challenging behaviors of clients may not be because of clients' severe addiction problems or aggressive and antisocial personalities, but because of their trauma history and experiences. To increase treatment success, substance abuse providers must take the lead and be sensitive and respond appropriately to the clients' traumatic experiences (Brown, Harris, et al., 2013; SAMHSA, 2014).

SAMHSA (2014) has identified 19 specific issues that can trigger agencies' re-traumatization on their clients: (a) having no insight regarding the possible significant impact of trauma history on a client's life; (b) developing a treatment plan without screening for trauma history; (c) discounting clients' reports of traumatic experience or abuse; (d) implementing physical restraints/isolation; (e) applying experiential activities that demean the individual; (f) supporting a confrontational counseling approach; (g) not intervening during the abusive conduct of one patient toward another patient; (h) tarnishing clients' behavior/feelings as pathological; (i) not providing adequate security within the treatment program; (j) limiting clients' participation in treatment planning and decisions; (k) discrediting or minimizing the client's responses; (l) disrupting worker-client relationships by altering workers' schedules and/or duty, (m) acquiring urine specimens in a public environment; (n) having clients unclothe in front of others; (o) enforcing rules with an inconsistent manner and tolerating chaos in the care system; (p) imposing and not giving clients opportunities to question agency policies; (q) executing new restrictions without staff-client communication; (r) restricting service access for ethnically different populations; and (s) allowing agency dysfunction, such as lack of competent leadership.

To achieve a trauma-informed environment, providers and treatment programs must address the above 19 issues. The major steps are to meet clients' needs in a secure, compassionate, and collaborative way; to prevent clients with a trauma history from being re-traumatized; to emphasize and enhance clients' strengths and resilience; and to endorse trauma-informed values and philosophies in the treatment settings through consultation, supervision of staff, and other support (SAMHSA, 2014). In addition, it is important for clinicians to address and heal from their own traumas. Many clinicians in addiction treatment field are trauma survivors themselves, but may have never tackled the issue; although they may be more able to be empathetic to trauma clients, they may also be in a more vulnerable

Purpose and Meaning in Life

Quality of life can comprise not only the dimensions of material poverty (e.g., homelessness, unemployment, and low family income) and interpersonal relationships/trauma, but also the dimension of meaning in life or a sense of purpose in life. Thompson stated, "Faced with a sober life infused with boredom, loneliness, and little direction, the substance addict used intoxication as way to feel vital and alive" (2016, p. 459). "Who am I?" "Why am I here?" "Is my life worthwhile?" These questions may have a significant bearing concerning a person's psychological well-being and recovery (Thompson, 2016). A widely cited longitudinal study that focused on a cohort of teenaged offenders and followed them up until their 70s helps to highlight the context of this issue. That study revealed two major factors that predict a person's desistence from committing a crime: (a) belonging to a family, and (b) having an employment that gives a sense of purpose and satisfaction (Laub & Sampson, cited in Best et al., 2016). Maslow's hierarchy of needs suggests that in addition to the basic needs, such as physiological needs and safety needs, human beings long for love (i.e., needs that involve "both giving and receiving love") and a sense of belongingness, self-esteem (i.e., needs to be "positively evaluated and complimented by others," and to gain self-esteem and self-respect) as well as self-actualization (i.e., desiring self-fulfillment, be it motherhood, art, athletics, creation, or other achievements) (Silton et al., 2011, p. 259). As mentioned previously, Alexander has also said, "the success story of the human species" requires that "all citizens recognize all other citizens as essential to the whole, and each is respected for his or her unique function" (2008, p. 319).

Both qualitative and quantitative studies have generated evidence indicating an association between possessing a sense of purpose in life and addiction recovery outcomes. For example, one major theme regarding recovery revealed from Vigilant's (2008) qualitative study of 45 methadone patients was "self-identity and actualization." Many participants in Vigilant's study consider recovery as transitioning from the "heroin junkie" identity into a more productive identity—they desired to acquire and sustain decent paying jobs, and perceive "their ability to retain employment as an index of having achieved a purposeful and actualizing recovery" (Vigilant, p. 287). Employment not only generates income and combats poverty, but also can fortify a person's positive self-identity and satisfy his or her self-actualization needs.

Various quantitative studies have also shown the impact of a sense of purpose in life on level of symptom severity or treatment outcomes. For example, using Project MATCH data, Roos and colleagues (2015, $n = 1,726$ individuals) reported that purpose in life was significantly negatively related to temptation to drink across time. In other words, they found that "higher initial levels of [purpose in life] and increases in [purpose in life] over time were associated with lower initial [temptation to drink] and decreases in [temptation to drink] over time" (p. 720). Furthermore, Roos and colleagues' findings showed that "Higher initial [purpose in life] and increases in [purpose in life] over time, as well as lower initial [temptation to drink] and decreases in [temptation to drink] over time, were significantly associated with lower drinking frequency and intensity and reduced alcohol-related consequences at the 15-month follow-up" (p. 720). Martin et al.'s study (2011, $n = 154$ cocaine-dependent patients attending an inner-city residential treatment program) reported that baseline purpose in life significantly predicted better treatment outcomes, including fewer relapse and alcohol and cocaine use frequency. These authors suggest that patients attending a community facility—like the participants in their study—may benefit more from the treatment if they have a higher regard to purpose in life.

In addition, research has also shown the impact of a sense of purpose in life on depression and borderline personality traits, both of which often co-occur with substance use disorder. Diaz et al.'s study (2014, $n = 77$ patients) found that higher meaning-in-life and existential purpose scores were related to lower depressive symptom scores among the substance-abusing patients. In the same vein, Horton et al.'s (2016) study ($n = 252$ clients attending a residential substance abuse treatment) revealed that higher meaning and purpose in life predicts lower borderline personality traits. Horton and colleagues suggest that this may be because having meaning and purpose in life is likely to alleviate feelings of loneliness and emptiness—one of the hallmark features of borderline personality disorder.

Following are principles for facilitating purpose and meaning in life among clients:

1. Assess clients' level of purpose and meaning in life and integrate it into treatment plan.

Some clients may have had a positive identity and life goals before their onset of drug use but lost those dreams and motivations after launching a drug career. Some other more socially isolated clients may not have had a life purpose or social identity to begin with, but only gained a "user identity" after engaging in drug use and associating with other drug users. It is beneficial to help the former renew their positive identities and the latter establish aspirational identities (Dingle et al., 2015).

2. Encourage clients to break from their old and using identities; facilitate opportunities for clients and link them with resources to pursue new and positive social identities.

According to Wasmuth et al. (2016), addiction may be considered an occupation, in that it offers clients benefits such as social connections, enjoyment, organization of time, and identity establishment. Addictive behaviors tend to occur among people who experience obstacles to participating in other types of occupations (Wasmuth et al., 2016). Clients may need a great deal of external support to transition from an addiction occupation and a user identity to a productive occupation and a recovery identity.

3. Instill meaning and purpose in life in clients through various treatments and methods.

Motivational interviewing and Acceptance and Commitment Therapy (see Chapter 6) are classic approaches to draw out clients' own values and motivations; the Twelve Step approach (see Chapter 6) can also facilitate a sense of purpose and meaning in clients; cognitive-behavioral therapy (see Chapter 8) enhances self-efficacy, which in turn fortifies self-competency and self-esteem (Martin et al., 2011). The community reinforcement approach (see Chapter 8) can also help create reward, meaning, and purpose in clients' lives. Frankl suggests that we can find meaning via creativity, experiences, and attitude (see Chapter 6). Along the same line, Thompson (2016) discussed meaning therapy to treat addiction as, he suggests, "addiction is a response to living a life that lacks personal meaning" (p. 478).

References

Afifi, T.O., Mota, N., Sareen, J., & MacMillan, H.L. (2017). The relationships between harsh physical punishment and child maltreatment in childhood and intimate partner violence in adulthood. *BMC Public Health, 17*, 493. doi: 10.1186/s12889-017-4359-8.

Alexander, B.K. (2008). *The globalization of addiction: A study in poverty of the spirit*. New York: Oxford University Press.

Arroyo, K., Lundahl, B., Betters, R., Vanderloo, M., & Wood, D.S. (2017). Short-term interventions for survivors of intimate partner violence: A systematic review and meta-analysis. *Trauma, Violence, & Abuse, 18*(2), 155–171.

Backhans, M.C., Balliu, N., Lundin, A., & Hemmingsson, T. (2016). Unemployment is a risk factor for hospitalization due to alcohol problems: A longitudinal study based on the Stockholm public health cohort (SPHC). *Journal of Studies on Alcohol and Drugs*, November, 936–942.

Barth, M.C. (2010). Healthy steps at 15: The past and future of an innovative preventive care model for young children. Retrieved on 02/19/2018 from www.commonweal thfund.org/~/media/Files/Publications/Fund%20Report/2010/Dec/1458_Barth_ Healthy_Steps_at_15.pdf.

Bennett, L.W., Prabhughate, P., & Gallagher, J.R. (2016). Accounting for intimate partner violence in the treatment of substance use disorders: Staff and agency readiness for screening and referral. *Alcoholism Treatment Quarterly, 34*(2), 126–142.

Best, D., Beckwith, M., Haslam, C., Haslam, S.A., Jetten, J., & Mawson, E. (2016). Overcoming alcohol and other drug addiction as a process of social identity transition: The social identity model of recovery (SIMOR). *Addiction Research & Theory, 24*(2), 111–123.

Breiding, M.J., Chen, J., & Black, M.C. (2014). *Intimate partner violence in the United States—2010*. Atlanta, GA: National Center for Injury Prevention and Control, Centers for Disease Control and Prevention.

Briggs, R.D., Silver, E.J., Krug, L.M., Mason, Z.S., Schrag, R.D.A., Chinitz, S., & Racine, A.D. (2014). Healthy Steps as a moderator: The impact of maternal trauma on child social-emotional development. *Clinical Practice in Pediatric Psychology, 2*(2), 166–175.

Brown, J., Barbarin, O., & Scott, K. (2013). Socioemotional trajectories in Black boys between kindergarten and the fifth grade: The role of cognitive skills and family in promoting resiliency. *American Journal of Orthopsychiatry, 83*(2, 3), 176–184.

Brown, S., Tracy, E.M., Jun, M., Park, H., & Min, M. (2015). Personal network recovery enablers and relapse risks for women with substance dependence. *Qualitative Health Research, 25*(3), 371–385.

Brown, V.B., Harris, M., & Fallot, R. (2013). Moving toward trauma-informed practice in addiction treatment: A collaborative model of agency assessment. *Journal of Psychoactive Drugs, 45*(5), 386–393.

Burke, N.J., Hellman, J.L., Scott, B.G., Weems, C.F., & Carrion, V.G. (2011). The impact of adverse childhood experiences on an urban pediatric population. *Child Abuse & Neglect, 35*(6), 408–413.

Calcaterra, S., Beaty, B., Mueller, S.R., Min, S.J., & Binswanger, I.A. (2014). The association between social stressors and drug use/hazardous drinking among former prison inmates. *Journal of Substance Abuse Treatment, 47*(1), 41–49.

Centers for Disease Control and Prevention (CDC) (2013). Retrieved on 05/05/2016 from www.cdc.gov/vitalsigns/pdf/2015-07-vitalsigns.pdf.

Centers for Disease Control and Prevention (CDC) (2015). Today's heroin epidemic. CDC Vitalsigns, July 2015. Retrieved on 04/25/2018 from www.cdc.gov/vitalsigns/pdf/2015-07-vitalsigns.pdf.

Choi, K.W., Sikkema, K.J., Vythilingum, B., Geerts, L., Faure, S.C., Watt, M.H., Roos, A., & Stein, D.J. (2017). Maternal childhood trauma, postpartum depression, and infant outcomes: Avoidant affective processing as a potential mechanism. *Journal of Affective Disorders, 211*, 107–115.

Claus, R.E., & Kindleberger, L.R. (2002). Engaging substance abusers after centralized assessment: Predictors of treatment entry and dropout. *Journal of Psychoactive Drugs, 34*(1), 25–31.

Collard, C.S., Lewinson, T., & Watkins, K. (2014). Supportive housing: An evidence-based intervention for reducing relapse among low income adults in addiction recovery. *Journal of Evidence-Based Social Work, 11*, 468–479.

Crane, C.A., & Easton, C.J. (2017). Integrated treatment options for male perpetrators of intimate partner violence. *Drug and Alcohol Review, 36*, 24–33.

Crane, C.A., Easton, C.J., & Devine, S. (2013). The association between phencyclidine use and partner violence: An initial examination. *Journal of Addictive Diseases, 32*(2), 150–157.

Diaz, N., Horton, E.G., & Malloy, T. (2014). Attachment style, spirituality, and depressive symptoms among individuals in substance abuse treatment. *Journal of Social Service Research*, 1–12.

Dingle, G.A., Cruwys, T., & Frings, D. (2015). Social identities as pathways into and out of addiction. *Frontiers in Psychology, 6*, 1795. doi: 10.3389/fpsyg.2015.01795.

Dube, S.R., Felitti, V.J., Dong, M., Chapman, D.P., Giles, W.H., & Anda, R.F. (2003). Childhood abuse, neglect, and household dysfunction and the risk of illicit drug use: The adverse childhood experiences study. *Pediatrics, 111*(3), 564–572.

Felitti, V.J., Anda, R.F., Nordenberg, D., Williamson, D.F., Spitz, A.M., Edwards, V., Koss, M.P., & Marks, J.S. (1998). Relationship of childhood abuse and household dysfunction to many of the leading causes of death in adults: The Adverse Childhood Experiences (ACE) Study. *American Journal of Preventive Medicine, 14*(4), 245–258.

Forster, M., Gower, A.L., Borowsky, I.W., & McMorris, B.J. (2017). Associations between adverse childhood experiences, student-teacher relationships, and non-medical use of prescription medications among adolescents. *Addictive Behaviors, 68*, 30–34.

Gilbert, L.K., Breiding, M.J., Merrick, M.T., Thompson, W.W., Ford, D.C., Dhingra, S.S., & Parks, S.E. (2015). Childhood adversity and adult chronic disease: An update from ten states and the District of Columbia, 2010. *American Journal of Preventive Medicine, 48*(3), 345–349.

Gilbert, L., El-Bassel, N., Manuel, J., Wu, E., Go, H., Golder, S., Seewald, R., & Sanders, G. (2006). An integrated relapse prevention and relationship safety intervention for women on methadone: Testing short-term effects on intimate partner violence and substance Use. *Violence and Victims, 21*(5), 657–672.

Glasser, W. (1976). *Positive addiction*. New York: Harper & Row, Publishers.

Green, J.G., McLaughlin, K.A., Berglund, P.A., Gruber, M.J., Sampson, N.A., Zaslavsky, A.M., & Kessler, R.C. (2010). Childhood adversities and adult psychopathology in the National Comorbidity Survey Replication (NCS-R) I: Associations with first onset of DSM-IV disorders. *Archieved of General Psychiatry, 67*(2), 113–123.

Green, T.C., Grimes Serrano, J.M., Licari, A., Budman, S.H, & Butler, S.F. (2009). Women who abuse prescription opioids: Findings from the Addiction Severity Index-Multimedia VersionR Connect Prescription Opioid database. *Drug and Alcohol Dependence, 103*(1-2), 65–73.

Hagen, E., Erga, A.H., Hagen, K.P., Nesvag, S.M., McKay, J.R., Lundervold, A.J., & Walderhaug, E. (2017). One-year sobriety improves satisfaction with life, executive functions and psychological distress among patients with polysubstance use disorder. *Journal of Substance Abuse Treatment*. Retrived from http://dx.doi.org/10.1016/j.jsat.2017.01.016.

Hammersley, R., Dalgarno, P., McCollum, S., Reid, M., Strike, Y., Smith, A., et al. (2016). Trauma in the childhood stories of people who have injected drugs. *Addiction Research & Theory, 24*(2), 135–151.

Han, Y., Lin, V., Wu, F., & Hser, Y.I. (2016). Gender comparisons among Asian American and Pacific Islander patients in drug dependency treatment. *Substance Use & Misuse, 51*(6), 752–762.

Henkel, D. (2011). Unemployment and substance use: A review of the literature (1990–2010). *Current Drug Abuse Reviews, 4*(1), 4–27.

Herts, K.L., McLaughlin, K.A., & Hatzenbuehler, M.L. (2012). Emotion dysregulation as a mechanism linking stress exposure to adolescent aggressive behavior. *Journal of Abnormal Child Psychology, 40*, 1111–1122.

Holtyn, A.F., DeFulio, A., & Silverman, K. (2015). Academic skills of chronically unemployed drug-addicted adults. *Journal of Vocational Rehabilitation, 42*, 67–74.

Horton, E.G., Luna, N., & Malloy, T. (2016). Exploring relationships between adult attachment, spirituality and personality disorder traits among individuals in in-patient treatment for substance use disorders. *International Journal of Social Work, 3*(1), 16–41.

Hubicka, B., Laurell, H., &Bergman, H. (2010). Psychosocial characteristics of drunk drivers assessed by the Addiction Severity Index, prediction of relapse. *Scandinavian Journal of Public Health, 38*, 71–77.

Humphreys, K., Blodgett, J.C., & Wagner, T.H. (2014). Estimating the efficacy of Alcoholics Anonymous without self-selection bias: An instrumental variables re-analysis of randomized clinical trials. *Alcoholism: Clinical and Experimental Research, 38*(11), 2688–2694.

Irons, R.R. (1996). Comorbidity between violence and addictive disease. *Sexual Addiction & Compulsivity, 3*(2), 85–96.

Jackson, J.S., Knight, K.M., & Rafferty, J.A. (2010). Race and unhealthy behaviors: Chronic stress, the HPA Axis, and physical and mental health disparities over the life course. *American Journal of Public Health, 100*(5), 933–939.

Johnson, J.E., Schonbrun, Y.C., Nargiso, J.E., Kuo, C.C., Shefner, R.T., Williams, C.A., & Zlotnick, C. (2013). "I know if I drink I won't feel anything": Substance use relapse among depressed women leaving prison. *International Journal of Prison Health, 9*(4), 169–186.

Jonzon, E., & Lindblad, F. (2006). Risk factors and protective factors in relation to subjective health among adult female victims of child sexual abuse. *Child Abuse & Neglect, 30*, 127–143.

Jones, L., & Sumnall, H. (2016). *Understanding the relationship between poverty and alcohol misuse.* Liverpool, UK: Center for Public Health, Liverpool John Moores University.

Kelly, J.F., Greene, M.C., & Bergman, B.G. (2016). Recovery benefits of the "therapeutic alliance" among 12-step mutual-help organization attendees and their sponsors. *Drug and Alcohol Dependence, 162*, 64–71.

Korotana, L.M., Dobson, K.S., Pusch, D., & Josephson, T., (2016). A review of primary care interventions to improve health outcomes in adult survivors of adverse childhood experiences. *Clinical Psychology Review, 46*, 59–90.

Larkin, H., Felitti, V.J., & Anda, R.F. (2014). Social work and adverse childhood experiences research: Implications for practice and health policy. *Social Work in Public Health, 29*, 1–16.

Laudet, A.B. (2011). The case for considering quality of life in addiction research and clinical practice. *Addiction Science & Clinical Practice, 6*(1), 44–55.

Laudet, A.B. (2012). Author reply to comment on the case for considering quality of life in addiction research and clinical practice. *Addiction Science & Clinical Practice, 7*, 2.

Laudet, A.B., Becker, J.B., & White, W.L. (2009). Don't wanna go through that madness no more: Quality of life satisfaction as predictor of sustained remission from illicit drug misuse. *Substance Use & Misuse, 44*(2), 227–252. doi: 10.1080/10826080802714462.

Lauritzen, G., & Nordfjærn, T. (2018). Changes in opiate and stimulant use through 10 years: The role of contextual factors, mental health disorders and psychosocial factors in a prospective SUD treatment cohort study. *PLoS ONE 13*(1), e0190381. Retrieved from https://doi.org/10.1371/journal.pone.0190381.

Leach, D., & Kranzler, H.R. (2013). An interpersonal model of addiction relapse. *Addictive Disorders & Their Treatment, 12*(4), 183–192.

Lipsky, S., Krupski, A., Roy-Byrne, P., Lucenko, B., Mancuso, D., & Huber, A. (2010). Effect of co-occurring disorders and intimate partner violence on substance abuse treatment outcomes. *Journal of Substance Abuse Treatment, 38*, 231–244.

Liu, Q.X., Fang, X.Y., Yan, N., Zhou, Z.K., Yuan, X.J., Lan, J., et al. (2015). Multi-family group therapy for adolescent Internet addiction: Exploring the underlying mechanisms. *Addictive Behaviors, 42*, 1–8.

Luty, J., & Arokiadass, S.M.R. (2008). Satisfaction with life and opioid dependence. *Substance Abuse Treatment, Prevention, and Policy, 3*, 2. doi: 10.1186/1747–597X-3–2.

Magura, S., Cleland, C.M., & Tonigan, S. (2013). Evaluating Alcoholics Anonymous's effect on drinking in Project MATCH using cross-lagged regression panel analysis. *Journal of Studies on Alcohol and Drugs, 74*, 378–385.

Martin, R.A., MacKinnon, S., Johnson, J., & Rohsenow, D.J. (2011). Purpose in life predicts treatment outcome among adult cocaine abusers in treatment. *Journal of Substance Abuse Treatment, 40*, 183–188.

Maslow, A.H. (1943) A theory of human motivation. *Psychological Review, 50*, 370–396.

Matto, H.C., & Cleaveland, C.L. (2016). A social-spatial lens to examine poverty, violence, and addiction. *Journal of Social Work Practice in the Addictions, 16*, 7–23.

McLaughlin, K.A. (2016). Future directions in childhood adversity and youth psychopathology. *Journal of Clinical Child & Adolescent Psychology, 45*(3), 361–382.

McMahon, K., Hoertel, N., Wall, M.M., Okuda, M., Limosin, F., & Blanco, C. (2015). Childhood maltreatment and risk of intimate partner violence: A national study. *Journal of Psychiatric Research., 69*, 42–49.

Metzler, M., Merrick, M.T., Klevens, J., Ports, K.A., & Ford, D.C. (2017). Adverse childhood experiences and life opportunities: Shifting the narrative. *Children and Youth Services Review, 72*, 141–149.

Mignone, T., Klostermann, K, & Chen, R. (2009). The relationship between relapse to alcohol and relapse to violence. *Journal of Family Violence, 24*, 497–505.

Milani, L., Osualdella, D., & Di Blasio, P. (2009). Quality of interpersonal relationships and problematic Internet use in adolescence. *Cyber Psychology & Behavior, 12*(6), 681–684.

Moos, R.H., & Moos, B.S. (2007). Protective resources and long-term recovery from alcohol use disorders. *Drug and Alcohol Dependence, 86*, 46–54.

Morgan, D., Grant, K.A., Gage, H.D., Mach, R.H., Kaplan, J.R., Prioleau, O., Nader, S.H., Buchheimer, N., Ehrenkaufer, R.L., & Nader, M.A. (2002). Social dominance in monkeys: Dopamine D_2 receptors and cocaine self-administration. *Nature Neuroscience, 5*(2), 169–174.

Mossakowski, K.N. (2008). Is the duration of poverty and unemployment a risk factor for heavy drinking? *Social Science & Medicne, 67*(6), 947–955.

Murphy, C.M., & Meis, L.A. (2008). Individual treatment of intimate partner violence perpetrators. *Violence and Victims, 23*(2), 173–186.

Najavits, L.M., Weiss, R.D., & Shaw, S.R. (1997). The link between substance abuse and posttraumatic stress disorder in women. *The American Journal on Addictions, 6*, 273–283.

Newman, R.G. (2012). Comment on the case for considering quality of life in addiction research and clinical practice. *Addiction Science & Clinical Practice, 7*, 2.

Nunn, J., Erdogan, M., & Green, R.S. (2016). The prevalence of alcohol-related trauma recidivism: A systematic review. *Injury, 47*(3), 551–558.

Ouimette, P.C., Kimerling, R., Shaw, J., & Moos, R.H. (2000). Physical and sexual abuse among women and men with substance use disorders. *Alcoholism Treatment Quarterly, 18*(3), 7–17.

Panebianco, D., Gallupe, O., Carrington, P.J., & Colozzi, I. (2016). Personal support networks, social capital, and risk of relapse among individuals treated for substance use issues. *International Journal of Drug Policy, 27*, 146–153.

Picci, R.L., Oliva, F., Zuffranieri, M., Vizzuso, P., Ostacoli, L., Sodano, A.J., & Furlan, P.M. (2014). Quality of life, alcohol detoxification and relapse: Is quality of life a predictor of relapse or only a secondary outcome measure? *Quality of Life Research, 23*, 2757–2767.

Poole, N., Greaves, L., Jategaonkar, N., McCullough, L., & Chabot, C. (2008). Substance use by women using domestic violence shelters. *Substance Use & Misuse, 43*, 1129–1150.

Rash, C.J., & Petry, N.M. (2015). Contingency management treatments are equally efficacious for both sexes in intensive outpatient settings. *Experimental and Clinical Psychopharmacology, 23*(5), 369–376.

Rivera, E.A., Phillips, H., Warshaw, C., Lyon, E., Bland, P.J., & Kaewken, O. (2015). *An applied research paper on the relationship between intimate partner violence and substance use.* Chicago, IL: National Center on Domestic Violence, Trauma & Mental Health.

Rodriguez, L.M., & Derrick, J. (2017). Breakthroughs in understanding addiction and close relationships. *Current Opinion in Psychology, 13*, 115–119.

Rollins, A.L., O'Neill, S.J., Davis, K.E., & Devitt, T.S. (2005). Substance abuse relapse and factors associated with relapse in an inner-city sample of patients with dual diagnoses. *Psychiatric Services, 56*(10), 1274–1281.

Roos, C.R., Kirouac, M., Pearson, M.R., Fink, B.C., & Witkiewitz, K. (2015). Examining temptation to drink from an existential perspective: Associations among temptation, purpose in life, and drinking outcomes. *Psychology of Addictive Behaviors, 29*(3), 716–724.

Saunders, D.G. (2008). Group interventions for men who batter: A summary of program descriptions and research. *Violence and Victims, 23*(2), 156–172.

Schmidt, L.A., Makela, P., Rehm, J., & Room, R. (2010). Alcohol: Equity and social determinants. In E. Blas & S. Kurup (Eds.) *Equity, social determinants and public health programmes* (pp. 11–29). Geneva, Switzerland: World Health Organization. Retrieved on 02/19/2018 from www.who.int/social_determinants/tools/EquitySDandPH_eng.pdf#page=21.

Schneider, F.D., Loveland Cook, C.A., Salas, J., Scherrer, J., Cleveland, I.N., & Burge, S.K. (2017). Childhood trauma, social networks, and the mental health of adult survivors. *Journal of Interpersonal Violence.* doi: 10.1177/0886260517696855.

Schneider, L.A., King, D.L., & Delfabbro, P.H. (2017). Family factors in adolescent problematic Internet gaming: A systematic review. *Journal of Behavioral Addiction, 6*(3), 321–333.

Silton, N.R., Flannelly, L.T., Flannelly, K.J., & Galek, K., (2011). Toward a theory of holistic needs and the brain. *Holistic Nursing Practice, 25*(5), 258–265.

Slopen, N., Kontos, E.Z., Ryff, C.D., Ayanian, J.Z., Albert, M.A., & Williams, D.R. (2013). Psychosocial stress and cigarette smoking persistence, cessation, and relapse over 9–10 years: A prospective study of middle-aged adults in the United States. *Cancer Causes & Control, 24*(10), 1849–1863.

Stein, M.D., Conti, M.T., Kenney, S., Anderson, B.J., Flori, J.N., Risi, M.M., & Bailey, G.L. (2017). Adverse childhood experience effects on opioid use initiation, injection drug use, and overdose among persons with opioid use disorder. *Drug and Alcohol Dependence, 179*, 325–329.

Stevens, S., Andrade, R., Korchmaros, J., & Sharron, K. (2015). Intergenerational trauma among substance-using Native American, Latina, and White mothers living in the Southwestern United States. *Journal of Social Work Practice in the Addictions, 15*, 6–24.

Substance Abuse and Mental Health Services Administration (SAMHSA) (2014). *Trauma-informed care in behavioral health services.* Treatment Improvement Protocol (TIP) Series 57. HHS Publication No. (SMA) 13–4801. Rockville, MD: SAMHSA. Retrieved on 02/19/2018 from https://store.samhsa.gov/shin/content//SMA14-4816/SMA14-4816.pdf.

Substance Abuse and Mental Health Services Administration (SAMHSA) (2015). *Behavioral health barometer: United States, 2015.* HHS Publication No. SMA-16-Baro-2015. Rockville, MD: SAMHSA. Retrieved on 02/15/2018 from www.samhsa.gov/data/sites/default/files/2015_National_Barometer.pdf.

Sun, A.P. (2000). Helping substance-abusing mothers in the child-welfare system: Turning crisis into opportunity. *Families in Society: The Journal of Contemporary Social Services, 81*(2), 142–151. Retrieved from https://doi.org/10.1606/1044-3894.1008.

Sun, A.P. (2006, May). The initial unequal footing to begin with: A challenge to the "free will" theory. Paper presented at the 14th Annual meeting of the Society for Prevention Research, San Antonio, TX.

Sun, A.P. (2007). Relapse among substance-abusing women: Components and processes. *Substance Use & Misuse, 42*, 1–21.

Sun, A.P. (2009). *Helping substance-abusing women of vulnerable populations: Effective treatment principles and strategies.* New York: Columbia University Press.

Sun, A.P. (2012). Helping homeless individuals with co-occurring disorders: The four components. *Social Work, 57*(1), 23–37.

Sun, A.P., & Cash, H. (2017). Factors related to the occurrence and recovery of internet use disorder. Paper presented at the 2017 National Association for Alcoholism and Drug Abuse Counselors Annual Conference, Denver, CO.

Sun, A.P., Chen, Y.C., & Marsiglia, F. (2016). Trauma and Chinese heroin users. *Journal of Ethnicity in Substance Abuse, 15*(2), 144–159.

Thompson, G.R. (2016). Meaning therapy for addictions: A case study. *Journal of Humanistic Psychology, 56*(5), 457–482.

Tonigan, J.S., McCallion, E.A., Frohe, T., & Pearson, M.R. (2017). Lifetime Alcoholics Anonymous attendance as a predictor of spiritual gains in the Relapse Replication and Extension Project (RREP). *Psychology of Addictive Behaviors, 31*(1), 54–60.

Torchalla, I., Linden, I.A., Strehlau, V., Neilson, E.K., & Krausz, M. (2014). "Like a lots happened with my whole childhood": Violence, trauma, and addiction in pregnant and postpartum women from Vancouver's downtown Eastside. *Harm Reduction Journal, 11*, 34. Retrieved from www.harmreductionjournal.com/content/11/1/34.

Tropiano, P. (2014). Treatment for drug and alcohol addiction—Rehabilitation or habilitation? Bulletin Board (/Pennsylvania/chestnuthill/bulletinboard). Retrieved on 03/08/2017 from http://patch.com/pennsylvania/chestnuthill/treatment-drug-and-alcohol-addiction-rehabilitation-or-habilitation.

Vadlin, S., Aslund, C., Hellstrom, C., & Nilsson, K. (2016). Associations between problematic gaming and psychiatric symptoms among adolescents in two samples. *Addictive Behaviors, 61*, 8–15.

vanDellen, M.R., Boyd, S.M., Ranby, K.W., MacKillop, J., & Lipkus, I.M. (2016). Willingness to provide support for a quit attempt: A study of partners of smokers. *Journal of Health Psychology, 21*(9), 1840–1849.

Ventura, A.S., & Bagley, S.M. (2017). To improve substance use disorder prevention, treatment and recovery: Engage the family. *Journal of Addictive Medicine, 11*(5), 339–341.

Vigilant, L.G. (2008). "I am still suffering:" The dilemma of multiple recoveries in the lives of methadone maintenance patients. *Sociological Spectrum, 28*, 278–298.

Wade, R., Becker, B.D., Bevans, K.B., Ford, D.C., & Forrest, C.B. (2017). Development and evaluation of a short adverse childhood experiences measure. *American Journal of Preventive Medicine, 52*(2), 163–172.

Walton, M.T., & Hall, M.T. (2016). The effects of employment interventions on addiction treatment outcomes: A review of the literature. *Journal of Social Work Practice in the Addictions, 16*, 358–384.

Wasmuth, S., Brandon-Friedman, R.A., & Olesek, K. (2016). A grounded theory of veterans' experiences of addiction-as-occupation. *Journal of Occupational Science, 23*(1), 128–141.

Widom, C.S., Czaja, S.J., & DuMont, K.A. (2015). Intergenerational transmission of child abuse and neglect: Real or detection bias? *Science, 347*(6229), 1480–1485.

World Health Organization (WHO) (1997). *WHOQOL: Measuring quality of life.* Division of Mental Health and Prevention of Substance Abuse, World Health Organization. Retrieved on 02/19/2018 from www.who.int/mental_health/media/68.pdf.

World Health Organization (WHO) (2014). *Global status report on alcohol and health.* Retrieved on 04/22/2018 from http://www.who.int/substance_abuse/publications/global_alcohol_report/msb_gsr_2014_1.pdf.

5

ADDICTION AND SOCIAL FACTORS

"It takes a village to raise a child," goes the common saying. Likewise, it takes many social sectors and systems to successfully deliver addiction treatment and prevention services. Similarly, the social aspect of the occurrence of new addictions or new faces of old addictions is closely related to cultural and political changes, as well as technological advancement, all of which have an impact on human behavior. Indeed, the relationships between human behaviors and the environment are bilateral: We affect our environment and in turn are affected by our environment. These macro-level factors are the 4th component in the ACQS model and important in the treatment formula. Although the macro factors—including ingrained historical roots, social values, policy changes (or resistance to change), and transformed lifestyles resulting from technological advancement—may sometimes appear to be subtle, slow, and distant, their impact can be enormous and hit close to home. Macro factors can precipitate or curb the occurrence and development of addiction problems, as well as strengthen or diminish the quality and function of addiction treatment service delivery. To effectively address these issues and challenges requires effort and collaboration among practitioners, the scientific research community, policymakers, and society in general.

The current opioid epidemic in the US demonstrates how these macro factors may precipitate the development of addiction and alter the nature of its occurrence. Studies have shown that the recent prescription opioid and heroin addiction crisis stems from an overall inadequate practice in pain management and the remedial, but inappropriate, prescription of opioid pain medications, leading to some patients' nonmedical use of prescription opioids and the subsequent transitioning into heroin use (Centers for Disease Control and Prevention [CDC], 2015). This iatrogenic phenomenon of prescription opioids, resulting in heroin dependence, is different from the heroin problems in the 1960s when people's heroin addictions originated with their initial heroin use. It's important to understand the nature and background of the current epidemic and develop corresponding strategies, such as guidelines for appropriate opioid prescribing and related training to physicians and medical school students (CDC).

The drug court system in the US is an example of how macro social factors may dilute or diminish the quality of addiction treatment service delivery. The drug court approach attempts to balance punishment and rehabilitation, and research indicates its success in reducing criminal recidivism among individuals with substance use disorder. However, the drug court system has been criticized for its racial bias in "cherry picking" qualified participants for treatment. Research reveals that after controlling for variables of demographics and arrest characteristics, White arrestees are more likely than African American arrestees to be referred to drug treatment in lieu of incarceration (Nicosia et al., 2013). Some statistics have shown that although African Americans accounted for 28% of arrestees, 28% of probationers and parolees, and 44% of prison inmates, they only accounted for 21% of drug-court participants (Marlowe, 2013). Judicial policies on treatment options are important, but detailed regulations and implemental procedures and standards are equally important to reduce racial inequality. Education, training, advocacy, creativity, and collaborations among various social systems and entities can also maximize treatment outcomes and benefits.

Chapter 5 explores first the impact of social factors on the occurrence of addiction, then their influence on the quality of addiction treatment services. Each of the two main sections contains four phenomena; all eight phenomena serve as examples to highlight the bearing of macro factors and are not exhaustive of the possible aspects.

Social Factors May Precipitate or Curb the Occurrence of Addiction

The impact of macro factors on addiction—whether substance or behavioral—may be gauged through time-space (cohort-country) variations. Researchers can focus on temporal contrasts and examine distinctions across different birth cohorts within one country; they can also examine spatial variations across different countries within one single cohort (Seedat et al., 2009). It's important to research and understand *current* epidemiology and prevalence of substance use and misuse problems, as well as the origins of those problems, so that updated and effective intervention can be developed accordingly. Likewise, the prevalence and nature of substance use problems may be distinct in different societies, countries, and regions; intervention strategies that emphasize localization and match the special needs of each unique society and community should be crafted.

I will discuss four major current phenomena in detail to illustrate the effects of macro social factors on the occurrence of addiction: (1) the current prescription opioid and heroin epidemic in the US; (2) the convergent trends of alcohol use and alcohol use disorder between men and women in the past decades in the US; (3) the emergence and heightening of various behavioral addictions such as internet gaming addiction, gambling disorder, shopping addiction, and sex addiction resulting from social change and easy access to computers and internet; and (4) the impact of legalization of medicinal and recreational marijuana. The discussions also include strategies to curtail the problems inherent in these four phenomena and the importance of integrating time-space variations in developing strategies.

The Current Prescription Opioid and Heroin Epidemic in the US

The consumption of opioid pain relievers and heroin—as well as the subsequent comorbidity and mortality—has dramatically increased in the US in the past two decades. For example, from 1999 to 2011, use of hydrocodone has more than doubled, and oxycodone use increased by almost 500% (Kolodny et al., 2015). Heroin use has also increased in the US—an expansion directly related to opioid pain reliever use—from 1 per 1,000 people in 2002 to 2 per 1,000 people in 2013, a 100% increase (NSDUH, 2002–2013). Specifically, from 2002–2004 to 2011–2013, there's a 50% increase of heroin use among men and 100% increase among women, an 109% increase among the age group 18–25 and 58% increase among the 26 or older age group (CDC, 2015). Growing use of opioid drugs and heroin have resulted in a higher prevalence of addiction, overdose death, and other implications such as neonatal abstinence syndrome, HIV and hepatitis C infections, emergency room visits, impairment of psychological conditions and social relationships, and loss of employment and productivity (Department of Health and Human Services, 2016; Kolodny et al.,

2015; Tolia et al., 2015). To curtail the crisis and its adverse consequences, it's important to research the origin of the epidemic surge and develop corresponding strategies.

Although it is not completely without dispute, research has pointed to a plausible direction: that insufficient pain management methods and inappropriate opioid prescribing practices is likely related to the nonmedical use of prescription opioids, which ultimately leads to heroin use because of heroin's easier access and lower costs (CDC, 2015, 2017b). According to the CDC (2017b), while there was no change in the volume or quantity of pain Americans reported during 1999–2014, the sale of prescription opioids in the US increased nearly fourfold during this period. In addition, Cicero et al.'s (2014) study on "the changing face of heroin use" in the US during the past half century found that 80% of their study participants who began using heroin in the 1960s reported heroin to be their first opioid, whereas 75% of the more recent users in the study reported that they started via prescription drugs (p. 821). Similarly, based on the National Epidemiologic Survey on Alcohol and Related Conditions, Martins et al. (2017) found that the percentage of individuals who reported "initiation of nonmedical use of prescription opioids before initiating heroin use" escalated from 35.83% (2001–2002) to 52.83% (2012–2013) (p = .01) among Whites. Therefore, the nature or underlying impetus of the current heroin epidemic in the US seems to be different compared to the heroin problems of the 1960s, demonstrating how conditions and circumstances change over time (one of the social macro factors).

It would be interesting and insightful to compare the current heroin epidemic in the US with heroin problems in China as a way to exemplify the affects of geography and the social construct of nations (that is, macro factors). The current US heroin epidemic looks different when compared to the heroin problems in China that can be traced to social changes in the early 1990s. Deng Xiaoping introduced economic reforms in 1978 and the Shanghai stock market—which had been closed since 1949—reopened in December, 1990 (Hirst, 2015). China's Open Door policy successfully helped the country achieve an economic transformation, but some people believe this Open Door policy also brought in vices from outside like heroin and rising crime. Although more systematic studies are needed, the preliminary findings of my own qualitative interviews (Sun et al., in progress) reveal that some Chinese heroin users in the 40–60 age group, who started using heroin during the early 1990s, perceived themselves as "victims" of the Open Door policy. They stated that the "white powder" was carried into China from Hong Kong, Burma, and other countries once China's iron curtain was raised, and that during that period of time, heroin consumption was considered a high-class recreational activity symbolizing social status and prestige (Sun et al., in progress). In contrast are the precipitators of today's new and younger cohort of Chinese heroin users who started in the 2010s. Anecdotal information gathered by this author reveals that some younger heroin users in China tend to be laborers or workers who left rural hometowns and migrated to urban regions for better job opportunities. Often naïve about the addictive nature of heroin, these homesick young people were likely to seek comfort from heroin or other substances.

To target the current prescription opioid and heroin crisis in the US, the Department of Health and Human Services (HHS) began the Opioid Initiative in 2015 and the National Pain Strategy in 2016 (www.hhs.gov/sites/default/files/opioid-report-v4-remediated.pdf). Three areas are highlighted by the HHS and experts.

1. Improve Opioid Prescribing Practices

The current prescription opioid and heroin epidemic is very much associated with physicians who widely prescribed opioid pain medications in the past two decades to help their patients afflicted with chronic pain. Munzing (2017) offers a historical background to explain why there was, until very recently, such extensive opioid prescribing—prescribing for pain was emphasized during the 1990s and the beginning of 2000s; pain was considered "the fifth vital sign" and many organizations advocated, unrealistically, "getting pain to zero." On top of that, pharmaceutical companies created more long-acting and potent opioids and aggressively marketed these products to physicians while downplaying the potential risks. Munzing concludes, "Physicians wield the power to heal and relieve pain. However, the same power has the potential to contribute to harm, especially in the case of prescribed opioids" (p. 1).

We now know that not only are illegal opioids, such as heroin, highly addictive, but so are prescription opioids. It is estimated that about 1.9 million individuals were dependent on or abused prescription opioid analgesics in 2013 (Panther et al., 2017). As mentioned above, some individuals who are addicted to prescription opioids eventually transition into heroin or other illicit opioid use, such as illegally manufactured fentanyl. Many physicians, although well-meaning, prescribed potent opioids because of a lack of accurate education and experience in this area; other clinicians in primary care indicated apprehension about treating patients' chronic pain, and patients' misuse of and addiction to opioid pain medication, expressing concern regarding their inadequate training in the area (Munzing, 2017; Panther et al., 2017).

Various actions have been taken to improve opioid prescription practices. For example: the Food and Drug Administration put a boxed warning on the label of benzodiazepines and prescription opioids to call attention to their serious risks; Vivek Murthy, the US Surgeon General, wrote a letter to US physicians asking them to help reverse the tide on the opioid crisis; the White House organized a summit of many leaders regarding this topic; and the CDC developed 12 recommendations, based on input from various stakeholders, experts, peer reviewers, the general public, and an advisory committee (Munzing, 2017). More recently, President Trump in late 2017 declared the opioid crisis a national emergency.

The CDC's 12 recommendations for prescribing opioids for noncancer chronic pain touch upon three areas—"determining when to initiate or continue opioids for chronic pain," "opioid selection, dosage, duration, follow-up, and discontinuation," and "assessing risk and addressing harms of opioid use"—and can be retrieved from www.cdc.gov/drugoverdose/prescribing/guideline.html (2017a). They are summarized and directly quoted below:

- Nonpharmacologic therapy and nonopioid pharmacologic therapy are preferred for chronic pain.
- Before starting opioid therapy for chronic pain, clinicians should establish treatment goals with all patients. Clinicians should continue opioid therapy only if there is clinically meaningful improvement in pain and function that outweighs risks to patient safety.
- Before starting and periodically during opioid therapy, clinicians should discuss with patients known risks and realistic benefits . . . and patient and clinician responsibilities for managing therapy.
- When starting opioid therapy for chronic pain, clinicians should prescribe immediate-release opioids instead of extended-release/long-acting opioids.

- When opioids are started, clinicians should prescribe the lowest effective dosage. Clinicians should use caution when prescribing opioids at any dosage, should carefully reassess evidence of individual benefits and risks when considering increasing dosage to ≥50 morphine milligram equivalents (MME)/day, and should avoid increasing dosage to ≥90 MME/day or carefully justify a decision to titrate dosage to ≥90 MME/day.
- Long-term opioid use often begins with treatment of acute pain. When opioids are used for acute pain, clinicians should prescribe the lowest effective dose of immediate-release opioids and should prescribe no greater quantity than needed for the expected duration of pain severe enough to require opioids. Three days or less will often be sufficient; more than seven days will rarely be needed.
- Clinicians should evaluate benefits and harms with patients within 1 to 4 weeks of starting opioid therapy for chronic pain or of dose escalation. Clinicians should evaluate benefits and harms of continued therapy with patients every 3 months or more frequently. If benefits do not outweigh harms of continued opioid therapy, clinicians should optimize other therapies and work with patients to taper opioids to lower dosages or to taper and discontinue opioids.
- Before starting and periodically during continuation of opioid therapy, clinicians should evaluate risk factors for opioid-related harms. Clinicians should incorporate into the management plan strategies to mitigate risk, including considering offering naloxone when factors that increase risk for opioid overdose, such as history of overdose, history of substance use disorder, higher opioid dosages (≥50 MME/day), or concurrent benzodiazepine use are present.
- Clinicians should review the patient's history of controlled substance prescriptions using state prescription drug monitoring program (PDMP) data to determine whether the patient is receiving opioid dosages or dangerous combinations that put him or her at high risk for overdose. Clinicians should review PDMP data when starting opioid therapy for chronic pain and periodically during opioid therapy for chronic pain, ranging from every prescription to every three month.
- When prescribing opioids for chronic pain, clinicians should use urine drug testing before starting opioid therapy and consider urine drug

testing at least annually to assess for prescribed medications as well as other controlled prescription drugs and illicit drugs.

- Clinicians should avoid prescribing opioid pain medication and benzodiazepines concurrently whenever possible.
- Clinicians should offer or arrange evidence-based treatment (usually medication-assisted treatment with buprenorphine or methadone in combination with behavioral therapies) for patients with opioid use disorder.

Compared to the old guidelines, the changes in new recommendations include: lower dosages as a means of caution; safety precautions that are applicable to all patients rather than high-risk patients; encouraging clinicians to use state prescription drug monitoring programs; more specific recommendations on overseeing and stopping opioids when harms outweigh benefits (CDC, 2017a).

Other experts have also suggested guidelines for better practice of pain management: (a) The treatment should be individualized, based on a detailed history, a thorough evaluation, and physical examination. (b) The physician needs to weigh the pros and cons, and comply with the ethical code regarding "doing no harm." (c) Treatment should be multimodal, and contain both nonpharmacologic and pharmacologic approaches. Nonpharmacologic treatment may contain massage, exercise, physical therapy, ice, heat, cognitive behavioral therapy, meditation, and co-occurring disorder treatment. Pharmacologic approaches may include nonopioid medications (e.g., acetaminophen, nonsteroidal anti-inflammatory drugs, tricyclic antidepressants, etc.) and topical medications (Munzing, 2017).

2. Increase Naloxone Use to Reverse Opioid Overdoses

Overdoses and related deaths that accompany the current opioid epidemic are a major public health crisis; it is critical to make the opioid overdose remedy, naloxone, more available. In 2015, 16.3 per 100,000 population died of drug overdose—an increase from 12.3 in 2010. Among the 52,404 persons who died of drug overdose during 2015, 63.1% were affected by an opioid. The death rates increased by 72.2% for synthetic opioids (mainly illegally manufactured fentanyl, not methadone), 20.6% for heroin, and

2.6% for natural and/or semisynthetic opioids. In other words, the increased death rates were primarily driven by illicitly manufactured opioid synthetics, such as fentanyl, and heroin (Rudd et al., 2016).

In addition to improving opioid prescribing practice and pain management, one direct strategy that can be implemented within a short period of time to curb opioid overdoses is to expand delivery of the opioid overdose antidote (Panther et al., 2017). Naloxone—an opioid-receptor antagonist that can overturn the depression of the central nervous system and reinstate respiration—has been the primary medication to treat opioid overdose. Naloxone needs to enter the circulatory system directly and there are various routes to administer naloxone—including intranasal, intravenous, intramuscular, subcutaneous, endotracheal, and intraosseus (Robinson & Wermeling, 2014). Although paramedics traditionally administer naloxone via intravenous or intramuscular route, intranasal is considered a better route than intravenous (Robinson & Wermeling, 2014) for several reasons. Compared to intranasal route approach, an intravenous route approach may have increased risks of blood-borne infectious diseases or other injury to first responders. In addition, many IV drug users may have damaged veins because of their overuse of injection sites, which makes it difficult to obtain intravenous access. Use of intranasal route approach, however, also has its contraindications. For example, intranasal approach cannot be used if a person has intranasal abnormalities, nasal trauma, extreme nasal mucus, and/or intranasal damage (e.g., caused by cocaine use) (Robinson & Wermeling, 2014).

3. Increase Access to Medication-Assisted Treatment (MAT)

Voluminous studies have shown the effectiveness of medication-assisted treatment (MAT) for helping opioid-addicted patients, particularly when the pharmacotherapy is combined with psychosocial counseling, behavioral therapy, comorbid mental disorder treatment, and other case management services such as medical services and vocational rehabilitation (Center for Substance Abuse Treatment [CSAT], 2011). CSAT considers opioid addiction a chronic disease that is best treated with maintenance medication and behavioral intervention; a combination of both can enhance patients' treatment compliance and decrease the rates of treatment dropout and opioid relapse. CSAT said, "discontinuation of maintenance medication [e.g., methadone] often results in dropout from other services and a return to previous levels of opioid abuse, with its accompanying adverse medical and psychosocial consequences" (p. 4).

Although research recommends that medications such as methadone and buprenorphine should be available as options for all opioid or heroin addicted patients, the utilization of these medications is inconsistent and low (Oliva et al., 2011; Robertson & Swartz, 2017). Barriers to medication-assisted treatment are found in at least four areas: decisions made by drug courts, stigma against opioid agonist treatment, costs of medication and insurance policies, and different treatment philosophies.

Drug Court Factor Although the treatment outcomes of drug court programs are not completely consistent, systematic reviews have indicated evidence that participation in drug courts reduces recidivism. However, evidence also shows that drug court programs have high dropout rates, such that about 40% of their participants leave treatment prematurely and only about 50% of participants complete the program (Robertson & Swartz, 2017). In addition to low motivation for treatment, the high dropout rates may be related to participants' heroin use (Robertson & Swartz, 2017). Many drug courts do not allow their opioid-addicted participants to receive pharmacotherapy such as methadone. Matusow et al.'s study (2013) showed that about 98% of all drug courts involved opioid-addicted clients, yet only 47% of them offered an agonist (e.g., methadone) for treatment. The problems may be getting worse as nationwide the proportions of drug court participants with opioid dependence have greatly increased in the past decade. To take one drug court in North Carolina as an example, the rate of opioid dependence among its participants has increased to over 50% today, compared to about 25% during the past decades (Robertson & Swartz, 2017).

The resistance to pharmacotherapy by drug courts and the criminal justice system may stem from people's inadequate knowledge regarding the benefits of medication-assisted treatment, inflexible perceptions of addiction being a non-medical problem, and concerns about participants' possible medication diversion (Robertson & Swartz, 2017). To expand medication-assisted treatment (MAT) in general, one strategy is to make MAT available to opioid-addicted drug court participants. It is important to promote positive views on pharmacotherapy via public education campaigns supported by government; it may also be helpful to ask leaders who support pharmacotherapy to advocate and change facility culture in this regard (Oliva et al., 2011). Based on scientific findings that opioid-addicted offenders who received medication-assisted treatment show better outcomes, the National Association of Drug Court Professionals (NADCP, n.d) has declared its support for the use of medication-assisted treatment in its 2013 Guidelines for Adult Drug Courts. The NADCP encourages MAT use—including agonist (e.g., methadone), antagonist (e.g., naltrexone), and partial agonist (e.g., buprenorphine)—to help drug court participants who are afflicted with opioid addiction (Parrino et al., 2015).

Stigma of Opioid Agonist Treatment It is not only drug courts' staff and judges, but also many professionals in other settings and the general public, who may oppose using opioid agonists, e.g., methadone, to treat opioid addiction. To them, it is not a true treatment and not a true recovery for a patient to use one opioid (methadone) to replace another (heroin). They are blind to the facts that methadone encourages abstinence from heroin, reduces HIV/AIDS and transmission of other infectious diseases, decreases crimes, and enables many addicted individuals to become functional again in their daily lives, such as by maintaining employment and positive social relationships (Csete & Catania, 2013; Parrino et al., 2015). No matter how assured of its successful treatment outcomes by scientific research findings, opioid agonist treatment has always had a stigma attached and encounters more obstacles compared to other models of treatment such as detoxification, psychotherapy, and drug-free rehabilitation (Parrino et al., 2015). It is not easy to change the biased attitude and culture toward opioid agonist treatment, considering half of the countries on earth—including Russia—prohibit methadone treatment. Media can play a significant role to help overturn the general public's biased perceptions of opioid agonist treatment; politicians should also make agonist treatment resources more accessible to people in need. In addition, clinicians, medical students, family members, and policymakers should all be exposed to the knowledge that "a correct agonist opioid treatment" is effective and can help people afflicted with heroin or other opioid addiction problems (Parrino et al., 2015, p. 261).

Medication-assisted treatment is not limited only to agonists such as methadone, it may include antagonists (e.g., naltrexone)—an approach that is probably more acceptable to people who oppose agonist treatment. Regular naltrexone (an oral form) has been criticized for the problem of patient noncompliance, but extended release naltrexone (XR-NTX, an injectable form) has proven to be as effective as buprenorphine-naloxone (a partial agonist) in helping patients maintain abstinence from heroin and other illicit drugs (Tanum et al., 2017). Lee et al.'s study (2018) did find that it is more challenging to induct patients with XR-NTX than buprenorphine-naloxone; however, once initiated, both medications tended to be equally effective. Lee and colleagues suggested that future efforts should target strategies for facilitating initiation of XR-NTX and enhancing treatment retention for both XR-NTX and buprenorphine-naloxone. For drug court participants, studies have found that XR-NTX can be applied and yield effective treatment outcomes (Finigan et al., 2011).

Costs of Medications and Insurance Policies Another barrier to expanding medication-assisted treatment is the costs of both the medications and insurance. Without insurance, XR-NTX may cost a person about $1000 monthly out-of-pocket; in contrast, a person may only need to be responsible for a monthly co-pay of $3 if his or her Medicaid insurance covers the medication (Robertson & Swartz, 2017). To return to the subject of drug court, most drug courts have difficulty allocating funds to cover participants' medications, especially the more expensive medications such as XR-NTX (Robertson & Swartz, 2017). Therefore, it is critical that health insurance or Medicaid includes medication coverage for addiction treatment (Oliva et al., 2011; Robertson & Swartz, 2017). To tackle the barrier of high medication costs, several issues must be addressed and improved, including disparity in insurance coverage, insurance reimbursement obstacles, complicated rules related to Medicaid pharmacotherapy coverage, and other limits on coverage (Oliva et al., 2011).

Different Treatment Philosophies The medication-assisted therapy (MAT) has been strongly advocated to treat heroin addiction in the past decades, yet some private or voluntary treatment programs uphold the values of total abstinence. They adopt a combination of detoxification, counseling, and self-help group to treat their patients who are addicted to prescription pain medication or who have transitioned from prescription pain medication to heroin addiction. They believe methadone and suboxone are also addictive and that naltrexone is not without side effects and other risks. They also believe certain demographic variables may play a role regarding the issue. They ask questions such as: Is MAT more suitable for traditional heroin users than the newly emerged patient group who are addicted to prescription pain medication? Are younger patients and patients with a shorter opioid addiction career more likely to be successful with the total abstinence approach? Will patients with a higher level of recovery capital, such as education, employment, and social support, be more likely to recover without MAT than their counterparts who have low recovery capital? More research is needed to answer all of these questions, especially longitudinal studies measuring treatment outcomes at follow-ups, recovery status, and the type of aftercare received post discharge.

The Trend of Gender Convergence in Substance Use

Many scientific studies across the globe have consistently identified a trend of gender convergence in alcohol use and its related harm and problems, including research from Norway (e.g., Bratberg et al., 2016), five developing and ten developed countries (Seedat et al., 2009), North America, Europe, Asia, Oceania, and other places (Slade et al., 2016), and the US (White et al., 2015). Some evidence of gender convergence has also been found for marijuana use (e.g., Chapman et al., 2017; Johnson et al., 2015). It is not clear exactly what has driven the convergence, but the fact is that more women—particularly the younger cohorts—are using. The implications of the increased number of women users are multifold. Although not completely consistent (e.g., Lewis & Nixon, 2014), many studies suggest the "telescoping effect," meaning that women are faster to progress from initial use to regular and severe use (e.g., Haas & Peters, 2000; Khan et al., 2013; Schepis et al., 2011). Women may be more vulnerable to the negative biological, psychological, and social consequences of substance abuse than men, including, for example, liver cirrhosis, cancers, fetal alcohol spectrum disorder, and violence (Eagon, 2010; Ekwueme et al., 2017; Feldman et al., 2012; La Flair et al., 2012; Rehm et al., 2010; Simapivapan et al., 2016; Wilsnack et al., 2014). More evidence-based substance treatment and prevention services that are tailored to the biopsychosocial needs of female patients are needed to increase treatment retention and efficacy.

The Time/Cohort Factor

The analysis of Slade and colleagues (2016) showed that the sex ratios for alcohol use and its related harms decreased over time, such that the male/female ratio for alcohol use was 2.2 (i.e., for every 2.2 male alcohol users, there is 1 female alcohol user) among people born in the early 1900s vs. 1.1 among people born in the late 1900s. That is, women born in earlier times were less likely to drink than modern women. For problematic alcohol use, the male/female ratio was 3.0 for the early 1900s birth cohort versus 1.2 for the late 1900s birth cohort. Although not completely consistent, gender convergence was also found in marijuana use among later cohorts. For example, Chapman and colleagues' (2017) systematic review shows that the male/female ratio of cannabis use prevalence decreased from 2.0 among individuals who were born in 1941 to 1.3 among people born in 1995. Based on data from the National Youth Risk Behavior Survey—a national school-based survey targeting students in 9th to 12th grades, Johnson and colleagues (2015) also found that the male/female marijuana use prevalence ratio narrowed over time in the last 15 years. On the other hand, Carliner's research team (2017) studied the 2002–2014 National Survey on Drug Use and Health data that suggested the marijuana use gap between genders is widening and that such a divergence is mainly due to increased use prevalence among low-income men. They believe their findings are in line with the literature that suggests that people, especially men, are more likely to engage in substance use during times when the economy is bad; the occurrence of the Great Recession and higher unemployment rates in 2007 are related to the increase of marijuana use among low-income men, resulting in a wide gender gap in marijuana use (Carliner et al., 2017). The major difference between Carliner et al.'s study and the other two studies cited here is that Carliner et al. looked for the gender gap trend by mixing all age groups whereas the other two studies either focused on a comparison between an older and a younger cohort or primarily on adolescent groups. In addition, Johnston et al.'s (2015) observations may also help explain the discrepancy; they found that when the overall rates of marijuana and other drug use declined, the gender ratio tends to be narrow, while the gender ratio is more likely to widen during periods when the overall rates of use are high. Johnson et al. wrote that the gender convergence found in their study could reflect the overall low level of marijuana use during the period.

The Space/Geographical Factor

Macro or societal factors can be related to time (e.g., comparing younger cohorts with older cohorts) or space (e.g., comparing the Americas and European regions with Asian regions). According to World Health Organization 2010 data (WHO, 2014), the male/female ratio for "current drinkers" is 1.3 for the Americas and 1.2 for Europe, but is 4.3 for Southeast Asia and 1.8 for the Western Pacific region. Such differences are even more pronounced for "heavy episodic drinking among drinkers," in that it is 2.4 for the Americas and 2.5 for Europe, whereas it's 10.9 for Southeast Asia and 7.3 for the Western Pacific region. Similar patterns occur for alcohol use disorders. For example, the gender gap is 46.5 for China, compared to 2.38 for Sweden. For tobacco smoking, again, the gender gaps are vastly different when comparing most Asian countries with European countries. For example, the male/female ratio is 36.85 for Vietnam, 22.17 for China, and 18.35 for Indonesia, whereas it is only 1.35 for France, 1.20 for the Netherlands, and 1.06 for Norway (WHO, 2015).

Another noticeable theme is the interactive effect between age and gender on the rate of tobacco smoking. For most Asian countries, not only do men have a much higher tobacco-smoking rate than women, the two genders reveal a different trend as they become older. The trend for Asian men is like a bell curve, such that the rate gradually increases from age 15 to 24, reaches the peak at around age 40 to 54, and gradually declines afterwards. For Asian women, however, the rate gradually and consistently increases as they grow older. For most European countries, not only are the gender gaps narrower, but also the two genders share a similar bell curve trend.

Underlying Mechanism for Gender Convergence

Although many studies confirmed the narrowing gender gap in alcohol or other substance use and related harm, those researchers were uncertain about, and requested more research on, the underneath mechanism that drives the change and the corresponding implications for treatment and prevention efforts (e.g., Bratberg et al., 2016; White et al., 2015). The evidence, however, indicates that the gender convergence on alcohol use is a result of more females becoming current drinkers, whereas the numbers for men stayed relatively the same (White et al., 2015).

Although the research on a causal relationship between the increase in the number of female drinkers is difficult to obtain, some relational studies show that "gender role traditionality" (GRT, meaning the gender ratios on employment, education, marital timing, and birth control) may have a bearing on gender convergence with alcohol use (Seedat et al., 2009). For example, Seedat et al.'s study—an analysis of the WHO World Mental Health surveys that cover five developing and ten developed countries—found that the sex differences in the prevalence rates of substance use disorder across birth cohorts tend to be closer among countries where the roles of women and men are converging over time. In other words, as women's gender roles become less traditional, they start to draw near to men in their rates of substance use disorder.

If the observable prevalence gap in substance use between genders in the West is related to the impact of a society's structure and values in general, and its double standard toward the two genders in particular, such an environmental effect appears to impact many more Asians in a more profound way, as their such gap is much further apart between men and women. For example, for about every 37 Vietnamese male tobacco smokers, there is only 1 Vietnamese female tobacco smoker. This is in stark contrast with the statistics that for every 1.2 Dutch male tobacco smokers, there is 1 Dutch female tobacco smoker. The fact that Asian women demonstrate a consistent and climbing trend of tobacco-smoking rates as they grow older—as opposed to the bell-shape curve demonstrated by Asian men, Western men, and Western women—is interesting. Perhaps this is also a reflection of social and cultural influences, in that Asian society may grant more privileges and respect to older people, especially older women who have given birth to sons, which directly and indirectly relaxes many of the restrictions previously prescribed for younger women, as well as increases older women's access to substances and their purchasing ability. Compared to Asian women, most Asian men and Western men and women may be early-onset tobacco smokers and may cut down or quit smoking during their middle age for health reasons, or they may have died because of smoking- related illnesses.

Researchers are also unclear why cannabis liberalization is more likely to affect women's marijuana use than men. Rapidly changing marijuana policy may also affect the gender gap in marijuana use. For example, Miller and colleagues (2017) investigated the impact of recreational marijuana legalization on marijuana use among college undergraduates, using National College Health Assessment data. They found that Washington State University students (Washington state legalized recreational marijuana use in 2015) not only had a larger increase in marijuana use than the predicted national trend but also that such a change was most pronounced among women, African Americans, and Latino students. Shi et al. (2015) also reported that the connection between cannabis use and cannabis liberalization was larger for girls than for boys, although they were uncertain why. I think one possible explanation could be that women, overall, are less willing to engage in deviant or illegal behaviors than men; recreational marijuana legalization eliminates the illegal and deviant aspect of the substance, making cannabis more acceptable for women to consume.

Gender Specific Practice and Treatment

SBIRT and Prevention The gender convergence in substance use and substance use disorders points to the ways that we should target both young men and women when providing prevention and intervention (Chapman et al., 2017), as the traditional landscape with regard to alcohol or other substance consumption among men and women has changed. This gender convergence further calls attention to the fact that women are more vulnerable to the negative consequences of problematic drinking. For example, women are at risk for physical illnesses such as ovarian and breast cancer, liver cirrhosis, and fetotoxic effects or birth defects (Eagon, 2010; Ekwueme et al., 2017; Feldman et al., 2012; Rehm et al., 2010; Simapivapan et al., 2016). When at a high level of alcohol consumption, women may suffer a more severe consequence than men (Lewis & Nixon, 2014). Women may also suffer a faster progression from initial use to severe addiction (Blanco et al., 2006; Greenfield et al., 2010; Schepis et al., 2011). In addition, women are vulnerable to becoming victims of violence when substance use or abuse is involved (La Flair et al., 2012; Wilsnack et al., 2014). Therefore, it is critical to prevent and detect early substance abuse or other addictive behavioral problems among women; to achieve this goal, evidence-based Screening, Brief Intervention, and Referral to Treatment (SBIRT) can be implemented in primary care settings and prenatal care programs (Shogren et al., 2017).

SBIRT can be applied to screen not only for heroin and prescription opioid use problems to reduce the negative impact of the rising opioid epidemic, but also to detect and intervene early with cannabis use disorder among adolescents and young adults, as well as drinking problems among women who correspond to the phenomenon of gender convergence on drinking. The appropriate screening tools for women may include the NIAAA Single Question, AUDIT, AUDIT-C, CRAFFT, T-ACE, and TWEAK (Shogren et al., 2017; Sun, 2009). Women can be provided with education or brief advice if screening results show low risk. Topics of education can include, for example, the effects of alcohol consumption, definition of a standard drink, number of drinks per day safe for a woman, and so on. For pregnant women and those considering pregnancy, it's important to address the negative effects of alcohol on the fetus, that there is no safe amount of alcohol consumption during pregnancy, and that total abstinence should be the guideline. If a woman's SBIRT screening result indicates at-risk alcohol use, brief intervention in addition to education should be provided to her. Brief intervention can be exemplified by a FLO model (feedback, listen, and options) (Shogren et al., 2017). Based on the motivational interviewing approach, the clinician gives the patient *feedback* regarding her screening results, where they indicate at-risk behavior, and the consequences of heavy drinking. The clinician then *listens* to the woman's response to the feedback, encourages her decision-making process, and explores *options* regarding behavior change if she chooses. If the SBIRT screening result indicates an alcohol use disorder, the clinician in the generalist practice setting should adopt motivational interviewing skills to encourage and refer the woman for further specialized treatment (Shogren et al., 2017).

Gender-Informed and Gender-Specific Treatment In addition to prevention, gender-informed and gender-specific treatment can better help women who are already afflicted with addiction problems. Research has revealed some gender-specific insights with respect to women and addiction, including: (1) Different characteristics, compared to men, at admission for addiction treatment. For example, women indicate worse scores than men in the areas of psychiatric/psychological issues, health/medical problems, family/social difficulties, and employment obstacles. (2) Different factors, compared to men, that contribute or relate to initial use and/or relapse. For example, women seem to be more likely than men to self-medicate negative emotions. Women are also are more likely to be affected by their family and spouse with regard to use and relapse. (3) Other biopsychosocial risk factors that are specifically pertinent to women, such as menstrual cycles, telescoping effects, prenatal alcohol and/or drug exposure, and other biological factors. Knowledge of all these factors enables practitioners to have a better understanding of women's needs, and therefore conduct a gender-sensitive and gender-specific assessment as well as develop an effective treatment plan to promote long-term recovery among women (Sun, 2016).

Let's examine each of these factors in detail.

1. Different Characteristics Between Men and Women at Admission

Among the eight studies reviewed concerning psychiatric/psychological problems (e.g., depression, anxiety) at admission, seven suggest that women present worse than men (Burch et al., 2015; Rash & Petry, 2015; Han et al., 2016; Fernandez-Montalvo et al., 2014; DeVito et al., 2014; Karpyak et al., 2016; Green et al., 2009); only one study (Levine et al., 2015) showed no significant difference between the two genders. Among the six studies that considered health/medical matters, three (Burch et al., 2015; Fernandez-Montalvo et al., 2015; Haas & Peters, 2000) indicate women present worse than men, while three studies (Rash & Petry, 2015; Han et al., 2016; DeVito et al., 2014) show no significant difference. Among the seven studies that examined the family/social area, six (Burch et al., 2015; Han et al., 2016; Rash & Petry, 2015; Fernandez-Montalvo et al., 2014; Green et al., 2009; Levine et al., 2015) indicate that women are worse than men in this regard, while one study (DeVito et al., 2014) suggests no significant difference between the two genders. Among the nine studies reviewed for employment situations, seven (Burch et al., 2015; DeVito et al., 2014; Fernandez-Montalvo et al., 2014; Han et al., 2016; Kennedy et al., 2013; McNeese-Smith et al., 2009; Rash & Petry, 2015) suggest women are worse than men, while two studies (Greenfield et al., 2010; Maxwell, 2014) indicate no significant difference between the two genders. Among the seven studies that assessed legal troubles (incarceration) and/or antisocial personality disorder, five (Devito et al., 2014 [antisocial personality disorder]; Fernandez-Montalvo et al., 2014; Green et al., 2009; Rash & Petry, 2015) show that men are worse than women and two (DeVito et al., 2014 [legal]; Han et al., 2016) suggest no significant difference between the two genders.

2. Different Factors Related to Use and Relapse Comparing Women and Men

Enhanced positive emotions are a major relapse/use trigger. Four studies indicate that men and women are equally vulnerable to this trigger—e.g., seeking a high, fun, and more energy in the cases of methamphetamine use (Lee et al., 2015; Maxwell, 2014); drinking during pleasant times with others or when having pleasant emotions (Levy et al., 2016); and feeling "optimism about winning" among individuals with gambling disorder (Hodgins & el-Guebaly, 2004). Three studies show that men are more likely to use methamphetamines to increase libido or seek more pleasure during sex (Cheng et al., 2009; Lee et al., 2015; Maxwell, 2014).

While men are more or equally likely than women to use or relapse in pursuit of positive emotions, women are more likely to use or relapse because they want to reduce negative feelings, such as unpleasant emotions, physical discomfort, childhood or adulthood trauma, stress, work difficulties, and conflict with others (Heffner et al., 2011; Hodgins & el-Guebaly, 2004; Karpyak et al., 2016; Sun, 2007). Heffner et al.'s study revealed that childhood and adulthood trauma predicted relapse among women but not among men. Karpyak et al. found that alcoholic women—with or without comorbid depression or anxiety disorder—are likely to drink when facing unpleasant emotions, whereas only alcoholic men with comorbid major depression, substance-induced depression, or anxiety disorder tend to drink to cope with negative emotions. On the other hand, men with schizophrenia spectrum disorder are more likely than their female counterparts to use tobacco to self-medicate, both in Canada (Johnson et al., 2010) and China (Zhang et al., 2010). Negative emotion can be a use/relapse trigger not only for substance-abusing women but also for women with gambling disorder. Hodgins and el-Guebaly (2004) found that women are more likely than men to relapse to pathological gambling because of negative emotions or situations (7% of the male subjects vs. 18% of the female subjects). Negative emotions may include anxiety, loneliness, anger, frustration, and guilt; negative situations may include feeling the "need to get away from problems with children, work difficulties, and so forth" (p. 77).

Influence of spouse or other family members is another major trigger for use or relapse among women. Studies have indicated that a larger percentage of women with alcoholism problems report having one or both parents alcoholic and/or having an alcoholic spouse, as compared to their male counterparts (Lewis & Nixon, 2014; Morgan et a al., 2010; see Sun's review, 2009). For example, Lewis and Nixon found that 73% of their female subjects, compared to 61% of male subjects, had alcoholic parents; that 58% of their female subjects, yet only 38% of male subjects, had an alcoholic spouse. Lewis and Nixon stated that the association between alcoholic women and their alcoholic spouses could be due to assortative mating or that alcoholic women may have a lower likelihood of leaving their alcoholic partners. Other studies have also suggested that women are more likely to be initiated into drug use by their spouse than vice versa (Cheng et al., 2009; Sun, 2007), and that women tend to be affected by their male spouses with regard to use, stopping use, and relapse (Sun, 2000; 2007). These data suggest that familial and/or spousal relationships are important topics to address when helping substance-abusing women.

3. Other Factors Specifically Related to Women

Women's using and quitting behaviors may be affected by their menstrual cycle, in that it may be more difficult to quit using if begun during a certain phase of the menstrual cycle. Some studies suggest that there is a heightened nicotine withdrawal symptomatology during the late luteal phase, and that this could be "an additive . . . combination of withdrawal and premenstrual sensations" (Hudson & Stamp, 2011, p. 429). Other studies report that women experience enhanced craving for cocaine during the late follicular/early luteal phase, whereas they indicate a reduced level of craving during the mid luteal phase (Moran-Santa Maria et al., 2014).

Telescoping is another gender-specific phenomenon. Some studies suggest that women progress faster from initial use to addiction or treatment seeking; the telescoping effect applies to drinking, cannabis use, and even gambling. For example, studies reveal a shorter period of time from initial drinking to the stage of alcohol dependence for women than men (Johnson et al., 2005; Piazza et al., 1989; Randall et al., 1999). Studies have also found that women have a shorter lapse between initial cannabis use and the development of cannabis use disorder (Ehlers et al., 2010; Hernandez-Avila et al., 2004; Schepis et al., 2011). Telescoping has also been indicated among female pathological gamblers (Grant et al., 2012). Unfortunately, research findings on telescoping are not consistent. Some suggest that it occurs only among clinical or treatment-seeking populations but not general populations (Keyes et al., 2010). Some researchers suggest that the telescoping effect may be substance-specific, in that it may occur with certain but not other substances (Khan et al., 2013). Some find that telescoping happens, comparing men with women, regarding the length of time from initial use to treatment seeking rather than from initial use to problematic use or addiction. For example, Lewis and Nixon (2014) reported that women enter treatment more swiftly by about four years; however, there is no difference between men and women when comparing the length of time from initial drinking to the development of alcohol problems or alcohol dependence. It is not clear why women are more vulnerable to telescoping; possible explanations are that men and women may have different vulnerabilities—e.g., sexual hormones may play an important role—when experiencing reinforcement (Fattore, 2015; Fattore et al., 2014) and that they may have different risks for comorbid drug and mental disorders (Lopez-Quintero et al., 2011). The telescoping effect has implications for substance abuse treatment and prevention for men and women; gender-informed treatment and prevention practice for girls and boys should be emphasized. (Schepis et al., 2011).

Social and Technological Change and the Emergence of Behavioral Addiction

The enormous and rapid technological advancement as well as social change of recent years have altered the landscape of the addiction problem and its occurrence. Addiction is no longer limited to just problematic alcohol and drug consumption; addiction can happen through various behaviors or processes that "repeatedly reinforc[e] the reward, motivation and memory circuitry" of the brain—a "revolutionary paradigm shift" (Grant et al., 2010; Love et al., 2015, p. 389; Yau & Potenza, 2015). Compared to many decades ago, we now have *new* addictions, such as addiction to food or addiction to the internet. We also have new forms of old addictions, such as internet pornography and online gambling. The accompanying challenges are multifold, including the most basic: both the general public and some mental health professionals hesitate to consider behavioral addiction as true addiction, despite that more and more clients and their families are seeking help for such problems. Although there is some evidence showing similarities between substance addiction and behavioral addiction in terms of their neurobiological mechanism, the field demands more evidence from rigorous scientific studies showing that behavioral addiction is in and of itself an addiction, not symptoms secondary to other primary mental disorders. Research is also needed for pharmacotherapy for behavioral addiction, as there is no FDA-approved medication to treat behavioral addiction so far, unlike substance addiction (see Chapter 7). In addition, research can target and expand behavioral-addiction-specific cognitive behavioral therapy and psychosocial treatment strategies, albeit many treatment methods and skills for substance addiction appear to be effective for behavioral addiction.

Scholars have used the Public Health Model to explain substance addiction, in that the occurrence of addiction is viewed as involving a host (a vulnerable addicted person), an agent (drugs in the case of substance use disorder), a vector (the drug dealer or enticement to drug use), and an environment (the physical setting where the drug use takes place) (Leshner, 2001). The behavioral or process addiction is consistent with the Public Health Model as well; that is, if there had been no invention of computer and internet, there would be no "agent" to cause new addiction such as internet addiction or internet gaming addiction. Although the internet has benefited most people, its detrimental effects on a group of at-risk population, who overuse and eventually become addicted to it, should not be underestimated or ignored. Internet-related addiction has been noticed in many countries globally, including North American, Asia, and Europe. Although this phenomenon is most prominent in some Asian countries such as China, Korea, and Taiwan—where internet addiction has been coined as "digital dope" or new "opiate war" and considered a public health crisis—more media reports and mental health professional discourse have appeared in the US in the past decade regarding internet-related addiction or internet use disorder. The prevalence rates of internet addiction is somewhat inconsistent, possibly because of different researchers' adopting different operational definitions for the concept of internet use disorder, different measurement tools and research designs, and different age groups (Sun, 2013a). Two US studies (on nongeneral populations, basically on adolescents and young adults) found the rates to be 8.1% (Morahan-Martin & Schumacher, cited in Sun, 2013a) and 8.5% (Gentile, cited in Sun, 2013a). Other studies found the rates in the US and Europe to be between 1.5% and 8.2% (cited in Cash et al., 2012). Sun's review of several non-US studies (nongeneral populations, mostly young adults and adolescents) found the rates to be between 6% and 23%.

The advent of the computer and the internet, likewise, have created new vectors and new environments to promote the old addictions like pornography or gambling. To take pornography as an example: Although evidence has indicated the attraction to pornographic materials in ancient Indian, Greek, and Roman art, people's contact with such content was limited by various factors, such as geography and social status (Pappas, cited in Sirianni & Vishwanath, 2016). However, owing to the internet, pornography today has become much more accessible, with an "unprecedented dissemination." It was estimated that the internet porn audience is between about 40 million and 100 million in the US (Sirianni & Vishwanath, 2016). Cooper's (1998) often-cited Triple-A Engine—accessibility, affordability, and anonymity—explains the global dissemination of internet pornography. The availability of mobile phones and other portable devices has further made porn access easier, which could lead to more frequent use and subsequently addiction and negative consequences in the areas such as emotion, couple relationships, and work performance (Sirianni & Vishwanath, 2016). Moreover, Wood (2011) suggests that the internet sex path not only increases access to pornographic materials but also may affect a person's ego and superego functioning among a small group of those who access internet sex, facilitating escalation from casual use to compulsive use to illegal use, and eventually to contact and sexual offending against a minor. Food addiction has also been linked to social change. For example, there was exponential growth in the number of fast-food restaurants in the US from about 600 in 1958 to 140,000 by 1980, and to an estimated 222,000 in 2010 (Paeratakul et al., 2003; Fortuna, 2012). One of the factors contributing to the corresponding obesity epidemic may be binge eating / food addiction as the restaurants provide easy and affordable access to high consumption of palatable foods (Fortuna, 2012; Volkow & Wise, 2005).

Despite that more and more mental health and addiction treatment professionals have encountered patients who seek help for their behavioral addiction problems—such as addiction to technology, internet gaming, social media, internet pornography, and sex—or families who seek such help for their significant others (Duffy et al., 2016; Sun & Cash, 2017), that mainstream media in the US has reported actual cases of digital addiction (for example, the ABC's May 19, 2017, "20/20 special: Digital Addiction?"), and that more and more MRI, fMRI, and other studies have revealed evidence on the similarities between how both the substance addiction and the behavioral addiction affect our brains (Ko et al., 2009; Ko et al., 2013; Love et al., 2015; Luijten et al., 2014; Weinstein et al., 2017), the journey to shift the paradigm from the notion that addiction only pertains to substance addiction to the notion that addiction can include both substance addiction and behavioral addiction is not without roadblocks.

Although suggesting "some evidence has been found for similar neural deficits" between substance dependence and behavioral addictions, Luijten and colleagues' review (2014) concluded that "however, studies are scarce and results are not yet conclusive" (p. 149). Based on literature review, Sun (2013b) identified several roadblocks that contribute to the ambivalence and struggle with regard to the recognition of behavioral addiction as bona fide addiction. In addition to concerns such as how the existing studies on behavioral addiction lack scientifically rigorous designs and that behavioral addiction—such as internet gaming disorder—usually co-occurs with other psychiatric or mental disorders, and therefore it's important to disentangle the two and ascertain the internet gaming disorder not as just a by-product of some other mental disorder such as depression, ADHD, or autism spectrum disorder, one major issue is that labeling "behavioral addiction" as addiction may involve too low of a threshold—if every satisfied urge or desire (for example, from an illicit drug to fashionable handbags) can be considered as a symptom manifested from addiction, the term "addiction" will explain everything but then also virtually nothing. This perspective may be related to the relatively lower prevalence rates of various behavioral addictions compared to substance addiction. It could also be because of society's stereotypical views on behavioral vs. substance addiction. On one hand, society may perceive many abused drugs as illegal and therefore vicious and harmful, and excessive drinking as posing hazards to public health such as drunk driving. On the other hand, society may view many behavioral addictions—such as food addiction (binge-eating disorders), hypersexual disorder, internet use disorder, pathological gambling, or compulsive shopping—as extensions of normal human needs and behavior, and are therefore personal lifestyles or less harmful leisure activities.

Not only does society have some concern, but also some mental health professionals and scholars have similar unease about the possibility of over-prescribing. They fear that the identification and targeting of behavioral addiction may pathologize everyday life behavior and create "diagnostic inflation" and "false epidemics" (e.g., Frances & Widiger, 2012). Allen Frances, a psychiatrist and the chair of the 1994 DSM-IV task force, said that the *DSM-5* task force members are completely naïve regarding how the contents in the book are converted to the real world. Recently, Billieux et al. (2015) also raised a similar concern in their article, "Are we overpathologizing everyday life? A tenable blueprint for behavioral addiction research." They discuss "how the use of atheoretical and confirmatory research approaches may result in the identification of an unlimited list of 'new' behavioral addiction" and propose that more research is needed to help us shift "from a mere criteria-based approach toward an approach focusing on the psychological process involved" (p. 119). In fact, researchers have established at least 3 dimensions to determine the existence of a true addiction. To establish a "new addiction," we must have data to support its existence phenomenologically (clinical features), neurobiologically, and genetically (Potenza, 2015). In his commentary on Billieux et al.'s article, Potenza (2015) used gambling disorder as an example to reconcile the issue. He states,

a systematic approach should be undertaken when considering whether a behavior may constitute the focus of an addiction. Such an approach was taken in the re- classification of pathological gambling (now gambling disorder) from a category of 'Impulse-control Disorders . . . Not Elsewhere Classified' in DSM-IV-TR . . . to one of 'Substance-related and Addictive Disorders' in DSM-5 . . . In this case, several research workgroups considered pathological gambling and other disorders characterized by impaired impulse control. Similarities with and differences from substance-use disorders (conditions well established as addictions) were reviewed, systematically considering data from epidemiological, clinical, phenomenological, psychological, genetic, neurobiological, cultural and other domains . . .

Such an approach, one that focuses on incorporating findings from a broad range of domains, will be important pursue with a range of potentially addictive behaviors (e.g., gaming, forms of Internet use, sex, shopping and eating) to consider the extent to which each one may have addictive potential.

(p. 140)

Thege et al.'s (2015) recently published study, "Natural Course of Behavioral Addictions: A 5-Year Longitudinal Study," raises yet another doubt about behavioral addiction being a bona fide addiction. Based on their study findings, these authors assert that "self-identified excessive exercising, sexual behavior, shopping, online chatting, video gaming, and/or eating tend to be fairly transient for most people" (p. 1, online publication) and that "The overall patterning of the results concerning help-seeking and symptom trajectories over time suggests that the largest part of the change in symptom severity of excessive behaviors . . . is to be considered as spontaneous and not (professionally) assisted recovery. This aspect of our results is against a conceptualization of addictions as progressive without treatment" (p. 12, online publication). To many researchers and clinicians (including the author of this book), Thege and colleagues' assertion seems like déjà vu. Similar debate has occurred previously, such as arguing whether alcohol and drug use disorder is a (brain) disease or simply a disorder of choice. For example, some scholars found that many individuals afflicted with substance abuse problems actually do not experience the problems chronically and they have unassisted recovery; they therefore suggest "addiction" to be a choice rather than a chronic disease (Heymen, 2009; also see discussions in Chapter 2). To reconcile this issue, it is reasonable to say that substance use disorder involves a continuum ranging from mild, moderate, to severe, with only a small portion of clients falling into the severe category (Volkow & Koob, 2015). Only those individuals who fall into the high severity category should be considered addicted, and it is usually only them who end up in treatment. The same notion can be applied to behavioral addiction. *Excessive* users—be it gamblers, gamers, or pornography consumers, for example—are not necessarily *addicted* users. To become addicted, excessive use is necessary; however, excessive use does not equal addiction and will not necessarily result in addiction. Excessive use has the potential to lead to addiction only among a smaller group of individuals who are vulnerable to or at risk for addiction genetically and environmentally. Excessive users may be more likely to recover on their own, whereas addicted users often suffer the progressive course of a chronic disease and require professional treatment.

Although the concept of behavioral addiction still faces challenges in its being recognized as a formal addiction today, the issue of "behavioral addiction" has drawn more attention and discourse from society and the field has made some progress in addressing the behavioral addiction issue in the past decade. The American Society of Addiction Medicine (ASAM; Mee-Lee, et al., 2013) has recognized behavioral addiction as addiction along with substance addiction. According to ASAM (2013, pp. 10–11), "Addiction is a primary, chronic disease of brain reward, motivation, memory and related circuitry. Dysfunction in these circuits leads to characteristic biological, psychological, social and spiritual manifestations. This is reflected in an individual pathologically pursuing reward and/or relief *by substance use and other behaviors*" and that addiction can also involve impaired control over behaviors (such as gambling) that do not involve psychoactive substance use. Likewise, in its 2013 update, the *Diagnostic and Statistical Manual of Mental Disorders* (5th ed.; *DSM-5*; American Psychiatric Association [APA], 2013) moved gambling disorder from the previous category of "Impulse-Control Disorder, Not Elsewhere Classified" to under the same umbrella of "Substance-Related and Addictive Disorders" with substance use disorders. Moreover, the *DSM-5* acknowledges the high prevalence of "internet use disorder," specifically internet gaming disorder, stating that "the seemingly high prevalence rates, both in Asian countries and, to a lesser extent, in the West, justified inclusion of this disorder in Section III of DSM-5" (p. 796). The reason the *DSM-5* includes internet gaming disorder only in Section III, which contains "emerging measures and models," rather than in Section II, which covers formal diagnoses, was because the APA committees felt the field still has insufficient knowledge about this disorder and especially that "an understanding of the natural histories of cases [afflicted with internet addiction], with or without treatment, is still missing" (p. 796).

Additional progression includes research, funding, and establishment of treatment programs. For example, behavioral addiction research has been bourgeoning since the time when Isaac Marks introduced the concept of "non-chemical addictions" in 1990. There were about 250 behavioral addiction papers published in key addiction-related journals in 1990; in 2000, more than 500 were published; in 2010, close to 2000 were published; and in 2013, more than 2500 were published. Moreover, the *Journal of Behavioral Addictions* was established in 2012, with the aim being "to create a forum for the scientific information exchange with regard to behavioral addictions. The journal is a broad focused interdisciplinary one that publishes manuscripts on different approaches of non-substance addictions, research reports focusing on the addictive patterns of various behaviors, especially disorders of the impulsive-compulsive spectrum" (*Journal of Behavioral Addictions* website, n.d.). Also, in 2017, for the first time the National Institutes of Health is funding a research project that targets internet addiction to be conducted at the University of Connecticut School of Medicine, with an aim to help determine whether internet addiction, especially online gaming, should be considered a true independent mental health disorder in the *DSM* (Booth, 2017).

To advance the behavioral addiction movement, it's critical to continue and expand more sound research, as well as provide training in the area. Research is needed to justify the inclusion of behavioral addiction, such as internet gaming or sex addiction, in the formal classification in the *DSM*, which in turn will get the treatment programs or clinicians reimbursed by patients' health insurance. Although behavioral addiction affects all walks of life, it's likely that only those who are more well-to-do can afford the treatment expenses, as most internet addiction or sex addiction treatment programs cannot get reimbursed from insurance for services rendered and patients have to pay out of pocket (personal communication with Dr. Hilarie Cash, reSTART Life, October, 2017). Research is critical also because studying both behavioral and substance addictions may synergistically potentiate our understanding of the phenomenon of addiction overall as well as each category specifically (Sun, 2013b). In addition, although treatment methods and strategies for substance addiction, such as cognitive behavioral therapy, can be applied to treating behavioral addiction such as internet addiction, and although patients can participate in various addiction-specific self-help groups, such as Gamblers Anonymous, Technology Addiction Anonymous, and Love and Sex Addiction Anonymous, still behavioral addiction specific treatment strategies need to be developed. For example, we have pharmacotherapy for alcohol addiction and heroin addiction, but no FDA-approved medications for treating behavioral addiction so far. Training is another urgent issue facing the professional community. Clinicians are encountering more patients who are afflicted with internet use disorder or who have co-occurring disorders, such as ADHD + internet gaming addiction or Autism spectrum disorder + internet addiction, but they do not know how to treat those problems. Likewise, many clinicians have faced the situations that more clients are revealing their habitual use of pornography in counseling sessions. Although these clinicians perceive addiction to pornography a problem worth treating, they often are underprepared to treat patients with such addiction (Ayres & Haddock, 2009; Pyle & Bridges, 2012). Training clinicians to more competently treat their pornography-addicted clients is important because without appropriate knowledge and skills in pornography addiction management, clinicians are more likely to be guided by their own personal beliefs and biases in helping their clients regarding the issue, which may increase the risk of unethical treatment (Sniewski et al., 2018).

The Legalization of Medicinal and Recreational Marijuana

The legalization of medical and recreational marijuana in the recent decades has changed the landscape of marijuana use in the US rapidly and may create large implications for the field of addiction treatment and prevention, especially because such a social movement of putting an end to marijuana prohibition is grassroots based, promoted and facilitated via the voters and the general public with no significant feedback from the scientific, medical, or research communities (Weiss et al., 2017). As of 2017, there are 29 states plus the District of Columbia (DC) in the US that have legalized medicinal marijuana; furthermore, eight states—Alaska, California, Colorado, Maine, Massachusetts, Nevada, Oregon, and Washington—and DC have legalized recreational marijuana use for adults aged 21 and older. In other words, in spite of marijuana being a Schedule I illegal drug under the federal law, over 63% of the US population now live in a state where medicinal marijuana is legal, and over 21% of the US population currently reside in a state where they can use marijuana for recreational purposes (Carnevale et al., 2017). Although many factors may have propelled the marijuana legalization movement, such as the general public's perceptions that the existing prohibition policy has been unsuccessful as marijuana was the most-used illegal drug, that the existing prohibition policy has led to an unequal imprisonment of racial and ethnic minorities (Cerdá et al., 2012; Weiss et al., 2017), and that marijuana legalization and sale can increase tax revenue, as well as decrease crimes and therefore decrease costs related to the criminal justice system (Cerdá et al., 2012), one critical factor is that more and more Americans have come to believe that marijuana is not as harmful as it was previously perceived by society. They believe, on the contrary, that marijuana actually possesses various therapeutic functions, such as helping prevent nausea and vomiting for cancer patients receiving chemotherapy, increasing appetite for HIV/AIDS patients, reducing chronic pain, and decreasing seizures among children epilepsy problems (Issitt, 2014).

Although we should be more open-minded with regard to conducting more rigorous research to verify (or nullify) both cannabis' positive and negative effects on human beings, we should not deemphasize or dismiss what scientific data have already informed us. Scientific research findings have consistently suggested that heavy use, frequent use, adolescent onset use, and high levels of tetrahydrocannabinol (THC) can result in adverse consequences (Volkow et al., 2014; Volkow et al., 2016). Some proponents of marijuana legalization equate marijuana to alcohol, arguing that marijuana should be legalized if alcohol is legalized. What should also be accentuated in the similar context is that just like the phenomena of alcohol use disorders, underage drinking, and drunk driving, we need to address the subsequent implications of marijuana legalization to cannabis use disorders, underage use, and driving under the influence. Among all the issues, underage use is worth a great amount of attention. One very important concern is whether youths now will be more likely to perceive marijuana as less harmful and/or whether the underage use will now increase (like underage drinking).

The Impact of the Medicinal and Recreational Marijuana Legalization on Adolescent and Young Adult Marijuana Use

One very relevant concern of marijuana legalization is whether it will promote adolescent and young adult use. This issue is important because the brains of youths have not completely developed and are more vulnerable to the detrimental effects of drugs, and a person is more likely to develop cannabis use disorder or addiction with early onset use (Volkow et al., 2014; Volkow et al., 2016). Research findings so far seem to suggest that *medical* marijuana legalization has very little or no effect on precipitating marijuana use among youths (e.g., Choo et al., 2014), whereas the impact of *recreational* marijuana legalization is less conclusive and appears to point to the direction of increasing use among certain subpopulations of youths and young adults (e.g., Cerda et al., 2017; Kerr et al., 2017; Miller et al., 2017).

For example, although Wall et al.'s (2011) cross-sectional study showed that teenagers in states with medical marijuana legalization (MML) had a higher marijuana use rate compared to their counterparts in states without MML, these authors also suggested that teenagers in states with MML actually already had a higher cannabis use rate than those in states without MML in prior to the legalization. Hasin's review (2018) found that 16 of the 17 large surveys—including the Monitoring The Future 1991–2014 data, National Survey on Drug Use and Health 2002–2012 data, and other large databases that controlled for various individual- and state-level confounders—showed that adolescent marijuana use rates are not impacted by medical marijuana legalization. Hasin (2018) concluded that although the studies employed different research methodologies, their findings were consistent, in that they all indicate that there is no significant difference comparing adolescent cannabis use before and after instituting the policy of medical marijuana legalization.

On the other hand, study findings on the impact of recreational marijuana legalization (RML) are less conclusive and tend to suggest that RML increases youths' or young adults' cannabis use, especially among certain subpopulations. For example, Kerr et al. (2017) compared college students in Oregon state—where its RML became in effect in 2015—with college students in six other universities in states without RML, with regard to their cannabis use from before and after 2015 Oregon's RML. These researchers found that overall, there was an increase of marijuana use from before to after 2015 among students of six of the seven universities, and that such an increase was significantly larger among students in Oregon than in the universities in states without RML. However, the greater increase of cannabis use in Oregon occurred only for students who also had recent heavy alcohol use. Using the data from the National College Health Assessment, Miller and colleagues (2017) found that Washington State University students had a significant increase in cannabis use after its RML and such increase was greater than the predicted nationwide trends. Moreover, Miller and colleagues found that the groups of female students, African American students, and Latino students had the greatest change. Cerdá et al.'s study (2017) indicated that youths (8th and 10th graders) in Washington had a lowered perception of harmfulness related to marijuana use and an increased marijuana use after the state's RML. These authors also found that youths in Colorado did not show differences in the two regards after the state's RML. One possible interpretation is that youths in Colorado have been exposed to the pro-marijuana values and atmosphere in their communities.

Although marijuana legalization targets adults 21 or older, the decriminalization of cannabis use overall as well as the subsequent social acceptance have created an environment that may cause young people to assume marijuana is safe, acceptable, and therapeutic (Carnevale et al., 2017; Ryan et al., 2017). Ryan and colleagues state, "Although it is common for adolescents and young adults to try psychoactive substances, it is important that this experimentation not be condoned, facilitated, or trivialized by adults. Even the first use of a psychoactive substance may result in tragic consequences, such as injury, victimization, or even fatality" (p. e2). Moreover, Johnston et al.'s Monitoring the Future national survey results on drug use, 1975–2015 data, showed that the percentages of 12th graders who "perceived regular cannabis use as risky" have decreased from 78.6% in 1991, to 46.8% in 2010, and to 31.9% in 2015 (cited in Weiss et al., 2017).

What should clinicians and providers do in face of the rapid shift of marijuana legalization status? Brooks and colleagues' study (2017) found that most providers and clinicians consider marijuana to have high potential to be harmful, but they perceive themselves not sufficiently knowledgeable about cannabis and its health risks, do not feel comfortable discussing cannabis health risks with their patients, and want more training about marijuana. Brooks et al. commented that, "This uncertainty may reflect the state of the marijuana health literature, which currently show mixed results for a number of marijuana-related health measures" (pp. 4–5).

Adverse Consequences of Marijuana

Under the new era of marijuana legalization, it is critical for the clinicians, especially those who work with adolescents and their parents, to understand and convey information regarding adverse consequences of marijuana (Brooks et al., 2017; Hopfer, 2014); the detrimental consequences of marijuana use are most pertinent to adolescent onset users. Not only are the general public vague about the adverse consequences of marijuana, but also many clinicians and practitioners are unclear about these consequences and often do not feel comfortable discussing with their patients cannabis health risks and other safety issues (Brooks et al., 2017). Many clinicians have indicated that they want more education and training on marijuana (Brooks et al., 2017). Although research findings are not completely consistent regarding the adverse consequences of marijuana use, and although the research designs of some studies suffer from limitations in controlling for hidden rival variables (e.g., the negative outcomes could be due to other drugs if the marijuana user happens to also be a poly drug user) (Volkow et al., 2014; Wood & Salomonsen-Sautel, 2016), there is strong scientific evidence pointing to negative consequences among *heavy* or *regular users* and *adolescent onset users* (Volkow et al., 2014). Marijuana's detrimental effects may include following:

(1) Risk of becoming addicted to marijuana or developing cannabis use disorder (CUD). There is very strong evidence showing that a subset of marijuana users will develop addiction (Volkow et al., 2014; Weiss et al., 2017). Like alcohol, tobacco, or some other drugs, marijuana is addictive and can create addiction in a vulnerable person. Marijuana use may be a recreational activity, but cannabis use disorder or marijuana addiction constitutes a psychiatric disorder. As mentioned in Chapter 2, addiction or substance use disorder encompasses pathological behaviors such as impaired control (e.g., "persistent desire or unsuccessful efforts to cut down or control cannabis use"), social impairment (e.g., "recurrent cannabis use resulting in a failure to fulfill major role obligations at work, school, or home"), risky use (e.g., cannabis "use is continued despite knowledge of having a persistent or recurrent physical or psychological problem that is likely to have been caused or exacerbated by cannabis"), and pharmacological criteria (e.g., a "need for markedly increased amounts of cannabis to achieve intoxication or desired effect") (American Psychiatric Association [APA], 2013, p. 509).

Research has shown that about 1 in every 10 marijuana users will develop cannabis dependence syndromes (Hall & Degenhardt, 2009) or about 9% of individuals who engage in experimenting marijuana will develop addiction (Lopez-Quintero et al., 2011). The ratio increases when the onset of use is during early age as well as when the use is frequent—about 1 in every 6 marijuana users who start using as adolescents will become addicted, and about 25 to 50% of daily marijuana smokers will become addicted

(Hall & Degenhardt, 2009). Hasin (2018) says that many people consider the risk of development of CUD is rare, and this is probably based on the research findings dated back 25 years ago. Her review suggests that CUD is not only not rare but can be serious. She reports that more recent US data indicate about 3 out of 10 cannabis users developed DSM-IV CUD. Furthermore, among those who had used cannabis in life, about 19.5% met diagnostic criteria for *DSM-5* CUD; of those, 23% met the threshold for the severe category (> 6 criteria); of these, about 48% were unable to fulfill a major role (for example, work) (Hasin, 2018).

Factors fostering marijuana addiction may include marijuana withdrawal syndrome, early age onset of use, regular use, and high THC level of the marijuana. Marijuana can create bona fide withdrawal syndrome when a user stops using abruptly, including symptoms like sleeping difficulties, irritability, dysphoria, anxiety, and craving, all of which contribute to cessation difficulty and relapse (Volkow et al., 2014). Studies have also indicated that compared to individuals who start using marijuana during adulthood, the likelihood of developing marijuana addiction within 2 years post initial use is 2 to 4 times greater for those who start active using during adolescence (Volkow et al., 2014). It is well established that an adolescent's brain has not fully developed and is vulnerable to addiction (Gogtay et al., 2004; Mechoulam & Parker, 2013; Volkow et al., 2014).

In addition to augmenting depression, anxiety, or psychosis (Di Forti et al., 2009; Pierre et al., 2016), some research suggests that high tetrahydrocannabinol (THC) potency may also precipitate the risk of cannabis dependence (Hall & Degenhardt, 2009; Panlilio et al., 2015). Cannabis that is bred from a higher level of THC may contain a very low level of cannabidiol (CBD) content; research has shown that cannabis that contains low CBD may generate greater reinforcing effects and make the users like and want the cannabis more, potentially increasing the addictive nature of the cannabis (Panlilio et al., 2015). This factor is relevant considering the fact that, based on confiscated marijuana samples, the THC potency has been increasing from 3% to 12%, from the 1980s to 2012 (ElSohly, cited in Volkow et al., 2014). The THC potency can be even higher among cannabis in some stores in states where medical and recreational marijuana are legal. For example, THC for a retailer in Washington state in 2015 was 21.25%; in Colorado state, THC of some strains ranges from 28% to 32%

ADDICTION AND SOCIAL FACTORS

(Hasin, 2017). Furthermore, although Colorado legislators tried to reduce the THC level of the state's marked cannabis to about 16% during 2016, the local community did not support their efforts (Hasin, 2018).

(2) Risks for causing motor-vehicle accidents. Experimental (lab) studies have indicated that marijuana use severely damages driving skills. It impairs all areas that are practically linked to safe driving, including visual functions, cognitive functions (memory and perception of time), motor coordination, and complex tasks execution that demands divided attention (Ramaekers et al.; Sewell et al., cited in Romano et al., 2017; Volkow et al., 2014). In contrast, the epidemiological studies have shown that the risks of marijuana use resulting in car crashes range from low to high. Some epidemiological studies revealed only very modest contribution of marijuana to motor-vehicle accident risk or that "most marijuana-intoxicated drivers show only modest impairments on actual road tests" (e.g., Rogeberg & Elvik, 2016; Romano et al.'s review, 2017, p. 316). Other studies have demonstrated that the risks for a car-crash related fatality or injury are increased because of driving under the influence of marijuana or driving while intoxicated with marijuana (e.g., see Hasin's review, 2017; Salomonsen-Sautel et al., 2014; Volkow et al.'s review, 2014; Wettlaufer et al., 2017). The inconclusiveness could be due to the imperfect data used for the analysis and the imperfect models used to analyze the data (Romano et al., 2017). The inconclusiveness could also be because some cannabis users may intentionally drive slowly to avoid accidents, knowing that one's driving ability might be affected by the cannabis (Hartman & Huestis, 2013; Ronen et al., 2008).

Multiple studies have revealed evidence showing that cannabis-use impairment is dose-related (Ramaekers et al., 2004). One study reports that individuals testing THC positive, especially those who showed high blood levels of THC, were up to sevenfold more likely to be responsible for a traffic accident compared to people who had not consumed alcohol or drugs prior to driving (Ramaekers et al., cited in Volkow et al., 2014). This is concerning considering the trend of the increasing level of THC—the psychoactive component of marijuana that causes the impairment—potency over the years and under the current pro-cannabis culture. Studies have shown that the THC level has increased from approximately 3% to 12%, from the 1980s to 2012, respectively (Volkow et al., 2014). In addition, Washington state passed its recreational marijuana legalization in 2012, and it was found that the overall marijuana flower THC potency for a retailer in Seattle was 21.2% in 2015 (Hasin, 2018).

Combining cannabis with alcohol and/or other drugs also worsens the situation (Carnevale et al., 2017; Hartman & Huestis, 2013). Studies have shown that a combination of alcohol use and marijuana use results in a greater risk than only using one of the two (Carnevale et al., 2017; Hartman et al., cited in Volkow et al., 2014). Wood and Salomonsen-Sautel's (2016) study of Colorado's DUI citations found that although marijuana was the drug most cited among driving under the influence cases, marijuana tends to be used in combination with alcohol and/or other drugs. These authors therefore suggest that the current DUI laws must increase penalties for violations that involve polydrug use or a combination of a drug and alcohol. Liu et al.'s study (2016) found that "Unbelted drivers were over 4 times more likely to die in the crash compared to belted drivers . . . These are notable for drivers with both alcohol and cannabis who were 3.7 times more likely to be unbelted and drivers on alcohol were 3.5 times more likely to be unbelted" (p. 4).

(3) Risk for cognitive impairment / reduced school performance and lifetime achievement. The adolescence stage involves dramatic brain development; drug use, especially heavy and frequent use, during this stage and into young adulthood may lead to cognitive impairment (Hall & Lynskey, 2016; Meier et al., 2012; Volkow et al., 2014). One longitudinal study (43 healthy subjects and 22 treatment-seeking teenagers with cannabis use disorder) found compelling evidence that repeated marijuana exposure may result in harmful effects on adolescents' brain development, including brain resting functional connectivity, cognitive function, and intelligence (Camchong et al., 2017). However, stronger scientific evidence is still needed and studies replicated to verify a causal relationship between early onset of marijuana use and cognitive impairment, as the two variables could both be related to a third factor; or it could be that cognitive impairment has taken place prior to an adolescent's onset of use (Hasin, 2018).

Volkow and colleagues (2014) ranked the level of confidence "Medium" in the evidence in support of abnormal brain development as a result of marijuana use (as opposed to "High" in the evidence in support of developing marijuana addiction among users and in support of involving motor vehicle crashes among users). To better ascertain a causal relationship between early onset marijuana use and cognitive impairment, the National Institutes of Health (NIH) has launched a large-scale, longitudinal Adolescent Brain Cognitive Development (ABCD) Study (Hasin, 2018). The ABCD study is recruiting approximately 10,000 children aged 9–10 from 21 sites in the US (NIH, 2018), with the goal to implement brain imaging and neurocognitive research on children before the onset of cannabis use, and continue to evaluate them—some do and some do not use marijuana—repeatedly over a period of 10 years to verify their neurocognitive and various other outcomes (Hasin, 2018).

Various studies have verified the association between marijuana use and negative outcomes in multiple other domains in life (Hall & Degenhardt, 2009; Hurd et al., 2014; Volkow et al., 2014). The detrimental effects are dose related and especially prevalent among heavy and frequent users who start using during adolescence and into young adulthood; daily users are most affected (Hurd et al., 2014). These users are more likely to have a lower academic performance and educational attainment, lower later life achievement and less life satisfaction, worse mental health wellbeing, and an increased tendency to use illicit drugs, some of which could be related to their drug-affected brain function and structure as well as cognitive abilities (Hall & Degenhardt, 2009; Hall & Lynskey, 2016; Weiss et al., 2017).

Again, although there is an association between marijuana use and worse outcomes in several life domains, such relationships are not necessarily causal relationships, and more research is needed to clarify these issues (Hall & Degenhardt, 2009; Hasin, 2018). To take the effects of marijuana use on educational attainment as an example, Lynskey and Hall's review (2000) suggests that the poorer educational attainment is not necessarily caused by cannabis use per se but by the contexts that facilitate not only marijuana use but also other problematic behaviors conducive to low educational achievement. These social contexts foster cannabis use, as well as an anti-conventional lifestyle and gang affiliation, association with substance-abusing peers, and leaving school education and parental home early to assume adult roles. Verweij et al.'s twin study (2013) found that the relationship between early-onset marijuana and early school leaving is not causal—i.e., marijuana does not cause early school dropout or vice versa—rather, they both are affected by the third variable(s), i.e., the shared environmental factors or overlapping familial problem. Again, more studies are needed to clarify the issue, and perhaps, the ABCD longitudinal study (Lisdahl et al., 2018) that covers brain imaging and other areas of investigations can shed some lights on this.

(4) Risk for mental health issues in general and schizophrenia in particular. Although some studies have shown a linkage between chronic marijuana use and various mental health consequences, such as depression, anxiety, and suicidal ideation, research findings on such a linkage are not consistent (Weiss et al.'s review, 2017). On the other hand, there is strong evidence linking cannabis use to psychosis or full blown schizophrenia (Andreasson et al., 1987; Arseneault et al., 2002; Volkow et al., 2016; Weiss et al., 2017). The linkage between marijuana use and development of psychosis or schizophrenia is enhanced by factors like frequent use, heavy use, early-onset use, and cannabis use with high THC potency (Hall & Degenhardt, 2009; Volkow et al, 2016), as well as the factor of genetic susceptibility or a family history of schizophrenia (Caspi et al., 2005; Di Forti et al., 2012; Hall & Lynskey, 2016; van Winkel et.al., 2011; Volkow et al., 2016; Weiss et al., 2017).

Studies have shown the association between the level of cannabis use and the risk of developing schizophrenia, in that "ever use of cannabis" is shown to increase the schizophrenia risk by about twofold, and that "frequent use" or "use of cannabis with high THC potency" augments the schizophrenia risk by about sixfold (see Volkow et al.'s review, 2016). Considering the high THC potency contained in current marijuana, the subsequent negative consequence of marijuana use could be worse (Brady, cited in Volkow et al., 2014; ElSohly, cited in Volkow et al., 2014).

Genetic susceptibility also plays an important role in the connection between marijuana use and development of schizophrenia (Caspi et al., 2005; Di Forti et al., 2012; Hall & Lynskey, 2016; van Winkel et al., 2011; Volkow et al., 2014; Weiss et al., 2017). Three insights emphasized by Volkow et al. (2014) are that "cannabis use is neither necessary nor sufficient for the development of schizophrenia," that "most individuals who use cannabis do not develop schizophrenia," and that "having a close family member with schizophrenia is the strongest known risk factor for schizophrenia" (p. 294). Studies have revealed that the impact of cannabis use on development of schizophrenia is more relevant for cannabis users who are genetically vulnerable to schizophrenia, who have a family history of schizophrenia, or who have a history of psychotic symptoms (Caspi et al., 2005; Hall & Lynskey, 2016; Weiss et al., 2017). For example, Caspi and colleagues' study found that "[a] functional polymorphism in the COMT gene moderated the influence of adolescent cannabis use on developing adult psychosis" and that "[c]arriers of the *COMT valine* [158] allele were most likely to exhibit psychotic symptoms and to develop schizophreniform disorder if they used cannabis. Cannabis use had no such adverse influence on individuals with two copies of the methionine allele" (Caspi et al., 2005, p. 1117). Another study by Di Forti and colleagues indicates that "Carriers of the *AKT1* C/C genotype with a history of cannabis use showed a greater than twofold increased likelihood of a psychotic disorder . . . when compared with users who were T/T carriers" and that "[a]mong daily users, C/C carriers demonstrated a sevenfold increase in the odds of psychosis compared with T/T carriers" (p. 811). On the other hand, Volkow et al. (2016) considered an alternative theory, in that they suggest people who are at risk for schizophrenia may also be at risk for marijuana use. In other words, their theory states that marijuana use does not trigger schizophrenia, but both marijuana use and schizophrenia are triggered by the same or similar genes. Therefore, research is critical to ascertain the bona fide causal relationship between exposure to cannabis and the increased risk of development of schizophrenia among marijuana users with genetic vulnerability to or a family history of schizophrenia. Findings of these studies can help identify the population who should not use marijuana (Di Forti et al., 2012).

(5) Risks of negative effects on health. Research findings so far have not been consistent regarding marijuana's negative impact on a person's physical health. For example, Volkow et al. (2014) assigned a "Low" confidence level regarding the evidence showing a correlation between lung cancer and marijuana use. Hall and Degenhardt (2009) also found no links between marijuana use and the development of cancers of upper respiratory tracts. However, Hall and Lynskey (2016) detected

chronic bronchitis and diminished respiratory function among regular cannabis smokers. More research is needed in this regard.

(6) Increased odds of use of other illicit drugs. The question of whether marijuana is a gateway drug is a complicated question, and multiple theories are involved in an attempt to explain this issue. (a) Research has shown cannabis use does tend to take place prior to other substance use, with nicotine as an exception. (b) Marijuana is illegal for underage users, and underage users are likely to gain access to other illegal drugs via dealers or drug-using peers. (c) The same or similar genetic and environmental factors may serve as common liability for cannabis use and other drug use. (d) Exposure to marijuana use may alter an adolescent's neurobiological pathways, and subsequently makes the person more vulnerable to use other drugs. Regardless, research indicates that among most users of other drugs, marijuana often is the first drug they use, and that most marijuana users do not continue using other drugs (Weiss et al., 2017).

Treatments of Cannabis Use Disorder

SBIRT and Other Prevention Strategies The legalization of medical and recreational marijuana reduces both cannabis product prices and the social costs of cannabis use—in that cannabis becomes more affordable to purchase, it is safer and easier to acquire cannabis, its use will no longer involve criminal penalties for adults aged 21 or older, and, subsequently, after legal acceptance, cannabis use also becomes more socially acceptable—and have facilitated an atmosphere for society to increasingly view marijuana use as "acceptable, safe, and therapeutic" (Caulkins et al., 2012; Hall & Lynskey, 2016; Ryan et al., 2017, p. e1). Although research findings so far seem to suggest that *medical* marijuana legalization has very little or no effect on precipitating marijuana use among youths (Choo et al., 2014; Hasin, 2018), the impact of *recreational* marijuana legalization is less conclusive and appears to point to the direction of increasing use among certain subpopulations of youths and young adults (e.g., Cerdá et al., 2017; Kerr et al., 2017; Miller et al., 2017).

In addition to equipping oneself to become more conversant with laws related to cannabis use and more knowledgeable about cannabis and its health and other risks, clinicians can help prevent cannabis use among youths, as well as cannabis use disorders among (young) adults by implementing marijuana screening, such as SBIRT (Brooks et al., 2017; Levy et al., 2016; Ryan et al., 2017). Although there has been evidence indicating SBIRT's effectiveness for helping adults, there has not been sufficient evidence to suggest whether SBIRT is effective or not for helping adolescents (Ryan et al., 2017). However, considering SBIRT's available limited evidence and its low cost, the American Academy of Pediatrics and the National Institute on Alcoholism and Alcohol Abuse still recommend SBIRT to be part of routine procedures among pediatric practices (Ryan et al., 2017).

As mentioned earlier under the subsection of gender convergence in substance use, SBIRT represents screening, brief intervention, and referral for treatment. Based on the screening results, clinicians can decide what intervention needs to be provided to the patients, including education, brief advice, or referral for specialist treatment. (See above subsection "The Trend of Gender Convergence in Substance Use" for a more detailed description of SBIRT.) Alcohol and other drug (including marijuana) screening tools used for adolescents may include the CRAFFT (see Appendix A) and AUDIT (see Appendix B). Marijuana-specific screening tools may include CUDIT-R (Cannabis Use Disorders Identification Test-Revised, 8 items; Adamson et al., 2010) (see Appendix C) and CAST (Cannabis Abuse Screening Test; Legleye et al., 2013). CRAFFT was endorsed by the American Academy of Pediatrics and includes 6 yes/no items; a score of 2 or more is considered positive (Mitchell et al., 2013). A computer version of Brief Intervention (BI) can also be conducted with adolescents who usually prefer technology and consider technology salient (Walton et al., 2014). Walton et al. found that computer BI may be more efficacious than therapist BI, yielding clinically meaningful albeit small effect sizes in cannabis use prevention.

Marijuana legalization also makes it relevant and important to apply SBIRT among (young) adults. Historically, about 50% of treatment referrals that involve marijuana as the primary substance abused are related to the criminal justice system (Pacula, cited in Carnevale et al., 2017). The legalization of marijuana will dramatically decrease the exposure of adult cannabis users to the criminal justice system. In lieu of the criminal justice system as a main referral source for people in need of treatment for cannabis use disorder, now other mechanisms such as emergency rooms and primary health care settings should pick up the role to identify early people with cannabis use disorder and refer them for specialist treatment. Routine applications of SBIRT among patients in those settings will be one major strategy in this regard (Carnevale et al., 2017).

In addition to SBIRT and other BI techniques, clinicians can provide parents, especially those who use cannabis themselves, with guidelines regarding preventing their offspring from using cannabis. For example, education and counseling can be offered to make parents aware of how their own recreational cannabis use behavior may serve as a role model affecting their child's cannabis use—"actions speak louder than words" (Ryan et al., 2017, p. e4). In addition, parents' cannabis use may decrease their ability to perform the parental role fully when they are "high" on cannabis, as well as increase the risks of their child ingesting cannabis and secondhand smoke (Ryan et al., 2017). Parents should keep marijuana products and edibles—like other toxic items or medications—away from minors. Ryan et al. also suggested that parents discuss drug use case scenarios in general rather than share their own drug use history with their children.

Cannabis Use Disorder Treatment

In response to the movement of marijuana legalization and its potential impact, clinicians should not only better equip themselves with the updated knowledge regarding cannabis and its risks, as well as implement SBIRT or other prevention practices, but also be familiar with the available effective cannabis use disorder (CUD) treatment methods. Regarding pharmacotherapy, there is no clear efficacious treatment available for marijuana. This is similar to the fact that there is a lacking of pharmacotherapy for cocaine dependence; this is also in contrast with opioid, alcohol, and nicotine dependence where there is large evidence backing pharmacotherapy (Sherman & McRae-Clark, 2016). Although so far no medications have been approved by the FDA for CUD treatment, research in the area is active. For example, some promising medications may include zolpidem (Ambien), which is a sleep aid; buspirone (BuSpar), which is an anti-stress/anti-anxiety medication; and gabapentin (Horizant, Neurontin), which can help manage insomnia and possibly improve executive function (NIDA, 2018). CUD seems to be similar to other substance use disorders, but with less severe long-term clinical consequences; regarding behavioral therapy or psychosocial treatment, no unique treatment approach or modality has been developed for cannabis dependence (Banys & Cermak,

2016; NIDA, 2018). Similar to treatments for other substance use disorders, the behavioral or psychotherapeutic treatment strategies for CUD may involve motivational enhancement therapy (MET), cognitive behavioral therapy (CBT), and contingency management (CM) (Budney et al., 2007; NIDA, 2018). Although MET, CBT, and CM all show evidence of treatment efficacy, a combination of all three yields the most potent effectiveness for cannabis use disorder and fosters a longer term of abstinence (Budney et al., 2007).

The motivational enhancement therapy (MET) is not necessarily used to treat the person, but rather inspire the person's inner motivation to engage in treatment or to change (NIDA, 2018). Via the OARS approach—i.e., the clinician asks open questions; affirms patients' strengths; reflects patients feelings, perceptions, and points of view; and summarizes the themes and insights occurring in the counseling sessions—MET focuses on adopting nonconfrontational interviewing skills, building trust relationship with patients, addressing their ambivalence about change or quitting using, mobilizing and enhancing their internal resources and motivation for change, and developing goals and plans to help them achieve the change (Budney et al., 2007; Miller & Moyers, 2006; NIDA, 2018). (See Chapter 6 for a more detailed description of MET). Cognitive behavioral therapy (CBT) helps patients learn functional analysis, including identifying their problematic behaviors and antecedents that trigger their marijuana use or relapse, as well as developing strategies to avoid or counteract these triggers. CBT also teaches patients drug refusal skills and increases their problem-solving abilities (Budney et al., 2007; NIDA, 2018). CBT for marijuana dependence can be delivered in weekly group or individual sessions—each lasts 45 to 60 minutes, with a total ranging from 6 to 14 sessions (Budney et al., 2007). (See Chapter 8 for a more detailed description of CBT.) Adopting the evidence-based CM model for cocaine users, the marijuana CM intervention gives marijuana patients vouchers when they obtain negative urine analysis (UA) testing results, which are conducted twice weekly. The value of the rewards or vouchers increases with each succeeding negative drug testing result. Clients can use the vouchers for prosocial services or item purchase (Budney et al., 2007). (See Chapter 8 for a more detailed description of CM.)

For adolescent clients, the multiple dimensional family therapy (MDFT) and adolescent community reinforcement approach (A-CRA) can be additionally considered. Research evidence has shown that, although both approaches worked, the MDFT approach resulted in better treatment outcomes over 12 months compared to the individual psychotherapy approach among adolescents with cannabis use disorder (CUD); the MDFT recipients had fewer drug-using days and stayed in treatment longer (Banys & Cermak, 2016). Other studies have shown that age and co-occurring disorders may also play a role moderating the efficacy of MDFT and cognitive behavioral therapy (CBT). For example, Hendriks et al. (2012) found that younger adolescents may benefit more from MDFT, whereas older adolescents (e.g., 17 to 18 years of age) may benefit more from cognitive behavioral therapy. These authors also found that adolescents with oppositional defiant or conduct disorder or internalizing problems had better treatment outcomes in MDFT, whereas their counterparts without such co-occurring psychiatric problems tended to gain more from CBT. Schaub et al.'s study (2014) revealed that MDFT outperformed individual psychotherapy in treating CUD adolescents who came from conflict-susceptible families and adolescents who had both substance use and other externalizing problems. Developed by Liddle and colleagues, MDFT is an empirically supported, family based treatment approach for adolescents with substance use disorders. MDFT targets major domains in an adolescent's life, including the adolescent him- or herself, his or her parent(s), other family members, peers and friends, leisure time, and school and/or work (Schaub et al., 2014). A detailed description of MDFT can be found in the manual of *Multidimensional Family Therapy for Adolescent Cannabis Users* (Liddle, 2002). A detailed description of A-CRA can be found in the manual of *The Adolescent Community Reinforcement Approach for Adolescent Cannabis Users* (Godley et al., 2001).

Social Factors Affect Quality of Addiction Treatment Service Delivery

Social and macro factors can precipitate or curb the occurrence of addiction problems, as discussed above; these factors can also affect the quality of addiction treatment service delivery. Social policies or other macro factors may affect the types of addiction treatment available—for instance, some countries (e.g., the US) offer methadone treatment for opioid addicted patients, while other countries (e.g., Russia) prohibit it. The macro factors may also affect how the treatment is delivered—for instance, among the countries that do offer methadone programs, some countries (e.g., the US) allow both public/government and private ownership of the programs, while others (e.g., China) restrict ownership only to the public/government. The implications of these various cultural, social, and political factors and policies can have huge impacts on the wellbeing and recovery of addicted patients. This section includes four cases to explain the bearing of macro factors on service provision: (1) drug courts, (2) methadone clinics, (3) subsidized housing, and (4) the "five clocks." These four cases are not exhaustive, but are able to demonstrate the issues.

Drug Courts

Drug courts started in 1989 in Miami-Dade County, Florida, and were sparked by a group of visionary justice professionals who were "tired of the same faces and the same cases repeatedly appearing before the court" and who "decided that the system as it existed was broken and there had to be a better way" (National Association of Drug Court Professionals [NADCP], p. 1, n.d.). Also as a response to the overpopulation of prisons, drug courts reached every US territory and state by June 2012, and there were approximately 3,000 drug courts operating in the US by June 2015 (NADCP, n.d.; Tiger, 2011; US Department of Justice [DOJ], 2017). A drug court treatment approach consists of three main features: (a) it uses legal pressure to mandate individuals to get substance treatment; (b) it heavily monitors the treatment progress of the defendant through drug testing and providers' reports; and (c) it implements various incentives to reinforce progress (e.g., judge's praise, ceremonies acknowledging moving to the next phase of treatment, reduced required number of court appearances, and program graduation) and strategies to swiftly punish noncompliance (e.g., more frequent drug testing, fines, jails, and termination of drug court treatment and prison sentence) (Tiger, 2011). The types of drug courts may include adult, juvenile, family (child welfare), veterans, DWI (driving while intoxicated), tribal, co-occurring, campus, and so on (US DOJ). Perhaps because of the different historical background with respect to drug treatment policies and the varying cultural, social, and political environments, drug court treatment options are not available to addicted individuals in many countries. Today, 15 other countries in addition to the US, including Australia, Brazil,

Canada, Ireland, Mexico, and United Kingdom, have adopted a drug court treatment system (Gallagher et al., 2017; NADCP, n.d.).

Although it attempts to balance punishment and rehabilitation, and research evidence has shown its success in reducing criminal recidivisms among individuals with substance use disorder, drug court treatment in the US has encountered criticisms, including its "cherry picking" bias and low completion rates—both of which are related to the impact of macro factors on treatment service delivery.

Research has indicated that although a disproportionate amount of African Americans are arrested because of drug charges, racial distributions of drug court participants do not accurately reflect this disproportionality and the majority of the participants are Caucasians. Some statistics have shown that although African-Americans accounted for 35% of drug-offense arrestees, they only accounted for 21% of drug-court participants; in contrast, Caucasians accounted for 63% of drug-offense arrestees, and they accounted for 62% of drug-court participants (Huddleston & Marlowe, 2011). Racial bias may exist in picking qualified individuals for drug court treatment. Nicosia et al. (2013) found disparities in criminal court referrals to drug treatment between racial minority and White arrestees, such that, after controlling for variables like demographics and arrest characteristics, the odds ratios for diversion to drug treatment for African American arrestees were 0.68–0.73 versus 1 for the White arrestees (meaning for every one White arrestee referred to drug treatment in lieu of incarceration, only 0.68 to 0.73 African American arrestees received the same referrals, $p < .001$). Nicosia et al., therefore, suggested that disparities in diversion to drug treatment among drug-related offenders affect a great number of people and might fortify inequities in health and criminal justice outcomes, and that standardized policies are needed to improve drug treatment access and alleviate these disparities.

In addition to the fact that African Americans have unequal opportunity for selection into the diversion drug court treatment, another criticism facing drug court treatment is the low completion rate. As mentioned previously, traditionally, the resistance of drug court professionals to allow their opioid addicted participants to engage in medication assisted treatment (MAT)—such as methadone—may have led to some participants' dropping out of drug court programs. Another main factor is unemployment. Research has shown that African American participants in some drug courts seem to have a lower treatment completion rate than their White counterparts, and various factors may be involved, including unemployment (Brown & Zuelsdorff, 2009; DeVall & Lanier, 2012). Gallagher and colleagues' (2017) qualitative study of 31 African American drug court participants revealed that participants considered compassion and respect from the judge and case managers, and the camaraderie with other program participants, as the positive factors that supported them in completing the program. On the other hand, these participants suggested that it is important to help participants gain and sustain employment. They felt that people who are employed are more motivated to complete the treatment; in addition, they also felt that an imbalance between the requirements of drug court and the person's work responsibilities may adversely affect the preservation of a person's job. Gallagher and colleagues suggested that drug court treatment programs should emphasize helping African Americans with employment, both gaining and maintaining employment. These authors further suggested adding employers into the multijudicial treatment team—which basically comprises judges, defense and prosecuting attorneys, probation officers, case managers, and counselors—to maximize treatment benefits among African American drug court participants.

Methadone Clinics

Although methadone has been considered as gold standard treatment for opiate addiction in the US and other Western countries, about half of the countries globally prohibit such use (WHO, 2008). This is perhaps because some countries and societies—due to different cultural, social, and political environments—perceive methadone as being an opioid agonist itself and believe that it is not a true treatment and may possibly bring about more risks and negative implications, if using one agonist to "substitute" another agonist, such as heroin or other opioids. For example, the US legalized methadone use to treat opioid addiction in the early 1970s, while China only lifted its methadone ban in 2004 after facing the HIV/AIDS epidemic (Sun et al., 2016). Today, the Russian Federation still prohibits using methadone—an opioid agonist—to treat heroin or opioid addiction, and instead only allows naltrexone—an opioid antagonist (Woody et al., 2016).

Research evidence has shown that methadone not only relieves opiate withdrawal, but also diminishes the sedating and euphoric effects of opiates when methadone is at steady state, thus reducing both the negative and the positive reinforcing functions of heroin or other short-acting opiates (Bart, 2012). In other words, appropriately prescribed methadone can benefit opioid-addicted patients, allowing them to focus on activities that do not involve drugs, resume normal employment, no longer engage in criminal behavior to acquire opiates to curb urges, and avoid many dangerous drug-associated risks, such as HIV/AIDS and other contractual diseases (Bart, 2012; Marsch, 1998; Russolillo et al., 2017). Although methadone is an evidence-based pharmacotherapy, the macro factor may be one major force that prevents many opioid-addicted patients, globally, from accessing and benefiting from it (WHO, 2008). Even within the US, where not only methadone is legal but medication-assisted treatment is recommended to treat opioid addiction, macro factors may still play a role, blocking patients from receiving it. For example, as mentioned previously, some drug courts in the US stick to total abstinence principle and disallow their participants from obtaining methadone treatment (Matusow et al., 2013).

Macro factors can also affect how methadone treatment is delivered and subsequently how it affects the wellbeing of methadone recipients. For example, patients in some Asian countries may not be as fortunate as their American counterparts in this regard—they do not have a take-home methadone privilege system in place; it is not required for the clinic to provide psychosocial treatment in addition to methadone, and the methadone clinics do not offer flexible operating office hours. In the US, methadone clinics' operating hours usually are flexible—e.g., from 3 am to 12 noon—to meet the needs of patients who need to be at work before 9 am. In contrast, in China or Taiwan, the methadone clinics provide services adopting regular company operating hours, i.e., from 9 am to 5 pm, with 12 noon to 1 closed for a lunch break. This has created many time conflicts, struggles, and challenges for patients with employment. Some patients have complained that not only is it inconvenient that they have to come to the clinic *daily* to get the "juice," but also they suffer job-loss risks because of their frequent tardiness to work or that they lose employment opportunities simply because of the incompatible scheduling (Sun et al., 2016; Sun et al., in progress). This seemingly minute inconvenience caused by the macro system can actually have a huge impact on a patient's employment and quality of life, and in turn, his or her long-term recovery.

Subsidized Housing

This is an example demonstrating how policies may have been changed, but people who implement the policies have not—a macro factor that can jeopardize the goal and quality of the service delivery. The US Department of Housing and Urban Development (HUD) has recognized the importance of integrating people with criminal backgrounds back into the community to prevent homelessness for discharged inmates and their future re-incarceration. Although HUD has amended its stance toward housing applicants with criminal histories from one strike to second chance policies, many public housing authorities (PHAs) still stick to the one strike philosophy and have not updated the way they administer the program, i.e., they exclude people with drug conviction or a criminal history with violence (Tran-Leung, 2015; Walter et al., 2017). In 2011, the HUD Secretary Shaun Donovan emphasized that PHAs should give ex-offenders "second chances" and help them obtain housing (Tran-Leung, 2015). However, "nearly all PHAs institute more stringent bans than required by federal law" (Curtis et al., 2013, p. 37; Tran-Leung, 2015; Walter et al., 2017). As a result, some vulnerable populations who desperately need housing assistance but who have criminal histories are denied access, based on PHAs' "discretion."

Angelina was one of them. Angelina was a 30-year old Latina who used to abuse cocaine, and because of that, her four children, including a newborn, were taken away from her by child protective services. She was told by her social worker that one of the criteria that would qualify her to take her kids back was having a place, a home, for the kids. She had been living at a transitional housing, which is only a one-bedroom apartment without a kitchen and is too small for four kids plus one adult. Her external resources were scarce—both her mother and brother used drugs; she lost contact with her children's father, who was found later, but was sentenced to one year in prison for DUI and was unable to financially support the family; she, herself, has no car and has never previously been employed. She applied for the subsidized housing for low-income families but was denied because of her previous shoplifting criminal history (Sun, 2014).

Policies are important, but detailed regulations and implemental procedures and standards are equally important to successfully deliver the service and achieve the intended goal of the policy. Education, training, advocacy, creativity, and collaborations among various social systems and entities can also maximize treatment benefits. For example, in the case of Angelina, the substance abuse treatment system can work with public housing authorities and the child welfare system to best help her and her family.

The Five Clocks

The widely cited concept of "four clocks" is an example that illustrates how an addicted caretaker in the child welfare system may fall into service delivery cracks because of the different philosophies, rules, and timetables held by the various involved systems. The four clocks are: (a) the child welfare system (CWS) timetable, which requires parents to be evaluated by 6 months and a permanency hearing conducted at 12 months; (b) the alcohol and other drug treatment timetable, which often adopts the philosophy "one day at a time, for the rest of your life"; (c) the Temporary Assistance for the Needy Families (TANF), which imposes a timetable requiring clients to find jobs with 24 months; and (d) the developmental timetable for young children during their first 18 months, which is often a critical period for the child and mother to build bonding and attachment (Young et al., 1998). These different philosophies and conflicting timetables often create challenges and obstacles for recovering parents. Young and Gardner (2002) later proposed a fifth clock: she suggests different disciplines and systems should be flexible in their operating principles and should work together to maximize treatment benefits for the clients.

References

Adamson, S.J., Kay-Lambkin, F.J., Baker, A.L., Lewin, T.J., Thornton, L., Kelly, B.J., & Sellman, J.D. (2010). An improved brief measure of cannabis misuse: The Cannabis use disorders identification test—Revised (CUDIT-R). *Drug and Alcohol Dependence, 110*, 137–143.

American Psychiatric Association [APA]. (2013). *Diagnostic and statistical manual of mental disorders*, Fifth Edition. Arlington, VA: American Psychiatric Association.

Andreasson, S., Allebeck, P., Engstrom, A., & Rydberg, U. (1987). Cannabis and Schizophrenia: A longitudinal study of Swedish conscripts. *The Lancet*, December 26, 1483–1486.

Arseneault, L., Cannon, M., Poulton, R., Murray, R., Caspi, A., & Moffitt, T.E. (2002, November 23). Cannabis use in adolescence and risk for adult psychosis: Longitudinal prospective study. *BMJ, 325*, 1212–1213.

Ayres, M.M., & Haddock, S.A. (2009). Therapists' approaches in working with heterosexual couples struggling with male partners' online sexual behavior. *Sexual Addiction & Compulsivity, 16*(1), 55–78.

Banys, P., & Cermak, T. (2016). Clinical treatment of cannabis use disorders in adolescents. In *Marijuana legalization and youth: Briefings for California policy makers* (pp. 1–18). California Society of Addiction Medicine.

Bart, G. (2012). Maintenance medication for opiate addiction: The foundation of recovery. *Journal of Addictive Diseases, 31*(3), 207–225.

Billieux, J., Schimmenti, A., Khazaal, Y., Maurage, P., & Heeren, A. (2015). Are we over-pathologizing everyday life? A tenable blueprint for behavioral addiction research. *Journal of Behavioral Addictions, 4*(3), 119–123.

Blanco, C., Hasin, D.S., Petry, N., Stinson, F.S., & Grant, B.F. (2006). Sex differences in subclinical and DSM-IV pathological gambling: results from the National Epidemiologic Survey on Alcohol and Related Conditions. *Psychological Medicine, 36*(7), 943–953.

Booth, B. (2017). Internet addiction is sweeping America, affecting millions. CNBC. Published 10:45 AM ET Tue, 29 Aug 2017/Updated 12:12 PM ET Tue, 29 Aug 2017. Retrieved on 04/29/2018 from www.cnbc.com/2017/08/29/us-addresses-internet-addiction-with-funded-research.html

Bratberg, G.H., Wilsnack, S.C., Wilsnack, R., Haugland, S.H., Krokstad, S., Sund, E.R., & Bjorngaard, J.H. (2016). Gender differences and gender convergence in alcohol use over the past three decades (1984–2008), The HUNT Study, Norway. *BMC Public Health, 16*, 723.

Brooks, E., Gundersen, D.C., Flynn, E., Brooks-Russell, A., & Bull, S. (2017). The clinical implications of legalizing marijuana: Are physician and non-physician providers prepared? *Addictive Behaviors, 72*, 1–7.

Brown, R.T., & Zuelsdorff, M. (2009). Treatment retention among African-Americans in the Dane County drug treatment court. *Journal of Offender Rehabilitation, 48*(4), 336–349.

Budney, A.J., Roffman, R., Stephens, R.S., & Walker, D. (2007, December). Marijuana dependence and its treatment. *Addiction Science & Clinical Practice*, 1–16.

Burch, A.E., Rash, C.J., & Petry, N.M. (2015). Sex effects in cocaine using methadone patients randomized to contingency management interventions. *Experimental and Clinical Psychopharmacology, 23*(4), 284–290.

Camchong, J., Lim, K., & Kumra, S. (2017). Adverse effects of cannabis on adolescent brain development: A longitudinal study. *Cerebral Cortex, 27*(3), 1922–1930.

Carliner, H., Mauro, P.M., Brown, Q.L., Shmulewitz, D, Rahim-Juwel, R., Sarvet, A.L., et al. (2017). The widening gender gap in marijuana use prevalence in the U.S. during a period of economic change, 2002–2014. *Drug and Alcohol Dependence, 170*, 51–58.

Carnevale, J.T., Kagan, R., Murphy, P.J., & Esrick, J. (2017). A practical framework for regulating for-profit recreational marijuana in US states: Lessons from Colorado and Washington. *International Journal of Drug Policy, 42*, 71–85.

Cash, H., Rae, C.D., Steel, A.H., & Winkler, A. (2012). Internet addiction: A brief summary of research and practice. *Current Psychiatry Reviews, 8*, 292–298.

Caspi, A., Moffitt, T.E., Cannon, M., McClay, J., Murray, R., Harrington, H., et al. (2005). Moderation of the effect of adolescent-onset cannabis use on adult psychosis by a functional polymorphism in the catechol-o-methyltransferase gene: Longitudinal evidence of a gene x environment interaction. *Biological Psychiatry, 57*, 1117–1127.

Caulkins, J.P., Hawken, A., Kilmer, B., & Kleiman, M. (2012). *Marijuana legalization: What everyone needs to know.* New York: Oxford University Press.

Centers for Disease Control and Prevention (CDC) (2015). Today's heroin epidemic. CDC Vitalsigns, July 2015. Retrieved on 04/25/2018 from www.cdc.gov/vitalsigns/pdf/2015-07-vitalsigns.pdf.

Centers for Disease Control and Prevention (CDC) (2017a). CDC guideline for prescribing opioids for chronic pain. Retrieved on 04/20/2018 from www.cdc.gov/drugoverdose/prescribing/guideline.html.

Centers for Disease Control and Prevention (CDC) (2017b). Prescribing data. Retrieved on 04/20/2018 from www.cdc.gov/drugoverdose/data/prescribing.html.

Center for Substance Abuse Treatment (CSAT) (2011). *Medication-assisted treatment for opioid addiction in opioid treatment programs.* Treatment Improvement Protocol (TIP) Series 43. HHS Publication No. (SMA) 08–4214. Rockville, MD: Substance Abuse and Mental Health Services Administration.

Cerdá, M., Wall, M., Keyes, K.M., Galea, S., & Hasin, D. (2012). Medical marijuana laws in 50 states: Investigating the relationship between state legalization of medical marijuana and marijuana use, abuse and dependence. *Drug and Alcohol Dependence, 120*(1-3), 22–27.

Cerdá, M., Wall, M., Feng, T., Keyes, K.M., Sarvet, A., Schulenberg, J., et al. (2017). Association of state recreational marijuana laws with adolescent marijuana use. *JAMA (The Journal of the American Medical Association) Pediatrics, 171*(2), 142–149.

Chapman, C., Slade, T., Swift, W., Keyes, K., Tonks, Z., & Teesson, M. (2017). Evidence for sex convergence in prevalence of cannabis use: A systematic review and meta-regression. *Journal of Studies on Alcohol and Drugs, 78,* 344–352.

Cheng, W.S., Garfein, R.S., Semple, S.J., Strathdee, S.A., Zians, J.K., & Patterson, T.L. (2009). Differences in sexual risk behaviors among male and female HIV-Seronegative heterosexual methamphetamine users. *American Journal of Drug and Alcohol Abuse, 35*(5), 295–300.

Choo, E.K., Benz, M., Zaller, N., Warren, O., Rising, K.L., & McConnell, K.J. (2014). The impact of state medical marijuana legislation on adolescent marijuana use. *Journal of Adolescent Health, 55,* 160–166.

Cicero, T.J., Ellis, M.S., Surratt, H.L., & Kurtz, S.P. (2014). The changing face of heroin use in the United States: A retrospective analysis of the past 50 years. *JAMA Psychiatry, 71*(7), 821–826.

Cooper, A.L. (1998). Sexuality and the Internet: Surfing into the new millennium. *Cyber-Psychology & Behavior, 1*(2), 187–193.

Csete, J., & Catania, H. (2013). Methadone treatment providers' views of drug court policy and practice: A case study of New York State. *Harm Reduction Journal, 10,* ArtID: 35.

Curtis, M.A., Garlington, S., Schottenfeld, L.S. (2013). Alcohol, drug, and criminal history restrictions in public housing. *Cityscape: A Journal of Policy Development and Research, 15*(3), 37–52.

Department of Health and Human Services (2016). HHS opioid research portfolio brief—Translating science into action. July 1. Retrieved on 05/10/2017 from www.hhs.gov/sites/default/files/opioid-report-v4-remediated.pdf.

DeVall, K.E., & Lanier, C.L. (2012). Successful completion: An examination of factors influencing drug court completion for White and non-White male participants. *Substance Use & Misuse, 47*(10), 1106–1116.

DeVito, E.E., Babuscio, T.A., Nich, C., Ball, S.A., & Carroll, K.M. (2014). Gender differences in clinical outcomes for cocaine dependence: Randomized clinical trials of behavioral therapy and disulfiram. *Drug Alcohol Depend, 156*–167. doi: 10.1016/j.drugalcdep.2014.10.007.

Di Forti, M., Iyegbe, C., Sallis, H., Kolliakou, A., Falcone, M.A., Paparelli, A., et al. (2012). Confirmation that the *AKT1* (rs2494732) genotype influences the risk of psychosis in cannabis users. *Biol Psychiatry, 72,* 811–816.

Di Forti, M., Morgan, C., Dazzan, P., Pariante, C., Mondelli, V., Marques, T.R., et al. (2009). High-potency cannabis and the risk of psychosis. *The British Journal of Psychiatry, 195*(6), 488–491.

Duffy, A., Dawson, D.L., & das Nair, R. (2016). Pornography addiction in adults: A systematic review of definitions and reported impact. *The Journal of Sexual Medicine, 13*(5), 760–777.

Eagon, P.K. (2010). Alcoholic liver injury: Influence of gender and hormones. *World Journal of Gastroenterology, 16*(11), 1377–1384.

Ehlers, C.L., Gizer, I.R., Vieten, C., Gilder, D.A., Stouffer, G.M., Lau, P., et al. (2010). Cannabis dependence in the San Francisco Family Study: Age of onset of use, DSM-IV symptoms, withdrawal, and heritability. *Addictive Behaviors, 35*(2), 102–110.

Ekwueme, D.U., Allaire, B.T., Parish, W.J., Thomas, C.C., Poehler, D., Guy, G.P., et al. (2017). Estimation of breast cancer incident cases and medical care costs attributable to alcohol consumption among insured women aged < 45 years in the U.S. *American Journal of Preventive Medicine, 53*(3S1), S47–S54.

Fattore, L. (2015). Reward processing and drug addiction: Does sex matter? *Frontiers in Neuroscience, 9*(329). doi: 10.3389/fnins.2015.00329.

Fattore, L., Melis, M., Fadda, P., & Fratta, W. (2014). Sex differences in addictive disorders. *Frontiers in Neuroendocrinology, 35,* 272_284.

Feldman, H.S., Jones, K.L., Lindsay, S., Slymen, D., Klonoff-Cohen, H., Kao, K., et al. (2012). Prenatal alcohol exposure patterns and alcohol-related birth defects and growth deficiencies: A prospective study. *Alcoholism: Clinical and Experimental Research, 36*(4), 670–676.

Fernandez-Montalvo, J., Lopez-Goni, J.J., Azanza, P., & Cacho, R. (2014). Gender differences in drug-addicted patients in a clinical treatment center of Spain. *The American Journal on Addictions, 23,* 399–406.

Finigan, M.W., Perkins, T., Zold-Kilbourn, P., Parks, J., & Stringer, M. (2011). Preliminary evaluation of extended-release naltrexone in Michigan and Missouri drug courts. *Journal of Substance Abuse Treatment, 41,* 288–293.

Fortuna, J.L. (2012). The obesity epidemic and food addiction: Clinical similarities to drug dependence. *Journal of Psychoactive Drugs, 44*(1), 56–63.

Frances, A.J., & Widiger, T. (2012). Psychiatric diagnosis: Lessons from the DSM-IV past and cautions for the DSM-5 future. *Annual Review of Clinical Psychology, 8,* 109–130.

Gallagher, J.R., Nordberg, A., & Dibley, A.R. (2017). Improving graduation rates for African Americans in drug court: Importance of human relationships and barriers to gaining and sustaining employment. *Journal of Ethnicity in Substance Abuse, *(0), 1–15. https://doi.org/10.1080/15332640.2017.1381661.

Godley, S.H., Meyers, R.J., Smith, J.E., Karvinen, T., Titus, J.C., Godley, M.D., et al. (2001). *The adolescent community reinforcement approach for adolescent cannabis users.* Cannabis Youth Treatment (CYT) Series, Volume 4. DHHS Pub. No. (SMA) 07-3864. Rockville, MD: Center for Substance Abuse Treatment, Substance Abuse and Mental Health Services Administration (reprinted 2002, 2003, and 2007).

Gogtay, N., Giedd, J.N., Lusk L., Hayashi, K.M., Greenstein, D., Vaituzis, A.C., et al. (2004). Dynamic mapping of human cortical development during childhood through early adulthood. *Proceedings of the National Academy of Sciences of the United States of America, 101,* 8174–8179.

Grant, J.E., Odlaug, B.L., & Mooney, M.E. (2012). Telescoping phenomenon in pathological gambling: Asociation with gender and comorbidities. *Journal of Nervous and Mental Disease, 200*(11), 996–998.

Grant, J.E., Potenza, M.N., Weinstein, A., & Gorelick, D.A. (2010). Introduction to behavioral addictions. *American Journal of Drug and Alcohol Abuse, 36*(5), 233–241.

Green, T.C., Grimes Serrano, J.M., Licari, A., Budman, S.H, & Butler, S.F. (2009). Women who abuse prescription opioids: Findings from the Addiction Severity Index-Multimedia VersionR Connect Prescription Opioid database. *Drug and Alcohol Dependence,* 103(1–2), 65–73.

Greenfield, S.F., Back, S.E., Lawson, K., & Brady, K.T. (2010). Substance abuse in women. *Psychiatric Clinics of North America, 33*(2), 339–355.

Haas, A.L., & Peters, R.H. (2000). Development of substance abuse problems among drug-involved offenders: Evidence for the telescoping effect. *Journal of Substance Abuse, 12,* 241–253.

Hall, W., & Degenhardt, L. (2009). Adverse health effects of non-medical cannabis use. *Lancet, 374,* 1383–1391.

Hall, W., & Lynskey, M. (2016). Evaluating the public health impacts of legalizing recreational cannabis use in the United States. *Addiction, 111,* 1764–1773.

Han, Y., Lin, V., Wu, F., & Hser, Y.I. (2016). Gender comparisons among Asian American and Pacific Islander patients in drug dependency treatment. *Substance Use & Misuse, 51*(6), 752–762.

Hartman, R.L., & Huestis, M.A. (2013). Cannabis effects on driving skills. *Clinical Chemistry, 59*(3), 478–492.

Hasin, D.S. (2018). U.S. epidemiology of cannabis use and associated problems. *Neuropsychopharmacology, 43,* 195–212.

Heffner, J.L., Blom, T.J., & Anthenelli, R.M. (2011). Gender differences in trauma history and symptoms as predictors of relapse to alcohol and drug use. *American Journal on Addictions, 20*(4), 307–311.

Hendriks, V., van der Schee, E., & Blanken, P. (2012). Matching adolescents with a cannabis use disorder to multidimensional family therapy or cognitive behavioral therapy: Treatment effect moderators in a randomized controlled trial. *Drug and Alcohol Dependence, 125,* 119–126.

Hernandez-Avila, C.A., Rounsaville, B.J., & Kranzler, H.R. (2004). Opioid-, cannabis- and alcohol-dependent women show more rapid progression to substance abuse treatment. *Drug and Alcohol Dependence, 74,* 265–272.

Heyman, G.M. (2009). *Addiction: A disorder of choice.* Cambridge, MA: Harvard University Press.

Hirst, T. (2015). A brief history of China's economic growth. *World Economic Forum.* Retrieved on 05/11/2017 from www.weforum.org/agenda/2015/07/brief-history-of-china-economic-growth/.

Hodgins, D.C., & el-Guebaly, N. (2004). Retrospective and prospective reports of precipitants to relapse in pathological gambling. *Journal of Consulting and Clinical Psychology, 72*(1), 72–80.

Hopfer, C. (2014). Implications of marijuana legalization for adolescent substance use. *Substance Abuse, 35,* 331–335.

Huddleston, W., & Marlowe, D.B. (2011). Painting the current picture: A national report on drug courts and other problem-solving court programs in the United States. Retrieved on 04/29/2018 from www.ndci.org/sites/default/files/nadcp/PCP%20Report%20FINAL.PDF.

Hudson, A., & Stamp, J.A. (2011). Ovarian hormones and propensity to drug relapse: A review. *Neuroscience and Biobehavioral Reviews, 35,* 427–436.

Hurd, Y.L., Michaelides, M., Miller, M.L., & Jutras-Aswad, D. (2014). Trajectory of adolescent cannabis use on addiction vulnerability. *Neuropharmacology, 76*, 416–424.

Issitt, M. (2014). Preface: The State of marijuana reform. In *Marijuana reform, the reference shelf* (pp. ix–xiii) (Volume 86, Number 5). Ipswich, Massachusetts: H.W. Wilson, a Division of EBSCO Information Services, Grey House Publishing.

Johnson, B.A. (2007). Naltrexone long-acting formulation in the treatment of alcohol dependence. *Therapeutics and Clinical Risk Management, 3*(5), 741–749.

Johnson, J.L., Ratner, P.A., Malchy, L.A., Okoli, C.T.C., Procyshyn, R.M., Bottorff, J.L., et al. (2010). Gender-specific profiles of tobacco use among non-institutionalized people with serious mental illness. *BMC Psychiatry, 10*(101). www.biomedcentral.com/1471-244X/10/101.

Johnson, P.B., Richter L., Kleber, H.D., McLellan, A.T., & Carise, D. (2005). Telescoping of drinking-related behaviors: Gender, racial/ethnic, and age comparisons. *Substance Use & Misuse, 40*(8), 1139–1151.

Johnson, R.M., Fairman, B., Gilreath, T., Xuan, Z., Rothman, E.F., Parnham, T., & Furr-Holden, C.D.M. (2015). Past 15-year trends in adolescent marijuana use: Differences by race/ethnicity and sex. *Drug and Alcohol Dependence, 155*, 8–15.

Johnston, L. D., O'Malley, P. M., Miech, R. A., Bachman, J. G., & Schulenberg, J. E. (2015). Monitoring the Future national survey results on drug use: 1975–2014: Overview, key findings on adolescent drug use. Ann Arbor: Institute for Social Research, The University of Michigan.

Journal of Behavioral Addictions website (n.d.). Retrieved on 04/29/2018 from akademiai.com/loi/2006.

Karpyak, V.M., Biernacka, J.M., Geske, J.R., Abulseoud, O.A., Brunner, M.D., Chauhan, M., et al. (2016). Gender-specific effects of comorbid depression and anxiety on the propensity to drink in negative emotional states. *Addiction, 111*, 1366–1375.

Kennedy, A.P., Epstein, D.H., Phillips, K.A., & Preston, K.L. (2013). Sex differences in cocaine/heroin users: Drug-use triggers and craving in daily life. *Drug and Alcohol Dependence, 132*, 29–37.

Kerr, D.C.R., Bae, H., Phibbs, S., & Kern, A.C. (2017). Changes in undergraduates' marijuana, heavy alcohol and cigarette use following legalization of recreational marijuana use in Oregon. *Addiction, 112*(11), 1992–2001.

Keyes, K.M., Martins, S.S., Blanco, C., & Hasin, D.S. (2010). Telescoping and gender differences in alcohol dependence: New evidence from two national surveys. *American Journal of Psychiatry, 167*(8), 969–976.

Khan, S.S., Secades-Villa, R, Okuda, M., Wang, S., Perez-Fuentes, G., Kerridge, B.T., et al. (2013). Gender differences in cannabis use disorders: Results from the National Epidemiologic Survey of Alcohol and Related Conditions. *Drug and Alcohol Dependence, 130*, 101–108.

Ko, C.H., Liu, G.C., Hsiao, S., Yen, J.Y., Yang, M.J., Lin, W.C., Yen, C.F., & Chen, C.S. (2009). Brain activities associated with gaming urge of online gaming addiction. *Journal of Psychiatric Research, 43*(7), 739–747.

Ko, C.H., Liu, G.C., Yen, J.Y., Chen, C.Y., Yen, C.F., & Chen, C.S. (2013). Brain correlates of craving for online gaming under cue exposure in subjects with internet gaming addiction and in remitted subjects. *Addictive Biology, 18*(3), 559–569.

Kolodny, A., Courtwright, D.T., Hwang, C.S., Kreiner, P., Eadie, J.L., Clark, T.W., & Alexander, G.C. (2015). The prescription opioid and heroin crisis: A public health approach to an epidemic of addiction. *Annual Review of Public Health, 36*, 559–574.

La Flair, L.N., Bradshaw, C.P., Storr, C.L., Green, K.M., Alvanzo, A.A.H., & Crum, R.M. (2012). Intimate partner violence and patterns of alcohol abuse and dependence criteria among women: A latent class analysis. *Journal of Studies on Alcohol and Drugs, 73*, 351–360.

Lee, J.C., Nakama, H., Goebert, D., & Alicata, D. (2015). Gender differences in reasons for methamphetamine use in an ethnically diverse population in Hawaii. *Journal of Substance Use, 20*(2), 93–96.

Lee, J.D., Nunes, E.V, Novo, P., Bachrach, K., Bailey, G.L., Bhatt, S., et al. (2018). Comparative effectiveness of extended-release naltrexone versus buprenorphine-naloxone for opioid relapse prevention (X:BOT): A multicentre, open-label, randomised controlled trial. *Lancet, 391*(10118), 309–318.

Legleye, S., Piontek, D., Kraus, L., Morand, E., & Falissard, B. (2013). A validation of the Cannabis abuse screening test (CAST) using a latent class analysis of the DSM-IV among adolescents. *International Journal of Methods in Psychiatric Research, 22*(1), 16–26.

Leshner, A.I. (2001, May). When the question is drug abuse and addiction, the answer is 'all of the above.' *NIDA Notes, 16*(2). National Institute on Drug Abuse.

Levine, A.R., Lundahl, L.H., Ledgerwood, D.M., Lisieski, M., Rhodes, G.L., & Grenwald, M.K. (2015). Gender-specific predictors of retention and opioid abstinence during methadone maintenance treatment. *Journal of Substance Abuse Treatment, 54*, 37–43.

Levy, S.J.L., Williams, J.F., & Committee on Substance Use and Prevention (2016). Substance use screening, brief intervention, and referral to treatment. *Pediatrics, 138*(1), e20161211.

Lewis, B., & Nixon, S.J. (2014). Characterizing gender differences in treatment seekers. *Alcoholism: Clinical and Experimental Research, 38*(1), 275–284.

Liddle, H.A. (2002). *Multidimensional family therapy for adolescent cannabis users.* Cannabis Youth Treatment Series, Volume 5. DHHS Pub. No. 02-3660. Rockville, MD: Center for Substance Abuse Treatment, Substance Abuse and Mental Health Services Administration.

Lisdahl, K.M., Sher, K.J., Conway, K.P, Gonzalez, R., Feldstein Ewing, S.W., Nixon, S.J., et al. (2018). Adolescent brain cognitive development (ABCD) study: Overview of substance use assessment methods. *Developomental Cognitive Neuroscience.* Retrieved on 04/19/2018 from https://doi.org/101016/j.dcn.2018.02.007.

Liu, C., Huang, Y., & Pressley, J.C. (2016). Restraint use and risky driving behaviors across drug types and drug and alcohol combinations for drivers involved in a fatal motor vehicle collision on U.S. roadways. *Injury Epidemiology, 3*(9). doi 10.1186/s40621-016-0074-7.

Lopez-Quintero, C., Perez de los Cobos, J., Hasin, D.S., Okuda, M., Wang, S., Grant, B.F., & Blanco, C. (2011). Probability and predictors of transition from first use to dependence on nicotine, alcohol, cannabis, and cocaine: Results of the national epidemiologic survey on alcohol and related conditions (NESARC). *Drug and Alcohol Dependence, 115*(1–2), 120–130.

Love, T., Laier, C., Brand, M., Hatch, L., & Hajela, R. (2015). Neuroscience of internet pornography addiction: A review and update. *Behavioral Sciences, 5*, 388–433. doi: 10.3390/bs5030388.

Luijten, M., Machielsen, M.W.J., Veltman, D.J., Hester, R., de Haan, L., & Franken, I.H.A. (2014). Systemaatic review of ERP and fMRI studies investigating inhibitory control and error processing in people with substance dependence and behavioural addictions. *Journal of Psychiatry Neuroscience, 39*(3), 149–169.

Lynskey, M., & Hall, W. (2000). The effects of adolescent cannabis use on educational attainment: A review. *Addiction, 95*(11), 1621–1630.

Marlowe, D.B. (2013). Achieving racial and ethnic fairness in drug courts. *Court Review, 49*, 40–47.

Marsch, L.A. (1998). The efficacy of methadone maintenance interventions in reducing illicit opiate use, HIV risk behavior and criminality: A meta-analysis. *Addiction, 93*(4), 515–532.

Martins, S.S., Sarvet, A., Santaella-Tenorio, J., Saha, T., Grant, B.F., & Hasin, D.S. (2017). Changes in US lifetime heroin use and heroin use disorder prevalence from the 2001–2002 to 2012–2013 National Epidemiologic Survey on Alcohol and Related Conditions. *JAMA Psychiatry, 74*(5), 445–455.

Matusow, H., Dickman, S.L., Rich, J.D., Fong, C., Dumont, D.M., Hardin, C. et al. (2013). Medication assisted treatment in US drug courts: Results from a nationwide survey of availability, barriers and attitudes. *Journal of Substance Abuse Treatment, 44*(5), 473–480.

Maxwell, J.C. (2014). A new survey of methamphetamine users in treatment: Who they are, why they like "meth," and why they need additional services. *Substance Use & Misuse, 49*, 639–644.

McNeese-Smith, D.K., Wickman, M., Nyamathi, A., Kehoe, P., Earvolino-Ramirez, M., Robertson, S., et al. (2009). Gender and ethnicity group differences among substance abuse treatment clients insured under managed care. *Journal of Addictions Nursing, 20*, 185–202.

Mechoulam, R., & Parker, L. A. (2013). The endocannabinoid system and the brain. *Annual Review of Psychology, 64*, 21–47.

Mee-Lee, D., Shulman, G.D., Fishman, M.J., Gastfriend, D.R., Miller, M.M., et al. (2013). *The ASAM criteria: Treatment criteria for addictive, substance-related, and co-occurring conditions.* 3rd ed. Carson City, NV: The Change Companies.

Meier, M.H., Caspi, A., Ambler, A., et al. (2012). Persistent cannabis users show neuropsychological decline from childhood to midlife. *Proceedings of the National Academy of Science, 109*(40), E2657–E2564.

Miller, A.M., Rosenman, R., & Cowan, B.W. (2017). Recreational marijuana legalization and college student use: Early evidence. *SSM—Population Health, 3*, 649–657.

Miller, W.R., & Moyers, T.B. (2006). Eight stages in learning motivational interviewing. *Journal of Teaching in the Addictions, 5*(1), 3–17.

Mitchell, S.G., Gryczynski, J., O'Grady, K.E., & Schwartz, R.P. (2013). SBIRT for adolescent drug and alcohol use: Current status and future directions. *Journal of Substance Abuse Treatment, 44*(5), 463–472.

Moran-Santa Maria, M.M., Flanagan, J., & Brady, K. (2014). Ovarian hormones and drug abuse. *Current Psychiatry Reports, 16*(11), 511. doi:10.1007/s11920-014-0511-7.

Morgan, P.T., Desai, R.A., & Potenza, M.N. (2010). Gender-related influences of parental alcoholism on the prevalence of psychiatric illnesses: Analysis of the National Epidemiologic Survey on Alcohol and Related Conditions. *Alcoholism: Clinical and Experimental Research, 34*(10), 1759–1767.

Munzing, T. (2017). Physician guide to appropriate opioid prescribing for noncancer pain. *The Permanente Journal, 21*, 16–169.

National Association of Drug Court Professionals (NADCP) (n.d.). History: Justice professionals pursue a vision. Retrieved on 12/10/2017 from www.nadcp.org/learn/what-are-drug-courts/drug-court-history.

National Institute on Drug Abuse (NIDA) (2018). *Marijuana*. Retrieved on 04/19/2018 from d14rmgtrwzf5a.cloudfront.net/sites/default/files/1380-marijuana.pdf.

National Institutes of Health (NIH) (2018). Adolescent brain cognitive development study. Retrieved on 04/19/2018 from https://abcdstudy.org/about.html.

Nicosia, N., MacDonald, J.M., & Arkes, J. (2013). Disparities in criminal court referrals to drug treatment and prison for minority men. *American Journal of Public Health, 103*(6), e77–e83.

Oliva, E.M., Maisel, N.C., Gordon, A.J., & Harris, A.H.S. (2011). Barriers to use of pharmacotherapy for addiction disorders and how to overcome them. *Current Psychiatry Report, 13,* 374–381.

Paeratakul, S., Ferdinand, D., Champagne, C., Ryan, D., & Bray, G.A. (2003). Fast food consumption among US adults and children: Dietary and nutrient intake profile. *Journal of American Dietetic Association, 103*(3), 1332–1338.

Panlilio, L.V., Goldberg, S.R., & Justinova, Z. (2015). Cannabinoid abuse and addiction: Clinical and preclinical findings. *Clin Pharmacol Ther, 97*(6), 616–627.

Panther, S.G., Bray, B.S., & White, J.R. (2017). The implementation of a naloxone rescue program in university students. *Journal of the American Pharmacists Association, 57,* S107–S112.

Parrino, M.W., Maremmani, A.G., Samuels, P.N., & Maremmani, I. (2015). Challenges and opportunities for the use of medications to treat opioid addiction in the United States and other nations of the world. *Journal of Addictive Diseases, 34*(2–3), 255–262.

Piazza, N.J., Vrbka, J.L., & Yeager, R.D. (1989). Telescoping of alcoholism in women alcoholics. *International Journal of the Addictions, 24*(1), 19–28.

Pierre, J.M., Gandal, M., & Son, M. (2016). Cannabis-induced psychosis associated with high potency "wax dabs." *Schizophrenia Research, 172,* 211–212.

Potenza, M. (2015). Commentary on: Are we overpathologizing everyday life? A tenable blueprint for behavioral addiction research. *Journal of Behavioral Addictions, 4*(3), 139–141.

Pyle, T.M., & Bridges, A.J. (2012). Perceptions of relationship satisfaction ad addictive behavior: Comparing pornography and marijuana use. *Journal of Behavioral Addictions, 1*(4), 171–179.

Ramaekers, J.G., Berghaus, G., van Laar, M., & Drummer, O.H. (2004). Dose related risk of motor vehicle crashes after cannabis use. *Drug and Alcohol Dependence, 73,* 109–119.

Randall, C.L., Roberts, J.S., del Boca, F.K., Carroll, K.M., Connors, G.J., & Mattson, M.E. (1999). Telescoping of landmark events associated with drinking: A gender comparison. *Journal of Studies on Alcohol, 60,* 252–260.

Rash, C.J., & Petry, N.M. (2015). Contingency management treatments are equally efficacious for both sexes in intensive outpatient settings. *Experimental and Clinical Psychopharmacology, 23*(5), 369–376.

Rehm, J., Taylor, B., Mohapatra, S., Irving, H., Baliunas, D., Patra, J., et al. (2010). Alcohol as a risk factor for liver cirrhosis: A systematic review and meta-analysis. *Drug and Alcohol Review, 29,* 437–445.

Robertson, A.G., & Swartz, M.S. (2017). Extended-release naltrexone and drug treatment courts: Policy and evidence for implementing an evidence-based treatment. *Journal of Substance Abuse Treatment.* Retrieved from http://dx.doi.org/10.1016/j.jsat.2017.02.016.

Robinson, A., & Wermeling, D.P. (2014). Intranasal naloxone administration for treatment of opioid overdose. *American Journal of Health-System Pharmacy, 71,* 2129–2135.

Rogeberg, O., & Elvik, R. (2016). The effects of cannabis intoxication on motor vehicle collision revisited and revised. *Addiction, 111*, 1348–1359.

Romano, E., Torres-Saavedra, P., Voas, R.B., & Lacey, J.H. (2017). Marijuana and the risk of fatal car crashes: What can we learn from FARS and NRS data? *The Journal of Primary Prevent, 38*, 315–328.

Ronen, A., Gershon, P., Drobiner, H., Rabinovich, A., Bar-Hamburger, R., Mechoulam, R., et al. (2008). Effects of THC on driving performance, physiological state and subjective feelings relative to alcohol. *Accident Analysis & Prevention, 40*, 926–934.

Rudd, R.A., Seth, P., David, F., & Scholl, L. (2016). Increases in drug and opioid-involved overdose deaths—United States, 2010–2015. *MMWR, 65*(50&51), 1445–1452.

Russolillo, A., Moniruzzaman, A, McCandless, L.C., Patterson, M., & Somers, J.M. (2017). Associations between methadone maintenance treatment and crime: A 17-year longitudinal cohort study of Canadian provincial offenders. *Addiction, 113*, 656–667.

Ryan, S.A., Ammerman, S.D., & Committee on Substance Use and Prevention (2017). Counseling parents and teens about marijuana use in the era of legalization of marijuana. *Pediatrics, 139*(3), e1–e6.

Salomonsen-Sautel, S., Min, S.J., Sakai, J.T., Thurstone, C., & Hopfer, C. (2014). Trends in fatal motor vehicle crashes before and after marijuana commercialization in Colorado. *Drug and Alcohol Dependence, 140*, 137–144.

Schaub, M.P., Henderson, C.E., Pelc, I., Tossmann, P., Phan, O., Hendriks, V., Rowe, C., & Rigter, H. (2014). Multidimensional family therapy decreases the rate of externalizing behavioural disorder symptoms in cannabis abusing adolescents: Outcomes of the INCANT trial. *BMC Psychiatry, 14*, 26. Retrieved from www.biomedcentral.com/1471-244X/14/26.

Schepis, T.S., Desai, R.A., Cavallo, D.A., Smith, A.E., McFetridge, A., Liss, T.B., et al. (2011). Gender differences in adolescent marijuana use and associated psychosocial characteristics. *Journal of Addiction Medicine, 5*(1), 65–73.

Seedat, S., Scott, K.M., Angermeyer, M.C., Berglund, P., Bromet, E.J., Brugha, T.S., Demyttenaere, K. et al. (2009). Cross-national associations between gender and mental disorders in the WHO World Mental Health Surveys. *Archieved of General Psychiatry, 66*(7), 785–795.

Sherman, B.J., & McRae-Clark, A.L. (2016). Treatment of cannabis use disorder: Current science and future outlook. *Pharmacotherapy, 36*(5), 511–535.

Shi, Y., Lenzi, M., & An, R. (2015). Cannabis liberalization and adolescent cannabis use: A cross-national study in 38 countries. *PLoS ONE 10*(11): e0143562.doi:10.1371/journal.pone.0143562.

Shogren, M.D., Harsell, C., & Heitkamp, T. (2017). Screening women for at-risk alcohol use: An introduction to screening, brief intervention, and referral to treatment (SBIRT) in women's health. *Journal of Midwifery & Women's Health, 62*, 746–754. doi: 10.1111/jmwh.12659.

Simapivapan, P., Boltong, A., & Hodge, A. (2016). To what extent is alcohol consumption associated with breat cancer recurrence and second primary breast cancer? A systematic review. *Cancer Treatment Reviews, 50*, 155–167.

Sirianni, J.M., & Vishwanath, A. (2016). Problematic online pornography use: A media attendance perspective. *Journal of Sex Research, 53*(1), 21–34.

Slade, T., Chapman, C., Swift, W. Keyes, K., Tonks, Z., & Teesson, M. (2016). Birth cohort trends in the global epidemiology of alcohol use and alcohol-related harms in men and women: Systematic review and metaregression. *BMJ Open, 6*(10): e011827. doi: 10.1136/bmjopen-2016-011827.

Sniewski, L., Farvid, P., & Carter, P. (2018). The assessment and treatment of adult heterosexual men with self-perceived problematic pornography use: A review. *Addictive Behaviors, 77*, 217–224.

Sun, A.P. (2000). Direct practice with substance abusing mothers in the child welfare system: A system perspective. *Smith College Studies in Social Work, 70*(3), 441–457.

Sun, A.P. (2007). Relapse among substance-abusing women: Components and processes. *Substance Use & Misuse, 42*, 1–21.

Sun, A.P. (2009). *Helping substance-abusing women of vulnerable populations: Effective treatment principles and strategies.* New York: Columbia University Press.

Sun, A.P. (2013a). Internet Addiction. In A.P. Sun, L. Ashley, & L. Dickson, *Behavioral addiction: Screening, assessment, and treatment* (pp. 131–161). Las Vegas, Nevada: Central Recovery Press.

Sun, A.P. (2013b). Historical Background of Behavioral Addiction and the Trend Today. In A.P. Sun, L. Ashley, & L. Dickson, *Behavioral addiction: Screening, assessment, and treatment* (pp. 9–33). Las Vegas, Nevada: Central Recovery Press.

Sun, A.P. (2014). Angelina: The story of a substance-abusing woman and its analysis. *Journal of Womens Health Care, 3*, 171. doi: 10.4172/2167–0420.1000171.

Sun, A.P. (2016). The gender factor in addiction prevalence, assessment, and treatment. Paper presented at the 2016 NAADAC Annual Conference, Minneapolis, MN.

Sun, A.P., & Cash, H. (2017). Factors related to the occurrence and recovery of internet use disorder. Paper presented at the 2017 National Association for Alcoholism and Drug Abuse Counselors Annual Conference, Denver, CO.

Sun, A.P., Chen, Y.C., & Marsiglia, F. (2016). Trauma and Chinese heroin users. *Journal of Ethnicity in Substance Abuse, 15*(2), 144–159.

Sun, A.P., Marsiglia, F., Ling, L. (in progress). Substance abuse among the Chinese: An examination of risk factors and treatment strategies.

Tanum, L., Solli, K.K., Latif, Z., Benth, J.S., Opheim, A., Sharma-Haase, K., Krajci, P., & Kunoe, N. (2017). Effectiveness of injectable extended-release naltrexone vs daily buprenorphine-naloxone for opioid dependence: A randomized clinical noninferiority trial. *JAMA Psychiatry, 74*(12), 1197–1205.

Thege, B.K., Woodin, E.M., Hodgins, D.C., & Williams, R.J. (2015). Natural course of behavioral addictions: A 5-year longitudinal study. *BMC Psychiatry.* doi 10.1186/s12888-015-0383-3.

Tiger, R. (2011). Drug courts and the logic of coerced treatment. *Sociological Forum, 26*(1), 169–182.

Tolia, V.N., Patrick, S.W., Bennett, M.M., Murthy, K., Sousa, J., Smith, P.B., Clark, R.H., & Spitzer, A.R. (2015). Increasing incidence of the neonatal abstinence syndrome in U.S. neonatal ICUs. *The New England Journal of Medicine, 372*, 2118–2126.

Tran-Leung, M.C. (2015). When discretion means denial: A national perspective on criminal records barriers to federally subsidized housing. Sargent Shriver National Center on Poverty Law. Retrieved on 04/26/2018 from http://povertylaw.org/files/docs/WDMD-final.pdf.

U.S. Department of Justice (DOJ) (2017). Drug courts. Retrieved on 04/19/2018 from www.ncjrs.gov/pdffiles1/nij/238527.pdf.

Van Winkel, R., Kahn, R.S., Linszen, D.H., Van Os, J., Wiersma, D., Bruggeman, R., Cahn, W., De Haan, L., Krabbendam, L., & Myin-Germeys, I. (2011). Family-based analysis of genetic variation underlying psychosis-inducing effects of cannabis: Sibling analysis and proband follow-up. *Archives of General Psychiatry, 68*(2), 148–157.

Verweij, K.J.H., Huizink, A.C., Agrawal, A., Martin, N.G., & Lynskey, M.T. (2013). Is the relationship between early-onset cannabis use and educational attainment causal or due to common liability? *Drug and Alcohol Dependence, 133*(2). doi: 10.1016/j.drugalcdep.2013.07.034.

Volkow, N.D., Baler, R.D., Compton, W.M., & Weiss, S.R.B. (2014). Adverse health effects of marijuana use. *The New England Journal of Medicine, 370*(23), 2219–2227.

Volkow, N.D., & Koob, G. (2015). Brain disease model of addiction: Why is it so controversial? *Lancet Psychiatry, 2*(8), 677–679.

Volkow, N.D., Swanson, J.M., Evins, E., DeLisi, L.E., Meier, M.H., Gonzalez, R. et al. (2016). Effects of cannabis use on human behavior, including cognition, motivation, and psychosis: A review. *JAMA Psychiatry, 73*(3), 292–297.

Volkow, N.D., & Wise, R.A. (2005). How can drug addiction help us understand obesity? *Nature Neuroscience, 8*(5), 555–560.

Wall, M.M., Poh, E., Cerda, M., Keyes, K.M., Galea, S., & Hasin, D.S. (2011). Adolescent marijuana use from 2002 to 2008: Higher in states with medical marijuana laws, cause still unclear. *AEP, 21*(9), 714–716.

Walter, R.J., Viglione, J., & Tillyer, M.S. (2017). One strike to second chances: Using criminal backgrounds in admission decisions for assisted housing. *Housing Policy Debate*. doi:10.1080/10511482.2017.1309557.

Walton, M.A., Resko, S., Barry, K.L., Chermack, S.T., Zucker, R.A., Zimmerman, M., Booth, B.M., & Blow, F.C. (2014). A randomized controlled trial testing the efficacy of a brief cannabis universal prevention program among adolescents in primary care. *Addiction, 109*(5), 786–797.

Weinstein, A., Livny, A., & Weizman, A. (2017). New development in brain research of internet and gaming disorder. *Neuroscience and Biobehavioral Reviews, 75*, 314–330.

Weiss, S.R.B., Howlett, K.D., & Baler, R.D. (2017). Building smart cannabis policy from the science up. *International Journal of Drug Policy, 42*, 39–49.

Wettlaufer, A., Florica, R.O., Asbridge, M., Beirness, D., Brubacher, J., Callaghan, R., Fischer, B., et al. (2017). Estimating the harms and costs of cannabis-attributable collisions in the Canadian provinces. *Drug and Alcohol Dependence, 173*, 185–190.

White, A., Castle, I.P., Chen, C.M., Shirley, M., Roach, D., & Hingson, R. (2015). Converging Patterns of Alcohol Use and Related Outcomes Among Females and Males in the United States, 2002 to 2012. Alcoholism: *Clinical & Experimental Research, 39*(9), 1712–1726.

Wilsnack, S.C., Wilsnack, R.W., & Wolfgang Kantor, L. (2014). Focus on: Women and the costs of alcohol use. *Alcohol Research: Current Reviews, 35*(2), 219–228.

Wood, E., & Salomonsen-Sautel, S. (2016). DUID prevalence in Colorado's DUI citations. *Journal of Safety Research, 57*, 33–38.

Wood, H. (2011). The internet and its role in the escalation of sexually compulsive behavior. *Psychoanalytic Psychotherapy, 25*(2), 127–142.

Woody, G.E., Krupitsky, E., & Zvartau, E. (2016). Antagonist models for relapse prevention and reducing HIV risk. *Journal of Neuroimmune Pharmacology, 11*, 401–407. doi: 10.1007/s11481-016-9659-8.

World Health Organization (WHO) (2008). Bulletin of the World Health Organization. The methadone fix. Retrieved on 04/17/2018 from www.who.int/bulletin/volumes/86/3/08-010308/en/.

World Health Organization (2014). *Global status report on alcohol and health 2014*. Geneva, Switzerland: World Health Organization. Retrieved on 04/13/2018 from www.who.int/substance_abuse/publications/global_alcohol_report/msb_gsr_2014_1.pdf.

World Health Organization (2015). WHO global report on trends in prevalence of tobacco smoking. Retrieved on 03/05/2018 from http://apps.who.int/iris/bitstream/10665/156262/1/9789241564922_eng.pdf?ua=1

Yau, Y.H.C., & Potenza, M.N. (2015). Gambling disorder and other behavioral addictions: Recognition and treatment. *Havard Review of Psychiatry, 23*(2), 134–146.

Young, N.K., & Gardner, S.L. (2002). *Navigating the pathways: Lessons and promising practices in linking alcohol and drug services with child welfare.* SAMHSA Publication No. SMA-02-3639. Rockville, MD: Center for Substance Abuse Treatment, Substance Abuse and Mental Health Services Administration.

Young, N.K., Gardner, S.L., & Dennis, K. (1998). *Responding to alcohol and other drug problems in child welfare: Weaving together practice and policy.* Washington, DC: CWLA Press.

Zhang, X.Y., Zhang, R.L., Pan, M., Chen, D.C., Xiu, M.H., & Kosten, T.R. (2010). Sex difference in the prevalence of smoking in Chinese schizophrenia. *Journal of Psychiatric Research, 44*, 986–988.

PART II

6

SPIRITUALITY, CONNECTEDNESS, AND HOPE

THE HIGHER POWER CONCEPT, SOCIAL NETWORKS, AND INNER STRENGTHS

The compulsive, chronic, and destructive nature of addiction has created enormous challenges for patients, their significant others, and clinicians; patients often are physically, emotionally, and spiritually drained by the time they seek treatment. They lose confidence that they can ever defeat addiction and turn their lives around. They mourn the loss of their precious youth and irreplaceable times in life, which have been mostly wasted in meaningless and futile addiction. The addicted person suffers stigma, trauma, rejection, isolation, loneliness, insecurity, shame, and guilt. This is a life in pain and despair, a life that is helpless and hopeless, and a life that desperately needs support, compassion, encouragement, and wisdom from sources outside of him- or herself. While the person benefits from "professional treatment"—such as evidence-based pharmacotherapy (Chapter 7) and behavioral/psychosocial treatment (Chapter 8), in addition the person needs to have his or her spirituality rekindled and hope re-instilled. It may take time to develop severe addiction; likewise, it demands an extended time to get out of addiction—for many, a lifetime with possible recurrence of relapse. With or without pharmacotherapy and behavioral therapy, to *initiate* and *sustain* the journey of recovery requires spirituality, connectedness, and hope. It is extremely difficult for an addicted individual without hope—and therefore without motivation and stamina—to pursue, engage in, and comply with pharmacotherapy or behavioral therapy, regardless of how evidence-based these treatments are.

This chapter focuses on instilling hope in our addicted patients by connecting them with a higher power, a supportive and caring social network, and/or their own inner strengths. Belief in a higher power is soothing and comforting, especially during difficult times. It provides hope and direction, increases a person's hardiness, and buffers the stressors and suffering in a person's life. However, "higher power" is a controversial concept that is subject to multiple interpretations and differing receptivity. For individuals who do not believe in a divine or mysterious higher power, a compassionate, affirmative, and instrumental non-using or recovering social network can be as inspiring and empowering. Such a social network can satisfy a person's needs for belonging and attachment, facilitate problem-solving, and uplift the person's spirit and hope. Furthermore, spirituality and hope can come from patients' inner strengths, which can be enhanced by helping them explore the meaning of life and deep personal values and encouraging their actualization of life goals, as well as teaching them skills to regulate emotion and live healthy and enjoyable lives.

Many patients with severe addiction hesitate to stop using, or to enter and complete treatment, because of the acute and protracted withdrawal symptoms, some of which are extremely painful (e.g., heroin) or even fatal (e.g., alcohol). They worry they would not be able to function normally once they cease use. One patient told me, "The pain and discomfort you get from heroin withdrawal is similar to if you get a bad flu, only 20 times worse!" They also show low self-efficacy with regard to relapse avoidance, and do not feel they are psychologically strong enough to resist the insidious drug craving and triggers, which are closely associated with cues of people, places, things, and stresses in their daily lives. They do not believe that their addiction is treatable and that their downward swirling lives will ever be turned around. Their brains and minds are completely occupied by concerns of when and how to find the next fix so they can "live normally," leaving no room for anything else, including aspiration and dreams for life. They consider "this life" to have been wasted and not worth fighting for; they submit themselves to helplessness, hopelessness, and despair. The prolonged addiction career not only erodes their internal resources—such as ambition, self-confidence, health, and dignity—and their external resources—such as properties, vocations, and relationships—but also

SPIRITUALITY, CONNECTEDNESS, AND HOPE

negatively affects their cognitive functions such that their "bottom up" brain systems may override their "top down" brain systems. Because of addiction, the individuals' views of themselves and others, as well as decision-making capacities, may have been severely twisted, and their subsequent behaviors may be against their core moral values, precipitate their "burning many bridges," and/or involve crimes. As Mustain and Helminiak (2015) explain, "As a symptom of addiction, addicts often experience an internal fragmentation. . . . [A]ddicts have little intimate understanding of themselves in terms of morals, values, beliefs, individuality, interpersonal relationships, and social roles" (p. 366). The destructive nature of addiction has driven addicted people to alienation and detachment from society (Mustain & Helminiak, 2015).

Spirituality, love, and compassion are important dimensions to be integrated with science on the way to well-being and health (Friedland, 2014). Friedland describes the story of Archie Cochrane from Cochrane's book, *One Man's Medicine*, underscoring the notion that spirituality and science are not necessarily mutually exclusive and, on the contrary, science alone is not enough: "[Cochrane] shared how as a doctor in a prisoner of war camp he cared for a dying patient who he initially believed was screaming in pain from pleurisy. With no medications at hand to care for the patient, he simply held the patient in his arms and noted that the screaming stopped almost at once. He recognized that loneliness, not pleurisy, was likely the cause of the screaming and that the needed balm was love and compassion rather than morphine" (p. 3). Wiklund's study (2008) suggests that it is important to address patients' spirituality and fulfill their needs for "a sense of community and attachment, confirmation and acceptance" when caring for patients with addiction problems, and that it is important that "patients feel alive and in communion with others" (p. 2435).

It is clear that spirituality does not equate to religion but may include religion; however, there is no consensus within the research and clinical practice community regarding the definition of spirituality other than it is multidimensional and diverse (Chen, 2010; Cook, 2004; Treloar et al., 2014). Spiritual well-being typically includes religious well-being and existential well-being. The religious aspect focuses on whether a person has a satisfying relationship with God, whereas the existential aspect addresses a person's perception of his or her life purpose and life satisfaction (Paloutzian & Ellison, 1982). Spirituality is about "responding to the deepest questions prompted by an individual's existence" (Chen, p. 365). Cook's review of 265 books and articles on addiction and spirituality revealed 13 concepts related to spirituality. Most frequent were "relatedness" (e.g., relationships, connectedness) and "transcendence" (e.g., a higher power outside self, "God as we understand him"), followed by "core/force/soul" (e.g., "inner feeling of strength," inner resources) and "meaning/purpose" (e.g., "meaning and purpose in life," "will to meaning") (p. 545). Johann Hari said it well: the opposite of addiction is connection. Many scholars seem to agree with him. For example, some researchers define spirituality as concepts "characterized by relatedness to self, to the environment, to the existence of a 'Higher Power' (that is not necessarily associated with God) and to the meaning in life that enables self-transcendence" (Chen, p. 367). Treloar et al. (2014) suggest that spirituality can be integrated into a person's recovery journey as "connectedness with self, others, and a broader perspective" (p. 36).

Following are three main approaches that clinicians can consider to instill hope in their addicted clients during their journey to recovery: the higher power approach, the social network approach, and the inner strengths approach. Specifically, the higher power approach involves (a) the Twelve Step philosophy and guidance and (b) spiritual well-being. The social network strategy encompasses (a) clinicians' unconditional and genuine regards and acceptance, (b) family-oriented treatment or psychoeducation, and (c) Twelve Step-oriented self-help groups (e.g., AA, NA) and non-Twelve-Step-oriented self-help groups (e.g., SMART Recovery). The inner strengths method targets (a) the will to meaning, (b) a developmental model, (c) emotion regulation, (d) the motivational interviewing (MI), and (e) the acceptance and commitment therapy (ACT). These ten units are singled out to highlight their functions in facilitating motivation and hope; their utility, however, is not limited to just lifting spirits and creating optimism among clients.

The Higher Power Approach

When everything has failed, it's soothing and heartening to know that one still has a place to turn to and rely on—that is, a higher power. According to the Merriam-Webster dictionary, a higher power is "a spirit or being (such as God) that has great power, strength, knowledge, etc., and that can affect nature and the lives of people." Human beings have inclination to rely on faith for support and strength (Laudet, 2006). As Alcoholics Anonymous (AA) has long preached, "A Power greater than ourselves could restore us

SPIRITUALITY, CONNECTEDNESS, AND HOPE   213

to sanity" (Alcoholics Anonymous World Services, Inc., 2001). Via the impact of AA and other Twelve Step self-help groups such as Narcotics Anonymous (NA), spirituality and a higher power have long been accentuated in the addiction field (Miller, 2013). Clinicians and researchers over the past several decades have shown a renewed interest in spirituality and its impact on treatment for addiction (Cook, 2004; DiClemente, 2013).

The Twelve Steps

AA's Twelve Steps include two major themes: to do God's/a higher power's will (e.g., "turn our will and lives to the care of God," "have God remove our . . . defect of character," and "carry this message to alcoholics") and to be empowered by God/a higher power (e.g., "sought through prayer and meditation to improve our conscious contact with God"). Alcoholics Anonymous was originally influenced by the Oxford Group—a Christian evangelical organization that emphasized "self-examination, acknowledgment of character defects, restitution for harm done, and sharing with others" (AA World Services, cited in Dermatis & Galanter, 2016, p. 511). DiClemente (2013) also states, "It is not a coincidence that the notion of 'hitting bottom' and the finding of a higher power in Alcoholics Anonymous are linked. This connection was supported by the notion particularly in some American Protestant traditions that success in business and life was a reward for living a righteous life and turning to God was the only way to turn failure into recovery or righteousness" (p. 1260). AA considers pathological narcissism—"selfishness-self-centeredness"—to be the root of alcoholics' problems (Sachs, 2009). Therefore, to reverse or repair the moral, psychological, and social damages caused by addiction, as well as make a healthy lifestyle sustainable and long-term, alcoholics are required to have a new frame of reference and must have an overhaul in their attitudes, mindsets, and behaviors. AA lays out 12 concrete steps or strategies in guiding its members through a process of surrendering to a higher power, including cultivating humility, making amends, and offering services to others.

The Twelve Steps of Alcoholics Anonymous

1. We admitted we were powerless over alcohol—that our lives had become unmanageable.
2. Came to believe that a Power greater than ourselves could restore us to sanity.

214 SPIRITUALITY, CONNECTEDNESS, AND HOPE

3. Made a decision to turn our will and our lives over to the care of God *as we understood Him.*
4. Made a searching and fearless moral inventory of ourselves.
5. Admitted to God, to ourselves, and to another human being the exact nature of our wrongs.
6. Were entirely ready to have God remove all these defects of character.
7. Humbly asked Him to remove our shortcomings.
8. Made a list of all persons we had harmed, and became willing to make amends to them all.
9. Made direct amends to such people wherever possible, except when to do so would injure them or others.
10. Continued to take personal inventory and when we were wrong promptly admitted it.
11. Sought through prayer and meditation to improve our conscious contact with God, as we understood Him, praying only for knowledge of His will for us and the power to carry that out.
12. Having had a spiritual awakening as the result of these steps, we tried to carry this message to alcoholics, and to practice these principles in all our affairs.[1]

To actualize the Twelve Steps—i.e., "doing the Steps," as many AA members refer to the process—demands courage, energy, and perseverance. The concept of a higher power not only provides directions and guidance but also communion and empowerment, all of which can inspire a person who is in anguish, confusion, and misery. The AA's Twelve Steps offer a new way of thinking and living. Its inclusion of "connecting with the higher power via prayer and meditation" further inspires its members to have faith, trust, courage, wisdom, spirit, and perseverance to continue "doing the steps" and actualize the essential principles and value orientation in their daily lives. A connection with God/a higher power and feeling close to this source of strength can soothe a person's anxiety and empower the person to engage in challenging but positive goals and tasks. AA's co-founder, Bill W., wrote of the recovering alcoholic,

> He finally realizes that he has undergone a profound alteration in his reaction to life; that such a change could hardly have been brought about by himself alone . . . With few exceptions our members find

that they have tapped an unsuspected inner resource which they presently identify with their own conception of a Power greater than themselves. Most of us think this awareness of a Power greater than ourselves is the essence of spiritual experience. Our more religious members call it 'God-consciousness.

(Alcoholics Anonymous World Services,
Inc., 2001, pp. 567–568)

Spiritual Well-Being

Although spirituality is intangible and its existence cannot be verified by science, research has shown that spirituality can be beneficial to health. Spirituality is associated with reductions in HIV progression, depression, anxiety, substance abuse, and gambling (Center for Spirituality, Theology and Health, Duke University Research Library, cited in Friedland, 2014). Spirituality can be considered as social support from the divine (Underwood & Teresi, cited in Laudet et al., 2006). The literature has consistently found that higher existential well-being is associated with higher self-esteem and lower depression (Ellison, 1983; Fehring et al., 1987; Genia, 2001). A safe and stable attachment to God associates with less distress, but an anxious attachment to God (i.e., uncertain of God's presence) associates with more distress (Bradshaw et al., 2010). Numerous studies have found that spiritual and religious beliefs and practices can mediate the relationship between stressors and quality of life, including buffering insecurity and vagueness when facing chronic illness, such as cancer, an HIV positive diagnosis, or AIDS (See Laudet et al.'s review, 2006). Those findings suggest that spiritual well-being can enhance a person's resilience and hardiness, especially when confronted with harsh reality or difficult situations.

Many studies have also shown the impact of spiritual well-being on addicted patients' recovery, including how it may reduce stress and subsequently decrease relapse. For example, Langman and Chung (2013) suggest that spirituality can help people deal with distress and buffer against the occurrence of psychological comorbidity. Noormohammadi and colleagues' study (2017) reported that the relapse group of opioid-addicted patients had lower scores of spiritual well-being compared to their non-relapse counterparts ($p. < .001$). Jones (2014, $N=113$ substance abuse patients in recovery) found that attachment to God and spirituality protect people from stress that could lead to relapse—people who perceive God as close and responsive reported a lower level of stress, whereas those who perceive God as unreachable or who are uncertain of God's existence reported a higher level of stress.

The story of Coss Marte, the founder and CEO of ConBody, perhaps can serve as a close-up of how faith in a higher power can turn a person's life around. Mr. Marte grew up poor and had made a living by selling marijuana, cocaine, and heroin during his teen and young adulthood years. He ended up in prison and later was sent to a painful solitary confinement because of an altercation with a prison officer. His sister wrote to him and suggested he read Bible Psalm 91—which, he said, totally changed his perspective on life. He stated in a CNN interview, "I began to believe that my purpose was to give back instead of destroying individuals around me. I realized selling drugs was wrong. What I was doing was not only affecting my son and family, but the thousands of people I sold drugs to as well." Today, Marte is successfully running a prison-style fitness boot camp. He also hires ex-convicts to teach the classes in order to give formerly incarcerated people a second chance and help them construct a bridge with society ("Ex-con transforms", 2016).

It is beneficial if a person embraces the higher power concept, as it can give a person guidance, strength, and hope. However, belief in a higher power or supreme being can be a very subjective and personal matter, and not all people are open to it. In addition, an initially very religious and spiritual person may lose faith in God because of significant trauma or crisis. For example, a young veteran who was a highly devoted believer may suffer from severe PTSD and may totally lose trust in God after exposure to excruciating killings in the battlefields. The person may never regain faith in God or it may take a long time for him or her to do so. Nonetheless, spirituality and fulfillment of the spirit can have broader meanings that embody love, compassion, wisdom, support, communion, affirmation, empowerment, and hope. They are not limited only to a divine and mysterious God, supreme being, or higher power. Spirituality or spirit can come from the empirical world, embodied in a supportive and caring social network, as well as a wholesome and mature inner self. For addicted individuals who oppose or do not prefer the concepts of a higher power or the Twelve Steps, clinicians could target these two areas to facilitate inspiration and hope.

The Social Network Approach

Human beings need both autonomy and community—"to feel free and still belong"; relatedness and connectedness are not only primary emotional and social needs, but in the broader sense also spiritual needs of a human being (Alexander, 2012, p. 1479). As Alexander states, "This is probably why forced dislocation (in the form of ostracism, excommunication, exile, and solitary confinement) has been a dreaded punishment from ancient times until the present, and is an essential part of the most up-to-date technology of torture" (p. 1479). Severe dislocation can cause anxiety, depression, rage, shame, boredom, and suicide (Alexander, 2012). Many addicted clients, whose relationships with families, significant others, and non-using social networks have been severely damaged as a result of their chronic, drug-related destructive behaviors, often end up associating only with substance-abusing social networks. Furthermore, addicted people may feel inadequate, inferior, or ashamed to interact with non-using people because of their involvement with drugs, addiction, or illegal activities. For example, a woman once told me, "I knew my aunt would accept me . . . but I felt so ashamed to go back to her 'cause I have not listened to her . . . I am a failure. I don't know how I can face her." Another woman who "chose to stay with dope friends and drug dealers one after another," said it's not because of drugs per se, but because these people always accept anyone and they were her only friends. A third woman said, "I never had any friends who were not using . . . Although not all of them, [nonusers] may look down on me" (Sun, 2007, p. 14). A man who avoided eye contact throughout the entire interview said, "I am more at ease interacting with drug users; I can be myself and talk about anything. I am very vigilant when interacting with nonusers. When people become aware of our past, they will discriminate against us. They may not know your past in the beginning, but soon they will" (Sun et al., 2016, p. 155). Although association with using peers may satisfy the need of belongingness and fill the communal void, research has indicated a relationship between support for substance use among an addicted patient's social network and his or her risk for relapse. That is, the more support for substance use within a person's social network, the higher the risk for the person to relapse (Longabaugh et al., 2010; Litt et al., 2009; Zywiak et al., 2009). Addicted individuals tend to have few or no social networks as they have "burned bridges" with most of their significant others or social circle, or they associate with peers who are also using, both of which deter their seeking treatment and hinder their recovery.

Many individuals become addicted to alcohol, drugs, gambling, or gaming because of their self-medication to cope with a lack of social support or dysfunctional relationships with others in the first place. Their active addiction brought in criticisms and stigma from society and non-using people, which further exacerbates isolation and alienation. Social networks can provide a person with concrete help and emotional support. Various scientific studies have indicated that a stronger and more supportive social network is related to better treatment outcomes (Dobkin et al., 2002; Fals-Stewart et al., 2004; Klostermann & O'Farrell, 2013; Rowe, 2012). In addition, the more non-using friends in a person's social support system, the less likely it is for the person to relapse (Longabaugh et al., 2010; Litt et al., 2009; Zywiak et al., 2009). Relatedness and connection to a healthy and beneficial social network can be enhanced through various formal and informal channels. Sometimes it can be as informal as media like radio or TV programs. Recently while driving home and listening to a radio show called *Delilah*, I heard a woman call in and send her gratitude to the show hostess, Delilah. This listener proclaimed the hostess as her champion because the hostess's broadcasts gave her the courage to finally leave an extremely abusive relationship. Although not a licensed therapist, Delilah's genuine caring and common-sense wisdom obviously moved the woman. Similarly, a former client of mine had a severe addiction problem, no family, and very limited social connection. Although he had never claimed to be an atheist, he did express that he had no concept of spirituality nor of a higher power. One day, unexpectedly, he mentioned to me how much he enjoyed Joe Osteen's TV program. He said Osteen's messages were "very uplifting!"

Systematic research has shown that clients can benefit from at least three types of formal social networks: alliances with clinicians, with the family or significant others, and with self-help groups and peers.

Alliance Between Patients and Clinicians

Social workers, counselors, and therapists are trained professionals whose cardinal values include that all individuals are born with uniqueness and dignity and should be treated with respect; that they have a desire

SPIRITUALITY, CONNECTEDNESS, AND HOPE   219

to grow and become better; that they have strengths; and that they are entitled to actualize their potentials and live a fulfilling life (Hepworth et al., 2002). When everyone rejects or gives up on the addicted person, the helping professionals will not and should not. The training of helping professionals—the knowledge, skills, and values—enable and obligate them to establish a "therapeutic alliance" with the clients in addition to providing major and specific interventions, treatments, and services. Therapeutic alliance or bonding involves empathy, trust, unconditional regards and acceptance, relatedness, affirmation, and hope, all of which facilitate an opportunity to connect the addicted patient with another human being, when all fails. My qualitative research on substance-abusing mothers in the child welfare system reveals the critical role of social workers/counselors to help clients turn a crisis into opportunity. When asked what made them change, one of the recurrent factors mentioned by these mothers was their social workers/counselors. One mother, for example, replied, "Because my social worker cares . . . She cares about me. Having someone care about me makes me care about myself." Another said, "Her faith in me . . . My social worker has faith in me . . . which, in turn, gives me confidence in myself" (Sun, 2000, p. 148).

Numerous studies regarding psychotherapy in general or addiction treatment in particular have consistently indicated that a therapeutic alliance increases treatment retention and promotes effective treatment outcomes (Miller & Moyers, 2015; Moos, 2007). Clients are more likely to explore problems enthusiastically, feel less stress and more positive mood, refrain from drugs, and achieve long-term treatment effects (Moos, 2007). The clinician–patient therapeutic alliance can be considered a spiritual or generic ingredient that cuts across various treatment theories, methods, and orientations; it makes those treatments more effectively delivered by the clinician and better taken in by the client (Kelly et al., 2016). The positive linkage between the patient-client alliance and treatment outcomes appears to operate across various addiction treatment approaches, including motivational enhancement therapy, cognitive behavioral therapy, and the Twelve Step facilitation approach (Connors et al., Lebow et al., and Martin et al., cited in Moos, 2007). It is important to establish a patient-clinician alliance because research has shown that the alliance is related to better treatment engagement and improved substance use treatment outcomes outside of the supposedly "major" components of treatment (e.g., applying cognitive behavioral therapy and teaching patients relapse prevention strategies; Orlinsky et al., cited in Kelly, 2016).

Clinicians not only can instill hope and lift spirits in their patients through a strong patient-clinician therapeutic alliance, they are also instrumental in facilitating connections between patients and their families and significant others. They help repair damaged relationships, recruit family members to participate in treatment, and conduct family-oriented treatments, all of which contribute to patients' treatment and recovery success. Clinicians also connect patients with self-help groups, which not only provide patients with abstinence-emphasis messages and recovery role models, but also expand patients' non-using social networks and help satisfy patients' needs to socially belong. Clinicians are also critical in motivating patients, enhancing their inner strengths and resilience. All of these qualities and achievement are contingent upon clinicians' professional education and training, countertransference management, self-care, and compassion fatigue prevention.

Families and Other Social Support

Social support that includes family and friends can provide material and emotional support to a person in recovery, satisfy needs to belong and connect, and enhance his or her well-being and happiness. Traditionally, addiction treatment has focused only on the addicted person while excluding his or her family, or it may consider family as mere "adjuncts" in treatment (Csiernik, 2002; Kourgiantakis et al., 2017; Orford et al., 2013). However, research in the past two decades has shown strong evidence that social support, family dynamics, interpersonal functions, and relationships are related to the origin and maintenance of the addiction problem, as well as treatment engagement, retention, outcomes, and the patient's long-term recovery (Fals-Stewart et al., 2004; Rowe, 2012). Meta analyses of randomized clinical trials revealed that family- and partner-involved treatments result in better treatment outcomes—including improved family functioning and decreased substance use—compared to treatments that focus only on the addicted person (Klostermann & O'Farrell, 2013). The family member, for instance, can be an adolescent addicted to substances or internet gaming and who needs the psychological support from his parents; an adult addicted to heroin who longs for his aging parents' forgiveness and his adult siblings' acceptance; or an alcoholic wife who needs to have a better relationship and communications with her spouse.

Dobkin and colleagues' study (2002) revealed that patients who have higher social support at admission tend to have a higher level of treatment retention, as well as a lower degree of severity of substance abuse at the 6-month follow up. The study of McPherson and colleagues (2017) reported that patients with family participation in treatment had 6.32 more days residential retention than patients without family participation, and that the former group had a 9.62% higher program completion rate than the latter group. Family involvement is also critical for gambling addiction. Ingle and colleagues (2008) found that participation of a significant other increases the odds of a successful treatment completion by gamblers. Likewise, a study that interviewed gamblers and their families found that families with high involvement tend to have better family and individual functioning, as well as more effective treatment outcomes (Kourgiantakis et al., 2017).

Lassiter and colleagues (2015) suggest that no history, rapport, or connection are comparable to the ones with loving family members, and therefore, counselors should recruit the family in the treatment to help the addicted person. While it's true that not all families are appropriate to get involved in patients' treatment, many families love and support their members and will never give up on them regardless of the circumstances, including their addiction. In reality, however, the initially strong "history, rapport, and connection" with a loving family are often eroded, little by little, and eventually damaged badly, by the addicted person's chronic and destructive addictive behaviors—repeated lies, stealing, manipulation, impulsivity, compulsivity, irresponsibility, disregard of negative consequences, meaningless and senseless decisions and behaviors . . . the list goes on. Many once-loving families become exhausted, indifferent, and ultimately give up on their once-beloved family members. The addicted person has burned the bridges!

While the family suffers from the dysfunctional and destructive behaviors of the addicted person, that person also suffers from the distance and rejection of their family. This may be especially true in certain family-oriented cultures and societies. Qualitative research on Chinese substance users has shown that the relationship between the drug user and his or her family is often full of tension and alienation, despite it being the time when the drug user needs his or her family most (Sun et al., 2016). "The participants [of the study] perceived the family's rejection [as] especially hurtful and agonizing. In addition to the frustrations related to the participant's repeated relapses, stigma exacerbates the family's rejection" (Sun et al., 2016, p. 153). For instance, one participant said, "I feel that my siblings will not change their negative attitudes toward me even if I do change. They will still look down on me. If I were a little closer to their kids, they would think I am going to impose some kind of bad influence on their kids! . . . I couldn't accept the way they treated me" (p. 153). A study on male methadone recipients in Iran (a country that has the highest rate of heroin use disorder globally) conducted by Aghakhani and colleagues (2017) indicated that "participants also reported the need for psychological support from their families but family members were not always willing to provide this support because they believed the person was beyond help." For example, one participant said, "We need help from our family to solve our problems. We need psychological support from them . . . but everybody prefers our death and believes that any kindness for us is wasting time and money" (p. 4).

Although research has shown the urgency of an addicted person's longing for his or her family's support during the course of the addiction disease (Aghakhani et al., 2017; Kourgiantakis et al., 2017; Patel, 2016; Sun et al., 2016) and the instrumental role a family can play in facilitating treatment and recovery success, nonetheless not all families want to get involved. Researchers have suggested at least five barriers hindering family involvement in its member's addiction treatment (Kourgiantakis et al., 2017; Patel, 2016):

(1) **Blame/Conflict:** Patel's qualitative study (2016) of 11 US clinicians' perceptions/assessment of barriers to a family's involvement found the most frequent theme to be that the "family blames the addict." For example, one participant said, "I know that they [the family] immediately want to dump all these things on the addict when they start the recovery process. They have all this anger and they have all these

resentments . . . and I try to say, 'listen, it's important that you do express these things and process these things'" (pp. 93–94). Another clinician perceived that "blaming and scapegoating is big" and described families' typical strong reaction: "'We've tried and we've tried and we've gotten nowhere. . . . Well, it's not our problem anymore. It's his problem. He needs to get better. This has nothing to do with us'" (Patel, p. 94). Kourgiantakis and colleagues' 2017 research on perceptions of problem gamblers and their families found that conflict between the addicted person and his or her family could be a barrier to the family's involvement in treatment. For instance, one addicted woman said, "the gambling caused (my husband) and I to be more uptight. I would describe it to be stressful . . . We are on edge a lot which impacts how we see each other . . . We are not as supportive as we should be" (p. 12 [online publication]).

(2) **Family Resistance/Isolation:** Families may refuse to participate in treatment because they have been too disappointed at the nonprogress of the addicted member, have exhausted their energy and hope, have worried about stigma and struggled with shame, have been in denial, and/or had the issues of codependency and enabling, as it is too painful to face the problem. One clinician in Patel's study said, "The family [is] unwilling to become involved in the recovery process. . . [F]amilies are not honest about what's going on. So that can be very difficult, too, because you're trying to figure out what's going on in the family dynamic, but they're not putting it out there." (2016, p. 95). Kourgiantakis et al.'s (2017) study showed that some families may be alienated from one another and from other support networks—they separated themselves from the person that has the gambling disorder because they feel interactions and discussions are likely to be burdensome; they hesitate to seek help from professionals because they feel ashamed addressing pathological gambling issues. One clinician in Patel's study targeted the issue of denial: "but then I need the cooperation of the parents and the parents don't want to admit their child has a drug problem or an alcohol problem because, after all, it affects their persona" (2016, p. 100).

(3) **Family Members' Own Abuse, Substance Abuse, and Mental Health Issues:** Some families struggle with their own addiction, violence, and mental health issues that may sabotage the treatment and

recovery of the addicted person. It's not appropriate to involve them in the addicted person's treatment; they require treatment themselves. For instance, one clinician in Patel's study explained, "[I]f your family is using and they don't believe in recovery and they don't understand recovery. That can be very problematic. Again, it really depends on how much contact the person has with their family" (2016, p. 99). Kourgiantakis et al. (2017) found that some family members may have mental health issues that decrease their coping skills and limit their abilities to support the addicted person. Furthermore, a family member may choose not to be involved in the addicted person's treatment because that may force the member to change his or her own addictive behavior. For example, one participant in Kourgiantakis et al.'s study said, "Part of our problem is we both have addictions . . . which I think now that I've accepted, but unfortunately, his drinking and my gambling don't fit. He tells me go to Bingo cause he wants to sit home and drink. So we're not helping each other that way, but it's almost like you know he wants to be by himself" (p. 14, online publication).

(4) **Communication:** The communication among family members and the addicted person is usually poor, although families that participate in their addicted member's treatment usually have more positive communication. One clinician in Patel's study said, "[T]hey're often not good at expressing themselves very directly and they tend to use more passive-aggressive ways of expressing themselves. And to a certain extent addiction can be like a passive-aggressive way of dealing with things" (2016, p. 97). Another stated, "Feelings are not discussed. Feelings are not talked about how to process them" (p. 97). Participants in Kourgiantakis et al.'s (2017) study found that learning communication skills enabled family involvement in the addicted member's treatment through increased and improved communication and discussion. Via treatment they learned ways of "listening to one another, remaining calm, and focusing on positive change" (p. 10, online publication). For instance, one family member said, "I think it was just a feeling of relief that she could be honest and she feels good that she could tell me straight away. She feels good that I could give her the support she needs and that I wasn't punishing" (p. 10, online publication).

(5) **Family Coping Skills and Family Self Care:** One family member explained the effort to better deal with the problem as "Trying to kind

of get out of that space of negative thinking and being angry towards him all the time. Just kind of looking at the positives and focusing on what he's done to improve the situation" (Kourgiantakis et al., 2017, p. 10, online publication). Another family member said, "I'm not his therapist right so I have a tendency to want to fix things immediately if there's something wrong . . . so I think the main thing has been you know holding back. Not always verbalizing what I'm thinking because those comments could be hurtful and detrimental to our relationship and to his progress. Also just trying to let go of the anger that I have and just focus on the positive with him'" (Kourgiantakis et al., 2017, p. 11, online publication). In Patel's study (2016), one clinician said, "Empowering families. This—these are the things that you can do. You can't control the addict. You can't lock them in a room. You can't do those things as much as you would want to. These are the things that you can do. Look at the limits that you can set. That's where their power is" (pp. 106–107).

Clinicians can enhance families' participation in addicted patients' treatment, as well as help facilitate a connection and positive relationship between addicted persons and their families with several strategies. To reduce families' blaming, scapegoating, and judgmental attitudes, at least two areas can be targeted: clinicians can help the families process their frustration, resentment, and other negative feelings; in addition, they can convey information to the families regarding the science-based brain disease model of addiction, and the impulsive, compulsive, relapsing, and chronic nature of addiction. Improving the communication skills, emotional coping strategies, and problem solving abilities for both the addicted persons and their families can be critical as well. Clinicians will find it beneficial to balance an emphasis on the families' vital roles in facilitating patients' treatment and recovery while also stressing the families' own needs for services, therapy, and self-care. Many family-based treatments for substance abuse—for adolescents or adults—have emerged in the past decades (Rowe, 2012). For example, two widely cited approaches are the multidimensional family therapy (MDFT) for substance abusing adolescents and the behavioral couples therapy (BCT) for adults. There are other approaches, such as the community reinforcement and family training (CRAFT) that focuses on teaching family members skills to get the reluctant patient to enter treatment, as well as skills to enhance their own lives regardless of the patient's commencing treatment or not (Dutcher et al., 2009; Kirby et al., 2015; Meyers et al., 1999). A multifamily approach adopts a group formed of several families with similar problems, aiming to help families reduce stigma, receive feedback, and gain insights and solutions from each other (Garrido-Fernández et al., 2017; Springer & Orsbon, 2002). Following are more detailed descriptions of MDFT and BCT.

Multidimensional family therapy (MDFT) is an empirically supported treatment approach that combines individual therapy, family therapy, substance use disorder counseling, and multiple systems-oriented involvements (Liddle, 2013; Rowe, 2012). MDFT targets four areas: adolescent focus, parent focus, parent-adolescent interaction focus, and a focus on social systems external to the family (Liddle, 2013). In the area of adolescent focus, clinicians build a working alliance with the adolescent—a relationship that is unique from, yet related to, the client's relationship with their parents. The goal is to help the adolescent to replace a delinquent and substance-using lifestyle with a new emphasis on his or her life and its meaning and direction (Liddle, 2013). For the area of parent focus, the goals include accentuating the past efforts of the parents, recognizing difficult past and current circumstances, enriching feelings of emotional connection and parental love, changing the relationship between the parents and the adolescent, improving parenting skills, and generating hope. When concentrating on the parent-adolescent bond, clinicians can shape more positive and functional family interactions by facilitating discussions on relationship topics while coaching and assisting family members to communicate and solve problems in new and healthy ways. In social arenas outside of the family—for example, school, employment, legal systems, mental and physical health facilities—clinicians can help the family and adolescent more effectively negotiate these organizations, which often has a bearing on the youth's short- and long-term treatment outcomes.

Meta-analysis of behavioral couples therapy (BCT) trials indicated that BCT has a medium effect size over individual treatments, and the effects are especially strong at follow-ups (Powers et al., 2008). Evidence shows that BCT yields more substance abstinence and improved relationship functioning than individual-based treatment; it additionally reduces emotional problems of children of the couple's (O'Farrell & Schein, 2000). BCT has three goals: to reduce substance abuse, to involve the family in support of the patient's efforts to recover, and to improve couple interaction patterns leading to long-term abstinence (Fals-Stewart et al., 2004). BCT is suitable either for couples with only one substance-abusing partner or couples who both use and both want to pursue abstinence (Fals-Stewart et al., 2004). BCT is not suitable for couples who report severe violence or when either partner fears the other physically; in such cases, violent partners may be referred to domestic violence programs and the substance-abusing partners to substance abuse counseling (Fals-Stewart et al., 2004). O'Farrell and Schein (2000) write about BCT methods in details. The first step is to promote abstinence, using a Daily Recovery Contract, which begins with the "trust discussion" where the patient states his or her intent to maintain abstinence that day ("one day at a time") and the partner shows supports for the patient's efforts. The contract may further include abstinence-facilitated activities such as taking medications (e.g., disulfiram, naltrexone), attending self-help group meetings, and receiving urine screens. Both partners also agree not to talk at home about past substance use problems nor their fear of future problems, and will discuss these issues only in professional sessions. After the patient becomes abstinent and the couple maintains appointments for some weeks, the BCT clinician can additionally improve the couple/family's relationship by enhancing their positive feelings and commitment toward each other, improving their communication skills to solve conflicts, and encouraging them to engage in shared rewarding recreational activities that do not involve alcohol or drugs.

The Self-Help Groups (Twelve Step or Non-Twelve Step)

Self-help groups can greatly contribute to addicted people's *long-term* recovery. Oftentimes, availability of professional treatment is time-limited, which may be a disadvantage to the recovery of an addicted patient who needs a more intensive and lifelong support and help. A self-help group is a free and powerful tool in this regard. A patient who can only meet with his or her therapist once a week can additionally attend a self-help group many days a week. A patient attending a 3-month intensive outpatient program for 4 days a week can continue the participation in a self-help group over a lifetime. Self-help groups can provide a safety net to fill the gaps that the professional treatment system cannot. For example, a Gamblers Anonymous member can call and seek help from some members—who voluntarily offer the service—to deal with urges anytime even after midnight; this is most likely a luxury that is not available from a professional therapist. The functions of self-help groups are multiple. Be it a Twelve Step-oriented AA group or a cognitive-behavioral-model focused SMART group, they all help members build a warm and welcoming, non-using, recovery-facilitating social network, which is desperately needed by a person who has suffered rejection, disconnection, loneliness, and despair. The group universality reduces stigma and isolation; the group comradeship satisfies the need to belong; the successful recovery experiences and stories of other members inspire hope; and the opportunities to offer services to other members are therapeutic and reinforce one's own recovery. All of these are conducive to help an addicted person reconnect with other human beings.

The Twelve Step self-help groups that are based on the AA model are the most common approaches to help an addicted person develop connectedness. Mustain and Helminiak (2015) have a detailed explanation on this. A newcomer typically develops a trust relationship with his or her sponsor—who offers unconditional regard and nonjudgmental acceptance, and with whom the addicted person can share intimate personal information without fear of being condemned. This serves as the foundation for the newly sober person to further develop trust relationships with others. Second, the newcomer is "encouraged to call his or her sponsor and other members daily and to expand her or his network with other recovering members, forging a sense of connectedness to others" (p. 367). Third, working on the Twelve Steps, which emphasizes humility and forgiveness in the individual's interpersonal history and context, helps to cultivate a mature and functional relationship with others. Finally, through meeting participation in self-help groups, a person eventually transitions to an established member who sponsors and helps others. This service and contribution also enhances the person's self-worth and develops connectedness. Kelly and colleagues' (2016) study (N=302 young adults from residential substance use disorder treatment) showed that having sponsor contact is related to increased Twelve Step participation, and that the stronger the sponsor alliance is, the greater the abstinence is.

Although research evidence indicates the efficacy of the Twelve Step program (Humphreys et al., 2014; Magura et al., 2013; Tonigan et al.,

2017), and there are many testimonials from AA members, as well as many courts and judges who mandate that offenders with addiction problems attend Twelve Step programs in lieu of prison times, the Twelve Step program and its related self-help groups are not embraced by everyone. While there are various ways to prepare a person to feel more comfortable with and benefit from the Twelve Step group, the concept of a higher power, God, or Supreme Being is subject to individual belief and receptivity. A higher power is not a tangible object and its existence cannot be empirically verified by science; many atheists, agnostics, or those of non-Abrahamic faiths have difficulty accepting the concept, despite the Twelve Step program's efforts to neutralize the concept of God by emphasizing "God-as we understood him." In 2013, the US 9th Circuit Court of Appeals ruled that a drug offender may not be mandated to attend a Twelve Step program, and Barry Hazle Jr., who sued his probation officers and the service provider for not allowing him to attend a secular treatment program, was subsequently awarded about two million dollars. For patients who prefer not to engage in the Twelve Step or groups oriented around a higher power but who can benefit from self-help group participation, there are non-Twelve Step or non-religious self-help groups available, such as the Self-Management and Recovery Training (SMART), the Secular Organizations for Sobriety/Save Our Selves (SOS), and the Women for Sobriety (WFS).

It's worth addressing the SMART groups in more details. The two major treatment methods in the addiction field are the Twelve-Step approach and the cognitive behavioral therapy approach. Not only do we have self-help groups that are based on the Twelve Steps, we also have professional treatment that either uses the Twelve Steps as its foundation (i.e., the Twelve Step facilitation approach) or refers its clients to a Twelve Step group as an adjunct service. Likewise, professional treatment has long adopted cognitive behavioral therapy (CBT) as one major model for relapse prevention, and now we have self-help groups that also espouse the CBT model. The SMART recovery group accentuates self-reliance rather than Twelve Steps and a higher power. It emphasizes the CBT model and incorporates updated scientific knowledge and tools to help its members recover (O'Sullivan et al., 2016). Although SMART groups are much less prevalent than AA groups—for example, there were only 1,500 SMART groups worldwide as of 2015, compared to 115,000 AA groups worldwide—they have been growing and gaining attention in the past two decades (Penn et al., 2016). Relatively new and paradigm shifting, the efficacy of SMART as a self-help group model awaits more research (Horvath & Yeterian, 2012; Penn et al., 2016).

The Inner Strengths Approach

In addition to a higher power and social networks—both of which can *indirectly* lead to enrichment of a person's inner strengths—clinicians can *directly* enhance a patient's inner strengths and resilience and therefore facilitate hope, courage, will, meaning, and spirituality within the patient to move him or her forward in life. An individual's inner strengths and resilience may be augmented by multiple strategies. I include here five of them: Helping patients explore and establish meaning in life (Chen, 2010; Frankl, 1946), employing the developmental model of recovery (Brown, 1996; Williams & Gressard, 2018), teaching patients emotion regulation skills (Linehan, 2015), applying motivational interviewing (Miller & Rose, 2009), and acceptance and commitment therapy (Harris, 2009; Hayes et al., 2006; Hayes et al., 2012). There are overlaps among the five strategies and they may complement each other. Of course, when available and appropriate, a combination of the inner strengths approach with a higher power method and/or social network strategy will obtain the optimal effects.

Exploring and Establishing Meaning in Life

Victor Frankl, an Austrian neurologist and psychiatrist who was also a Holocaust survivor, wrote a great deal regarding meaning in human life. He believed that "the will to meaning is the primary motivation for living and goes deeper than the will to pleasure . . . or the will to power," that "an individual who has no meaning in life" is in an existential vacuum, and that "meaning in life" is "self-transcendence that is reflected in one's ability to be useful" (1946/1959, quoted in Chen, 2010, p. 366). According to Frankl, there are two dimensions regarding meaning in life: a future-orientation that reflects a person's struggle to accomplish a social or spiritual goal, and a present-orientation that indicates he or she assigns meaning to actual occurrences or things. The three aspects of meaning suggested by Frankl are: (1) creativity—we can find meaning in life by creating something or implementing a mission; (2) experience—meaning exists in life if one

SPIRITUALITY, CONNECTEDNESS, AND HOPE   231

has a positive experience (such as a positive relationship) or experiences beauty (such as enjoying scenery or listening to music); (3) attitude—how we respond to life crises or things that happen to us can provide us with meaning in life—that is, "suffering has meaning if it generates change in the sufferer, as opposed to despair, which is meaningless suffering" (quoted in Chen, p. 366). Frankl's insights identified concrete directions that can assist a clinician seeking to help a patient find meaning in life and establish a sense of self.

Employing a Developmental Model of Recovery

Williams and Gressard (2018) emphasize a development model, including moral development, for addiction assessment, treatment, and recovery. They state that "individuals whose moral development has been hindered are less likely to exhibit complex moral decision-making processes and are more likely to focus on immediate gratification or self-preservation in making choices with moral implications" (p. 125). They suggest the importance of attention to a person's moral development stage both prior to and during their addiction career. Individuals whose original values, beliefs, and morals are compromised because of addiction may feel guilt and shame. The development model suggests that recovery should focus on reconnection and improvement in a person's biological and psychological areas, as well as the person's social and spiritual areas, all of which parallel developmental processes that foster taking personal responsibility, exercising moral reflection, and valuing meaning making. Williams and Gressard highlight Stephanie Brown's model in demonstrating the developmental model of recovery. Brown divides recovery into four stages: drinking, transition, early recovery, and ongoing recovery. During the drinking stage, a person emphasizes only the substance, not his or her interaction with the environment nor reflections on self or others. The person shows first step of "personal acceptance of responsibility" and moves to the transition stage once he or she admits and accepts the fact that he or she can no longer control the substance. Brown considers the transition stage "infant-like," in that the person needs a lot of external support and structures. The early recovery stage equates to adolescence, in that the person shifts from dependence to independence and has increased awareness of self, others, and the environment. If the transition stage concentrates on day-to-day survival, the early recovery stage brings into play sobering reflection on aspirations, short- and long-term goals, and plans (Brown, 1996, cited in Williams & Gressard, 2018). Ongoing recovery is the final stage and parallels adulthood, in that the goal is thriving instead of surviving. During this phase, the person focuses on matters such as fulfillment, self-transformation, meaningful relationships, spirituality, and personal contribution (Williams & Gressard, 2018).

Teaching Patients Emotion Regulation Skills/Dialectical Behavior Therapy

Emotion regulation enhances a person's inner strengths. Mustain and Helminiak (2015) consider emotion regulation as a part of spirituality. Emotions oversee human behavior and shape how a person perceives and reacts to his or her environment, as well as form meaning and direction (Neacsiu et al., 2017). Leaving negative emotions unmanaged can disrupt a person's daily activities and make it hard to enjoy life (Mustain & Helminiak, 2015). Furthermore, emotion dysregulation is believed to be associated with various psychopathologies such as borderline personality disorder, depression, anxiety disorder, eating disorders, and alcohol use disorder (Nolen-Hoeksema, 2012). Substance-abusing individuals are especially vulnerable in this regard, as they have the tendency to self-medicate their emotions, including boredom, emptiness, and anger (Mustain & Helminiak, 2015). Gratz and Tull (2010) found that, in their study sample, (a) the non-self-harming patients with substance use disorder (SUD) had a similar level of heightened emotion dysregulation compared to the self-harming samples in other studies; (b) the self-harming SUD patients had a significantly higher level of emotion dysregulation than the non-self-harming SUD patients; and (c) the association between emotion dysregulation and deliberate self-harm remained significant, even after controlling for psychiatric disorders or other risk factors such as childhood abuse, substance use level of severity, borderline personality disorder, and posttraumatic stress disorder.

Different people have different levels of emotional vulnerability and emotion regulation difficulties. Linehan's (2015) biosocial theory explains a person's emotional vulnerability from two perspectives. Biologically, some people are more vulnerable than others in emotion regulation because they are predisposed to be more impulsive and more sensitive to negative emotion and emotion cues, all of which could be related to factors of heredity,

SPIRITUALITY, CONNECTEDNESS, AND HOPE   233

intrauterine condition, physical insults that affect the brain during child-hood/adulthood, as well as early learning experiences that affect brain development. On the other hand, social environment, especially the family, also plays a role. For instance, some families tend to invalidate their members' emotions, are not able to model how to express emotion appropriately, and maintain a dysfunctional interaction pattern that continuously reinforces emotional arousal.

The emotion regulation process involves four domains: the person needs to (a) be aware and have clarity of his or her emotional responses; (b) accept his or her (negative) emotional responses; (c) have the ability to control his or her impulse and act according to desired goals when encountering negative emotions; and (d) have adequate access to effective emotion regulation strategies that can modulate his or her emotional responses to meet his or her goals and the demands of the situation (Gratz & Roemer, 2004). The nature of a person's emotion dysregulation may be related to one or a combination of several domains; interventions to enhance his or her emotion regulation abilities can target specific domains accordingly. For example, if the issue is related to a patient's nonacceptance of negative emotions, it is important to help the person find a nonevaluative and nonjudgmental stance toward his or her internal feelings and experiences, and thereby enable him or her to view these emotions as a normal part of the experience of human beings (Gratz & Tull, 2010). The time-honored serenity prayer—"God grant me the serenity to accept the things I cannot change, courage to change the things I can, and wisdom to know the difference" (Reinhold Niebuhr)—may also be beneficial in this regard. Psychological literature has developed comprehensive and systematic strategies and skills for emotion regulation. For example, Gross (1998) has developed some widely cited strategies. Matthias Berking and Brian Whitley's recommended *Affect Regulation Training: A Practitioners' Manual* (2014) and Martha Linehan's *DBT Skills Training Manual* (2015) also serve the function. It is critical, nonetheless, to be flexible in choosing different strategies to match different persons and their varied contexts (Aldao, 2013). Also, it's important to increase a patient's conscious control and elicit his or her sufficient practice so that the skills can become automatic eventually (Linehan, 2015).

The five strategies suggested by Gross (1998) are:

(1) **Situation Selection:** A person can decide to avoid or engage in a situation based on his or her knowledge or estimation of its resulting

emotional outcome. Although this strategy may appear simple and straightforward, it can also be complicated. For example, "a socially anxious person may avoid contact with others only to be pulled into further isolation," and therefore, Mustain and Helminiak (2015) emphasize that a person who has difficulty in emotion regulation should seek help from his or her sponsor or therapist to balance the conflict between short-term and long-term benefits (p. 368).

(2) **Situation Modification:** This refers to problem-focused coping, meaning a person can make an effort to modify the situation so that its negative emotional impact can be altered. Gross gave the example of "a flat tire on the way to an important appointment," which can be modified by "converting a meeting into a phone conference" (p. 283).

(3) **Attentional Deployment:** Examples in this category include distraction (take attention away from the situation altogether) and concentration (choose a task or a new internal situation that can captivate cognitive resources).

(4) **Cognitive Change:** A change of mind and/or context for the problem. "Downward social comparison" exemplifies this strategy, in that a person compares his or her situation with others less fortunate, which can therefore decrease the person's negative emotion.

(5) **Response Modulation:** This refers to "directly influencing physiological, experiential, or behavioral responding" (p. 285), and may include meditation, relaxation techniques, psychiatric treatment and medications, exercise, biofeedback, relaxation practice, and so on.

In her dialectical behavioral therapy skills training manual, Linehan (2015) gives detailed descriptions and discussions to address four major areas targeting emotion regulation: mindfulness, interpersonal effectiveness, emotion regulation, and distress tolerance. According to Linehan, mindfulness "has to do with the quality of awareness or the quality of presence that a person brings to everyday living" and is the foundation for the other three areas of skills (p. 151). Mindfulness constitutes three ingredients: observing, describing, and participating. Observing is attending to emotions, events, and other behaviors; describing is applying words to label these objects; and participating is "entering completely into the activities of the current moment" spontaneously and without self-consciousness (p. 154). Three more skills are suggested regarding how "observing,

SPIRITUALITY, CONNECTEDNESS, AND HOPE 235

describing, and participating" should be conducted. When observing, the person should be nonjudgmental, in that he or she may focus on the possible negative consequence a behavior may lead to and therefore change the behavior, but without judging the behavior as "bad." The person should also be of one mind, in that his or her attention should not be split among several things but focused only on the current activity. Effectiveness is the third skill, which emphasizes a person's doing what is truly needed in a situation rather than being stuck in wanting to be "right."

In the domain of interpersonal effectiveness skills, Linehan includes "effective strategies for asking for what one needs, for saying no, and for managing interpersonal conflicts skillfully" (p. 231). One example for "getting what you want" is summarized in the acronym DEAR MAN, representing "Describe, Express, Assert, Reinforce, (stay) Mindful, Appear confident, and Negotiate" (p. 248). The acronym GIVE represents skills targeting improving relationships while we interact with another individual and wish to achieve our objectives: "(be) Gentle, (act) Interested, Validate, (use an) Easy manner" (pp. 255–256). All these skill sets can greatly benefit our clients as many of them have never learned such life skills or they may have neglected and forgotten these skills because of their prolonged addiction career.

The domain of emotion regulation skills include "understanding and naming emotions," "changing unwanted emotions," "reducing vulnerability to emotion mind," and "managing extreme emotions" (Linehan, 2015, p. 318). It's important for a person to learn to identify and describe his or her current emotion as well as the context from which the emotion originates. Second, our emotions may be reactions to our subjective thoughts or interpretations of events, which may not be a factual reflection of the events. Linehan suggests checking the facts and correcting appraisals to match the facts. Problem solving can also change unwanted emotions—i.e., "to control emotions is to control the events that set off emotions" (p. 319). One skill to reduce vulnerability to emotion mind is self-care, including a balanced diet and nutrition, adequate sleep and exercise, and having physical illness treated. To manage extreme emotions, a person can apply mindfulness to decrease emotional pain; the person can also learn to identify "the skills breakdown point" and turn to the skill set for distress tolerance.

For skills to enhance distress tolerance, Linehan suggests, for example, distracting, self-soothing, and working to IMPROVE the moment.

Distracting can be facilitated by the skills codified by ACCEPTS: engage in Activities that can take the focus away from the crisis; do things that serve others and therefore Contributing; Compare the current crisis with a time in life that was worse or compare self with other people who suffer more than oneself; replace the negative Emotion with its opposite emotion (for example, watching a comedy when feeling upset); Push away the crisis or issue by imagination; occupy the brain with Thoughts that leave no space for the issue or crisis; and distract by provoking Sensations (e.g., taking a cold shower). Self-soothing can be achieved via vision (e.g., scenery), hearing (e.g., music), smell (e.g., lavender oil), taste (e.g., favorite food, but one should be cautious to not overeat), and touch (e.g., massage). The "IMPROVE the moment" skill set includes Imagery, Meaning, Prayer, Relaxation, One thing in the moment, Vacation, and Encouragement.

Motivational Interviewing

Spirituality plays a critical role for many people who fight addiction—from the early stage of initiating change to the later stages of maintaining recovery—as it is empowering to find a source of strength and optimism. At the same time, a person who hopes to heal from addiction at some point must mobilize his or her inner resources and strengths to take tangible action in the direction of recovery (Mustain & Helminiak, 2015). Most patients seen by health professionals do take action to seek treatment for themselves. However, for many clients with addiction problems, ambivalence and resistance to change are not uncommon, owing to the chronic and compulsive nature of addiction. The classic book *Intervention: How to Help Someone Who Doesn't Want Help*, by Vernon Johnson (1986), speaks to the core of the challenge among chemically dependent patients. Some clinicians, on the other hand, may simply give up and dismiss their "involuntary," "difficult to reach," "unmotivated," and "noncompliant" clients, telling them, "Come back when you're serious about changing" (Miller & Rose, 2015, p. 130), which sometimes is equivalent to when they "hit the bottom."

The motivational interviewing (MI) approach takes a very different philosophical stance, compared to the passive and authoritative mentality of frustrated therapists. MI does not reject clients who "are not ready for change"; rather, its mission is to facilitate change in clients. An evidence-based treatment approach, MI can be applied to help various types of

SPIRITUALITY, CONNECTEDNESS, AND HOPE   237

client populations—especially patients afflicted with addiction—to take actions to change. The word *motivation* originates from the Latin *movere*, which means "to move" or "be moved" (Ryan et al., 2011, p. 197). Ryan and colleagues suggest that motivation can be "defined broadly as that which moves people to act" and that it "implies both the *energy* and *direction* of action" (pp. 197–198). Adopting the transtheoretical model of stages of change (Prochaska & DiClemente, 1984)—which range from pre-contemplation (the person does not consider change), to contemplation (the person is ambivalent about change), to preparation (the person has resolved the ambivalence and is planning for action), to action (the person actually engages in action and treatment), and finally to maintenance (the person maintains abstinence and sobriety)—MI clinicians focus on assessing their client's current stage of the change continuum, then facilitating change and promoting action in the client accordingly.

Two major components of motivational interviewing explain its underlying mechanism and processes that help move a client to change: a relational element, which involves client-clinician rapport and alliance, and a technical element, which encompasses techniques such as elicitation and reinforcement of a client's "change talk" (Miller & Rose, 2009). Let's examine these two components.

(1) **A Relational Component:** According to the self-determination theory, human beings have three essential psychological needs—autonomy, competence, and relatedness—which if filled can result in integrity, well-being, and continuous psychological growth. Satisfaction of these three needs also form the foundation for psychological energy required to motivate the start and long-term preservation of healthy behaviors (Silva et al., 2014). Autonomy refers to a person's feeling of "being the origin of one's own behaviors"; competence represents self-efficacy and a person's "feeling effective"; relatedness means a person's "feeling understood and cared for by others" (p. 172). Motivational interviewing emphasizes client-centeredness, in that a genuine, warm, egalitarian, and respectful stance is highlighted to support a client's autonomy. MI also accentuates its opening strategies, including open-ended questions, affirmations, reflections, and summaries (Miller & Rollnick, 2013). Among these, affirmations serve to recognize a client's strengths and positive characteristics; this is one

way to instill self-confidence in the client and increase his or her self-efficacy, and thus help fulfill a person's need for competence. A sense of competency is conducive to a client's decision to change or not, as many clients hesitate to change not because they don't want to, but because they don't believe they have the capability (Hepworth et al., 2002). Open-ended questions, reflections, and summaries are interviewing strategies that facilitate empathy from a clinician to a client, which helps to build an alliance and a sense of relatedness between the client and the clinician.

(2) **A Technical Component.** Unlike Carl Roger's famous non-directive client-centered approach where the clinician does not manipulate the direction of the therapy session, motivational interviewing is a *directive* client-centered approach. Being "directive" involves many specific techniques on the part of a clinician, especially in guiding a client to pass through the different stages of change to achieve sobriety. For example, to facilitate a client moving from the pre-contemplation stage—where he or she is not aware of the problem or does not want to change—to the contemplation stage, the clinician can help a client examine the discrepancies between the client's and others' perceptions of the presenting problems. Or, the clinician can help a client develop discrepancies between what he or she is now and what he or she wants or hopes to be, and explore the roles that alcohol, drugs, gambling, or gaming play in this context. To help clients resolve their ambivalence during the contemplation stage, and facilitate transition to the preparation stage, a clinician may want to identify, evoke, and reinforce a client's "change talk" (that is, any client language that supports movement toward change) rather than his or her "sustain talk" (that is, any client language that supports status quo) (Miller & Rollnick, 2013). Furthermore, change talk may include two subcategories: the DARN (desire, ability, reason, and need) and the CAT (commitment, activation, and taking steps). Research has indicated that first, the strength of DARN predicts the strength of CAT; and second, the CAT or the commitment language predicts effective treatment outcomes, whereas the DARN or the preparatory change talk did not. Therefore, to promote change, a clinician should evoke and reinforce commitment language (Miller & Rose, 2009).

SPIRITUALITY, CONNECTEDNESS, AND HOPE

Acceptance and Commitment Therapy

Both motivational interviewing (MI) and acceptance and commitment therapy (ACT) help clients identify and draw out their aspirations, life purpose, and goals. MI concentrates on facilitating clients to move from where they are now to where they want to be; whereas ACT focuses on helping clients to, on one hand, accept pain or sufferings that are not avoidable in a human life and, on the other hand, encouraging them to commit their energy and efforts to pursue their life goals that are based on their values, that are most dear to their heart, and that are what matters (Harris, 2009). Both MI and ACT can inspire clients and rekindle hope.

Hayes et al. (2012) emphasize that ACT "is not based on the psychology of abnormality" and clients are not viewed as beyond hope or damaged. Empowerment is the foundation of ACT, with three emphases: (a) everyone has a meaningful and values-based life available to him or her; (b) pain is part of life, which we should learn to accept and diffuse; and (c) progress should not be measured by "an absolute level of achievement but rather by the incremental choice to embrace the present and to step forward toward a life worth living" (p. 985). Hayes and colleagues use an analogy to explain their thoughts: A person who struggles with psychotic disorders choosing to walk to a store may actually indicate more vitality and bravery than a high-paid CEO who holds forth assertively at a multinational corporation board meeting.

Although ACT is the acronym of acceptance and commitment therapy, it is not pronounced as the letters A, C, and T, but as one word: "act." The intention is to encourage clients to take action guided by their own core values. While ACT helps clients explore those core values, change their behaviors based on their core values, and guide them to pursue their life purpose and dreams, it also teaches clients psychological knowledge and skills such as mindfulness and emotion regulation so that they can more effectively manage painful thoughts and feelings in life, with the result that those thoughts and feelings are much less impactful (Harris, 2009).

Six processes are focused in ACT: being here and now; acceptance of difficult and painful thoughts and feelings; observing and experiencing these thoughts and feelings without being controlled by them; self as context; discovering what matters in life; taking action and committing self to pursue goals that matter in life (Harris, 2009; Hayes et al., 2012; Ungar &

Bukstein, 2017). "Monsters on a Bus" is a simple analogy that actually well demonstrates the philosophy and methods of ACT. While driving along the journey, a bus driver suffers a great deal of noise, disturbances, assaults, and other terrible behaviors from his many monster riders on the bus. If the driver chose to attend to all these nuisances and uproars, he would be most likely not to be able to arrive his destination (Hayes et al., 1999). This analogy can be applied to many situations and cases, highlighting the strategy of letting go of not-so-important frustrations and negative events and taking actions to pursue the life goals that we treasure and value (Ungar & Bukstein, 2017).

Note

1 The Twelve Steps are reprinted with permission of Alcoholics Anonymous World Services, Inc. ("A.A.W.S."). Permission to reprint the Twelve Steps does not mean that A.A.W.S. has reviewed or approved the contents of this publication, or that A.A. necessarily agrees with the views expressed herein. A.A. is a program of recovery from alcoholism only - use of the Twelve Steps in connection with programs and activities which are patterned after A.A., but which address other problems, or in any other non-A.A., does not imply otherwise.

References

Aghakhani, N., Lopez, V., & Cleary, M. (2017). Experiences and perceived social support among Iranian men on methadone maintenance therapy: A qualitative study. *Issues in Mental Health Nursing, 38*(9), 692–697.

Alcoholics Anonymous World Services, Inc. (2001). Appendix II: Spiritual experience. In Alcoholics Anonymous: The story of how many thousands of men and women have recovered from alcoholism (the Big Book, fourth edition, pp. 567-568). Retrieved on 04/28/2018 from www.aa.org/pages/en_US/alcoholics-anonymous.

Aldao, A. (2013). The future of emotion regulation research: Capturing context. *Perspectives on Psychological Science, 8*(2), 155–172.

Alexander, B.K. (2012). Addiction: The urgent need for a paradigm shift. *Substance Use & Misuse, 47*, 1475–1482.

Berking, M., & Whitley, B. (2014). *Affect regulation training: A practitioners' manual.* New York: Springer.

Bradshaw, M., Ellison, C.G., & Marcum, J.P. (2010). Attachment to God, images of God, and psychological distress in a nationwide sample of Presbyterians. *Internationla Journal for Psychology of Religion, 20*(2), 130–147.

Brown, S. (1996). *Treating the alcoholic: A developmental model of recovery.* New York: Wiley.

Chen, G. (2010). The meaning of suffering in drug addiction and recovery from the perspective of existentialism, Buddhism and the 12-step program. *Journal of Psychoactive Drugs, 42*(3), 363–375.

Cook, C. (2004). Addiction and spirituality. *Addiction, 99*(5), 539–551.

Csiernik, R. (2002). Counseling for the family: The neglected aspect of addiction treatment in Canada. *Journal of Social Work Practice in the Addictions, 2*(1), 79–92.

Dermatis, H., & Galanter, M. (2016). The role of twelve-step-related spirituality in addiction recovery. *Journa of Religion and Health, 55*, 510–521.

DiClemente, C.C. (2013). Paths through addiction and recovery: The impact of spirituality and religion. *Substance Use & Misuse, 48*, 1260–1261.

Dobkin, P.L., De Civita, M., Paraherakis, A., & Gill, K. (2002). The role of functional social support in treatment retention and outcomes among outpatient adult substance abusers. *Addiction, 97*, 347–356.

Dutcher, L.W., Anderson, R., Moore, M., Luna-Anderson, C., Meyers, R.J., Delaney, H.D., et al. (2009). Community reinforcement and family training (CRAFT): An effectiveness study. *Journal of Behavior Analysis in Health, Sports, Fitness and Medicine, 2*(1), 80–90.

Ellison, C.W. (1983). Spiritual well-being: Conceptulization and measurement. *Journal of Psychology and Theology, 11*(4), 330–338.

"Ex-con transforms to entrepreneur behind bars," interview with Coss Marte. Cable News Network, 10:30 am ET, 4 October 2016.

Fals-Stewart, W., O'Farrell, T.J., & Birchler, G.R. (2004). Behavioral couples therapy for substance abuse: Rationale, methods, and findings. *Science & Practice Perspectives*, 30–41.

Fehring, R.J., Brennan, P.F., & Keller, M.L. (1987). Psychological and spiritual well-being in college students. *Research in Nursing & Health, 10*, 391–398.

Frankl, V.E. (1946/1959). *Man's search for meaning.* Vienna, Austria: Verlag fur Jugend und Vol/Boston, MA: Beacon Press.

Friedland, D. (2014). Evidence-based medicine: A framework for emotional regulation, intuition, and conscious engagement. *Global Advances in Health and Medicine, 3*(2) 3–4. doi: 10.7453/gahmj.2014.026.

Garrido-Fernández, M, Marcos-Sierra, J.A., López-Jiménez, A., & Ochoa de Alda, I. (2017). Multi-family therapy with a reflecting team: A preliminary study on efficacy among opiate addicts in methadone maintenance treatment. *Journal of Marital and Family Therapy, 43*(2), 338–351.

Genia, V. (2001). Evaluation of the spiritual well-being scale in a sample of college students. *The International Jouranl for the Psychology of Religion, 11*(1), 25–33.

Gratz, K.L., & Roemer, L., (2004). Multidimensional assessment of emotion regulation and dysregulation: Development, factor structure, and initial validation of the difficulties in emotion regulation scale. *Journal of Psychopathology and Behavioral Assessment, 26*(1), 41–54.

Gratz, K.L., & Tull, M.T. (2010). The relationship between emotion dysregulation and deliberate self-harm among inpatients with substance use disorders. *Cognitive Therapy and Research, 34*, 544–553.

Gross, J.J. (1998). The emerging field of emotion regulation: An integrative review. *Review of General Psychology, 2*(3), 271–299.

Harris, R. (2009). *ACT made simple: An easy-to-read primer on acceptance and commitment therapy.* Oakland, CA: New Harbinger Publications, Inc.

Hayes, S.C., Luoma, J.B., Bond, F.W., Masuda, A., & Lillis, J. (2006). Acceptance and commitment therapy: Model, processes and outcomes. *Psychology Faculty Publications*, Paper 101. Retrieved from http://scholarworks.gsu.edu/psycho_facpub/101.

Hayes, S.C., Pitorello, J., & Levin, M.E. (2012). Acceptance and commitment therapy as a unified model of behavior change. *The Counseling Psychologist, 40*(7), 976–1002.

Hayes, S.C., Strosahl, K.D., Wilson, K.G. (1999). *Acceptance and commitment therapy: An experiential approach to behavior change.* New York: Guilford.

Hepworth, D.H., Rooney, R.H., & Larsen, J.A. (2002). *Direct social work practice: Theory and skills.* Pacific Grove, CA: Cole-Thomson Learning.

Horvath, A.T., & Yeterian, J. (2012). SMART recovery: Self-empowering, science-based addiction recovery support. *Journal of Groups in Addiction & Recovery, 7*(2–4), 102–117.

Humphreys, K., Blodgett, J.C., & Wagner, T.H. (2014). Estimating the efficacy of alcoholics anonymous without self-selection bias: An instrumental variables re-analysis of randomized clinical trials. *Alcoholism: Clinical and Experimental Research, 38*(11), 2688–2694.

Ingle, P.J., Marotta, J., McMillan, G., & Wisdom, J.P. (2008). Significatn others and gambling treatment outcomes. *Journal of Gambling Studies, 24,* 381–392.

Johnson, V.E. (1986). *Intervention: How to help someone who doesn't want help.* Center City, MN: Hazelden Publishing.

Jones, B.A. (2014). *Spirituality as positive predictor of coping with stress for individuals in recovery from alcohol and other drug addictions.* Dissertation, Capella University.

Kelly, J.F., Greene, M.C., & Bergman, B.G. (2016). Recovery benefits of the "therapeutic alliance" among 12-step mutual-help organization attendees and their sponsors. *Drug and Alcohol Dependence, 162,* 64–71.

Kirby, K.C., Versek, B., Kerwin, M.E., Meyers, K., Benishek, L.A., Bresani, E., et al. (2015). Developing community reinforcement and family training (CRAFT) for parents of treatment-resistant adolecents. *Journal of Child & Adolescent Substance Abuse, 24*(3), 155–165.

Klostermann, K., & O'Farrell, T.J. (2013). Treating substance abuse: Partner and family approaches. *Social Work in Public Health, 28*(3–4), 234–247.

Kourgiantakis, T., Saint-Jacques, M., & Tremblay, J. (2017). Facilitators and barriers to family involvement in problem gambling treatment. *International Journal of Mental Health Addiction, 16,* 291–312. doi: 10.1007/s11469-017-9742-2.

Langman, L., & Chung, M.C. (2013). The relationship between forgiveness, spirituality, traumatic guilt and posttraumatic stress disorder (PTSD) among people with addiction. *Psychiatric Quarterly, 84,* 11–26.

Lassiter, P.S., Czerny, A.B., & Williams, K.S. (2015). Working with addictions in family therapy. In M. Stauffer & D. Capuzzi (Eds.) *Foundations of couples, marriage, and family counseling* (pp. 389–417). Hoboken, NJ: Wiley.

Laudet, A.B., Morgen, K., & White, W.L. (2006). The role of social supports, spirituality, religiousness, life meaning and affiliation with 12-step fellowships in quality of life satisfaction among individuals in recovery from alcohol and drug problems. *Alcoholism Treatment Quarterly, 24*(1–2), 33–73.

Liddle, H.A. (2013). Multidimensional family therapy for adolescent substance abuse: A development approach. In: *Interventions for addiction* (Comprehensive addictive behaviors and disorders, Volume 3, Chapter 10, pp. 87–96). New York: Academic Press.

Linehan, M.M. (2015). *DBT skills training manual,* Second Edition. New York: Guilford.

Litt, M.D., Kadden, R.M., Kabela-Cormier, E., & Petry, N.M. (2009). Changing network support for drinking: Network support project two-year follow-up. *Journal of Consulting and Clinical Psychology, 77*(2), 229–242.

Longabaugh, R., Wirtz, P.W., Zywiak, W.H., & O'Malley, S.S. (2010). Network support as a prognostic indicator of drinking outcomes: The combine study. *Journal of Studies on Alcohol and Drugs*, 837–846.

Magura, S., Cleland, C.M., & Tonigan, J.S. (2013). Evaluating alcoholics anonymous's effect on drinking in project MATCH using cross-lagged regression panel analysis. *Journal of Studies on Alcohol and Drugs*, *74*(3), 378–385.

McPherson, C., Boyne, H., & Willis, R. (2017). The role of family in residential treatment patient retention. *International Journal of Mental Health Addiction*, *15*, 933–941.

Meyers, R.J., Miller, W.R., Hill, D.E., Tonigan, J.S. (1999). Community reinforcement and family training (CRAFT): Engaging unmotivated drug users in treatment. *Journal of Substance Abuse*, *10*(3), 291–308.

Miller, W.R. (2013). Addiction and spirituality. *Substance Use & Misuse*, *48*, 1258–1259.

Miller, W.R., & Moyers, T.B. (2015). The forest and the trees: Relational and specific factors in addiction treatment. *Addiction*, *110*, 401–413.

Miller, W.R., & Rollnick, S. (2013). *Motivational interviewing: Helping people change*. New York: Guilford.

Miller, W.R., & Rose, G.S. (2009). Toward a theory of motivational interviewing. *Amrican Psychologist*, *64*(6), 527–537.

Miller, W.R., & Rose, G.S. (2015). Motivational interviewing and decisional balance: Contrasting responses to client ambivalence. *Behavioral and Cognitive Psychotherapy*, *43*, 129–141.

Moos, R.H. (2007). Theory-based active ingredients of effective treatments for substance use disorders. *Drug and Alcohol Dependence*, *88*(2–3), 109–121.

Mustain, J.R., & Helminiak, D.A. (2015). Understanding spirituality in recovery from addiction: Reintegrating the psyche to release the human spirit. *Addiction Research & Theory*, *23*(5), 364–371.

Neacsiu, A.D., Smith, M., & Fang, C.M. (2017). Challenging assumptions from emotion dysregulation psychological treatments. *Journal of Affective Disorders*, *219*, 72–79.

Nolen-Hoeksema, S. (2012). Emotion regulation and psychopathology: The role of gender. *Annual Reviw of Clinical Psycholofy*, *8*, 161–187.

Noormohammadi, M.R., Nikfarjam, M., Deris, F., & Parvin, N. (2017). Spiritual well-being and associated factors with relapse in opioid addicts. *Journal of Clinical and Diagnostic Research*, *11*(3), VC07–VC10.

O'Farrell, T.J., & Schein, A.Z. (2000). Behavioral couples therapy for alcoholism and drug abuse. *Journal of Substance Abuse Treatment*, *18*(1), 51–54.

Orford, J., Velleman, R., Natera, G., Templeton, L., & Copello, A. (2013). Addiction in the family is a major but neglected contributor to the global burden of adult ill-health. *Social Science & Medicine*, *78*, 70–77.

O'Sullivan, D., Watts, J.R., Xiao, Y., & Bates-Maves, J. (2016). Refusal self-efficacy among SMART recovery members by affiliation length and meeting frequency. *Journal of Addictions & Offender Counseling*, *37*, 87–101.

Paloutzian, R.F., & Ellison, C.W. (1982). Loneliness, spiritual well-being and the quality of life. In L.A. Peplau LA and D. Perlman (Eds.) *Loneliness: A sourcebook of current theory, research and therapy* (pp. 224–237). New York: Wiley.

Patel, J.R. (2016). *Perspectives of addiction treatment professionals regarding family involvement in adult substance abuse treatment: A qualitative study*. Doctoral Dissertation, Capella University.

Penn, P.E., Brooke, D, Brooks, A.J., Gallagher, S.M., & Barnard, A.D. (2016). Co-occurring conditions clients and counselors compare 12-step and smart recovery mutual help. *Journal of Groups in Addiction & Recovery, 11*(2), 76–92.

Powers, M.B., Vedel, E., & Emmelkamp, P.M.G. (2008). Behavioral couples therapy (BCT) for alcohol and drug use disorders: A meta-analysis. *Clinical Psychology Review, 28,* 952–962.

Prochaska, J.O., & DiClemente, C.C. (1984). *The Transtheoretical approach: Crossing traditional boundaries of therapy.* Homewood, IL: Dow Jones Irwin.

Rowe, C.L. (2012). Family therapy for drug abuse: Review and updates 2003–2010. *Journal of Marital and Family Therapy, 38*(1), 59–81.

Ryan, R.M., Lynch, M.F., Vansteenkiste, M., & Deci, E.L. (2011). Motivation and autonomy in counseling, psychotherapy, and behavior change: A look at theory and practice. *The Counseling Psychologist, 39*(2), 193–260.

Sachs, K.S. (2009). A psychological analysis of the 12 steps of alcoholics anonymous. *Alcoholism Treatment Quarterly, 27*, 199–212.

Silva, M.N., Marques, M.M., & Teixeira, P.J. (2014). Testing theory in practice: The example of self-determination theory-based interventions. *The European Health Psychologist, 16*(5), 171–180.

Springer, D.W., & Orsbon, S.H. (2002). Families helping families: Implementing a multifamily therapy group with substance-abusing adolescents. *Health & Social Work, 27*(3), 204–207.

Sun, A.P. (2000). Helping substance-abusing mothers in the child-welfare system: Turning crisis into opportunity. *Families in Society, 81*(2), 142–151.

Sun, A.P. (2007). Relapse among substance-abusing women: Components and processes. *Substance Use & Misuse, 42*(1), 1–21. doi: 10.1080/10826080601094082.

Sun, A.P., Chen, Y.C., & Marsiglia, F. (2016). Trauma and Chinese heroin users. *Journal of Ethnicity in Substance Abuse, 15*(2), 144–159.

Tonigan, J.S., McCallion, E.A., Frohe, T., & Pearson, M.R. (2017). Lifetime Alcoholics Anonymous attendance as a predictor of spiritual gains in the Relapse Replication and Extension Project (RREP). *Psychology of Addictive Behaviors, 31*(1), 54–60.

Treloar, H.R., Dubreuil, M.E., & Miranda, R. (2014). Spirituality and treatment of addictive disorders. *Rhode Island Medical Journal*, March, 36–38.

Ungar, A.K., & Bukstein, O.G., (2017). Mindfulness-based interventions for substance use disorder treatment. In E. Zerbo, A. Schlechter, S. Desai, & P. Levounis (Eds.) *Becoming mindful: Integrating mindfulness into your psychiatric practice* (pp. 134–146). Arlington, VA: American Psychiatric Association.

Wiklund, L. (2008). Existential aspects of living with addiction—Part II: Caring needs. A hermeneutic expansion of qualitative findings. *Journal of Clinical Nursing, 17*, 2435–2443.

Williams, A.E., & Gressard, C.F. (2018). A developmental approach to addiction theory and treatment. In P.S. Lassiter & J.R. Culbreth (Eds.) *Theory and practice of addition counseling* (pp. 117–140). Los Angeles: SAGE.

Zywiak, W.H., Neighbors, C.J., Martin, R.A., Johnson, J.E., Eaton, C.A., & Rohsenow, D.J. (2009). The important people drug and alcohol interview: Psychometric properties, predictive validity, and implications for treatment. *Journal of Substance Abuse Treatment, 36*(3), 321–330.

7

WITHDRAWAL MANAGEMENT AND RELAPSE PREVENTION

PHARMACOTHERAPY

How and where do we begin helping an addicted person and his or her family? Before we discuss the focus of this chapter—withdrawal management and relapse prevention through pharmacotherapy, and through behavioral therapy/psychosocial treatment in the next chapter—we should remember the treatment ingredient of hope instillation. As mentioned in Chapter 6 and elsewhere, many addicted clients (and their families) are in despair and have lost confidence in fighting addiction by the time they reach out for help. An important overarching practice guideline, therefore, is to instill hope in them when they initiate treatment and throughout their entire recovery processes. Hope can be facilitated and actualized via warm and unconditional positive regards from clinicians and treatment programs, as well as the individual or group sessions of motivational interviewing that brings out a client's inner strengths and raises his or her motivation to take action to change. Participation in a Twelve Step self-help group, which emphasizes spirituality, higher power, and fellowship and peer support, is another powerful tool to generate hope in an addicted person. For atheists, agnostics, and people who do not accept the Twelve Step concept, many non-Twelve Step mutual-aid groups, such as the SMART (Self-Management and Recovery Training) recovery groups, Women for Sobriety groups, and the WRAP (Wellness Recovery Action Plan) groups are available to serve similar important functions as well.

With *hope* being the overarching climate, there are multiple methods and strategies to help a person combat addiction and achieve long-term recovery. Scientific data have emphasized the importance of both pharmacotherapy and behavioral therapy/psychosocial treatment in treating substance abuse and addiction problems (National Institute on Drug Abuse [NIDA], 2018; Substance Abuse and Mental Health Services Administration and National Institute on Alcohol Abuse and Alcoholism [SAMHSA & NIAAA], 2015). One of the 13 principles of effective treatment for substance abuse and addiction organized by NIDA is that "medications are an important element of treatment for many patients, especially when combined with counseling and other behavioral therapies" (2018, para. 7). Pharmacotherapy or medication-assisted treatment (MAT) has been underutilized for addiction treatment (Mark et al., 2009; Oliva et al., 2011). This chapter is written primarily for addiction-treatment social workers and counselors, as well as other practitioners who cannot prescribe medications but need to have basic knowledge and skills with regard to the nature and function of various relevant pharmacotherapies and their related issues in order to effectively facilitate communications between patients, physicians, and other treatment team members to best serve the patients.

Pharmacotherapy should not be provided in isolation, but should be combined with behavioral therapies or psychosocial treatment to reach an optimal treatment outcome (National Collaborating Centre for Mental Health, The Royal College of Psychiatrists, 2011; SAMHSA & NIAAA, 2015). Behavioral therapies and psychosocial treatment can help a client deal with issues related to his or her psychological/social areas and overall quality of life, all of which have a bearing to indirectly help the person combat the neurobiological aspect of the fundamentals of addiction. Furthermore, a combination of pharmacotherapy and psychosocial treatment can optimize treatment outcomes because, on one hand, psychosocial treatments can increase a patient's compliance with the overall treatment plan and with the prescribed medications in particular; on the other hand, via medication's reduction of a patient's withdrawal symptoms and cravings, the patient can be more receptive to and, therefore, benefit more from the behavioral therapy and psychosocial interventions (SAMHSA & NIAAA, 2015).

To give readers a more coherent insight, I organize the materials first based on the sequence of treatment and recovery phases a patient usually goes through, then we follow with specific treatment methods and strategies that correspond to each treatment phase. This chapter, therefore, focuses on two major sequential phases: first, detoxification or withdrawal management during patients' initial phase of treatment; second, their rehabilitation and aftercare with a goal of relapse prevention. Although the withdrawal management phase occurs prior to the relapse prevention phase, addicted people may relapse during the relapse prevention phase and return to the withdrawal management phase. Pharmacotherapies that are relevant to each phase are addressed. This chapter includes discussions related to addicted patients in general; therefore, some of the contents may be applied to both addicted patients with and without co-occurring disorders (COD), whereas other contents may pertain only to those without COD and may require modifications to help patients with COD. (Chapter 3 addresses currently available pharmacotherapy and behavioral therapy for treating addicted patients with co-occurring disorders.)

Alcohol and opioid addictions are highlighted in this chapter because many patients seek treatment, especially withdrawal, for one of the two addictions. Pharmacotherapy is better developed for alcohol and opioid addiction than many other addictive drugs such as cocaine, amphetamines, and marijuana (Kranzler et al., 2014) and currently there is a heroin epidemic (Centers for Disease Control and Prevention [CDC], 2017), that has driven development of effective treatments of opioid use disorder as well as chronic pain to be a national priority (Connery' review, 2015; Dowell et al., 2016).

Withdrawal Management

What is withdrawal? Not everyone with substance use disorder will develop withdrawal syndrome, and some substances tend to result in more apparent physical withdrawal symptoms than others. For example, only people with heavy and prolonged use of alcohol may develop withdrawal symptoms once they cease or reduce alcohol consumption, as their bodies have adapted to the presence of alcohol (American Psychiatric Association [APA], 2013). Also, substances in the categories of central nervous systems depressants or "downers," like alcohol, sedatives, hypnotics, anxiolytics, and opioids are likely to have common physical withdrawal symptoms (APA, 2013). On the other hand, although withdrawal symptoms may also happen to central nervous system stimulants (such as amphetamines and cocaine), tobacco, and cannabis, their signs and symptoms tend to be less apparent (APA, 2013). In addition, not everyone who shows withdrawal symptoms will have severe withdrawal symptoms; only a small portion of individuals among those with withdrawal symptoms will have severe symptoms.

Withdrawal is uncomfortable and can be dangerous (Mee-Lee et al., 2013). To take alcohol as an example, the diagnosis of alcohol withdrawal disorder requires at least 2 of the 8 criteria—"autonomic hyperactivity" (e.g., sweating, pulse rate > 100 bpm); "increased hand tremor"; "insomnia"; "nausea or vomiting"; "transient visual, tactile, or auditory hallucinations or illusions"; "psychomotor agitation"; "anxiety"; and "generalized tonic-clonic seizures" (APA, 2013, p. 499). Alcohol withdrawal symptoms usually occur "within several hours" to "a few days" after a person stops or decreases alcohol use. However, protracted withdrawal symptoms, such as lower intensities of anxiety, autonomic dysfunction, and insomnia may follow acute withdrawal and last for 3–6 months. The opioid withdrawal symptoms may not be as potentially fatal as the alcohol withdrawal syndrome (Gordon & Dahl, 2011), but they can be extremely uncomfortable and painful. To meet the *DSM-5* diagnosis of opioid withdrawal, a person needs to present at least 3 of the 9 symptoms: "dysphoric mood"; "nausea or vomiting"; "muscle aches"; "lacrimation or rhinorrhea"; "pupillary dilation, piloerection, or sweating"; "diarrhea"; "yawning"; "fever"; and "insomnia" (APA, 2013, pp. 547–548). The acute opioid withdrawal symptoms (e.g., for heroin) usually last for about 7 days, with a peak during days 1–3; the protracted withdrawal syndromes—i.e., less acute symptoms such as anxiety, insomnia, poor appetite, fatigue, anhedonia and bone pain—can extend for months (APA, 2013; O'Connor, 2005). One major obstacle that discourages a person from stopping use in the first place is these acute and protracted withdrawal symptoms. Because of the withdrawal symptoms, those individuals worry they might not function normally without alcohol or drugs. As the *DSM-5* states, "After developing withdrawal symptoms, the individual is likely to consume the substance to relieve the symptoms" (p. 484).

Who are more likely to develop withdrawal? As mentioned earlier, not all individuals with substance use disorder (SUD) may experience withdrawal symptoms when they stop or reduce use; only those with moderate or severe level of SUD are likely to encounter withdrawal. According to *DSM-5* (APA, 2013), "the ICD-10-CM code [reflects] the fact that alcohol withdrawal can only occur in the presence of a moderate or severe alcohol use disorder. It is not permissible to code a comorbid mild alcohol use disorder with alcohol withdrawal" (p. 500). A person is considered as having a mild alcohol use disorder (AUD) if the person has a presence of 2–3 symptoms among the 11 symptoms or criteria listed for AUD; a moderate AUD if 4–5 symptoms; and a severe AUD if 6 or more symptoms (APA, 2013, p. 491). The 11 symptoms or criteria are embedded in four groups of symptoms, including impaired control (e.g., "a persistent desire or unsuccessful efforts to cut down"), social impairment (e.g., recurrent use "resulting in a failure to fulfill major role obligations at work, school, or home"), risky use (e.g., continued use "despite knowledge of having a persistent or recurrent physical or psychological problem that is likely to have been caused or exacerbated by alcohol"), and pharmacological criteria (i.e., tolerance and withdrawal) (APA, 2013, pp. 490–491). About half of middle-class people with alcohol use disorder have developed a full alcohol withdrawal; the rates are higher for people who are homeless or hospitalized, which can be 80% or more (APA, 2013). In addition, alcohol withdrawal is rare among people younger than 30 years of age, and more likely to happen to heavy drinkers (APA, 2013; Maldonado et al., 2014).

Furthermore, not all individuals with alcohol withdrawal symptoms will develop severe or dramatic withdrawal. Less than 10% of individuals who experience withdrawal may develop *severe* withdrawal symptoms, such as severe autonomic hyperactivity, tremors, withdrawal delirium or seizures, and less than 3% will develop tonic-clonic seizures (APA, 2013). Risk factors for severe alcohol withdrawal may include older age, a dependence on both alcohol and other depressant drugs such as sedative-hypnotics, a history of previously many detoxification episodes, previous occurrence of blackouts, and previous alcohol withdrawal history (APA, 2013; Maldonado et al., 2014). Studies have shown that a history of previous occurrence of alcohol withdrawal or delirium tremens is among the strongest predictors for the occurrence of withdrawal syndromes (Maldonado et al., 2014).

How to help patients manage withdrawal syndromes? In this section, I will discuss: patient placement criteria—i.e., how we determine whether a patient should go to inpatient or outpatient detox program—and whether a patient should receive a medical or social detox, plus the contents of the two types of programs.

Traditionally, withdrawal management involves inpatient procedures. Today many withdrawal syndromes, except for the most severe ones, can be treated on an ambulatory or outpatient basis (Mee-Lee et al., 2013). At least two assessment systems are relevant to help guide clinicians with regard to a patient's placement: (1) the Clinical Institute Withdrawal Assessment for Alcohol, Revised (CIWA-Ar), which measures the severity of alcohol withdrawal, and the Clinical Opiate Withdrawal Scale (COWS), which measures the severity of opioid withdrawal, and (2) the ASAM's five levels of withdrawal management.

The CIWA-Ar (Sullivan et al., 1989) is a widely adopted scale that measures the severity of alcohol withdrawal symptoms (see Appendix D). The scale has high validity and reliability, is free, and takes only 2 to 5 minutes to complete. The CIWA-Ar covers 10 items—i.e., nausea and vomiting, tremor, paroxysmal sweats, anxiety, tactile disturbances, auditory disturbances, visual disturbances, headache, fullness in head, agitation, and orientation and clouding of sensorium—with a total maximum score of 67. Stephens and colleagues (2014) suggest three conditions to meet an inpatient detoxification admittance: (a) patient has a total CIWA-Ar score > 15; (b) patient has a total CIWA-Ar score of 8–15, but has a previous history of seizures or delirium tremens; or (c) patient has a decompensated chronic or acute medical disease, regardless of his or her CIWA-Ar score. Stephens and colleagues' suggestions are consistent with the ASAM's criteria.

Modeling the format and rating system of the CIWA-Ar scale, the Clinical Opiate Withdrawal Scale (COWS, Wesson & Ling, 2003) measures the severity of opioid withdrawal. It includes 11 items—i.e., resting pulse rate, sweating during past half hour (not accounted for by room temperature or physical activity), restlessness observed during assessment, pupil size, bone or joint aches, runny nose or tearing (not accounted for by cold symptoms or allergies), gastrointestinal upset during past half hour, tremor in outstretched hands, yawning observed during assessment, anxiety or irritability, and piloerection—with a total score of 5–12 points indicating mild; 13–24, moderate; 25 to 36, moderately severe; and greater than 36, severe (Wesson & Ling, 2003). The COWS takes about 2 minutes to complete while a clinician talks with the patient and observes his or her opioid withdrawal signs (Wesson & Ling, 2003).

The ASAM suggests that "The CIWA-Ar scale . . . has only been validated for tracking the withdrawal management process—not for making level of care decisions. Because it does not take into account the influence of the other five ASAM criteria dimensions, it should only be used as part of the decision-making process and *not as a stand-alone determinant* [italics added] for level of care decisions" (Mee-Lee et al., 2013, p. 146). ASAM includes six criteria dimensions to assess and determine at which level a patient should be placed; the "acute intoxication and/or withdrawal potential" is only one of the six dimensions and is the first dimension. The other five dimensions are: dimension 2: biomedical conditions and complications; dimension 3: emotional, behavioral, or cognitive conditions and complications; dimension 4: readiness to change; dimension 5: relapse, continued use, or continued problem potential; and dimension 6: recovery/ living environment (Mee-Lee et al., 2013, p. 43). The ASAM emphasizes that patient withdrawal management placement criteria (e.g., outpatient or inpatient) should take all dimensions into consideration. For example, a patient may only have a mild risk for his or her withdrawal potential— i.e., with only the symptoms of "mild anxiety, sweating, and insomnia, but no tremor" (p. 148)—and therefore indicate the need for an outpatient program; however, if the patient does not have adequate family or other support or if he or she satisfies residential criteria for other dimension(s), the patient may be placed in a residential program.

The ASAM does not just divide placement levels into inpatient versus outpatient, it categorizes adults in five different levels of withdrawal management. They are: 1-WM (withdrawal management): ambulatory withdrawal management without extended on-site monitoring; 2-WM: ambulatory withdrawal management with extended on-site monitoring; 3.2-WM: clinically managed residential withdrawal management; 3.7-WM: medically monitored inpatient withdrawal management; and 4-WM: medically managed intensive inpatient withdrawal management (Mee-Lee et al., 2013. p. 107).

There is no clear-cut definition for social detoxification but, in general, it is offered more for mild-to-moderate alcohol withdrawal. Social detoxification involves nonpharmacological treatment of alcohol withdrawal, including "frequent reassurance, reality orientation, monitoring of vital signs, personal attention, and general nursing care" (Kranzler et al., 2014, p. 20). Kranzler and colleagues, however, emphasize that some medical problems associated with alcoholism may complicate therapy and practitioners must take care to refer a patient whose condition indicates medical treatment. The ASAM considers its 3.2-WM level a "social detox" or "social setting detoxification," since it is "clinically managed" rather than "medically monitored" (3.7-WM) or "medically managed" (4-WM). According to the ASAM, social detox accentuates social and peer support instead of medical care; it offers treatment and services to patients whose intoxication or withdrawal symptoms and signs require 24-hour support but who do not need medically monitored or medically managed inpatient treatment (Mee-Lee et al., 2013).

Pharmacotherapy for Alcohol Detox

Medication is normally required for withdrawal symptoms only if a patient's CIWA-Ar score is greater than 10 (Kranzler et al., 2014; SAMHSA & NIAAA, 2015). However, Stephens and colleagues (2014) suggest that a CIWA score < 8 but with a prior history of delirium tremens or withdrawal seizures should lead to consideration of outpatient detoxification with fixed dose medications (Stephens et al., 2014, p. 589). The goal of pharmacotherapy during this alcohol detox stage is to prevent a patient's early withdrawal symptoms from progressing into more severe symptoms. Benzodiazepines are usually used to treat alcohol withdrawals because of their ability to modulate the $GABA_A$ receptor activities and therefore restrain the hyperexcitability related to alcohol withdrawal. Among benzodiazepines, oxazepam (Serax), chlordiazepoxide (Librium), or diazepam (Valium) are more frequently used. Diazepam relieves tremor, acute agitation, hallucinosis, and acute or impending delirium tremens in alcohol acute withdrawal (SAMHSA & NIAAA, 2015). Lorazepam may also be used and its intravenous dose can be used for speedy treatment of progressing delirium (Kranzler et al., 2014). Anticonvulsant medications can also decrease the central nervous system hyperexcitability caused by alcohol withdrawal; although they are used more often now, their use is still controversial and are not perceived as able to replace benzodiazepines during the early treatment phase (Minozzi et al., 2010). Patients in alcohol withdrawal should receive thiamine for the initial three to five days; multivitamin supplements (e.g., Vitamin B complex, Vitamin C) can be given during the acute stage of treatment (Kattimani & Bharadwaj, 2013; Perry, 2014). Thiamine supplementation and Vitamin B complex (folates included) are especially important to preventing Wernicke's encephalopathy (Mirijello et al., 2015).

Pharmacotherapy for Opioid Detox

Methadone, an opioid agonist, has been traditionally the typical medication for treatment of opioid withdrawal symptoms. Detoxification can be as long as six months in an outpatient methadone clinic; it can also be just several says in an inpatient setting. As mentioned earlier, opioid withdrawal symptoms can be extremely painful and the acute treatment can reduce a patient's distress rather than suppress all withdrawal symptoms (Renner et al., 2014). Buprenorphine, a partial opioid agonist, has also been considered as an effective medication to detoxify opioids; the office-based sublingual buprenorphine treatment has become one of the options for opioid detoxification treatment. Clonidine, an alpha 2 agonist, is also often used for detoxification as it can suppress many autonomic symptoms of withdrawal (Renner et al., 2014).

Relapse Prevention

When a person's addiction has progressed to physical dependence, withdrawal management treatment becomes the first priority (Mee-Lee et al., 2013). However, scientific studies have shown that withdrawal management or detoxification alone seldom helps a person reach a sustained and long-term recovery (Mee-Lee et al., 2013; NIDA, 2018). As mentioned earlier, acute withdrawal symptoms may only last for a week, protracted withdrawal symptoms—albeit with a lesser intensity—could last for 3 to 6 months. Furthermore, the phenomenon of craving or urge—which has caught more attention in the field in the past decades than previously, and which was added by the *DSM-5* in 2013 to be one of the 11 criteria for substance use disorder—can exist in an addicted person for years and can trigger relapse anytime. Craving is likely to be activated via withdrawal symptoms, stress, and/or cues associated with substance use and abuse (e.g., persons, things, and places). "Craving has also been shown to involve classical conditioning and is associated with activation of specific reward structures in the brain" (APA, 2013, p. 483). All of these comprise the hallmark of the nature of addiction—it is a chronic and relapsing disease. A withdrawal management treatment—inpatient or outpatient— is often short-term and only ranges from 3 to 5 days or a week, sometimes followed with a 28-day rehab program, and therefore insufficient. A post-detox aftercare planning and treatment that focuses on long-term recovery and relapse prevention is critical to help an addicted person achieve long-term recovery. These post-detox programs can be residential or outpatient, or be participation in community peer-supported self-help groups. Treatment strategies in this relapse prevention phase may include pharmacotherapy and behavioral/psychosocial treatment and intervention (including community self-help groups). In this section, I discuss pharmacotherapy, specifically focusing on alcohol and opioid use disorder. Behavioral/psychosocial treatment will be covered in Chapter 8. I include discussions on issues related to medications for relapse prevention, as well as currently approved medications for alcohol and opioid relapse prevention.

Pharmacotherapy for Relapse Prevention

Issues Related to Pharmacotherapy for Relapse Prevention

At least three issues are presently involved in pharmacotherapy targeting addiction relapse prevention. First, not enough medication options are available for addiction treatment. Scholars and practitioners have criticized the slow progress in the development of various efficacious medications to treat addiction. For example, Hall and colleagues (2015) state that few new medications have been approved in the past two decades and the most commonly used medications such as nicotine replacement therapy and methadone actually became available in the 1960s. Kranzler and colleagues (2014) say that "knowledge obtained from neurogenetics and neuroimaging has provided new insights into the etiology and pathophysiology of addiction, prompting a renewed interest in the pharmacological treatment of substance use disorders . . . Nonetheless, the high prevalence of these and other addictive disorders contrasts sharply with the limited pharmacological options that exist to treat them" and that "There are . . . many more medications to treat other psychiatric conditions than there are for addictive disorders" (p. xiii).

Second, the development of medications for addiction treatment is not even across the various addictive substances. For example, more medications have been designed and approved by the US Food and Drug Administration (FDA) for treating alcohol, tobacco, and opioid addiction than for other addictions such as cocaine, amphetamines, and cannabis (Kranzler et al., 2014). Also, currently there are no FDA approved medications for behavioral addiction such as gambling disorder, internet gaming addiction, and sex addiction.

Third, physicians appear conservative in prescribing, and patients in taking, medications for addiction treatment. To take alcohol dependence as an example, pharmacotherapy is more often used for detoxification/ withdrawal management and less so for relapse prevention. Physicians frequently use benzodiazepines to manage alcoholic patients' moderate or severe withdrawal symptoms, but they may be less prepared and less likely to prescribe—and some patients also are reluctant to take—relapse-prevention medications such as naltrexone, acamprosate, and disulfiram (Finlay et al., 2017; Goh & Morgan, 2017; Harris et al., 2013; Kranzler et al., 2014). Mark and colleagues' (2003) study revealed that addiction physicians prescribed naltrexone to only 13% of their alcoholic patients and disulfiram to only 9% of them, whereas they prescribed antidepressants to 44% of them. Based on the IMS National Prescription Audit (NPA) Plus database, Mark and colleagues (2009) found that alcoholism medication prescriptions increased from 393,000 in 2003 to about 720,000 in 2007, mainly attributable to the induction of acamprosate in 2005. In spite of the growth, these authors found that "overall substance abuse retail medication sales remain small relative to the size of the population that could benefit from treatment and relative to sales for other medications, such as antidepressants" (p. 345). They commented that "The extent to which substance dependence medications will be adopted by physicians and patients, and marketed by industry, remains uncertain" (p. 345).

Barriers to pharmacotherapy for relapse prevention of alcohol use disorder and strategies to improve such deficiencies have been suggested. For example, one barrier could be doctors' absence of knowledge and skills on addiction and its treatment and their lack of confidence on the efficacies of the medications (Finlay et al., 2017; Goh & Morgan, 2017;

Harris et al., 2013). Harris and colleagues (2013) surveyed Veterans Health Administration service providers and found that they perceived "low patient demand" as one major barrier, and that they would offer pharmacotherapy to patients if the patient "asked about a medication, showed interest, or requested it" (p. 417). Harris and colleagues stated that many providers still consider pharmacotherapy just an optional treatment for alcohol addiction, and "not something they are obligated to promote independently or perceived patient preference" and that the disease model of addiction should be emphasized "in hopes of persuading providers that alcohol dependence is a chronic illness that mandates treatment . . . even in the absence of patient initiative or overt interest, just as one might promote an antihypertensive for chronically elevated blood pressure" (pp. 417, 418). Four directions were revealed based on Harris et al.'s study: "more education to prescribing providers," "more education to patients," "increased involvement of physicians in alcoholism treatment," and "more compelling research on existing medication" (p. 418).

Pharmacotherapy for Relapse Prevention of Alcohol Use

Generally speaking, three major medications so far are accepted or licensed for relapse prevention of alcohol use in most countries that advocate the application of pharmacotherapy for alcohol dependence treatment; they are acamprosate, naltrexone, and disulfiram (Goh & Morgan, 2017). Meanwhile, new medications are under scientific investigation, such as baclofen, metadoxine, and topiramate (Goh & Morgan, 2017). A multisite, controlled clinical trial is evaluating the effectiveness and safety of a new medication, gabapentin enacarbil (HORIZANT), in reducing drinking among heavy drinkers or patients who met four or more symptoms of alcohol use disorder (NIAAA, 2015). Following are introductions to the three major medications approved by the US FDA for alcohol relapse prevention: acamprosate, naltrexone, and disulfiram.

Acamprosate

Multiple studies (although not all) and many meta-analyses have provided evidences of acamprosate being an efficacious and safe medication for alcohol relapse prevention (Kranzler et al., 2014; Mason & Heyser, 2010). The mechanism explaining how acamprosate reduces alcohol consumption and promotes abstinence in an addicted person is not yet completely clear, but theories suggest that acamprosate can lessen the excitability of and modulate the glutamatergic systems during the process of alcohol withdrawal, and thus ease the withdrawal symptoms and support abstinence (NIAAA, 2015; SAMHSA & NIAAA, 2015). Therefore, the primary function of acamprosate is its ability to decrease the undesirable symptoms associated with the phase immediately post alcohol detoxification (SAMHSA & NIAAA, 2015). As a medication promoting abstinence and relapse prevention, acamprosate also possesses many other advantages, such as low risks of abuse potential, tolerance, and overdose, as well as a low likelihood of interactions with other medications (National Collaborating Centre for Mental Health, The Royal College of Psychiatrists, 2011; SAMHSA & NIAAA, 2015).

Guidelines for adopting acamprosate are:

(1) Patients should be abstinent from alcohol at the time of taking acamprosate, as studies have shown that acamprosate is not efficacious for patients who have not completed detoxification or patients who have not reached abstinence before taking acamprosate (National Collaborating Centre for Mental Health, The Royal College of Psychiatrists, 2011).

(2) Acamprosate should be initiated as soon as possible following the withdrawal treatment phase because patients may relapse during the period between withdrawal treatment completion and acamprosate initiation, and because acamprosate may take 5 days to reach its steady levels (Mason, 2005).

(3) Because acamprosate is excreted mainly from kidneys and because it does not have significant interactions with other medications, it can benefit alcoholic patients who have hepatic diseases, who receive opioids treatment for addiction or pain, or who have to deal with multiple medical problems and take multiple medications. On the other hand, acamprosate is less appropriate for patients with severe renal impairment (SAMHSA & NIAAA, 2015).

(4) Although alcoholism medication prescriptions increased from 393,000 in 2003 to about 720,000 in 2007 and the growth is mainly attributable to the induction of acamprosate in 2005 (Mark et al., 2009), rates of adopting medications for alcohol relapse prevention are still much lower than those for other psychiatric medications. Kranzler and col-

leagues suggest more research is needed to find the patient attributes and treatment approaches that can optimize the function and effects of acamprosate (2014).

Naltrexone

Meta-analysis studies have found efficacy of naltrexone in treating alcohol use disorders (e.g., Bouza et al., 2004; Roozen et al., 2006). Although not all studies showed that naltrexone results in significant improvements in alcohol treatment outcomes, some clinical trials indicate that patients receiving naltrexone with behavioral treatments are less likely to relapse to alcohol use during treatment (Krishnan-Sarin et al., n.d.). There is also gradually more evidence suggesting naltrexone is particularly effective in some subgroups of alcoholic patients (Kranzler et al., 2014). Naltrexone is a pure opioid antagonist that can block brain opioid mu receptors, thereby preventing the receptors from being activated by an exogenous or endogenous opioid substance. This action not only attenuates euphoria associated with opiates or opioids (which will be discussed in the next section of pharmacotherapy for opioid relapse prevention) but also alcohol, making drinking less rewarding and reducing a person's craving for alcohol (Goh & Morgan, 2017; SAMHSA & NIAAA, 2015). Unlike disulfiram (Antabuse), naltrexone does not cause sickness if a person ingests alcohol. Another advantage is naltrexone tolerates well gastrointestinal side effects (Krishnan-Sarin et al., n.d.).

Guidelines for using naltrexone may include:

(1) Naltrexone has both the oral (e.g., Revia) and long-acting injectable (e.g., Vivitrol) forms. Both are effective for patients who are able to abstain from alcohol before treatment initiation; evidence does not show naltrexone is effective in alcoholic patients who are using at the initiation of treatment (SAMHSA & NIAAA, 2015).

(2) Poor naltrexone adherence may greatly reduce the medication's benefits and effectiveness. Oral naltrexone is therefore more appropriate for patients who have high motivation or have supports for daily dosing observed; extended-release injectable naltrexone has been developed to decrease the possible poor compliance to oral naltrexone (Kranzler et al., 2014). Although there are no formal comparisons between

the oral and the long-acting injectable naltrexone, the long-acting injectable form appears to have better adherence than the oral form (Gastfriend, 2011). The injectable naltrexone is given monthly or every four weeks, and should be administered intramuscularly—not intravenously or subcutaneously—with a specially designed needle (U.S. FDA, 2013). Also, physicians need to instruct patients to monitor possible reactions to the injection site (FDA, 2013).

(3) Side effects of naltrexone may include several. Since naltrexone is an opioid antagonist, the long-acting formulation Vivitrol is contraindicated among patients receiving opioid analgesics (Johnson, 2007). Also, when taking naltrexone, alcoholic patients who also have opioid dependence problems should be warned opioid withdrawal symptoms (such as nausea, insomnia, anxiety, muscle aches, and so on) could appear (SAMHSA & NIAAA, 2015). In addition, suicidal ideation or depression should be monitored among alcohol patients who are taking Vivitrol (Alkermes, Inc., cited in Johnson, 2007).

(4) Naltrexone may worsen liver toxicity; liver dysfunction has been found to be linked to injectable extended-release naltrexone treatment. Therefore, patients with acute liver impairment should not take naltrexone or patients who show symptoms/signs of acute hepatitis should discontinue use (National Collaborating Centre for Mental Health, The Royal College of Psychiatrists, 2011; SAMHSA & NIAAA, 2015). On the other hand, a dose of 50 mg naltrexone per day is very unlikely to result in hepatic toxicity and continued drinking actually is more likely to damage the liver (National Collaborating Centre for Mental Health, The Royal College of Psychiatrists, 2011). Naltrexone should also be used with caution among patients with severe or moderate renal problems (SAMHSA & NIAAA, 2015).

(5) Studies also showed three groups of alcoholic patients may experience greater naltrexone medication benefits: (a) patients who have more intense craving for alcohol than those with a lower level of craving; (b) patients who have a family history of alcoholism rather than those without such history; and (c) patients with opioid use disorder history and who are seeking treatment for alcohol problems, as naltrexone can curtail cravings for both alcohol and opioids (Krishnan-Sarin et al. 2007; Krishnan-Sarin et al., n.d; SAMHSA & NIAAA, 2015).

Disulfiram (Antabuse)

Compared to acamprosate and naltrexone, fewer scientific studies have been done regarding disulfiram's efficacy; in addition, it appears disulfiram is less frequently prescribed. For example, The U.K. National Institute for Health and Care Excellence (NICE) recommends disulfiram as second-line treatment, with acamprosate or naltrexone being the first-line treatment unless a patient prefers disulfiram (Goh & Morgan, 2017). Nonetheless, a recent systematic review by Jørgensen and colleagues (2011) showed that disulfiram had a better outcome on abstinence than other treatment, no treatment, or placebo in six of the 10 studies they reviewed and that the four studies that did not confirm this result showed no treatment to be better than disulfiram.

Disulfiram, the first US FDA-approved medication for relapse prevention of alcohol use disorder, became available in 1948. Naltrexone was approved by the FDA in 1994, followed by acamprosate in 2004. Today all three medications are adopted in major countries. Kranzler and colleagues believe the approval of disulfiram by FDA "preceded the implementation of rigorous requirements or efficacy that now must be satisfied for a drug to be marketed in the U.S." (2014, p. 24). On the other hand, Krampe and colleagues argued that the efficacies of disulfiram strongly depend on medication compliance and should be administered in a supervised way, but "the large-scale multicenter [randomized control trials] of Fuller and colleagues . . . investigated unsupervised disulfiram, resulting in a low compliance rate of 20% and no outcome differences between intervention and control groups. As a consequence, disulfiram was considered as an obsolete medication" (2011, p. 1732). This trend was even more apparent when new medications, naltrexone and acamprosate, became available. Krampe and colleagues advocate the value of supervised disulfiram as "the most successful pharmacological adjunct treatment to psychotherapy in alcoholism treatment" (p. 1733).

Disulfiram works in a very different manner compared to acamprosate (which decreases withdrawal discomforts), and naltrexone (which reduces craving). Disulfiram serves to create in an alcoholic patient a psychological deterrence to alcohol use via the patient's understanding of the fact that if he or she drinks on top of disulfiram, he or she will experience severe negative physiological consequences. Therefore, medication compliance and supervision as well as the role of psychotherapy and psychoeducation are extremely important for disulfiram to be efficacious. When a person drinks, alcohol is first metabolized by liver's alcohol dehydrogenase into acetaldehyde—a toxic compound, which then is converted into acetic acid by another liver enzyme called aldehyde dehydrogenase. The mechanism of the occurrence of interaction between alcohol and disulfiram is through disulfiram's inhibition of aldehyde dehydrogenase, which subsequently results in an accumulation of acetaldehyde and therefore, many unpleasant and uncomfortable symptoms, such as increased pulse, difficult breathing, facial flushing, palpitation, headache, nausea, vomiting, and rarely cardiovascular collapse (the worst of its symptoms) (Jørgensen et al., 2011; Krishnan-Sarin et al., n.d.; SAMHSA & NIAAA, 2015).

Guidelines for using disulfiram may include:

(1) Despite disulfiram's treatment efficacies, its prescription must be handled with care and safety issues taken into consideration (Kranzler et al., 2014; Mutschler et al., 2011). It is not recommended that disulfiram be administered to patients who (a) do not want to use disulfiram, (b) have medical or psychological contraindications (e.g., severe liver disease, diabetes, coronary artery disease, psychosis, etc.), and/or (c) do not want to pursue total abstinence from alcohol (Kranzler et al., 2014; SAMHSA & NIAAA, 2015). Use should also be with caution with patients who have hypothyroidism, nephritis, cerebral damage, or epilepsy, and who are over 60 years of age (SAMHSA & NIAAA, 2015). Patients should be warned about—and practitioners be sure the patients have the capacity to understand—possible risks involved with disulfiram use and its interaction with alcohol, and the need to avoid items that contain alcohol, such as perfumes, aerosols, some food, and so on (Kranzler et al., 2014; National Collaborating Centre for Mental Health, The Royal College of Psychiatrists, 2011). Ideal candidates may include those who want to abstain and also are willing to take this medication under the observation of treatment program or significant others (SAMHSA & NIAAA, 2015).

(2) Because of the disulfiram-ethanol interaction, a patient should receive disulfiram at least 24 hours after his or her last alcoholic drink and should not drink for at least one week or two weeks after his or her

last disulfiram ingestion (Kranzler et al., 2014; National Collaborating Centre for Mental Health, The Royal College of Psychiatrists, 2011).

(3) Supervision ensures medication compliance and enhances treatment efficacies (Kranzler et al., 2014). Supervised medication administration, by treatment program staff, significant others of a patient, or someone nominated by the patient, should be encouraged.

(4) A successful psychotherapeutic application of disulfiram requires therapists with knowledge on the pharmacological actions of disulfiram, its related adverse effects and safety issues, contraindications, and handling a disulfiram-alcohol reaction. Studies have shown that a supervised medication administration with an integration of behavioral therapy can significantly increase the efficiency of disulfiram in deterring alcohol use and achieving abstinence. Krampe and colleagues (2011) recommend disulfiram treatment be delivered in a supervised, low-dose (e.g., no more than 100 mg/day), and long-term form combined with behavioral therapy. The behavioral therapy can include components of psychoeducation, training patients to use disulfiram as a coping tool, broadening patients' coping skills, and helping patients eventually replace disulfiram with other effective new tools.

(5) Regular blood tests and medical examinations are necessary and side effects and adverse events of patients must be closely monitored, especially among polysubstance-using patients (Krampe et al., 2011; Specka et al., 2014). Patients may continue disulfiram long term if the treatment is successful and has relatively no side effects (Goh & Morgan, 2017).

Pharmacotherapy for Relapse Prevention of Opioid Use

There are three major medications for relapse prevention of opioid use: methadone, buprenorphine (oral or implant), and naltrexone (oral or injectable). To describe their nature and function, it is necessary to first explain the concepts of "opioid agonists," "opioid antagonists," and "partial opioid agonists." Agonists bind to and activate receptors in the brain; antagonists also bind to the receptors, but they block the receptors instead of activating them; and partial agonists bind to and activate the receptors, but they do not reach the same level full agonists do. Treatment Improvement Protocol (TIP) Series 40 provides the following information regarding the

PHARMACOTHERAPY

three concepts: There are various types of opioid receptors in the brain and the mu receptor is the most relevant type to opioid addiction and treatment. Mu receptors are turned on by full mu opioid agonists, which are the most addictive substances and include for example, morphine, heroin, oxycodone, hydromorphone, and methadone. On the other hand, opioid antagonists occupy and block receptors, preventing the receptors from being activated by agonists. Naltrexone and naloxone are examples of this category. Partial agonists hold some properties of full agonists and some of antagonists. Partial agonists involve a ceiling effect, such that their effects do not increase further after they reach a certain level, and that a higher dose will make them perform like antagonists as they occupy the receptors and block full agonists from activating the receptors. Buprenorphine is a mu opioid partial agonist (Center for Substance Abuse Treatment [CSAT], 2004).

To treat opioid agonist addiction, such as heroin addiction, an opioid antagonist approach would, theoretically and pharmacologically speaking, make more sense because the antagonists can occupy the receptors and block heroin away from activating the mu receptors, therefore reducing the reinforcing effects of heroin and patients' craving for heroin (Kleber, 2007). It may also appear to be counterintuitive to use an agonist, like methadone, to treat the addiction of another agonist, for example, heroin, because the person may just switch addiction from heroin to methadone. However, in reality so far, extensive research has suggested the contrary. Numerous scientific studies found that methadone (full agonist) is effective regarding treatment retention, decrease of heroin use (Marsch, 1998; Mattick et al., 2003, 2009), decrease of criminal activities (Marsch, 1998; Russolillo et al., 2017), and decrease of HIV transmission (Marsch, 1998). This may be related to the chronic and severe nature of opioid addiction on one hand, but on the other hand, treatment retention and medication compliance issues may play a key role. Patients are more likely to stay in methadone treatment or buprenorphine treatment; they are more likely to drop out of naltrexone treatment or abstinence-based treatment. Many patients are not interested in naltrexone because naltrexone—unlike methadone—does not contain opioid agonist activity and they experience cravings, therefore losing motivation to adhere to the medication and dropping out soon after the treatment (CSAT, 2004). Johansson and colleagues (2006) said, "Retention is always a key variable for efficacy of treatment and is itself a measure of efficacy. A treatment intervention with lower retention than a controlled condition is not effective" (p. 500). The apparent low treatment efficacy of naltrexone is explained by the patients' noncompliance of medication rather than by the medication's pharmacological effects per se. This phenomenon is somewhat similar to the situation of disulfiram in treating alcohol dependence, where medication supervision is involved and therefore medication adherence ensured, disulfiram either has better treatment outcomes than other treatments or no significant difference between the two (Jørgensen et al., 2011).

While the agonist model—especially methadone—has been the gold standard in treating opioid addiction since its inception about 60 years ago (Ayanga et al., 2016; Connery, 2015; Srivastava et al., 2017), more attention has been given to research on extended release naltrexone (XR-NTX) since the late 1990s. This was "when injecting opioid use and the rapid spread of HIV in the Russian Federation converged with an interest in exploring ways to control the HIV epidemic and led to meetings sponsored by the US National Institute on Drug Abuse (NIDA) and Pavlov State Medical University in St. Petersburg, Russian Federation" (Woody et al., 2016, p. 402). The AIDS epidemic has prompted many countries, such as China, India, and Taiwan, to legalize methadone for heroin addiction treatment, and the AIDS epidemic, although still facing many challenges, has been curbed dramatically in those countries. However, agonist treatment, such as methadone, is still illegal in many other countries, including the Russian Federation. During this period, Fidelity Capital in Russia developed a naltrexone implant that can block opioids for 3 months and Alkermes in the US developed extended release injectable naltrexone (XR-NTX) (Woody et al., 2016). The US FDA approved XR-NTX for opioid addiction treatment in 2010.

The development of XR-NTX is potentially of great benefit not only because it can enhance patients' medication adherence, but also for the following reasons: (a) owing to differing philosophical perspectives, many countries approve antagonists (e.g., naltrexone) but prohibit the use of agonists (e.g., methadone) to treat heroin addiction; (b) even within the countries where methadone is approved, methadone is not necessarily approved by all local regions and not all people who need it have access to it; (c) even where methadone is an approved treatment, some people, including patients themselves, may attach a stigma to methadone, which deters treatment; (d) agonist treatment might be less appropriate for patients of certain subgroups, such as patients who do not respond well to—or who do not prefer—methadone or buprenorphine, whose occupation bans opioid use, or who only have a short addiction history (Krupitsky et al., 2011; Nunes et al., 2015). Studies, including randomized controlled trials, have shown treatment efficacies of long-acting injectable naltrexone for opioid dependence (Kjome & Moeller, 2011; Krupitsky et al., 2011).

Extended research has recommended that methadone, buprenorphine, and extended-release naltrexone yield superior opioid addiction treatment outcomes compared to non-medication based treatment, and that the agonist model (e.g., methadone and buprenorphine) seems to be more effective than the antagonist model (e.g., naltrexone). However, much research is still needed regarding direct comparisons between methadone, buprenorphine, and oral and intramuscular naltrexone, as well as treatment paradigms and behavioral treatment that can optimize pharmacotherapy (Ayanga et al., 2016; Bart, 2012). Individualizing medication choice— i.e., who will respond to which medication best—is also a goal for future research. Before the goal is achieved in the scientific community and treatment field, patients should be informed of treatment options, their potential adverse and side effects, as well as expected outcomes, so that they can select the medication that might benefit him or her most (Bart, 2012). Following are introductions to each of the three major medications for opioid addiction treatment.

Methadone

As mentioned earlier, opioid substitution therapy (opioid agonist therapy) has been considered far more effective than abstinence-based treatment. Methadone was introduced in the US in 1964 and has become the most frequently used medicine for opioid relapse prevention in the US. Numerous scientific studies and meta-analyses—both from the US and other countries—have demonstrated methadone's efficacies in retaining patients in treatment, suppressing opioid withdrawal, decreasing craving for opioids, blocking other opioids' effects, reducing nonopioid drug use, improving employment, reducing criminal activities, bettering patients' social relationships and social functioning, decreasing needle sharing and

HIV transmission, enhancing patients' overall mental and physical health, and/or decreasing mortality (Johansson et al., 2007; Marsch, 1998; McLellan et al., 1993; Sun et al., 2015). Mattick and colleagues' (2009) systematic review of 11 qualified studies with randomized clinical trials (1,969 participants in total) also showed that methadone treatment is more effective than a treatment program that does not offer opioid substitution therapy in patients' treatment retention and reduction of heroin use, but the findings showed no significant difference on mortality or criminal activity between the two groups. These overall positive treatment outcomes of opioid substitution therapy may be especially prominent within the context that methadone patients additionally receive drug monitoring and individual/ family/group counseling, as well as needed medical, psychological, vocational, and social resources (CSAT, 2011).

Methadone is a synthetic mu-opioid receptor agonist that is taken orally. It is long acting, with a slow onset and long elimination half-life (t 1/2 = 24–36 h) and is used for both opioid withdrawal management and maintenance therapy (Ayanga et al., 2016; CSAT, 2011). Methadone prevents opioid withdrawal symptoms, reduces patients' opioid craving, and blocks illicit opioids' effects (NIDA). Methadone maintenance is not just a substitution of an illegal opiate; unlike illegal opiates, methadone rarely needs to increase its dose due to tolerance once a dose is stabilized (e.g., normally 60–120 mg daily) and a same dose can, in some cases, be held for more than 20 years (Bart's review, 2012; CSAT, 2011). In addition, methadone binds about 30% of mu-opioid receptors, which allows the remainder to conduct their normal physiological function regarding modulation of reward, mood, pain, and stress (see Bart's review, 2012). In addition to its pharmacological advantages, methadone has other advantages: it is administered under medical supervision, which is better than street opioids such as heroin that often have unknown purity; it is taken orally and reduces needle use and subsequently HIV transmission; patients usually do not experience euphoric or analgesic effects from methadone, which enables patients to resume a productive lifestyle, replacing their previous compulsive occupation of drug-seeking behavior and criminal activities to support their drug use (CSAT, 2011; WHO, 2009); and it has higher treatment retention than buprenorphine or naltrexone treatment (Schuckit's review, 2016; Srivastava et al., 2017).

Following are some guidelines regarding methadone treatment provision:

(1) Methadone is a controlled schedule II drug; to treat opioid addiction, it can only be dispensed by opioid treatment programs that are (a) registered as a narcotic treatment program by the US Drug Enforcement Agency (DEA) and (b) certified by Substance Abuse and Mental Health Services Administration (SAMHSA, 2014). Nurse practitioners or physician assistants may also deliver methadone to a patient as long as they are under the supervision of the SAMHSA-certified and DEA-registered medical director of the opioid treatment program (SAMHSA, 2014). Patients are eligible for methadone maintenance if they currently have an opioid use disorder that manifests physiologic features or who have high relapse risks (Schuckit, 2016). Also, patients cannot simultaneously participate in another maintenance treatment program (Schuckit, 2016). Eligible patients are required to get prescribed dose of methadone by going to the opioid treatment program daily, except Sundays and federal and state holidays. Take-home methadone may be allowed if the patient meets certain criteria specified by the Federal regulations (CSAT, 2011).

(2) Patients' preferences and characteristics should be taken into consideration when choosing agonists. In general, for patients with high risk of treatment dropout (e.g., injection drug users), methadone (a full agonist) may be considered as a higher-priority choice than buprenorphine (a partial agonist) or naltrexone (an antagonist) (Connery, 2015; Srivastava et al., 2017). If a patient receives buprenorphine-naloxone first and still persistently experiences withdrawal or craving symptoms or still uses opioids after an optimal dose of buprenorphine-naloxone is prescribed, a switch from buprenorphine-naloxone to methadone treatment may be considered (Srivastava et al., 2017).

On the other hand, although methadone has a better treatment retention than buprenorphine (Hser et al., 2014), buprenorphine has a lower risk of overdose. Safety should be the first priority for patients who are vulnerable to the risk of toxicity. Those may include, for example, the elderly, people who take high levels of sedating drugs or benzodiazepines, people with a severe respiratory medical condition or with prolonged QT interval (a heart rhythm condition), people with low level of tolerance, heavy drinkers, and so on (Schuckit, 2016; Srivastava et al., 2017). Buprenorphine-naloxone may be a more appropriate choice than methadone in these cases (Srivastava et al., 2017).

(3) Discuss with patients various treatment options and their implications, and document those discussions. As mentioned earlier, patients should be informed of treatment options, their potential adverse and side effects, as well as expected outcomes, so that they can select the medication that benefits him or her best (Bart, 2012). When agonists such as methadone or buprenorphine/naloxone maintenance are recommended, patients need to also be informed that they may re-experience opioid craving/withdrawal and may be at high risk for opioid relapse, or even fatal overdose, following termination of agonist therapy (Connery, 2015). In addition, although research evidence is not complete regarding the efficacy of antagonist treatment, for people with high treatment motivation and whose occupations do not favor or accept an agonist treatment model (e.g., physicians, pilots, professional athletes, and so on), antagonists may be considered. Also, antagonists may be considered for patients with co-occurring opioid use disorder and alcohol use disorder, as extended-release naltrexone treatment can benefit both. All of these should be integrated into a "collaborative informed consent process" and be carefully documented (Connery, 2015).

(4) Dosing guidelines, supervisions of high dosing cases, and patient education on overdose risks are important and can reduce mortality rates (Bart, 2012; Davoli et al., 2007). Although methadone safety has been established and recent methadone-related deaths tend to have occurred in pain treatment rather than in opioid addiction treatment, methadone, like other opioid agonists, can still cause fatal respiratory suppression when its dose exceeds a person's tolerance. Methadone overdose is more likely to occur during its induction phase (first 2 to 4 weeks) due to patients' multiple substance ingestion, and is even more likely to occur during methadone discontinuation because of patients' tolerance loss (Bart, 2012; Cornish et al., 2010). It is recommended to begin with the doses of 15–30 mg and increase by 10–15 mg every 3–5 days to 50–80 mg per day during the induction and early stabilization phase (about weeks 1–2), and to increase the dose during the late stabilization phase (about weeks 3–6) as tolerance is developed. It is suggested that a dose of 80–100 mg per day is most effective. Patient education should be provided regarding the high risk of methadone overdose during the induction phase and especially during the phase upon methadone discontinuation if they relapse. In addition, patients

receiving a dose greater than 100 mg per day should be monitored for side effects (Davoli et al., 2007).

(5) There is no universal agreement on the length of methadone maintenance treatment. Schuckit (2016) said that some clinicians favor helping their patients try to discontinue the medication around after one year, whereas others believe that methadone treatment should be unrestricted, accentuating the high risk of relapse and possible overdose deaths after patients' leaving methadone programs. While we discussed earlier the possible switch from buprenorphine to methadone, another related issue is how to help a patient switch from methadone to buprenorphine if he or she so desires, which will be discussed in next section on buprenorphine.

(6) Increase adequate coverage of and access to methadone treatment. Although methadone has demonstrated its superb treatment benefits and efficacy in treating opioid addiction, still globally "less than 650,000 people are thought to be receiving substitution treatment . . . less than 10% of those in need of treatment" (World Health Organization [WHO], 2008, para. 9). In the US, the rate of individuals with opioid use disorders receiving treatment was also low; it was about 18.8% in 2004–2008, and 19.7% in 2009–2013 (Saloner & Karthikeyan, 2015). In addition to the factors of differing philosophical perspectives and policies, factors such as stigma, costs, and inconvenience may have contributed to this phenomenon.

Certain sections of society, including some practitioners and addicted individuals themselves, may still attach a stigma to addiction in general, and agonist treatment in particular. CSAT (2011) states that stigma has isolated medication-assisted treatment (MAT) from mainstream medicine. Not only does society need to change its attitude toward MAT, treatment staff should do the same too. For example, staff should avoid the term "substitution treatment" because it "incorrectly implies that long-acting opioid medications act like heroin and other short-acting opioids" (in spite of this, many research publications associate the term "substitution therapy" with methadone or other agonist maintenance practices); they should also replace the drug-test specimens term "dirty" with "positive" and "clean" with "negative" (CSAT, 2011, p. 9). National education as well as clinical supervision and leadership efforts will facilitate reducing stigma.

Costs may also deter a person from seeking, or cause early discharge from, agonist maintenance treatment. For example, one factor leading to some patients' premature discharge from methadone maintenance was "nonpayment of fees," based on the qualitative study by Reisinger and colleagues (2009). Methadone maintenance treatment is not a covered benefit in 17 state Medicaid programs, although buprenorphine is covered to some level in every state Medicaid program. Worse is that some states that are currently offering coverage are challenging their future Medicaid coverage of methadone maintenance (Saloner et al., 2016). Saloner et al.'s study found that "Overall, 7.0% of Medicaid enrollees in treatment for opioid use received OAT [opioid agonist therapy] in states with no methadone coverage, whereas 46.6% received OAT in states with a Medicaid benefit that covers methadone maintenance, and 26.3% received OAT in states funding methadone only through a SAPT [Substance Abuse Prevention and Treatment] block grant" (p. 677). These authors suggest that Medicaid coverage of methadone maintenance therapy may facilitate entry to specialty treatment among particular populations such as heroin users.

Since methadone is a controlled substance, there are many regulations attached to its receipt, including going to the treatment program daily for the dose needed, which may cause a great deal of inconvenience for many patients. Renner and colleagues (2014) said "They resist the controls mandated in a methadone clinic and are often misinformed about methadone itself, factors that may make them reluctant to enter into this form of treatment" (p. 116). Some program-related reasons for early discharge from methadone programs may include "disagreement with program rules" and "schedule conflicts" (Reisinger et al., 2009). However, compared to methadone clinics in China and Taiwan where many methadone clinics operate from 9 am to 5 pm or 7 pm, with 12 noon to 1 pm being staff's lunch break, many of those in the US operate from 3 am to about 12 noon, which appears to be more accommodating to patients' needs in many regards, such as employment. Furthermore, there is no take-home medication policy in methadone programs in China and Taiwan (Sun et al., 2016). The take-home medication policy in the US allows a patient to have unsupervised doses more than just for Sundays or federal and state holidays. A medical director of the methadone clinic can decide if a patient meets all eight following criteria specified by the Federal regulations: "Absence of recent drug and alcohol abuse," "Regular [opioid treatment program]

(OTP) attendance," "Absence of behavioral problems at the OTP," "Absence of recent criminal activity," "Stable home environment and social relationships," "Acceptable length of time in comprehensive maintenance treatment," "Assurance of safe storage of take-home medication," and "Determination that rehabilitative benefits of decreased OTP attendance outweigh the potential risk of diversion" (CSAT, 2011, p. 81). The Federal regulations also specified maximum doses allowed for take-home based on the patient's length of treatment (CSAT, 2011).

Buprenorphine

As mentioned above, although methadone has superb proven efficacy, its treatment connotes stigma and it is isolated from mainstream medicine practice. In general, physicians cannot prescribe methadone at office-based settings and patients must go to licensed opioid treatment programs or methadone clinics to get the dose on a daily basis; as a result, the percentage of individuals with opioid use disorder getting treatment is low (CSAT, 2004). To remedy this problem, efforts to bring opioid treatment to mainstream medical practice started to take shape in the 1990s and resulted in the Drug Addiction Treatment Act (DATA) in 2000 (CSAT, 2004). Under DATA 2000, physicians who obtain a waiver can prescribe buprenorphine, a Schedule III medication, at their own office settings. Patients can get their doses on a monthly basis once they are on a stable buprenorphine dose, make progress, and show no illicit drug use (CSAT, 2004). Two forms of sublingual formulations of buprenorphine were approved by the US FDA in 2002 for opioid addiction treatment, including pure buprenorphine (Subutex) and buprenorphine/naloxone combination (Suboxone). Although Ling and colleagues stated that "As evidenced by its proven efficacy, its widespread uptake by clinicians, and its acceptance among patients, buprenorphine looks to be a success. It is arguably the most significant advance in the treatment of opioid addition since the introduction of methadone" (2011, p. 182), it is unclear whether the availability of buprenorphine has enhanced treatment rates and research shows that only about half of the waivered MDs actually were prescribing it (Kissin et al., 2006; Stein et al., 2012). Buprenorphine utilization among physicians has not been proportionate to the scale of the current opioid epidemic (Huhn & Dunn, 2017).

Many clinical trial studies and systematic reviews have confirmed the safety and efficacy of buprenorphine for withdrawal management and maintenance treatment (Ayanga et al., 2016; Fareed et al., 2012; Ling & Wesson, 2003; Ling et al., 2011; Webster et al., 2016). The advantages of buprenorphine are both its distinctive pharmacological properties and its safety profile (CSAT, 2004). As a partial opioid agonist, buprenorphine can reduce opioid withdrawal and cravings and therefore can attract individuals with opioid use disorder; on the other hand, because it is not a full agonist, buprenorphine creates a lower level of dose-dependent euphoria and thus has a lower addiction and abuse liability compared to methadone (CSAT, 2004; Ling et al., 2011). As a partial opioid agonist, it is also less likely to lead to respiratory depression or overdose than a full opioid agonist such as methadone (CSAT, 2004; Dahan, 2006). In addition, buprenorphine has minimal impact on serum transaminase levels and liver functions; it also seems to be as safe as methadone for treating opioid addiction among pregnant women (see review of Ayanga et al., 2016). Hser and colleagues' study (2014) showed that compared to methadone treatment group, the buprenorphine treatment group has a lower treatment retention rate, but also a lower continued illicit opioid use rate. Other advantages of buprenorphine include that it has less stigma than methadone treatment and is more convenient for patients to access treatment as they now can get it from a private doctor's office and for up to a one-month prescription. This option may have "attracted many individuals in the early stage of illness who have traditionally avoided methadone treatment" (Renner et al., 2014, p. 121).

Although buprenorphine is a partial agonist and, therefore, less likely to be abused than methadone or other agonists, it still has the potential to be diverted as it has the features of an agonist. To combat the concern of medication diversion and increase medication adherence, as well as reduce accidental exposure and poisoning, two measures were developed (Itzoe & Guarnieri, 2017; Ling et al., 2011). First, in addition to the buprenorphine monotherapy (containing only buprenorphine, e.g., Subutex), the combined buprenorphine and naloxone with a ratio of 4:1 (e.g., Suboxone) was created. Naloxone is an antagonist, which will not negatively interfere with the effects of buprenorphine when being taken sublingually; but naloxone may precipitate withdrawal syndromes if it is liquefied and injected (CSAT, 2004). Second, the US FDA approved Probuphine in 2016 to treat opioid addiction. Probuphine is a long-acting buprenorphine implant that delivers a steady low dose of buprenorphine over a 6-month course; such a subdermal (under skin) tool not only enhances medication adherence and steady drug amount in the body but also makes it difficult to divert the medication or create accidental exposure opportunities for children. Many studies have shown its efficacy and safety (Barnwal et al., 2017; Itzoe & Guarnieri, 2017). The buprenorphine implant procedure involves inserting four implants (each is 2.5 mm wide and 26 mm long) subdermally into the upper arm (inner side of either arm). The treatment is effective for six months; after that, the doctor can remove the implants and insert new implants into the patient's alternate arm (Chavoustie et al., 2017).

Following are some guidelines related to buprenorphine treatment and practice:

(1) Some clinicians suggested that buprenorphine-naloxone may be more appropriate for opioid-addicted patients who are socially stable, whose family or work responsibilities prevent them from going to opioid treatment programs on a daily basis, or whose occupations demand higher degrees of psychomotor and cognitive functioning (Srivastava et al., 2017). Srivastava and colleagues also suggested that buprenorphine-naloxone can be recommended for patients who are vulnerable to methadone toxicity, including heavy drinkers, high-dose benzodiazepine or sedating drug users, the elderly, and patients with risk of prolonged QT interval (a heart rhythm condition).

(2) Link a patient to buprenorphine only if he or she reviews all treatment options and agrees to accept buprenorphine treatment (CSAT, 2004). Patients should be informed of the potential adverse and side effects of each treatment option, and their expected benefits and outcomes should be discussed with the patients (Bart, 2012). Since buprenorphine (or methadone) is an agonist, when recommending buprenorphine/naloxone maintenance (or methadone maintenance), the clinicians should discuss with patients (including informed consent) about the difficulty of terminating agonist treatment (for example, a person may re-experience opioid withdrawal and/or craving), as well as the high likelihood of relapse following its cessation (Connery, 2015). In general, because buprenorphine is a partial agonist, the withdrawal is less severe when it is stopped than a full agonist such as methadone.

(3) Buprenorphine maintenance therapy begins with the induction phase, followed by a stabilization phase and a maintenance phase; a patient must discontinue his or her opioids abuse and exhibit mild to moderate withdrawal symptoms during the induction phase before administering buprenorphine (CSAT, 2004). In other words, because of its antagonist features despite of its being primarily an agonist, buprenorphine precipitates withdrawals if a patient takes buprenorphine while his or her opioid receptors are still filled with full agonists (e.g., heroin) (Westlake & Eisenberg, 2016). For a patient dependent on short-acting opioids (e.g., heroin, oxycodone), buprenorphine induction should not take place until the patient abstains for at least 12–24 hours from his or her last use (CSAT, 2004; Westlake & Eisenberg, 2016). "Patients who are not in active withdrawal because they have not abstained from using opioids for a sufficient period should receive a careful explanation of the advantages of waiting and should be urged to wait until they begin to experience the symptoms of withdrawal" (CSAT, 2004, p. 52). For a patient dependent on long-acting opioids (e.g., methadone) who wants to transition to buprenorphine, the procedure is more complicated and best handled by a physician who is experienced with this procedure and who also needs to, with the patient's signed consent, contact the patient's methadone clinic for information regarding the patient's exact time and quantity of his/her last methadone (CSAT, 2004). Methadone patients need to taper their methadone to 30 mg or less per day for at least 1 week and stop methadone use for at least 24 hours (CSAT, 2004), or taper methadone to 30 mg per day for at least 1–2 weeks and stop all opioids for about 96 hours (Westlake & Eisenberg, 2016), before buprenorphine induction. The Clinical Opiate Withdrawal Scale (COWS) can be used to evaluate a patient's withdrawal status, with a total score > 8 indicating a mild to moderate withdrawal state and making buprenorphine induction appropriate (Westlake & Eisenberg, 2016).

(4) Studies have shown both methadone (a full agonist) and buprenorphine (a partial agonist) are appropriate to treat pregnant women with opioid use disorder (Klaman et al., 2017; Tran et al., 2017). However, buprenorphine monotherapy, rather than buprenorphine-naloxone combined therapy, should be prescribed for pregnant women during all three stages including induction, stabilization, and maintenance (Tran

et al., 2017). For patients transitioning from a long-acting opioid (e.g., methadone) to buprenorphine, buprenorphine monotherapy should be used during the induction phase and, to minimize potential diversion, should be no more than two days before switching to buprenorphine-naloxone combined therapy. To minimize potential diversion, however, buprenorphine-naloxone combined therapy should be prescribed for most patients for all stages; justification should be noted in medical records if buprenorphine monotherapy is prescribed for long period (CSAT, 2004).

(5) Patients should be seen at least once a week during the stabilization phase to assess whether they take buprenorphine as prescribed and manage the medications responsibly. Once a steady dose of buprenorphine is achieved and toxicological tests show illicit opioids negative, the weekly visit can be changed to biweekly or monthly visits (CSAT, 2004). Buprenorphine patients should take toxicology tests for all relevant illicit drugs at least monthly (CSAT, 2004) and their adherence to treatment plan and their treatment progress should be reviewed periodically. If a patient shows clinical destabilization or toxicology tests still show illicit drug positive after 8 weeks, a physician may need to modify the treatment plan or consider referring the patient to a specialist opioid treatment program (CSAT, 2004; Stoller et al., 2016).

(6) Provide patients with both pharmacotherapy and psychosocial treatment. As mentioned previously, both pharmacotherapy and behavioral therapy/psychosocial treatment are important to help addicted patients reach the optimal treatment outcomes. Specialized opioid treatment programs (OTP) often provide individual counseling and group counseling in addition to pharmacotherapy to patients; office-based buprenorphine (OBB) practice should also take this into consideration. For their opioid addicted patients, physicians' responsibilities must also include offering or referring patients to psychosocial treatment, in addition to administering buprenorphine (CSAT, 2004). In fact, the DATA 2000 law specifies that when physicians apply for a waiver from the SAMHSA to practice buprenorphine treatment outside specialized OTP settings, they must demonstrate their capacity to link these patients with counseling and psychosocial services (CSAT, 2004).

(7) The buprenorphine implant should be applied to patients with clinical stability and they should be provided with psychosocial and

counseling support. The definition for clinical stability remains a pressing challenge (Chavoustie et al., 2017), but assessment may be directed at whether patients: (a) have sustained extended clinical stability on a dose of ≤ 8 mg/day of a transmucosal buprenorphine product for 3 months or longer with no need for adjustments; (b) have a stable period of time free of illicit opioid use; (c) have stable living environment or social support system, and participate in employment or structured activities; (d) participate consistently in peer support groups or behavioral therapy; (e) comply consistently with clinic's requirements; (f) have no or only minimal desire for illicit opioids; (g) have a stable period of time with no occurrence of emergency room episodes, hospitalization, or crisis interventions related to addiction or mental health concerns (Chavoustie et al., 2017). Buprenorphine implants should not be given to new-to-treatment patients or patients who have not demonstrated extended clinical stability (Chavoustie et al., 2017).

(8) Buprenorphine implants can only be available through a Risk Evaluation and Mitigation Strategy (REMS) program. It is a new procedure that may have its own risks, including irritation on the surgical site and possible movement and protrusion (Itzoe & Guarnieri, 2017). The REMS program conjoins with the FDA to decrease the risks of abuse and overdose, as well as to alleviate possible complication risks associated with the implant insertion and its removal such as migration, expulsion and nerve damage (Chavoustie et al., 2017, p. 37).

(9) Increase access to buprenorphine among individuals in need of opioid addiction treatment and facilitate the collaborative opioid prescribing model (CoOP). Buprenorphine waivers have not been fully utilized. For example, about 53.4% of US counties do not have waivered physicians, and the rate was even higher for rural counties, about 82.5% (Rosenblatt et al., 2015). Kissin and colleagues' study (2006) reported that among a random sample of 545 waivered physicians, buprenorphine had been prescribed only by 58% of them. Various surveys have identified barriers that prevent physicians' buprenorphine practice, including: induction logistics, limited counseling resources for patients, insufficient reimbursement, lack of time for more patients, concern about patients' poor compliance and medication diversion, and not having enough education about opioid use disorder, all of which may reinforce physicians' perception of substance use disorder treatment as

being difficult and time-consuming, best handled by specialty treatment programs (Huhn & Dunn, 2017; Kissin et al., 2006).

To increase physicians' obtaining and using buprenorphine waivers, Stoller and colleagues (2016) propose the collaborative opioid prescribing model (CoOP). The CoOP model connects office-based buprenorphine (OBB) sites with specialized opioid treatment programs (OTP), with the goal of enhancing the availability and efficacy of OBB. The model suggests OTP serve as a hub, providing collaborative stepped care, in addition to expert consultation, concurrent OTP-based counseling, and wrap-around services. The stepped care includes several components: (a) a patient receives the initial comprehensive substance use disorder assessment from an OTP hub; (b) if buprenorphine maintenance is suggested, the patient will receive buprenorphine induction and stabilization from the OTP through its medication dispensary; (c) once buprenorphine stabilization is achieved in the patient, he or she can be referred from the OTP hub to an OBB site to continue his or her buprenorphine maintenance, while still receiving counseling from the OTP hub; (d) if clinical destabilization occurs, such as positive toxicology tests or low counseling adherence, the hub OTP can increase the intensity of counseling; if necessary, the medication dispensing can be shifted back to the OTP from the OBB site; and (e) on the other hand, if the patient stabilizes again, the OTP can reduce his or her counseling intensity and receiving buprenorphine at the OBB site can be resumed.

To expand access to buprenorphine among needed individuals, studies suggest that potential buprenorphine sites—besides physicians' office-based settings—may also include general medical hospitals (Hassamal et al., 2017), harm reduction agencies (e.g., programs that provide social services and syringe exchange) (Fox et al., 2015), and infectious disease treatment doctors' offices (Westlake & Eisenberg, 2016), with the need for further evaluations of their efficacy and safety.

Naltrexone

Unlike methadone, an opioid agonist, and buprenorphine, a partial opioid agonist, naltrexone is an opioid antagonist, which blocks, rather than activates, mu receptors. The FDA approved oral naltrexone to treat opioid dependence in 1984, injectable depot naltrexone to treat alcohol dependence in 2006, and injectable depot (extended released) naltrexone to treat opioid dependence in 2010. The approval of naltrexone by FDA was based on its "pharmacologic profile since high dropout rates made it difficult to complete randomized trials" (Woody et al., 2016, p. 401). As mentioned earlier, naltrexone's antagonistic pharmacologic nature supposedly makes it a perfect treatment for opioid addiction—one 50 mg naltrexone tablet can block up to 24–36 hours of opioid effects (Kleber, 2007); however, one major concern with naltrexone is patients' treatment noncompliance/nonadherence and high treatment dropout rates. Johansson et al. (2006) stated it well, "Retention . . . is itself a measure of efficacy. A treatment intervention with lower retention than a controlled condition is not effective" (p. 500). The availability of the injectable depot, extended-release naltrexone (XR-NTX)—which allows patients to get treatment monthly instead of daily like methadone, buprenorphine, and oral naltrexone—has improved patients' noncompliance and shown treatment efficacy (Kjome & Moeller, 2011; Krupitsky et al., 2011). Compared to agonist treatment, advantages of naltrexone itself may include that it does not produce sedation, euphoria addiction, tolerance, or withdrawal, and has no potential to develop abuse or addiction (Krupitsky et al., 2011; SAMHSA, 2012). Its antagonist nature may also make some physicians feel more comfortable prescribing naltrexone than agonists such as buprenorphine or methadone (SAMHSA, 2012). In addition, naltrexone has no significant side effects, and its interactions with other medications tend to be low if it is used in prescribed doses (Kleber, 2007). One other major advantage is that naltrexone, being an opioid antagonist rather than an opioid agonist, has less stigma attached to it, and may match the needs of certain patients who hesitate to receive agonist treatment or whose occupations prohibit opioid use (Krupitsky et al., 2011).

Guidelines related to naltrexone prescription practice may include:

(1) Unlike methadone and buprenorphine—both of which are opioid agonists and require special approvals from SAMHSA and/or DEA to prescribe—naltrexone is an opioid antagonist and can be prescribed by "any healthcare provider who is licensed to prescribe medications. Special training is not required; the medication can be administered in OTP [opioid treatment program] clinics. Practitioners in community health centers or private office settings can also prescribe it for pur-

PHARMACOTHERAPY

chase at the pharmacy" (SAMHSA, 2012, p. 2). This factor can expand patient access to treatment (SAMHSA, 2012).

(2) Naltrexone may match the needs of certain client populations, including patients who do not prefer agonist therapy, who are new to treatment or have only short history of addiction, young people, or people whose employment does not allow agonist use, such as healthcare providers, military personnel, pilots, police, and so on (Krupitsky et al., 2011). Naltrexone can also be useful in those leaving prisons or detox facilities and have been off opioid agonists (Lesley Dickson, MD, Personal communication, February, 24, 2018).

(3) Although opioid agonist (e.g., methadone) treatment is the recommended treatment for pregnant women with opioid use disorder, naltrexone may be appropriate for selected pregnant patients. If a woman is already stable on extended-release naltrexone and later becomes pregnant, Saia and colleagues (2016) suggested she could be "reasonably continued on naltrexone through pregnancy" (p. 259). Researchers have consistently agreed that more research is needed to determine whether naltrexone is safe for and the degree it can benefit pregnant women (Saia et al., 2016; Tran et al., 2017). Naltrexone has been assigned as an "FDA Pregnancy Category C" medication, meaning that "animal studies have shown an adverse effect on the fetus and there are no adequate, well-controlled studies in humans, but potential benefits may warrant use of the drug in some pregnant women despite potential risks" (SAMHSA & NIAAA, 2015, p. 6).

(4) To begin naltrexone treatment, an opioid-dependent patient needs to have no physiological opioid dependence or have no acute withdrawal symptoms for at least seven days (Schuckit, 2016) or be completely withdrawn from all opioids for two weeks (CSAT, 2004). To determine an opioid-free status, Schuckit suggests it can be based on an opioid-free urine sample and "a challenge with 0.8 to 1.6 mg of intravenous or intramuscular naloxone with no withdrawal symptoms over the next 15 to 30 minutes before receiving naltrexone (at a dose of 50 mg) that same day" (Schuckit, 2016, p. 363). Some patients may need extra support during the withdrawal period, as many relapse to opioid use during this time and therefore unable to launch naltrexone treatment (CSAT, 2004).

(5) Provide psychoeducation to patients and their significant others regarding the risk of relapse and its associated high likelihood of

overdose if naltrexone is discontinued. There were reports of accidental overdoses and deaths among patients who were receiving naltrexone treatment (oral or depot) but who relapsed to opioids (Diguisto et al., 2004; U.S. FDA, 2013). Overdose is a serious concern for opioid-dependent patients; the most dangerous times for opioid overdose, if a person relapses, may include when a patient drops out of agonist treatment, completes detoxification, is discharged from a controlled environment (e.g., prison), and/or self-initiates termination of naltrexone (Sigmon et al., 2012). This is because patients tend to lose or develop a reduced level of tolerance to opioids, as well as grow a higher sensitivity to opioids during those time or situations; if they relapse, they may be unaware of this discrepancy and still use the same level of dosage they previously used, which may lead to an overdose and even life-threatening consequences (Degenhardt et al., 2015; Sigmon et al., 2012; SAMHSA, 2012). Sigmon and colleagues suggest a relapse contingency plan should be arranged initially with the patients and their significant others, indicating treatment team actions in the case of relapse.

(6) Enhance naltrexone adherence through various strategies and approaches, such as the extended-released form of naltrexone and psychosocial treatment. As mentioned earlier, naltrexone is an antagonist and patients are less likely to comply with treatment and easily drop out of treatment. Treatment compliance and adherence, therefore, is a key factor for treatment success for naltrexone. Research has shown that extended-released naltrexone tends to lead to better treatment outcomes compared to oral naltrexone and placebo (Comer et al., 2006; Ling et al., 2011; Krupitsky et al., 2011). Psychosocial treatment, such as psychosocial education, cognitive therapy, contingency management, and family-oriented treatment may also contribute to patients' adherence (Carroll et al., 2002; Ling et al., 2011; Preston et al., 1999).

References

American Psychiatric Association [APA]. (2013). *Diagnostic and statistical manual of mental disorders*, Fifth Edition. Arlington, VA: American Psychiatric Association.

Ayanga, D., Shorter, D., & Kosten, T.R. (2016). Update on pharmacotherapy for treatment of opioid use disorder, *Expert Opinion on Pharmacotherapy, 17*(17), 2307–2318.

Barnwal, P., Das, S., Mondal, S., Ramasamy, A., Maiti, T., & Saha, A. (2017). Probuphine [buprenorphine implant]: A promising candidate in opioid dependence. *Therapeutic Advances in Psychopharmacology, 7*(3), 119–134.

Bart, G. (2012). Maintenance medication for opiate addiction: The foundation of recovery. *Journal of Addictive Diseases, 31*(3), 207–225.

Bouza, C., Angeles, M., Munoz, A., & Amate, J.M. (2004). Efficacy and safety of naltrexone and acamprosate in the treatment of alcohol dependence: A systematic review. *Addiction, 99*(7), 811–828.

Carroll, K.M., Sinha, R., Nich, C., Babuscio, T., & Rounsaville, B.J. (2002). Contingency management to enhance naltrexone treatment of opioid dependence: A randomized clinical trial of reinforcement magnitude. *Experimental and Clinical Psychopharmacology, 10*(1), 54–63.

Centers for Disease Control and Prevention (2017). Drug overdose death data. Retrieved on 02/04/2018 from www.cdc.gov/drugoverdose/data/statedeaths.html (page last updated 19 December 2017).

Center for Substance Abuse Treatment (2004). *Clinical guidelines for the use of buprenorphine in the treatment of opioid addiction.* Treatment Improvement Protocol (TIP) Series 40. DHHS Publication No. (SMA) 07–3939. Rockville, MD: Substance Abuse and Mental Health Services Administration.

Center for Substance Abuse Treatment (2011). *Medication-assisted treatment for opioid addiction in opioid treatment programs.* Treatment Improvement Protocol (TIP) Series 43. HHS Publication No. (SMA) 08–4214. Rockville, MD: Substance Abuse and Mental Health Services Administration.

Chavoustie, S., Frost, M., Snyder, O., Owen, J., Darwish, M., Dammerman, R., & Sanjurjo, V. (2017). Buprenorphine implants in medical treatment of opioid addiction. *Expert Review of Clinical Pharmacology, 10*(8), 799–807. doi:10.1080/17512433.2017.1336434.

Comer, S.D., Sullivan, M.A., Yu, E., Rothenberg, J.L., Kleber, H.D., Kampman, K., et al. (2006). Injectable, sustained-release naltrexone for the treatment of opioid dependence: A randomized, placebo-controlled trial. *Archives of General Psychiatry, 63*(2), 210–218.

Connery, H.S. (2015). Medication-assisted treatment of opioid use disorder: Review of the evidence and future directions. *Harvard Review of Psychiatry, 23*(2), 63–75.

Cornish, R., Macleod, J., Strang, J., Vickerman, P., & Hickman, M. (2010). Risk of death during and after opiate substitution treatment in primary care: Prospective observational study in UK general practice research database. *BMJ, 341,* c5475. doi: 10.1136/bmj.c5475.

Dahan, A. (2006). Opioid-induced respiratory effect: New data on buprenorphine. *Palliative Medicine, 20*(Suppl. 1), s3–s8.

Davoli, M., Bargagli, A.M., Perucci, C.A., Schifano, P., Belleudi, V., Hickman, M., et al. (2007). Risk of fatal overdose during and after specialist drug treatment: The VEdeTTE study, a national multi-site prospective cohort study. *Addiction, 102,* 1954–1959.

Degenhardt, L., Larney, S., Kimber, J., Farrell, M., Hall, W., (2015). Excess mortality among opioid-using patients treated with oral naltrexone in Australia. *Drug and Alcohol Review, 34,* 90–96.

Digiusto, E., Shakeshaft, A., Ritter, A., O'Brien, S., Mattick, R.P., & the NEPOD Reserch Group (2004). Serious adverse events in the Australian National Evaluation of Pharmacotherapies for Opioid Dependence (NEPOD). *Addiction, 99,* 450–460.

Dowell, D., Haegerich, T.M., & Chou, R. (2016). CDC guideline for prescribing opioids for chronic pain—United States. *MMWR Recommendations Report, 65* (No. RR-1), 1–49. Retreived from http://dx.doi.org/10.15585/mmwr.rr6501e1.

Fareed, A., Vayalapalli, S., Casarella, J., & Drexler, K. (2012). Effect of buprenorphine dose on treatment outcome. *Journal of Addictive Diseases, 31*, 8–18.

Finlay, A.K., Ellerbe, L.S., Wong, J.J., Timko, C., Rubinsky, A.D., Gupta, S., Bowe, T.R., Burden, J.L., & Harris, A.H.S. (2017). Barriers to and facilitators of pharmacotherapy for alcohol use disorder in VA residential treatment programs. *Journal of Substance Abuse Treatment, 77*, 38–43.

Fox, A.D., Chamberlain, A., Frost, T., Cunningham, C.O. (2015). Harm reduction agencies as a potential site for buprenorphine treatment. *Substance Abuse, 36*(2), 155–160.

Gastfriend, D.R. (2011). Intramuscular extended-release naltrexone: Current evidence. *Annals of the New York Academy of Sciences, 1216*, 144–166.

Goh, E.T., & Morgan, M.Y. (2017). Pharmacotherapy for alcohol dependence—The why, the what and the wherefore. *Alimentary Pharmacology and Therapeutics, 45*, 865–882.

Gordon, D., & Dahl, J. (2011). Opioid withdrawal, #95, 2nd edition. *Journal of Palliative Medicine, 14*(8), 965–966.

Hall, W., Carter, A., & Forlini, C. (2015). The brain disease model of addiction: Is it supported by the evidence and has it delivered on its promises? *The Lancet Psychiatry, 2*(1), 105–110.

Harris, A.H.S., Ellerbe, L., Gordon, A., Hagedorn, H., Oliva, E., Lembke, A., &Kivlahan, D. (2013). Pharmacotherapy for alcohol dependence: Perceived treatment barriers and action strategies among Veterans Health Administration service providers. *Psychological Services, 10*(4), 410–419.

Hassamal, S., Goldenberg, M., Ishak, W., Haglund, M., Miotto, K., & Danovitch, I. (2017). Overcoming barriers to initiating medication-assisted treatment for heroin use disorde4r in a general medical hospital: A case report narrative literature review. *Journal of Psychiatric Practice, 23*(3), 221–229.

Hser, Y., Saxon, A.J., Huang, D., Hasson, A., Thomas, C., Hillhouse, M., et al. (2014). Treatment retention among patients randomized to buprenorphine/naloxone compared to methadone in a multi-site trial. *Addiction, 109*(1), 79–87.

Huhn, A.S., & Dunn, K.E. (2017). Why aren't physicians prescribing more buprenorphine? *Journal of Substance Abuse Treatment, 78*, 1–7.

Itzoe, M., & Guarnieri, M. (2017). New developments in managing opioid addiction: Impact of a subdermal buprenorphine implant. *Drug Design, Development and Therapy, 11*, 1429–1437.

Johansson, B.A., Berglund, M., & Lindgren, A. (2006). Efficacy of maintenance treatment with naltrexone for opioid dependence: A meta-analytical review. *Addiction, 101*, 491–503.

Johansson, B.A., Berglund, M., & Lindgren, A. (2007). Efficacy of maintenance treatment with methadone for opioid dependence: A meta-analytical study. *Nordic Journal of Psychiatry, 61*(4), 288–295.

Johnson, B.A. (2007). Naltrexone long-acting formulation in the treatment of alcohol dependence. *Therapeutics and Clinical Risk Management, 3*(5), 741–749.

Jørgensen, C.H., Pedersen, B., & Tønnesen, H. (2011). The efficacy of disulfiram for the treatment of alcohol use disorder. *Alcoholism: Clinical and Experimental Research, 35*(10), 1749–1758.

Kattimani, S., & Bharadwaj, B. (2013). Clinical management of alcohol withdrawal: A systematic review. *Industrial Psychiatry Journal, 22*(2), 100–108.

Kissin, W., McLeod, C., Sonnefeld, J, & Stanton, A. (2006). Experiences of a national sample of qualified addiction specialists who have and have not prescribed buprenorphine for opioid dependence. *Journal of Addictive Diseases, 25*(4), 91–103.

Kjome, K.L., & Moeller, F.G. (2011). Long-acting injectable naltrexone for the management of patients with opioid dependence. *Substance Abuse: Research and Treatment, 5,* 1–9.

Klaman, S.L., Isaacs, K., Leopold, A., Perpich, J., Hayashi,, S., Vender, J., Campopiano, M., & Jones, H. (2017). Treating women who are pregnant and parenting for opioid use disorder and the concurrent care of their infants and children: Literature review to support national guidance. *Journal of Addictive Medicine, 11*(3), 178–190.

Kleber, H.D. (2007). Pharmacologic treatments for opioid dependence: Detoxification and maintenance options. *Dialogues in Clinical Neuroscience, 9*(4), 455–470.

Krampe, H., Spies, C.D., & Ehrenreich, H. (2011). Supervised disulfiram in the treatment of alcohol use disorder: A commentary. *Alcoholism: Clinical and Experimental Research, 35*(10), 1732–1736.

Kranzler, H.R., Knapp, C.M., & Ciraulo, D.A. (2014). Alcohol. In H.R. Kranzler, D.A. Ciraulo, & L.R. Zindel (Eds.) *Clinical manual of addiction psychopharmacology* (pp. 1–70). Washington, DC: American Psychiatric Publishing.

Krishnan-Sarin, S., Krystal, J.H., Shi, J., Pittman, B., & O'Malley, S.S. (2007). Family history of alcoholism influences naltrexone-induced reduction in alcohol drinking. *Biological Psychiatry, 62,* 694–697.

Krishnan-Sarin, S., O'Malley, S., & Krystal, J.H. (n.d.). Treatment Implications: Using neuroscience to guide the development of new pharmacotherapies for alcoholism. Retrieved on 06/09/2017 from https://pubs.niaaa.nih.gov/publications/arh314/400-407.htm.

Krupitsky, E., Nunes, E.V., Ling, W., Illeperuma, A., Gastfriend, D.R., & Silverman, B.L. (2011). Injectable extended-release naltrexone for opioid dependence: A double-blind, placebo-controlled, multicentre randomized trial. *Lancet, 377,* 1506–1513.

Ling, W., Mooney, L., Zhao, M., Nielsen, S., Torrington, M., & Miotto, K. (2011). Selective review and commentary on emerging pharmacotherapies for opioid addiction. *Substance Abuse and Rehabilitation, 2,* 181–188.

Ling, W., & Wesson, D.R. (2003). Clinical efficacy of buprenorphine: Comparisons to methadone and placebo. *Drug and Alcohol Dependence, 70,* S49–S57.

Maldonado, J.R., Sher, Y., Ashouri, J.F., Hills-Evans, K., Swendsen, H., Lolak, S., & Miller, A.C. (2014). The "Prediction of Alcohol Withdrawal Severity Scale" (PAWSS): Systematic literature review and pilot study of a new scale for the prediction of complicated alcohol withdrawal syndrome. *Alcohol, 48,* 375–390.

Mark, T.L., Kassed, C.A., Vandivort-Warren, R., Levit, K.R., & Kranzler, H.R. (2009). Alcohol and opioid dependence medications: Prescription trends, overall and by physician specialty. *Drug and Alcohol Dependence, 99* (1–3), 345–349.

Mark, T.L., Kranzler, H.R., & Song, X. (2003). Understanding US addiction physicians' low rate of naltrexone prescription. *Drug and Alcohol Dependence, 71,* 219–228.

Marsch, L.A. (1998). The efficacy of methadone maintenance interventions in reducing illicit opiate use, HIV risk behavior and criminality: A meta-analysis. *Addiction, 93*(4), 515–532.

Mason, B.J. (2005). Acamprosate in the treatment of alcohol dependence. *Expert Opinion on Pharmacotherapy, 6*(12), 2103–2115.

Mason, B.J., & Heyser, C.J. (2010). Acamprosate: A prototypic neuromodulator in the treatment of alcohol dependence. *CNS & Neurological Disorders Drug Targets, 9*(1), 23–32.

Mattick, R.P., Breen, C., Kimber, J., & Davoli, M. (2003). Methadone maintenance therapy versus no opioid replacement therapy for opioid dependence. *Cochrane Database System Review,* (2), CD002209. doi: 10.1002/14651858.CD002209.

Mattick, R.P., Breen, C., Kimber, J., & Davoli, M. (2009). Methadone maintenance therapy versus no opioid replacement therapy for opioid dependence. *Cochrane Database System Review,* (3), CD002209. doi: 10.1002/14651858.CD002209.pub2.

McLellan, A.T., Arndt, I.O., Metzger, D.S., Woody, G.E., & O'Brien, C.P. (1993). The effects of psychosocial services in substance abuse treatment. *Journal of the American Medical Association, 269*(15), 1953–1959.

Mee-Lee, D., Shulman, G.D., Fishman, M.J., Gastfriend, D.R., & Miller, M.M. (Eds.) (2013). *The ASAM criteria: Treatment criteria for addictive, substance-related, and co-occurring conditions,* Third Edition. Carson City, NV: The Change Companies.

Minozzi, S., Amato, L., Vecchi, S., & Davoli, M. (2010). Anticonvulsants for alcohol withdrawal. *Cochrane Database of Systematic Reviews,* (3), CD005064. doi: 10.1002/14651858.CD005064.pub3.

Mirijello, A., D'Angelo, C., Ferrulli, A., Vassallo, G., Antonelli, M., Caputo, F., et al. (2015). Identification and management of alcohol withdrawal syndrome. *Drugs, 75*(4), 353–365.

Mutschler, J., Dirican, G., Gutzeit, A., & Rosshans, M. (2011). Safety and efficacy of long-term disulfiram aftercare. *Clinical Neuropharmacology, 34*(5), 195–198.

National Collaborating Centre for Mental Health, The Royal College of Psychiatrists (2011). *Alcohol-use disorders: The NICE guideline on diagnosis, assessment and management of harmful drinking and alcohol dependence.* London: The British Psychological Society and The Royal College of Psychiatrists. Retrieved on 02/04/2018 from www.nice.org.uk/guidance/cg115/evidence/full-guideline-136423405.

National Institute on Alcohol Abuse and Alcoholism (2015). NIH begins clinical trial of new medication for alcohol use disorder. NIH News (June 25, 2015).

National Institute on Drug Abuse (2018). *Principles of drug addiction treatment: A research-based guide,* Third Edition. Retrieved on 02/04/2018 from www.drugabuse.gov/publications/principles-drug-addiction-treatment-research-based-guide-third-edition/principles-effective-treatment (last updated January 2018).

Nunes, E.V., Krupitsky, E., Ling, W., Zummo, J., Memisoglu, A., Silverman, B.L., & Gastfriend, D.R. (2015). Treating opioid dependence with injectable extended-release naltrexone (XR-NTX): Who will respond? *Journal of Addictive Medicine, 9*(3), 238–243.

O'Connor, P.G. (2005). Methods of detoxification and their role in treating patients with opioid dependence. *JAMA, 294*(8), 961–963.

Oliva, E.M., Maisel, N.C., Gordon, A.J., & Harris, A.H.S. (2011). Barriers to use of pharmacotherapy for addiction disorders and how to overcome them. *Current Psychiatry Report, 13,* 374–381.

Perry, E.C. (2014). Inpatient management of acute alcohol withdrawal syndrome. *CNS Drugs, 28*(5), 401–410.

Reisinger, H.S., Schwartz, R.P., Mitchell, S.G., Peterson, J.A., Kelly, S.M., O'Grady, K.E., Marrari, E.A., Brown, B.S., & Agar, M.H. (2009). Premature discharge from methadone treatment: Patient perspectives. *Journal of Psychoactive Drugs, 41*(3), 285–296.

Renner, J.A. Jr., Knapp, C.M., Ciraulo, D.A., & Epstein, S. (2014). Opioids. In H.R. Kranzler, D.A., Ciraulo, & L.R. Zindel (Eds.) *Clinical manual of addiction psychopharmacology* (pp. 97–136). Washington, DC: American Psychiatric Publishing.

Roozen, H.G., de Waart, R., van der Windt, D., van den Brink, W., de Jong, C., & Kerkhof, A. (2006). A systematic review of the effectiveness of naltrexone in the maintenance treatment of opioid and alcohol dependence. *European Neuropsychopharmacology, 16*, 311–323.

Rosenblatt, R.A., Andrilla, C.H.A., Catlin, M., & Larson, E.H. (2015). Geographic and specialty distribution of US physicians trained to treat opioid use disorder. *Annals of Family Medicine, 13*(1), 23–26.

Russolillo, A., Moniruzzaman, A, McCandless, L.C., Patterson, M., & Somers, J.M. (2017). Associations between methadone maintenance treatment and crime: A 17-year longitudinal cohort study of Canadian provincial offenders. *Addiction, 113*, 656–667.

Saia, K.A., Schiff, D., Wachman, E.M., Mehta, P., Vilkins, A., Sia, M., et al. (2016). Caring for pregnant women with opioid use disorder in the USA: Expanding and improving treatment. *Current Obstetrics and Gynecology Reports, 5*, 257–263.

Saloner, B., & Karthikeyan, S. (2015). Changes in substance abuse treatment use among individuals with opioid use disorders in the United States, 2004–2013. *JAMA, 314*(14), 1515–1517.

Saloner, B., Stoller, K.B., & Barry, C.L. (2016). Medicaid coverage for methadone maintenance and use of opioid agonist therapy in specialty addiction treatment. *Psychiatric Services, 67*(6), 676–679.

Schuckit, M.A. (2016). Treatment of opioid-use disorders. *The New England Journal of Medicine, 375*(4), 357–368.

Sigmon, S.C., Bisaga, A., Nunes, E.V., O'Connor, P.G., Kosten, T., & Woody, G. (2012). Opioid detoxification and naltrexone induction strategies: Recommendations for clinical practice. *American Journal of Drug and Alcohol Abuse, 38*(3), 187–199.

Specka, M., Heilmann, M., & Scherbaum, N. (2014). Use of disulfiram for alcohol relapse prevention in patients in opioid maintenance treatment. *Clinical Neuropharmacology, 37*(6), 161–165.

Srivastava, A., Kahan, M., & Nader, M. (2017). Primary carte management of opioid use disorders: Abstinence, methadone, or buprenorphine-naloxone? *Canadian Family Physician, 63*, 200–205.

Stein, B.D., Gordon, A.J., Sorbero, M., Dick, A.W., Schuster, J., Farmer, C. (2012). The impact of buprenorphine on treatment of opioid dependence in a Medicaid population: Recent service utilization trends in the use of buprenorphine and methadone. *Drug and Alcohol Dependence, 123*, 72–78.

Stephens, J.R., Liles, E.A., Dancel, R., Gilchrist, M., Kirsch, J., & DeWalt, D.A. (2014). Who needs inpatient detox? Development and implementation of a hospitalist protocol for the evaluation of patients for alcohol detoxification. *Journal of General Internal Medicine, 29*(4), 587–593.

Stoller, K.B., Stephens, M.A.C., & Schorr, A. (2016). Integrated service delivery models for opioid treatment programs in an era of increasing opioid addiction, health reform, and parity. Retrieved on 06/21/2017 from www.aatod.org/wp-content/uploads/2016/07/2nd-Whitepaper-.pdf.

Substance Abuse and Mental Health Services Administration (SAMHSA) (2012). An introduction to extended-release injectable naltrexone for the treatment of people with opioid dependence. *SAMHSA Advisory, 11*(1), 1–8.

Substance Abuse and Mental Health Services Administration (SAMHSA) (2014). *Medicaid coverage and financing of medications to treat alcohol and opioid use disorders*. HHS Publication No. SMA-14–4854. Rockville, MD: SAMHSA.

Substance Abuse and Mental Health Services Administration and National Institute on Alcohol Abuse and Alcoholism (SAMHSA & NIAAA) (2015). *Medication for the treatment of alcohol use disorder: A brief guide*. HHS Publication No. (SMA) 15–4907. Rockville, MD: Substance Abuse and Mental Health Services Administration.

Sullivan, J.T., Sykora, K., Schneiderman, J., Naranjo, C.A., & Sellers, E.M. (1989). Assessment of alcohol withdrawal: The revised clinical institute withdrawal assessment for alcohol (CIWA-Ar). *British Journal of the Addictions, 84*(11), 1353–1357.

Sun, A.P., Chen, Y.C., & Marsiglia, F. (2016). Trauma and Chinese heroin users. *Journal of Ethnicity in Substance Abuse, 15*(2), 144–159.

Sun, H.M., Li, X.Y., Chow, E.P.F., Li, T., Xian, Y., Lu, Y.H., Tian, T., Zhuang, X., & Zhang, L. (2015). Methadone maintenance treatment programme reduces criminal activity and improves social well-being of drug users in China: A systematic review and meta-analysis. *BMJ Open, 5*, e005997. doi: 10.1136/bmjopen-2014-005997.

Tran, T.H., Griffin, B.L., Stone, R.H., Vest, K.M., & Todd, T.J. (2017). Methadone, buprenorphine, and naltrexone for the treatment of opioid use disorder in pregnant women. *Pharmacotherapy, 37*(7), 824–839.

U.S. FDA (2013). Vivitrol medication guide. Retrieved on 04/17/2018 from www.fda.gov/downloads/Drugs/DrugSafety/UCM206669.pdf.

Webster, L., Hjelmstrom, P., Sumner, M., & Gunderson, E.W. (2016). Efficacy and safety of a sublingual buprenorphine/naloxone rapidly dissolving tablet for the treatment of adults with opioid dependence: A randomized trial. *Journal of Addictive Diseases, 35*(4), 325–338.

Wesson, D.R., & Ling, W. (2003). The clinical opiate withdrawal scale (COWS). *Journal of Psychoactive Drugs, 35*(2), 253–258.

Westlake, A.A., & Eisenberg, M.P. (2016). What the ID clinician needs to know about buprenorphine treatment for opioid use disorder. Infectious disease (ID) Learning unit. *Open Forum Infectious Diseases, 4*(1), OFW251. doi: 10.1093/OFID/OFW251.

Woody, G.E., Krupitsky, E., & Zvartau, E. (2016). Antagonist models for relapse prevention and reducing HIV risk. *Journal of Neuroimmune Pharmacology, 11*, 401–407.

World Health Organization (WHO) (2008). Bulletin of the World Health Organization. The methadone fix. Retrieved on 04/17/2018 from www.who.int/bulletin/volumes/86/3/08-010308/en/.

World Health Organization (WHO) (2009). Clinical guidelines for withdrawal management and treatment of drug dependence in closed setting. Retrieved on 06/19/2017 from www.ncbi.nlm.nih.gov/books/NBK310658/?report=printable.

8

WITHDRAWAL MANAGEMENT AND RELAPSE PREVENTION

BEHAVIORAL THERAPY AND PSYCHOSOCIAL TREATMENT

Withdrawal Management

People addicted to substances may experience withdrawal symptoms once they abruptly stop using; the withdrawal may be particularly serous if the substance is heroin or a central nervous system depressant such as alcohol rather than stimulants. The goal of a detoxification program is twofold: (1) to provide treatment to help the patient go through withdrawal safely and humanely; (2) to link the patient to aftercare and long-term recovery (Center for Substance Abuse Treatment [CSAT], 2006). As mentioned in Chapter 7, to stabilize a patient's medical condition, pharmacotherapy is critical. On the other hand, behavioral therapy and psychosocial intervention play an important role in helping retain patients and facilitating detoxification completion as well as encouraging the patients to pursue aftercare and long-term recovery.

Following are strategies to retain patients and decrease dropout rates in the detoxification program; they can also promote patients' motivation to pursue aftercare post detoxification:

(a) Build a trust relationship and therapeutic alliance with patients. Literature has consistently established the significance of a therapeutic alliance in contributing to positive treatment outcomes (CSAT, 2006).

(b) Provide psychoeducation regarding the symptoms of withdrawal, the neurobiological base of addiction, and its chronic and relapsing nature. Withdrawal symptoms are usually the opposite of the drug's effects, which can cause patients anxiety and discomfort. Explaining to patients the rebound effects and typical withdrawal symptoms of the drugs can reduce the patients' concerns and chances of their leaving detox programs prematurely. The information about the chronic nature of addiction can instill in patients the importance of attending aftercare post detoxification services (CSAT, 2006).

(c) Enhance patients' motivation by applying "motivational intervention" or the notion of stages of change. Vederhus and colleagues (2014) found that compared to a brief advice intervention, a motivational intervention that targets enhancing involvement in Twelve Step groups is more successful regarding patients' affiliation with Twelve Step groups post detox and decreased substance use. Brief advice includes patients receiving local Twelve Step group meeting lists and their being briefly advised to go to meetings; whereas the motivational intervention includes treatment contents such as: patients attending sessions that help them understand the chronic nature of addition, patients watching an AA motivational DVD, exploring possible obstacles and misconceptions about Twelve Step meetings with patients, encouraging patients to call AA/NA and inviting their volunteers to the detox unit for conversation, and telling patients to make an appointment with the volunteer for going to the meeting post detox. In addition, detox staff should facilitate moving a patient to the next stage along the stages of change. For example, from pre-contemplation to contemplation, from contemplation to the preparation, action, and maintenance stages (CSAT, 2006).

(d) Involve family members, significant others, and/or peers. If available and appropriate, family members can be beneficially involved when the client is receiving detox services. Community Reinforcement and Family Training (CRAFT) is one approach to achieve the goal (CSAT, 2006). Brief family treatment intervention that involves both the patient and an adult family member (e.g., a parent or spouse) to review the patient's aftercare plans can also be useful (O'Farrell et al., 2008). Peer support has positive impact in reinforcing a patient's perception of needs and motivation to complete detox and pursue aftercare. Client advocates can help promote retention in detox programs for patients at risk for leaving treatment prematurely. If on-site Twelve Step or other group meetings are available, stabilized detox patients should be encouraged to attend (CSAT, 2006).

(e) Address patients' psychosocial needs, devise a solid discharge plan, and link patients to treatment and aftercare. Assess and address a patient's six ASAM dimensions (i.e., dimension 1, acute intoxication and/or withdrawal potential; dimension 2, biomedical conditions and complications; dimension 3, emotional, behavioral, or cognitive conditions and complications; dimension 4, readiness to change; dimension 5, relapse, continued use, or continued problem potential; and dimension 6, recovery/living environment), determine a level of placement for the patient post detox, and develop a discharge plan. Factors and triggers related to a patient's initiation and maintenance of addiction, as well as strategies to counteract them, need to be assessed and discussed (CSAT, 2006; National Collaborating Centre for Mental Health [NCCMH], 2008). Attending to patients' psychosocial needs can enhance their motivation to stay in detox and continue for aftercare (CSAT, 2006).

(f) Be flexible on treatment approaches. Not only motivational interviewing and cognitive behavioral therapy (introduced later in this chapter) are relevant to help patients in detox, contingency management (introduced at the end of this chapter) is also recommended to help patients during detox and 3–6 months post detox completion (NCCMH, 2008). Complementary or alternative medicine (e.g., acupuncture) can also be considered if they bring patients into detox and keep them there (CSAT, 2006).

(g) Make sure the detoxification facility is safe and drug free. Detox program staff should monitor visiting areas to prevent alcohol or other drugs from being brought in from outside. However, "personnel should be respectful in their efforts to maintain a drug-free environment" and should explain to patients and visitors prior to treatment why substances are not permitted in the setting (CSAT, 2006, p. 34).

A detoxification program is more than just helping patients to withdraw from substances safely; it should aim to smoothly transition the patients from detox to treatment or aftercare. Addiction is a chronic disease and detox alone usually does not help patients achieve long-term recovery (National Institute on Drug Abuse [NIDA], 2018). A patient is more likely to be readmitted to another detox service if he or she receives no treatment or aftercare following the initial detox discharge (Mark et al., 2006; Spear, 2014). Spear's study (2014) found that "patients who transitioned from detox to either residential or outpatient SUD treatment had 0.44 times the odds of readmission compared with patients who did not transition to SUD treatment" (p. 79). The "revolving door" phenomenon—patients frequently in and out of detox services—not only incurs more medical expenses in the systems but also reduces patients' own faith and self-efficacy in their pursue of recovery (NCCMH, 2008). In addition to the advantage of a lower detoxification readmission rate, studies have shown multiple other benefits when linking patients between detoxification services and aftercare, including a longer period of abstinence, a higher likelihood of employment, a lower chance of homelessness, and a lower rate of arrests (Ford & Zarate, 2010; Mark et al., 2006).

Despite the many advantages of linking detox patients to continued treatment post detox, the rates of transitioning from detoxification to addiction treatment/aftercare are usually modest or low, ranging from a quarter to less than half. For example, Lee and colleagues (2014) studied adult patients of publicly funded detoxification programs in five states regarding the percentage of patients who receive continuity of treatment within two weeks of discharge from their detoxification programs. The overall rates ranged from 13% (Connecticut) to 46% (New York's medically supervised withdrawal programs). Other rates were 21.3% for Massachusetts, 19.45% for Oklahoma, and 25.7% for Washington. Not much research has been done regarding how to decrease the detoxification readmission or how to enhance transitions of patients from detoxification to substance use disorder treatment/aftercare. Timko and colleagues (2016) conducted a qualitative study (N=30 providers from different Veterans Health Administration detoxification programs, USA) and generated several themes regarding the issue—at patient-, program-, and system-levels—all of which may provide insights to improve the transition of detoxification patients to continuing care.

Timko and colleagues (2016) found several factors at the patient level. Detoxification patients are more likely to transition to treatment/aftercare if they suffered negative consequences of substance abuse, experienced external support or pressure, were motivated, and/or were older. On the other hand, barriers included living too far away from treatment or no transportation to treatment; having responsibilities such as child care or employment that prevent them from attending treatment; having co-morbid disorders such as PTSD or personality disorders; criminal justice system involvement; and possible financial consequences of staying in treatment too long. At the program level, the factors related to the detoxi-fication program are practicing active discharge planning, offering patient education about benefits of attending addiction treatment/aftercare, and building rapport with patients. Factors related to the addiction treatment/aftercare program are: (a) offering evidence-based treatment, such as phar-macotherapy, motivational interviewing, cognitive behavioral therapy, relapse prevention, contingency management, PTSD treatment, dialecti-cal behavioral therapy, and harm reduction; (b) being patient-centered and providing care coordination, such as housing, outreach, peer support, case management, and aftercare; (c) being convenient in the areas of immediate access, office hours, telehealth, and transportation provision; and (d) staff that is professional and well-trained (Timko et al., 2016). At the system level, facilitators may include effective communication and a sound work-ing relationship between the detoxification program and the addiction treatment/aftercare program, as well as the integration of both programs in one single system. (Timko et al., 2016).

Relapse Prevention

As mentioned above, behavioral therapy and psychosocial intervention can enhance withdrawal service retention and facilitate the successful tran-sition from detoxification service to addiction treatment/aftercare. One major goal of addiction treatment/aftercare post detoxification is relapse prevention. Various evidence-based behavioral and psychosocial treat-ment strategies and approaches have been developed to help addicted patients prevent relapse and maintain long-term recovery. Many of these treatment methods are related to the framework of functional analysis, the A-B-C framework. A represents Antecedents; B, Behaviors; and C, Consequences. The A-B-C framework suggests that the occurrence of a person's behavior is associated with the antecedents or triggers that happen prior to the behavior, and such behavior is further reinforced or eliminated by the consequences following the behavior. Thus, to change the behavior—dysfunctional or addictive behavior in this context—we can target the antecedents and/or consequences. To target antecedents, at least three concepts are relevant: (a) classical conditioning; (b) cognitive restructuring, cognitive positive reappraisal, and schema healing; and (c) mindfulness. To aim at consequences, four concepts are relevant: (d) operant conditioning; (e) a rewarding recovery; (f) mindful savoring; and (g) quality of life.

This section, first introduces the functional analysis and skills training, followed by the seven important concepts. Various established evidence-based treatment approaches—such as cognitive behavioral therapy (CBT), mindfulness-based relapse prevention (MBRP), mindfulness-oriented recovery enhancement (MORE), community reinforcement approach (CRA), reinforcement-based treatment (RBT), contingency management (CM), and case management—will then be briefly discussed. Other treatment approaches that not only serve a relapse prevention function but also can enhance a person's spirit and hope—such as motivational interviewing, dialectic behavioral therapy, acceptance and commitment therapy, and the Twelve Step facilitation approach—are discussed and can be found in Chapter 6.

Functional Analysis and Skills Training

Although the field of addiction treatment adopted functional analyses (FA) somewhat later than other fields (Smith & Meyers, 2001), FA has become one major tool for relapse prevention in the field. Functional analysis basically demonstrates the context of why and how a behavior occurs and is subsequently sustained. A classic FA shows the logical linkages between <u>A</u>ntecedents, <u>B</u>ehaviors, and <u>C</u>onsequences (see Figure 8.1), in that it explains how antecedents may lead to dysfunctional and addictive behaviors, which may be further reinforced by the consequences. (Note: an A-B-C format may be used in different contexts, for example, the antecedents-beliefs-consequences model suggests that how a person interprets [beliefs] the event/situation [antecedents] will subsequently affect his/her emotion and behaviors [consequences].)

The antecedents can be external or internal triggers, both of which may contribute to the occurrence of the dysfunctional behavior. External triggers may include places, people, events, and times that are associated with

A (Antecedent)		B (Behavior)	C (Consequence)	
External triggers	Internal triggers	Behaviors	Short-term positive consequences	Long-term negative consequences
Who: Being alone; boyfriend has just left after a big fight. Where: at home When: Saturday night	Thoughts: Want to escape the negative and unpleasant feelings/want to have fun and to prove can still be happy being alone. Physical feelings: exhausted. Emotional feelings: humiliated, upset, lonely, and sad.	Gambling	Being able to forget about the unpleasant feelings because of the boyfriend. Being able to have some fun.	Feeling lousy physically next day from not sleeping for the entire night due to gambling. Losing all the money for rent and groceries. Feeling depressed that all the money is gone.

Figure 8.1 The A-B-C Diagram of Functional Analysis Diagram (Modified from Meyers & Miller, 2001)

substance use or gambling or other addictive behaviors. For example, being home alone during a weekend night after a big fight with a boyfriend who has just left. Internal triggers, on the other hand, may encompass thoughts, sensations, and emotional and/or physical feelings that facilitate the juncture for episodes of drinking or gambling or other addictive behaviors. For example, feeling humiliated, betrayed, upset, lonely, sad, and wanting to escape from those negative feelings. It is important to discuss with patients the antecedents preceding their dysfunctional or addictive behaviors, as many of them, when entering treatment, do not have a clear awareness regarding the influence of those antecedents on triggering the occurrence of the dysfunctional or addictive behaviors (Tuten et al., 2012).

The component of consequences can include short-term positive consequences (e.g., unpleasant feelings were blocked by the gambling activities and the casino's stimulating environment) and the long-term negative consequences (e.g., lost all the rent and grocery money). It's also important to explore the consequences of the dysfunctional or addictive behavior with patients to help them become aware of the fact that the positive consequence often is only short-lived and will be followed by long-term negative consequences.

Functional analysis (FA) usually involves a semi-structured interview and is usually conducted in the early sessions. A clinician can work with a patient to develop a treatment plan once the antecedents or triggers are recognized or discovered, and once the short-term positive and long-term negative consequences are explored. Different individuals may have different triggers; the clinician can (a) help patients to recognize their individual triggers or high-risk situations that activate their dysfunctional behaviors, (b) teach patients to avoid those high-risk situations in the first place, and (c) provide patients with skills training—for example, cognitive restructuring and reappraisal skills, mindfulness skills, communication skills, problem-solving skills, drug-refusal skills, parenting skills, budgeting skills, and so on—so that they can more effectively deal with the triggers if those triggers are unavoidable.

In the above case of the woman with a gambling disorder, for example, the clinician can help the woman identify the factors of interpersonal relationship conflicts with her boyfriend and the subsequent negative emotions, such as loneliness and depression, as her triggers for gambling. Possible corresponding treatment goals may be to improve the couple's communication skills and relationship. On the other hand, the clinician can also help the woman to more effectively regulate her negative emotion, and/or to explore, devise, and engage in non-gambling, rewarding, and healthy activities that can still bring fun and pleasure without involving gambling.

Functional analyses also emphasize the importance of reminding patients that the positive consequence of their dysfunctional behavior is often only short-lived and that there is a price to pay in the long term for their dysfunctional behaviors (Smith & Meyers, 2001). As they often say in the treatment field, "playing the tape through" is a method that alerts clients not to pause only at the initial, short-term euphoric effects of the dysfunctional behavior (e.g., drinking, gambling) but to "play the tape" all the way through to where the longer-term devastating effects emerge. Smith and Meyers suggest that long-term negative consequence assessments should be detailed and comprehensive, covering the areas of interpersonal, physical, emotional, legal, employment, financial, and other repercussions, all of which can also serve as factors motivating the patients to change their dysfunctional behaviors.

Avoid Triggers and Manage Them if Unavoidable: Classical Conditioning

Classical conditioning (Pavlovian conditioning) suggests that when an unconditioned stimulus with rewarding properties (e.g., drugs or food) is repeatedly paired with a conditioned stimulus that previously does not have the rewarding properties (e.g., places, people, objects, situations, times, moods, etc.), the conditioned stimulus is likely to acquire similar rewarding features possessed by the unconditioned stimulus. Specifically, there are two categories of conditioned stimuli. One is "proximal" or "discrete" cues, that "occur in close temporal proximity to the pharmacological effects of drugs," such as "sight, smell, taste . . . experienced with each sip of an alcoholic beverage" (Valyear et al., 2017, p. 26). The other is "environmental context," which can be defined as, for example, "a static configuration of multimodal stimuli that comprise the backdrop within which alcohol intake occurs" (Valyear et al., p. 28).

Exposure to these conditioned stimulus is likely to trigger relapse (Barry & Petry, 2009; Marlatt, 1985). Research has found the important role of classical conditioning in addiction (Conklin et al., 2013; Hoffmann et al., 2014). For example, Hoffmann and colleagues (2014) paired an odor with erotic film clips among men who engage in sex with men. They found that subjects with high sexual compulsivity are more conditionable and showed more intention to engage in sexual behavior when the odor is present. The study of Winkler and colleagues (2011) revealed that neutral cues, if paired with smoking, may acquire the power to prompt preparatory physiological reactions, which are presumed to trigger relapse. Stevenson and colleagues (2017) found that "exposure to smoking environments as compared to the nonsmoking environments resulted in greater craving, faster initiation of smoking, and more smoked cigarettes" (p. 49). Neuroimaging studies and quantitative meta-analysis of neuroimaging literature of cue-exposure/cue-reactivity have also shown that the brain's mesolimbic system is involved in processing alcohol cues and hyperactivity of the brain reward system occurs for alcohol-related cues among cases with alcohol use disorder as compared to controls (Kuhn & Gallinat, 2011; Schacht et al., 2013).

Several strategies have been proposed by researchers and clinicians to counteract the effects of classical conditioning. First is from a prevention perspective. To reduce the possibility of cravings and relapse, clinicians will teach patients to recognize "conditioned triggers"—including places, individuals, objects, events, and moods that are associated with substance use—and to avoid these high-risk situations altogether in the first place (Barry & Petry, 2009). It is a common practice for clinicians to help their addicted patient identify and keep away from individual triggers or high-risk situations that activate dysfunctional or addictive behaviors.

It is not unfamiliar to hear some clients say that they were able to quit heroin use altogether when they moved out of the city where they developed their addiction, but relapsed once they returned to the city, even for a short stay. While moving away does not guarantee there won't be relapse, it certainly reduces the impact and implications related to the factor of the Pavlovian classical conditioning. Likewise, some inmates will tell us that, while in the prison, they have been able to maintain sobriety, been totally awakened and sincerely want to live a drug-free life for the future, but found out that their dream and recovery plan could not resist the urge that emerged the moment they returned to their communities. Of course multiple factors are involved, but the *conditioned* neighborhood could be one of them. One research subject, a 65-year-old man who was addicted to heroin, once told me during our interview that he has stayed with the residential program for more than 8 years in a row and—although he could return to his hometown where his family, relatives, and friends are—he planned to stay there forever (with the permission of that program). He said he knew that was the safest and only way for him to not relapse. This may also echo Lee Robins' study findings on heroin-addicted Vietnam War veterans who returned to the US, although with a twist. Robins tracked down those veterans who were previously addicted in Vietnam and later returned to the US. She found that surprisingly only 5% of them became re-addicted within one year—the relapse rate was shockingly lower than that among general heroin users. One logical explanation is that addiction is heavily affected by contextual environment; leaving Vietnam where they developed their heroin addiction and leaving the environment that was full of triggers for heroin use, such as stress, heroin-using peers, and atrocious battlefield conditions, may have made it easier for these veterans to recover and not to relapse (Gupta, 2015). (Note: On the other hand,

Robins' findings that "addicts could quit heroin and remain drug-free" have been used to dismiss the belief that "once an addict, always an addict" and that "addiction is a chronic and relapsing brain disease" by some researchers, such as Satel and Lilienfeld [2014, p. 1, online publication]. I think those researchers may have oversimplified the phenomenon.)

Second, addicted individuals tend to develop attentional bias, propelling them to focus on drug-related cues in the environment and subsequently driving them to relapse. Therefore, teaching patients skills to change their automatic response to drug-related cues that trigger relapse will be beneficial (Hoffmann et al., 2014). Third, a clinician should not only help clients change their automatic response to craving/triggers, but also equip them with effective methods to cope with and manage these craving/triggers when these craving/triggers cannot be avoided. Strategies in this regard may include distractions such as taking a walk or taking a shower, calling a sponsor or a friend, surfing the urge, and so on (Kadden et al., 2003). In addition, depending on individual needs, clients can also benefit from improved communication skills, problem-solving skills, alcohol and drug-refusal skills, self-assertiveness skills, and skills in other areas.

Engage in Cognitive Restructuring, Positive Reappraisal, and Schema Healing

Functional analysis addresses both the antecedents (e.g., triggers) and consequences (e.g., a temporary relief of stress) that sustain a dysfunctional behavior (e.g., substance abuse or other addictive behaviors). To change or improve the dysfunctional behavior, we can target antecedents and/or consequences. A clinician can provide skills training to patients to help them more effectively deal with antecedents. For example, as mentioned above, patients can be taught to avoid places, persons, and things that are related to substance use to prevent relapse as the "classical conditioning" has paired these place, person, and thing with substance use, and they therefore may trigger relapse. The clinician can also teach patients problem solving skills, self-assertive skills, communication skills, emotion management skills, importance of a balanced life style, drug or alcohol refusal skills, and other relapse prevention skills (Rizeanu, 2012). Furthermore, treatment can accentuate cognitive reappraisal or cognitive restructuring, an evidence-based treatment. Schema healing may be another important factor in this context.

Meichenbaum (1977) began his chapter on cognitive restructuring with several quotes, including Epictetus' "Man is disturbed not by things but the views he takes of them," and Alfred Adler's "It is very obvious that we are influenced not by 'facts' but by our interpretation of facts." Dysfunctional thoughts lead to negative emotion and maladaptive behavior; one way to improve or reduce a person's maladaptive behavior (e.g., substance abuse) is to change or modify his or her related negative or erroneous thoughts. Cognitive reappraisal can be further divided into cognitive restructuring and positive reappraisal. The primary difference between the two is that cognitive restructuring replaces an *unrealistic* negative interpretation of an event or situation with an entirely new and *realistic* interpretation, whereas the positive reappraisal strives to accentuate and incorporate positive meaning into the initial negative appraisal (Nowlan et al., 2016).

Cognitive Restructuring

As mentioned earlier, a person's thoughts affect his or her emotion as well as behavior; a distorted thought tends to lead to negative emotion, which in turn, results in maladaptive behaviors. To change clients' maladaptive behaviors, a clinician should become familiar with their thoughts and help them identify and modify their distorted and unhelpful thinking patterns. Oftentimes, clients' thoughts or thinking patterns are heavily influenced by their assumptions, beliefs, and previous experiences interacting with other people. It is therefore important for a clinician to also explore and modify clients' assumptions, beliefs, and attitudes that are underneath these cognitions (Meichenbaum, 1977).

Beck and colleagues (1979) identified many common distorted thinking patterns that may negatively affect a person's emotions and behavior, including: (1) all-or-nothing thinking: a person perceives things as absolutistic, that is, they are either black or white, without the possibility of gray; (2) overgeneralization: based on the occurrence of only one negative event or a very small amount of experience, a person subsequently infers that many additional adverse situations will happen; (3) catastrophizing or magnification: similar to overgeneralization but to an even more extreme extent, a person makes negative predictions regarding the future with only little evidence or no basis; (4) emotional reasoning: a person determines whether something is true or not based on his or her feelings rather than objective evidence; (5) mental filtering: a person devalues positive information and focuses on negative information; and (6) personalization: a person believes that he or she plays a role in the occurrence of a negative event, regardless of how irrelevant the two are to each other.

In addition to the generic types of distorted thinking patterns outlined above, there are distorted thinking patterns that are specific to addiction, such as substance use disorder and gambling disorder. For substance use disorder, a distorted thought, for example, can be one rationalizing use: "One drink won't hurt me," "It has been a bad day; I deserve to use"; or giving up: "Why even try; I will always be an addict" (McHugh et al., 2010, p. 7). A clinician should elicit evidence from the clients regarding the degree of accurateness of their thoughts and discuss with clients alternative appraisals that may better portray their experience. Psychoeducation can also be provided to help clients understand the role these distorted thoughts play in sustaining the addictive behaviors. A clinician should also encourage clients to rehearse and practice drug-cue-related cognitive restructuring skills outside of sessions (McHugh et al., 2010).

Similarly, there are common gambling-related distorted cognitions. Raylu and Oei (2004) organized them into five factors: gambling expectancies (e.g., "Having a gamble helps reduce tension and stress"; "Gambling makes me happier"), illusion of control (e.g., "Specific numbers and colors can help increase my chances of winning"; "I have specific rituals and behaviors that increase my chances of winning"), predictive control (e.g., "Losses when gambling are bound to be followed by a series of wins"; "A series of losses will provide me with a learning experience that will help me win later"), inability to stop gambling (e.g., "I can't function without gambling"; "I am not strong enough to stop gambling"), and interpretive bias (e.g., "Relating my winnings to my skill and ability makes me continue gambling"; "Remembering how much money I won last time makes me continue gambling") (pp. 768–769). A clinician should help clients to challenge their gambling-specific erroneous thoughts and to develop more rational thinking, such as: gambling machines are programed by a computerized, randomized system and gamblers cannot control the outcomes on the machines; a person's luck rather than skills is more likely to determine gambling outcomes; there is no linkage between gambling outcomes and previous outcomes; gambling machines are designed to gain more from and pay less to the consumers; structural factors that are linked to gambling machines can foster continued gambling in a person even with his or her losses (Raylu & Oei, 2010; Rizeanu, 2012). Video or online gaming can be another example, with its related erroneous beliefs clustering in over-valuing the salience of gaming reward and experience, and a reliance on virtual or video-gaming for self-esteem, social status, and recognition (Delfabbro & King, 2015).

Positive Reappraisal

How we interpret a stressful situation determines how we feel and, subsequently, how we respond. Positive reappraisal is about whether a person can see the glass half full instead of half empty, or whether he or she can find the silver lining in a relatively and seemingly negative or bad situation. The literature has suggested that a positive reappraisal, a positive outlook to life, or an optimistic world view may increase a person's resilience, help him or her more effectively deal with challenging situations, and better maintain health and mental health (Moskowitz et al., 2012). Many empirical studies have shown the evidence. For example, a meta-analysis done by Moskowitz and colleagues (2009) reveals the positive reappraisal as a major factor associating new HIV patients with better outcomes. Troy and colleagues' study (2010) indicated that under a high level of stress—but not a low level—women with a cognitive-positive-reappraisal ability tend to exhibit less depressive symptoms than women without such an ability.

Moskowitz and colleagues (2012) organized several theoretically supported skills, including positive reappraisal, into a 5 weekly session positive affect intervention program. They gave a simple example demonstrating positive reappraisal: "a bus arriving late, being full and driving past 2 people at a bus stop. One person may interpret the situation as horrible, the bus driver refused to stop for her . . . The other person may think that the bus must have been very full for the driver not to even stop. Seeing it as no one's fault, she is less upset. The silver lining may be that the woman had time to call a friend she'd been meaning to catch up with and use the time she had productively" (p. 15, online publication). Moskowitz and colleagues found that this intervention program was acceptable for new HIV patients, that the retention and home-practice adherence were high, and that participants reported a significant increase in positive affect and a significant decrease in negative affect. The notion of teaching clients and asking them to practice positive reappraisal skills can be very relevant to addicted individuals and their families, as the chronic and relapsing nature of addiction has frequently created among them high-stress situations that are directly or indirectly related to the addictive behaviors, and that many of them have reached a state of despair and hopelessness.

Schema Healing

Although CBT, including cognitive restructuring and positive reappraisal, is an evidence-based treatment and has helped many clients, it is not a magic bullet and may not be effective for certain groups of people, especially those who have "significant characterological issues" under their major psychiatric disorders, have "full-blown personality disorders," or who are rigid in their cognition and thinking patterns. In other words, those clients may not necessarily be receptive or willing to change their distorted cognitions and erroneous thinking even after logical analysis and discourse. Young et al. (2003) state, "In our experience, their distorted thoughts and self-defeating behaviors are extremely resistant to modification solely through cognitive-behavioral techniques" (p. 4). These clients are inflexible and entrenched in how they view themselves, their relationships with others, and the world. They are usually unwilling and unable to comply with CBT treatment procedures—they do not practice assigned homework and are more interested in seeking support and solace from their therapists than learning strategies to help themselves. These clients tend to get stuck in prolonged therapeutic processes; they are not making progress even after months of therapy. Not only are they often labeled by clinicians as "difficult" clients, but also they themselves are pessimistic about change and frequently feel hopelessness (Young et al., 2003).

To more effectively help these clients, Young developed Schema Therapy by expanding the traditional cognitive behavioral therapy and integrating elements of attachment, Gestalt, constructivist, and psychodynamic schools (Young et al., 2003). Schema, specifically early maladaptive schema (EMS), is a pervasive theme that consists of memories, bodily sensations, emotions, and cognitions. Schemas are usually formed during childhood and are elaborated and reinforced throughout adolescence and adulthood years; schemas are stable, persistent, and difficult to change. How people view the world is based on their schemas. Schema therapy considers that people's dysfunctional behaviors originate from their maladaptive coping patterns, both of which are related to their rooted pathological schemas. Negative and problematic schemas are more likely to develop when children grow up in a dysfunctional or neglectful environment, with their essential emotional needs not being met. For example, the development of the mistrust schema may be related to a person's experience of abuse and mistreatment by parents or other people during childhood. A person with such a schema tends to perceive others to have bad intentions toward him- or herself and expects others to hurt him or her. Schema Therapy suggests that a clinician should make clients aware of their maladaptive schemas, help them heal these schemas, and encourage them to take responsibility to move on and live a healthy and fulfilling life.

There are about 18 early maladaptive schemas (EMS), including emotional deprivation, abandonment/instability, mistrust/abuse, social isolation/alienation, defectiveness/shame, failure, dependence/incompetence, vulnerability to harm and illness, enmeshment/undeveloped self, subjugation, self-sacrifice, emotional inhibition, unrelenting standards/hypercriticalness, entitlement/grandiosity, insufficient self-control/self-discipline, approval-seeking/recognition-seeking, negativity/pessimism, and punitiveness. Young's model further groups the 18 schemas into five "schema domains" of unmet emotional needs. Domain 1 is "disconnection and rejection." Clients with schemas in domain 1 usually believe that it's unlikely that their needs for safety, stability, love and belonging will be met. Many clients with schema in this domain had traumatic or adverse childhoods or come from unstable and abusive families. Domain 2 is "impaired autonomy and performance." Clients with schemas in this domain usually have impaired abilities to be autonomous and are less able to be independent from their families of origin as compared to their counterparts. They usually come from overprotected families, with their parents doing all for them. Or they could come from families at the totally opposite end— families that barely ever looked after them. Domain 3 is "impaired limits." Clients with schemas in this domain usually show characteristics of selfishness, irresponsibility, narcissism, entitlement, and grandiosity. They do not have sufficient internal limits, self-discipline, or the concept of reciprocity. They cannot restrain their impulse or delay immediate gratification for a later, longer-term but larger reward. It may be challenging for them to keep commitments and meet their long-term goals, or to cooperate with other people and respect other people's rights. They usually come from indulgent and overly permissive families. Or it could also be a form of overcompensation, in that they come from families that are not nurturing and they suffer the schema of emotional deprivation. Domain 4 is "other-directedness." Clients with schemas in this domain emphasize meeting others' needs instead of their own needs. Clients do so to seek approval, keep emotional connection, or prevent revenge. Clients with this category of schemas usually come from families with "conditional acceptance" or where "the parents value their own emotional needs or social 'appearances' more than they value the unique needs of the child" (p. 19). Domain 5 is "overvigilance and inhibition." Clients with schemas associated with this domain often endeavor to meet strict standards about their performance at the cost of relaxation, relationships, good health, and happiness. Growing up, they learned to be alert to and constantly careful about possible occurrence of negative events in life (Young et al., 2003). Research has indicated the relationship between early maladaptive schema (EMS) and the occurrence of various psychopathologies, such as depression, substance use, and anxiety. Shorey et al.'s (2015) research on 122 patients from a substance abuse treatment residential program found an association between major depressive disorder and the EMS areas of "disconnection and rejection" and "impaired limits," as well as an association between generalized anxiety disorder and the EMS area of "impaired autonomy and performance." Shorey and colleagues suggest that clinicians may want to include early maladaptive schemas in their assessment and treatment when working with substance-abusing clients with comorbid mental disorders.

In addition to modifying maladaptive schemas, Schema Therapy also emphasizes changing dysfunctional schema modes. Schema modes are "the current emotional, cognitive, and behavioral state that a person is in" (Farrell et al., 2014, p. 7). The four basic schema modes are: Innate Child Modes, Maladaptive Coping Modes, Dysfunctional Parent Modes, and Healthy Modes. The Innate Child Modes may include the role of a vulnerable, angry, or impulsive child. These dysfunctional modes are developed when a person's basic emotional needs during childhood—such as safety, love, nurturance, and autonomy—are not met. Maladaptive Coping Modes may include (a) the "avoidant protector" coping style, in that a person protects him- or herself from overwhelming painful feelings or fear by means of, for example, being "spacey" or by dissociation; (b) the "overcompensator," in that a person behaves contrary to the schema triggered; and (c) the "compliant surrenderer," in that a person gives in to the schema triggered; for example, if defectiveness is the schema, the person would choose not to take on challenges. Dysfunctional Parent Modes are a person's internalization of the punitive and demanding aspects of their parents or other attachment figures. The Healthy Modes includes both the healthy adult mode and happy child mode. The healthy adult mode represents rational thoughts and functional skills that lead to healthy behaviors. The happy child mode embodies resources for playful and gratifying activities (Farrell et al., 2014).

To heal maladaptive schemas and change dysfunctional schema modes, Schema Therapy uses three techniques: cognitive techniques, experiential techniques, and limited reparenting. The goal of cognitive techniques is to help clients invalidate their schema, as the clients will be unable to change as long as they believe their schemas are valid. The clinician helps the client look for evidence for and against the schema throughout his or her life and, oftentimes, the schema proves to be false. The therapist and the client will work together to summarize on flash cards messages that are against the schema. The client can hold and read the flash cards regularly, especially when encountering schema triggers. The experiential techniques focus on a patient's emotional level. For example, the imagery exercise enables people to revisit their childhood events or scenes where they were not being treated right by their significant others. In the imagery process, they are given a chance to rescript the outcomes by standing up for themselves. The strategy of "limited reparenting" is often considered as the heart of Schema Therapy (Farrell et al., 2014). In providing limited reparenting, a therapist acts as a good parent who would provide protection and validation to help the patient restore the Vulnerable Child Mode, allow the patient to vent and actively listen to the patient to heal his or her Angry Child Mode, and offer empathic and caring confrontation as well as set limits for the client's Impulsive Child Mode. Limited reparenting gives a patient an opportunity to have his or her missed early childhood emotional needs met (Farrell et al., 2014).

Practice Mindfulness

A Third Wave Behavioral Therapy

Mindfulness practice is perceived by some scholars as the third wave of behavior therapy, following the second wave of behavior therapy—i.e., cognitive behavioral therapy, and the first wave of behavior therapy—i.e., therapies that focus on behavioral principles, learning conditioning, and behavioral modification (Brown et al., 2011; Hayes, 2004). Although each newer wave can be considered as a paradigm shift to its previous wave, each is also built upon its previous wave (Brown et al., 2011; Hayes, 2004). One emphasis of cognitive behavioral therapy, also an addition to the first wave of behaviorism therapy, is the above discussed cognitive restructuring—i.e., changing maladaptive behavior and emotion through changing distorted and dysfunctional thoughts. Mindfulness therapies, however, encourage a person to be mindful of and accept his or her internal sensations, thoughts, and feelings, without changing them (Brown et al., 2011). As Hayes, who summarized various authors, says, "This shift undermined the idea that the form or frequency of specific problematic cognitions were key, focusing instead on the cognitive context and coping strategies related to these specific thoughts. More emphasis began to be given to contacting the present moment. . . [It is] possible to alter the function of thoughts without first altering their form" (p. 645). Hoppes (2006) says it well: "[The] paradigm shift from a more traditional cognitive-behavioral strategy of trying to eliminate pain by changing distorted thoughts, to a focus on changing one's relationship to dealing with pain and painful realities. This . . . shift is potentially more relevant to managing painful reality-based problems that are not based on distortions of thought, which individuals in recovery often have to endure as a result of their addiction histories" (p. 846).

Third wave behavioral therapies that integrate mindfulness in their strategies include dialectical behavior therapy (DBT; Linehan, 2015), mindfulness-based cognitive therapy (MBCT; Segal et al., 2002), acceptance and commitment therapy (ACT; Hayes et al., 2012), mindfulness-based relapse prevention (MBRP; Bowen et al., 2011), and mindfulness-oriented recovery enhancement (MORE; Garland, 2013). All treatment approaches of third wave behavioral therapy have their foundations in traditional cognitive behavioral therapy; each of them, however, also contribute new dimensions to and augment the standard cognitive behavioral therapy. All of them are relevant to addiction treatment, but MBRP and MORE are especially relevant.

Definition of Mindfulness

The concept of "mindfulness" originates from Buddhist philosophy, but has been embraced by Western psychology in the past decades (Chiesa et al., 2013; Creswell, 2017). There is growing evidence of mindfulness randomized control trials indicating its beneficial effects on physical conditions, mental health, cognitive outcomes, affective outcomes, and interpersonal outcomes (Chiesa & Serretti, 2014; Creswell, 2017; Ludwig & Kabat-Zinn, 2008). Regarding addiction specifically, preliminary evidence shows that mindfulness-based interventions are more effective in reducing craving and substance use, such as drinking and smoking, compared to control groups (see Chiesa & Serretti's review, 2014; and Creswell's review, 2017). Although there is no consensus about the exact definition of mindfulness, one commonly cited definition is "paying attention in a particular way: on purpose, in the present moment, and nonjudgementally" (Kabat-Zinn, 1994, p. 4). Creswell offers a working definition of mindfulness: "a process of openly attending, with awareness, to one's present moment experience" (p. 493). Creswell explains further, "This process of awareness of present moment experience contrasts with much of our daily life experience, in which we often find ourselves unintentionally letting our minds wander . . . running on automatic pilot . . . or suppressing unwanted experiences" (p. 493).

Break Automatic Pilot and Habituation

Mindfulness can have multiple functions in benefiting people with addiction problems. First, it may facilitate to stop automatic pilot and break habituation. Automatic pilot and habituation are mindlessness—an opposite of mindfulness that emphasizes focused attention, meta-awareness, and conscious intention and act (Garland, 2013). Addicted people often suffer not only impulsivity but also compulsivity, particularly during the late stage; they relapse because they react to craving or triggers automatically and habitually. Garland describes it well: "people struggling to recover from addiction often want to remain sober yet find themselves unconsciously compelled to use drugs or alcohol. Similarly, in spite of people's clear intentions to remain calm in the face of stress and pain, they may find themselves automatically lashing out in anger or yielding to hopelessness, only to suffer from pangs of guilt and shame at their uncontrolled reactions" (p. 5). A person engaged in automatic pilot does not have space and opportunity to make choices. Mindfulness trains a person to "practice pausing before reacting" (Bowen et al., 2011, p. 53), and thus allows

BEHAVIORAL THERAPY

307

a person space and opportunity to *consciously* observe oneself and make *choices*. Hoppes (2006) says that mindfulness enhances a person's ability to de-center from a strong urge, and the de-centering tactic to a craving or urge would make the person more able to shift away from the thoughts that it is impossible for me to ignore this urge to the thoughts that I can handle this urge, and that I will gain long-term advantages if I don't act on the urge.

Enhance Bottom-Up Emotion Regulation

The second major function of mindfulness is that it may enhance "bottom-up" regulation in addition to the function of stopping automatic pilot and habitual reaction. Bottom-up regulation cultivates equanimity, calmness, and contentment, without the need to act on "maladaptive" thoughts or to engage in cognitive reappraisal. A review by Chiesa et al. (2013) found that mindfulness practice could influence the bottom-up process, in that a person has a reduced activation in his or her limbic areas without the recruitment of the prefrontal cortex areas to regulate their emotional areas. In other words, mindfulness training could be associated with a person's "lower emotional reactivity to stimuli aimed at evoking emotion regulation strategies that is not meditated by enhanced top-down regulation of [prefrontal cortex] areas upon limbic areas, such as the amygdala and the striatum" (p. 89). Chiesa and colleagues' review of functional neuroimaging research that investigates mindfulness suggests that short-term mindfulness training may be related to top-down emotion regulation, whereas long-term mindfulness practice tends to associate with bottom-up emotion regulation. "One of the hallmarks of expert meditators is their ability to experience negative emotions without necessarily 'getting caught up' in them" (Treadway & Lazar, 2009, p. 53). Such a trait or skill can help a person more effectively deal with various psychopathology like depression and anxiety, which often involve a person's rumination of negative emotions.

Mindfulness practices focus on here and now experience, increasing a person's time "living in the moment," and thus decreasing his or her tendency to ruminate on negative thoughts and worries related to past or future (Treadway & Lazar, 2009). Furthermore, mindfulness emphasizes the values of being nonjudgmental, self-compassion, and acceptance

(Bowen et al., 2011)—all emotional and cognitive phenomena are only temporary mental events, and therefore we do not need to actively reappraise or regulate those experiences (Chiesa et al., 2013). Chiesa and colleagues' review shows that mindfulness training is related to brain pattern alteration, especially long-term mindfulness training that might produce structural change. Lutz and colleagues (cited in Chiesa et al., 2013) say this might elucidate why longstanding meditators often report augmented mental steadiness instead of continuous demand to regulate their mental processes.

Enhance Top-Down Emotion Regulation

Additionally, although one original major goal of mindfulness therapy is to help an individual to become more able to treat the internal negative thoughts and experiences as impermanent and accept them rather than restructuring or reappraising them, mindfulness or meditation practice seems to also be able to increase a person's ability to perform cognitive restructuring and reappraisal (Garland, 2013). Some studies have shown that people with dispositional mindfulness or those who receive mindfulness training are more likely to be aware of subtle changes, to make better distinctions, to become observant of new information, to adopt different perspectives, and to adapt their strategies to varying circumstances (Garland, 2013). Two interesting but preliminary studies reveal that regular meditation practice can protect against cortical thinning and enhance cognitive vitality among old people (Treadway & Lazar, 2009). Garland suggests that these increased top-down regulation, attentional capacity, and cognitive flexibility actually can fortify a person's cognitive reappraisal ability—a critical skill in cognitive behavioral therapy. It enables a person to modify his or her distorted or dysfunctional thoughts of an event or situation to more adaptive and functional thoughts, which in turn can positively affect his or her emotion and behavior. Chiesa et al.'s review (2013) concludes that mindfulness can enhance both a person's bottom-up and top-down brain regulations and that a person's negative and maladaptive emotion could be reduced by mindfulness practice through its concurrent function of observing and accepting it as well as reappraising and modifying it so that it becomes more adaptable.

Mindfulness Skills, Training, Exercises, and Practice

Because of mindfulness' multiple functions—including increasing self-control, cognitive flexibility, concentration, and psychological well-being—and its cost-efficiency and accessibility, many psychiatric, behavioral, and psychosocial treatment approaches have integrated mindfulness exercises and practices into their treatment sessions (Dunn et al., 2013). Dunn and colleagues suggest mindfulness as "a transtheoretical clinical process" that is applicable in psychotherapy. It would be appropriate to tailor mindfulness practice to meet the unique needs of specific client populations; for instance, addiction relapse prevention, pain reduction, or depression or anxiety reduction. A mindfulness practice program may include four basic components:

(a) Clients receive psychoeducation that explains the relationship between mindfulness and pain, stress, depression, anxiety, or addiction relapse. The concept of automatic pilot and how mindfulness practice can help a person step out of the automatic pilot are discussed. The concept of here and now is also introduced and emphasized. (b) Clients participate in formal mindfulness meditations during treatment sessions and practice such meditations outside of sessions. Formal mindfulness practice involves an allocation of time specifically for mindfulness practice—it may be 10 or 30 minutes or other length of time, usually daily, engaging in deep breath, use of the five senses experiencing internal states and surrounding environment, body scan, yoga, and/or lovingkindness. Many clients may rely on CD-guided meditation (e.g., Jon Kabat-Zinn's body scan meditation) initially but are able to transition to practice without guided instructions later (Bowen et al., 2011). (c) Clients are encouraged to not only engage in formal mindfulness in and out of treatment sessions but also practice informal mindfulness in daily activities. Informal mindfulness practice means "focusing on the details of the moment rather than rushing through it" and it is "the opposite of zoning out or going on 'autopilot'" (Moskowitz et al., 2012, p. 14, online publication). Informal mindfulness practice can be implemented during a person's daily life, while he or she is walking, at work, or at home; attention can be paid to the sensations of breathing, the feel of feet stepping on the ground (Moskowitz et al., 2012).

(d) Clients share their in-session or homework mindfulness practice experiences with, and receive feedback from, their therapists or group facilitators. The goal is to encourage clients and inspire them to avoid self-blame or self-criticisms when experiencing challenges or struggles while practicing mindfulness.

Mindfulness training emphasizes *practice*. To practice formal mindfulness meditation can enhance mindfulness ability, which is like going to the gym daily to strengthen muscles (Bowen et al., 2011; Moskowitz et al., 2012). A combination of formal mindfulness meditation and informal mindfulness practice in daily activities can better prepare a person and make him or her more able to apply mindfulness when encountering crises or high-risk situations (Bowen et al., 2011). Mindfulness training also accentuates the need for therapists or group facilitators to practice mindfulness themselves, suggesting this will not only enable them to become more effective in teaching clients mindfulness skills but also make them more able to be empathetic to clients (Bowen et al., 2011).

Risks of Mindfulness

Summarizing various studies, Creswell (2017) points out the possible occurrence of "dark night" experiences resulting from mindfulness intervention and offers the following insight: Although it is not uncommon for some people to experience unpleasant reactions while others sense contentment when engaged in formal mindfulness practice, such negative reactions tend to be benign and may actually help a person learn it is only a temporary experience, fostering understanding to more appropriately react to the difficult experiences. However, formal mindfulness intervention may trigger more severe adverse reactions in some people with trauma or who are at risk for psychosis; though more research is needed with respect to the prevalence and severity of these "dark nights." Furthermore, such severe adverse reactions only happen infrequently and most likely to people undergoing intensive and lengthy (two weeks to three months) residential mindfulness practice training; the present evidence-based mindfulness approaches—which adopt lesser doses and are offered by qualified instructors—bring low risks for severe negative reaction.

Make Recovery More Rewarding: The Operant Conditioning

Why It Is Necessary and Important to Make Recovery More Rewarding

Most addicted people use alcohol or drugs, or engage in gambling, internet gaming, or other addictive behaviors repeatedly to feel good or feel better, i.e., to seek reward, reduce pain, and relieve distress in the first place. Although abstinence and recovery will bring enormous advantages to some addicted people whose continued using will involve high stakes and costs (e.g., physicians or pilots), many other addicted people may lose enthusiasm for treatment or recovery once the negative consequences of their addiction—the crisis that brought them to treatment in the first place—dissipate (McKay, 2017). Unlike the more privileged groups such as physicians or pilots, they have no rewarding jobs to return to, no close relationships to rekindle, and no "fun" recreational activities available to them; they start to feel dull and isolated as the addictive agents have been taken away and so the rewards of those agents have gone. To them, the advantages brought in by abstinence do not exceed the disadvantages resulting from abstinence. According to behavioral choice theory, this context drives a person to relapse, as the person believes he or she has more to lose than to gain when abstaining. A rewarding lifestyle competes with and surpasses the reward produced by drug use or other addictive lifestyles; the key to help clients achieve a long-term recovery is to help them regain or cultivate a rewarding life during and post treatment. Many empirical studies have indicated that clients who engaged in rewarding, non-drug-related activities—such as employment, religious involvement, meaningful interpersonal relationships, and/or recreational pursuits—tend to have more positive treatment outcomes and lower relapse risks (Adamson et al., 2009; Higgins et al., 1993; Moos' review, 2007; Scherbaum & Specka, 2008).

Barriers to Make Recovery More Rewarding

Three barriers may block the way for an addicted person to develop a rewarding lifestyle without drugs or other addictive agents. First, a prolonged exposure to addictive agents may have resulted in brain neuroadaptation in a person, leading to his or her loss of interest in the rewards associated with everyday natural experiences, such as work achievement, interpersonal relationships, and pleasure from recreational activities. This underappreciation of reward from natural experiences can be acquired because of the brain's chronic exposure to drugs or other powerful addictive agents; it can also be genetically predisposed. Some patients are at risk genetically to "reward deficiency syndrome" that prompts them to be more sensitive to the reward effects of drugs or alcohol than the reward effects of ordinary everyday life experiences (Blum et al., 2014). Garland (2013) states that as addiction advances, alcohol and drugs or addictive behaviors will become the focus of the person and displace people, events, and activities that once the person treasured. This is "[m]uch like the anhedonia experienced by someone who is depressed, where once an addict might have felt pleasure from seeing a beautiful sunset or hearing the laughter of children, he or she may become increasingly dulled to the joy that can be experienced from these events. Addicts become more and more dependent on the addictive substance to get a feeling of reward and pleasure from life" (p. 60). It takes time, patience, and efforts for an addicted person to recover, rebuild life, and re-appreciate joy from natural activities and experiences. Some addicted people—especially those with low recovery capital or those who are impulsive and desire immediate reward—may need extra support and assistance to transition from a lifestyle that relies on drugs or other addictive agents for reward to a lifestyle that pursues reward based on productive, meaningful, everyday life activities.

Second, many addicted individuals have low recovery capital, poor quality of life, and few natural reinforcers—a situation that exists either before or after their drug career and that reduces the chance for them to obtain rewards (McKay, 2017). Addicted individuals, especially women, may have grown up in a dysfunctional family and environment, have never learned functional interpersonal skills and problem-solving skills, dropped out of school early and are equipped with no life skills or vocational skills (Henkel, 2011; Sun, 2006); they, therefore, need habilitation rather than rehabilitation. Or some may have had good relationships and occupations initially, all of which are severely impaired because of their prolonged addictions. McKay (2017) says it well: "In the absence of strong incentives for sustained behavior change, even the most effective medication or behavioral treatment is unlikely to be effective for very long" (p. 752). For many addicted people, recovery requires habilitation rather than rehabilitation; increasing recovery capital and enhancing quality of life is the key.

The third barrier is related to treatment programs' treatment philosophy and value orientation. Most treatment programs emphasize teaching and helping patients how to stop or cut down using, or to resist triggers of relapse; treatment programs seldom devote efforts and time to help patients learn how to embrace and celebrate life without using (McKay, 2017; Roozen, 2013). Roozen points out that addiction treatment programs typically practice motivational interviewing, which facilitates motivation in a person to stop or cut use; cognitive behavioral therapy, which teaches patients how to resist triggers and prevent relapse; and pharmacotherapy, which reduces the pleasure related to use (e.g., naltrexone to drinking) or increases pain if used (e.g., Antabuse to drinking). All these major treatment approaches enhance a person's ability to resist use and take away the pleasure of use. The problem is that treatment programs have overlooked the needs of patients to have pleasure in life while taking away the pleasure of use. It is important for treatment programs to simultaneously encourage and help patients engage in healthy and rewarding activities while guiding them to resist drug use; non-substance-related satisfying activities can counteract the reinforcing impact of drug and alcohol use (Roozen, 2013; Solinas et al., 2008; Volkow et al., 2003).

How to Make Recovery More Rewarding

Research has generated some insights, methods, strategies, and skills to make addicted patients' recovery more rewarding. Quality of life is one major factor impacting a patient's perception of whether his or her life has become better after treatment and abstinence. In other words, quality of life may determine whether a patient's recovery can be sustainable and long term. Quality of life includes many dimensions and areas, such as food and shelter, safety, health and mental health, interpersonal relationships and love, employment, self-esteem and self-actualization, and so on. Case management can be conducted to assess a patient's needs and interventions provided accordingly. (For details about quality of life, please refer to Chapter 4.) Other strategies treatment programs can adopt to reinforce patients' recovery and make their recovery more rewarding include: (a) strengthening patients' abilities to pursue healthy and pleasurable recreational activities; (b) encouraging and linking patients to employment and helping them to sustain it; and (c) teaching patients mindful savoring (Garland, 2013). Many established treatment approaches have also been developed to address the issue of a rewarding recovery, such as the Community Reinforcement Approach (Meyers & Miller, 2001), Reinforcement-based Treatment (Tuten et al., 2012), Contingency Management methods (e.g., Petry, 2012), and Mindfulness-Oriented Recovery Enhancement (Garland, 2013), which will be discussed in the next section of this chapter.

Most clinicians probably would think it is more important to help patients deal with substance use problems and prevent relapse than to help them engage in healthy, non-substance-related, pleasurable leisure activities. This not only underestimates the role healthy and rewarding recreational activities play to facilitate long-term recovery, but also overestimates the ability of a patient to engage in such activities. Many patients, after abstinence and during recovery, do feel bored and blunt; they miss the pleasure and excitement they previously had. However, they have been so used to using alcohol or drugs or engaging in gambling or online gaming to seek fun and relief, they become unfamiliar with pursuing other alternative recreational activities. Treatment programs thus should include a goal in the treatment plan of helping a patient to engage in healthy leisure activities on his/her own after discharge.

1. Recreational Activities

A treatment program can help a patient in this regard using at least two approaches. One is to create a "social club," where it offers healthy and rewarding social activities and both the present patients and alumni patients can attend periodically (e.g., once a week). Such a social club can further serve as a "lifeline" for some alumni patients (Tuten et al., 2012). The second approach is to prepare patients to develop their own repertoire of skills to pursue healthy and fun leisure activities after discharge. Tuten and colleagues suggest the following strategies: (a) Do not assume what activities would be reinforcing to the patients; rather, ask them. (b) Useful information may be derived by assessing the activities a patient had been participating in during a long abstinence period he or she had in the past. (c) Identify the activities that the patient truly enjoys and can regularly engage. (d) Encourage the patient to consider new activities to expand his or her activity repertoire. Because the patient may not find the new activity reinforcing, a mix of new and old activities is preferred instead of relying on just old or just new ones. (e) Diversify the activities to include those that can be implemented: alone—such as reading; with others—such as dinner with friends; in fine weather—such as taking a walk; in poor weather—such as playing a puzzle; when having money—such as watching a show in a theater; when the budget is tight—such as writing a letter to a friend. Tuten and colleagues also emphasize that the plan needs to be explicit, monitored, and discussed with the patient throughout treatment.

Although typical addiction treatment programs emphasize treatment related to stopping use and relapse prevention instead of recreational activities, several treatment programs in the US actually have centered their treatments with sports to raise holistic wellness among adolescent or adult patients in recovery (Harden & Walton, 2012). Sports are not only recreational, but also possess special qualities contributing to a person's recovery. Harden and Walton discovered parallels between a recovery journey and a flourishing athletic career. They suggest both require "open mindedness, discipline, time management, coaching/sponsorship, and learning from failure" (p. 355). An athlete needs to be open-minded to be aware of self-limitations and be willing to learn from coaches and other more experienced peers; likewise, a person in recovery needs to be flexible to forgo his or her previously fixed notions about substance use and learn about recovery. Discipline is essential to become a successful athlete; it is similarly critical for addicted people—who often lack internal discipline and accountability, especially among adolescents—to achieve long-term recovery.

2. Employment

Employment is another major ingredient contributing to a rewarding recovery. Numerous empirical studies have verified its significance to promote long-term recovery (Henkel, 2011; Walton & Hall, 2016). Employment is rewarding and contributes to long-term recovery because of its multiple significant functions: (a) It provides a structure for everyday life; a job normally will occupy the majority of time of the day, leaving the patient little room to indulge in drug use or gambling, as they previously did. (b) Working can enhance a person's self-efficacy and self-esteem, which can be very satisfying. (c) The earnings from employment can support a person's quality of life improvement, including better housing and more varieties of recreational activities. (d) Employment may also create opportunities for meeting new friends, expanding a person's social circle (Tuten et al., 2012). Tuten and colleague suggest clinicians encourage patients to pursue employment goals; they also accentuate the importance of clinicians giving patients a rationale for having a job as a goal and discuss with patients why a satisfying vocation can lead to a sustained sobriety and a rewarding life. Tuten and colleagues suggest that clinicians should initiate such a discussion, and perhaps begin with a statement like: "In drug abuse treatment, one of the predictors of long-term success is stable, satisfying employment. This relationship between abstinence and employment exists for the following reasons" (p. 83). Once a patient starts working, it is equally important for clinicians to help prepare the patient to stay on the job, including helping the patient to more effectively deal with interpersonal issues or other frustrations.

3. Mindful Savoring

Mindful savoring may also add joy, fun, and reward to a person's life, including during a person's recovery. Savoring experiences can involve both sensory and non-sensory events. Garland states that "We get so wrapped up in our thoughts, feelings, and memories that we often don't pay close attention to the many sights and sounds of the world . . . Especially when you are wrapped up in thoughts about drugs or about the stressors in your life, it can be hard to really notice the beauty of the world around you" (2013, p. 64). Garland suggests that there is inherent joy in a person's environment and clients can savor the enjoyable and rewarding perceptual qualities of a chosen object via the use of sights, sounds, smells, textures, and tastes. For example, attention to simple things in life such as beautiful scenery, a delicious chocolate cake, or the aroma of coffee, may all add rewarding elements to a person's life and enhance positive emotions. Savoring experiences are not limited to simple sensory events. Bryant and Veroff (2007) suggest that attentiveness to complex thoughts or targets can also be savored. For example, one can attend to "the wonderful elegance of a mathematical proof," or to "the joys of reading a suspenseful melodrama" (p. 27).

Three concrete strategies have been proposed by Bryant and Veroff (2007) to enhance savoring experiences and therefore add joy to life: (a) To prolong the moment. Bryant and Veroff say that it is puzzling regarding the usual duration of bad and good events—i.e., if unaffected, the good event often finishes on its own, whereas the bad event tends to persist on its own. They suggest that positive events of short duration—e.g., getting a promotion or raise or being given a kiss by a beloved one—tend to be more difficult to savor than those of long duration. People can revive their short-lived savored event through recall and reminiscence, sharing the story with others, or reviewing photos or other memorabilia. People can also use the strategy of "chaining," in that the discrete positive event can be prolonged via considering a constellation of associations related to the initial event. Bryant uses himself as an example. His experience of climbing to the top of a mountain is rewarding but only momentarily. Such exhilaration can be broadened and prolonged by the 360-degree scenery, the clean scent of mountain air, or even a contemplation of the meaning of the accomplishment. Celebration is another strategy to psychologically prolong the positive event; for example, people celebrate college graduation or birthday. (b) To intensify the moment. To achieve this, we can reduce distractions to the event. Bryant and Veroff give the example of how to strengthen the savoring of reading a book—we can tell others not to disturb us; position ourselves in a comfortable position; and prepare for ourselves a cup of tea. Sharing the moment or event with other people, especially a loved one or a close friend, can also boost the savoring, as the closeness and attachment that additionally take place during the process is itself something that can be savored. (c) "To shift gears to savoring." Bryant and Veroff suggest that people can elicit savoring when there are no positive feelings happening in their lives but they wish there were. Anticipating and planning for future events that will bring pleasure can produce feelings of control over a future positive event, as well as a portion of the version of that future event. Another strategy is to compare and refocus. People may feel better if they compare themselves with others who are less fortunate, or compare where they are now with a time when they were worse off.

Established/Evidence-Based Treatment Methods

Various established/evidence-based treatment methods and approaches relevant to addiction relapse prevention and recovery have been developed; all of them incorporate one or more of the above mentioned five essential notions—i.e., (a) functional analysis; (b) identifying and avoiding triggers, and managing them if they are unavoidable; (c) engaging in cognitive restructuring, positive reappraisal, and/or schema healing; (d) practicing mindfulness; and (e) making recovery more rewarding. These established treatment methods, for example, may include Cognitive Behavioral Therapy (e.g., Carroll & Onken, 2005; Carroll et al., 2008), Schema-Focused Cognitive Behavioral Therapy (e.g., Farrell et al., 2014; Young et al., 2003), Mindfulness-Based Relapse Prevention (e.g., Bowen et al., 2011), Acceptance and Commitment Therapy (e.g., Harris, 2009; Hayes, 2004), Dialectical Behavioral Therapy (e.g., Linehan, 2015), Mindfulness-Oriented Recovery Enhancement (e.g., Garland, 2013), Community Reinforcement Approach (e.g., Meyers & Miller, 2001), Contingency Management (e.g., Higgins & Rogers, 2009; Petry, 2012), and Reinforcement-Based Treatment (e.g., Tuten et al., 2012). Other methods such as Eye Movement Desensitization and Reprocessing (EMDR), Biofeedback, and so on, are not included in this book..

Cognitive Behavioral Therapy and Schema-Focused Therapy

Cognitive Behavioral Therapy (CBT) is one of the most researched, evaluated, and adopted evidence-based addiction relapse prevention treatment approaches (Magill & Ray, 2009). Numerous quantitative large trials and reviews have verified CBT's effectiveness in addiction relapse prevention (Dutra et al., 2008; Magill & Ray, 2009; McHugh et al., 2010). CBT combines functional analysis and skills training, helping patients to identify, avoid, and manage triggers, as well as to remember the fact that the positive effects of drug use are only temporary, which will be followed by long-term negative consequences. CBT also emphasizes helping patients recognize and change their distorted cognitions, as distorted thoughts often lead to negative emotions and maladaptive behaviors. For patients with characterological problems, who are psychologically rigid, or who have personality disorders and whose dysfunctional rooted core beliefs may prevent them from being receptive to cognitive restructuring in a relatively short time period, Schema-Focused CBT may be applied. Clinicians can use cognitive techniques, experiential techniques, behavioral pattern-breaking, empathic confrontation, and limited reparenting to help patients heal the schemas (Farrell et al., 2014; Young et al., 2003). Detailed descriptions and discussions regarding implementation of Schema Therapy can be found in Young and colleagues' book, *Schema Therapy: A Practitioner's Guide* (2003) or Farrell and colleagues' book, *The Schema Therapy Clinician's Guide* (2014).

CBT tends to have a long-lasting effect, in that patients continue using the skills they learned—e.g., self-monitoring and trigger recognition—and decreasing their substance use even after the treatment concluded (Carroll et al., 1994; NIDA, 2018). A meta-analysis indicates no difference comparing individual CBT with group CBT; group CBT may be the most economical option for clinical treatment (Magill & Ray, 2009). Schema-Focused CBT can also be delivered both in an individual and group format. In addition, CBT skills can be delivered to patients via computer, making CBT skills more widely available (Carroll et al., 2008). Carroll and colleagues' randomized clinical trial indicated that a biweekly approach to computer-based CBT training by patients in addition to the standard care enhances treatment engagement and effectiveness.

Mindfulness-Based Relapse Prevention

Mindfulness-Based Relapse Prevention (MBRP) is based on the traditional CBT framework of relapse prevention, but adds the component of mindfulness meditation practices (Bowen et al., 2011). Although more studies with more rigorous designs are needed, various empirical studies have verified the overall effectiveness of MBRP surpassing that of standard care or other control groups, and being equal to or exceeding that of CBT (Bowen et al., 2014; de Souza et al., 2015; Glasner-Edwards et al., 2017; Witkiewitz et al., 2014). There are multiple advantages the mindfulness component of the MBRP contributes to relapse prevention treatment: It enables patients to see the "big picture" and to pause before automatically reacting to triggers. It also facilitates in patients compassion toward self and others, so that discomfort and frustration become more tolerable and that acceptance replaces guilt, shame, blame, and stigma (Bowen et al., 2011). The mindfulness component is especially beneficial to help addicted individuals manage "painful reality-based problems that are not based on distortions of thought, which individuals in recovery often have to endure as a result of their addiction histories" (Hoppes, 2006, p. 846).

In addition to the basic CBT tasks, such as identifying, monitoring, and effectively dealing with relapse triggers, the MBRP encourages patients to practice formal and informal mindful activities. According to Bowen and colleagues (2011), the MBRP is suitable for patients attending an outpatient aftercare program and the goal is to help them maintain treatment gains and to promote long-term recovery. A detailed manual for implementing

MBRP can be found in Bowen and colleagues' book, *Mindfulness-Based Relapse Prevention for Addictive Behaviors: A Clinician's Guide* (2011). In addition to the MBRP, other mindfulness-related treatment methods may include Acceptance and Commitment Therapy (ACT), Dialectical Behavioral Therapy (DBT), and Mindfulness-Oriented Recovery Enhancement (MORE). ACT and DBT have been discussed in Chapter 6; MORE is worth highlighting here as it not only incorporates CBT and mindfulness, but also adds a new component, "mindfulness savoring."

Mindfulness-Oriented Recovery Enhancement

Mindfulness-Oriented Recovery Enhancement (MORE) was developed by Garland, who combined cognitive therapy, mindfulness, and positive psychology into the treatment model (2013). MORE has demonstrated a preliminary efficacy for treating patients with co-occurring chronic pain and prescription opioid use disorder (Garland et al., 2014). Two major theoretical values underlie the MORE approach. First, Garland (2013) suggests, citing research findings, that positive emotions—such as joy, contentment, and hope—have many advantages and functions, including broadening a person's cognition and attention; enabling him or her to think more innovatively and solve problems more effectively; enhancing a person's engagement in new behaviors and creating new social relationships; and building his or her physical, psychological, and social resources. Second, Garland and colleagues (2010) suggest, citing research evidence, that the more a person attends to painful or aversive stimuli, the more intense the person's subjective pain will be, whereas the person tends to experience greater pleasure if he or she focuses on the positive features of his or her environment. Based on these two themes and by using techniques related to mindfulness, cognitive restructuring, and life savoring, MORE's treatment strategies target: (a) positive reappraisal, and (b) mindful savoring.

For positive reappraisal, Garland (2013) emphasizes that MORE helps patients to develop a more positive and functional perspective of their life situations, which is in contrast to the traditional CBT cognitive restructuring in that patients typically are helped to correct their distorted cognitions into more accurate versions. Garland suggests that this approach endorses a person's strengths, empowers the person to face difficult situations in life, and helps him or her to realize that one can grow and become stronger from stressful and challenging situations. Garland further suggests the "mindful reappraisal" strategy and lays out steps that patients can practice, including: be aware of one's thoughts and feelings when facing a challenging situation; detect any negative thoughts and feelings, as well as practice mindful breathing to allow for alternative interpretations of the situations and choices for response; look for evidence that verifies and nullifies the negative interpretations; ask, "Is there a blessing in disguise here?" and consider possible positive outcomes that may result from the situation; and focus on positive thoughts (2013, p. 57). For mindful savoring, Garland (2013) encourages clients to learn mindfulness skills and pay close attention to beautiful and rewarding events in their environments as well as in their lives. Once a person is in intimate contact with the world and becomes appreciative of its sounds, sights, tastes, and smells, his or her mind will come to be quiet and body will settle down. Garland suggests this mindful savoring can help a person break automatic pilot, more effectively deal with craving, and cope with negative emotions and thoughts.

A detailed description and discussion of the MORE treatment approach can be found in Garland's book, *Mindfulness-Oriented Recovery Enhancement for Addiction, Stress, and Pain* (2013).

Community Reinforcement Approach

In addition to MORE, other treatment approaches that accentuate a rewarding recovery may include Community Reinforcement Approach (CRA), Contingency Management (CM), and the Reinforcement-Based Treatment (RBT). CRA, an evidence-based treatment approach, focuses on encouraging and helping addicted patients obtain pleasure from family and interpersonal relationships, employment, and recreational activities, rather than from alcohol or other drugs. The CRA comprises several elements: (a) Functional analysis of substance use, exploring both the antecedents of substance use and the consequences of substance use. This may also include relapse prevention, in that CRA helps clients to identify high-risk situations and strategies to cope with or counteract the risk factors or triggers. An unique feature of CRA is that its functional analysis not only examines substance use behaviors but also non-substance-use, pleasurable behavior. This is to encourage clients to engage in pleasurable behaviors that involve no substance use, in addition to a stoppage of substance use. (b) Sobriety sampling. CRA considers that an immediate total abstinence could be intimidating for some clients. To reduce dropout rate and move clients gently to long-term abstinence, the sobriety sampling strategy allows the client to negotiates with the therapist to agree to begin abstinence only for a time-limited period initially. (c) Happiness Scale and treatment plan. CRA uses a Happiness Scale to assess a client's needs or the areas that should be worked on, which then are incorporated into the client's treatment plan. The Happiness Scale contains 10 areas, such as substance use, job/education progress, money management, social life, personal habits, marriage/family relationship, legal issues, emotional life, communication, and general happiness. (d) Behavioral skills training. Using psychoeducation and role plays, CRA teaches clients problem solving skills, communication skills, and drink/drug refusal skills. (e) Employment skills. CRA provides training to help clients obtain and maintain a job. (f) Recreational and social counseling. CRA does not assume that clients will automatically know how to pursue non-substance-involved recreational activities or social circle; rather, CRA provides specific counseling in this area. (g) Relationship counseling. CRA help clients improve their relationships with their partners or significant others (Meyers & Miller, 2001; Meyers et al., 2011).

Based on the Community Reinforcement Approach, two other treatment approaches were developed. One is Adolescent Community Reinforcement Approach (A-CRA). Compared to CRA, A-CRA is different in several aspects. A-CRA is developmentally appropriate, in that its Happiness Scale contains items related to friends and school; its communication skills training additionally brings in an anger management element; and it involves parents or caregivers. Compared to many other treatment approaches for adolescents, A-CRA is equally effective but the most cost-effective (Meyers et al, 2011). Community Reinforcement and Family Training (CRAFT) is also based on CRA. The goal of CRAFT is to engage treatment-refusing people into treatment through working with their significant others. CRAFT does not directly pressure these people to get treatment; rather, it works via a Concerned Significant Other (CSO), usually a family member. Similar to CRA, CRAFT adopts the operant conditioning concept and teaches CSOs to reward clients' behaviors that support sobriety and withhold rewards when clients are using. CRAFT not only helps CSOs to encourage their addicted but treatment-resistant family members to attend treatment, but also focuses on increasing CSOs' own overall happiness. Studies have indicated the effectiveness of CRAFT in promoting treatment among treatment-refusing substance-abusing individuals; compared to the Johnson Intervention approach and Al-Anon model, CRAFT is two to three times more effective (Meyers et al., 2011).

A detailed description of CRA can be found in Meyers and Miller's book, *A Community Reinforcement Approach to Addiction Treatment* (2001).

Contingency Management/Motivational Incentives

Both the community reinforcement approach (CRA) and contingency management (CM), which is also called motivational incentives, are mainly based on the operant conditioning framework. Both treatments aim at increasing clients' frequency of reinforcement/reward for their abstinent behaviors while decreasing their frequency of reinforcement/reward obtained through substance-use related activities (Higgins & Rogers, 2009). The reward brought about to clients by CRA is naturalistic— including meanings and rewarding feelings from a partner or interpersonal relationships, employment, and recreational activities—whereas the reward brought about by CM comes from contrived sources. CM specifies an outcome behavior that can be measured objectively (such as treatment retention, negative urine testing results, medication compliance) and provides clients with an immediate and tangible positive reinforcement when they achieve the targeted behavior (Petry, 2012). Numerous studies have established the high efficacy of CM in treating addiction and its associated disorders (e.g., Blanken et al., 2016; Garcia-Fernandez et al., 2011; Kelly et al., 2014; Roll, 2007).

CM is usually combined with other treatment methods, such as CRA or cognitive behavioral therapy (CBT). Higgins and colleagues developed CRA+CM (vouchers) treatments for patients with cocaine dependence. Higgins and Rogers (2009) explain the rationale for the CRA+CM approach: Delivering contrived consequences via CM can promote a patient's abstinence during the initial treatment period, which grants both the clinician and the patient more time to work on more naturalistic alternatives that contribute to long-term recovery and abstinence. Indeed, the CM reinforcement is immediate and tangible, whereas it may take relatively longer time and more efforts for a client to experience the fruits of CRA. Esposito-Smythers and colleagues (2014) decided to integrate CBT with CM treatment for HIV-infected young people because of the literature's suggestions that young people living with HIV (YPLH) are less likely to attend treatment, be engaged, and respond to treatment. The preliminary results of Esposito-Smythers et al.'s study indicate that the CBT/CM intervention holds promise for helping YPLH, including excellent treatment attendance and retention, as well as the participants' reductions in alcohol use and its related problems over a 3-month course. Petry's (2012) review shows that CM can also benefit special populations, including substance-abusing patients with comorbid severe and persistent mental disorders, homeless populations, those enrolled in employment training, and pregnant substance-abusing women.

Three key principles of contingency management are: (a) frequently observe a client's targeted behavior; (b) provide the client with immediate and tangible positive reinforcers when he or she achieves the behavior; and (c) withhold the reinforcers when the behavior is not attained (Petry, 2012). Because most urine toxicology testing can detect use or no use over the window of 2 to 3 days, many CM programs adopt thrice-weekly urinalysis testing (i.e., Monday, Wednesday, and Friday). Petry suggests that "The key to a successful CM intervention is to select reinforcers that *all* patients will desire and work to achieve" (p. 12). Reinforcers can include clinic privileges, such as allowing clients to have take-home methadone. This is highly desirable for clients as they usually are required to go to the clinic to get their methadone on a daily basis. This is also beneficial to the clinic as it will incur no extra costs to reinforce clients' abstinence. However, taking medication home as a reinforcer may not be that straightforward, as there are more required criteria specified in federal regulations, such as "acceptable length of time in comprehensive maintenance treatment," "stable home environment and social relationships," "assurance of safe storage of take-home medication," and so on (CSAT, 2005, p. 81). Reinforcers can also be vouchers, prizes, or cash; studies have shown that the magnitude of reinforcers is strongly related to the efficacy of a CM system. Petry states that CM based on pure social reinforcers—such as receiving clinicians' praises or becoming a group leader of one's peers—has not been tested and suggests that social reinforcers alone normally are much less effective than monetary reinforcers. Furthermore, to reinforce clients' *continuous* abstinence, CM emphasizes the concept of "escalating magnitude of reinforcement" (Higgins & Rogers, 2009; Petry, 2012). For example, a client may earn a $2.50 value of voucher for her initial cocaine-negative specimen. The voucher value of each of her subsequent following cocaine-negative specimen will increase by $1.25. On the other hand, if she submits a cocaine-positive specimen or fails to submit a specimen, the rewarding system will be reset and the voucher value will be returned to the initial $2.50 (Higgins & Rogers, 2009).

A detailed guide for implementation of Contingency Management treatment can be found in Petry's (2012) book, *Contingency Management for Substance Abuse Treatment: A Guide to Implementing This Evidence-based Practice.*

Although voluminous research findings have established the high efficacy of CM in treating addition and its related disorders, only about 50% of addictions therapists show interest in using CM (Srebnik et al.'s review, 2013). Multiple reasons may explain this: despite its high efficacy, CM is less familiar to many clinicians compared to other evidence-based treatment methods; clinicians receive little CM training; it costs extra money to implement; it does not address the underlying issues of addiction; it undermines intrinsic motivation; and clinicians may have philosophical values incompatible to CM implementation (Ducharme et al., 2010; Petry, 2011; Srebnik et al., 2013). Srebnik and colleagues' (2013) study found 77% of 75 clinicians who work with patients with co-occurring mental health and substance use disorders at a multisite community mental health centers would implement CM if funding existed. The most endorsed strengths of CM by these clinicians are that "they focus on what is good in client behavior and that they provide abstinence motivation irrespective of underlying issues of addiction"; the most endorsed concern was "the cost of implementing incentives (particularly if the cost was $150/month" per person (p. 433). Strategies to raise funds for CM may include soliciting donations from companies or community institutions or writing national or regional grants. CM can also be self-sustaining. For example, a treatment program can use the "name-in-the-hat prize" CM procedure to increase its group members' motivational incentives for group attendance. Because of the increase of group members' attendance (e.g., by 20% to 40% more), the program may receive sufficiently more reimbursement to pay for the involved CM costs (Petry, 2012).

References

Adamson, S.J., Sellman, J.D., & Frampton, C.M.A. (2009). Patient predictors of alcohol treatment outcome: A systematic review. *Journal of Substance Abuse Treatment, 36*, 75–86.

Barry, D., & Petry, N.M. (2009). Cognitive behavioral treatments for substance use disorders. In P.M. Miller (Ed.) *Evidence-based addiction treatment* (pp. 159–174). New York: Academic Press.

Beck, A.T., Rush, A.J., Shaw, B.F., & Emery, G. (1979). *Cognitive therapy of depression.* New York: Guilford.

Blanken, P., Hendriks, V.M., Huijsman, I.A., van Ree, J.M., & van den Brink, W. (2016). Efficacy of cocaine contingency management in heroin-assisted treatment: Results of a randomized controlled trial. *Drug and Alcohol Dependence, 164*, 55–63.

Blum, K., Oscar-Berman, M., Demetrovics, Z., Barh, D., & Gold, M.S. (2014). Genetic addiction risk score (GARS): Molecular neurogenetic evidence for predisposition to reward deficiency syndrome (RDS). *Molecular Neurobiology, 50*, 765–796.

Bowen, S., Chawla, N., & Marlatt, G.A. (2011). *Mindfulness-based relapse prevention for addictive behaviors: A clinician's guide.* New York: Guilford.

Bowen, S., Witkiewitz, K., Clifasefi, S.L., Grow, J., Chawla, N., Hsu, S.H., et al. (2014). Relative efficacy of mindfulness-based relapse prevention, standard relapse prevention, and treatment as usual for substance use disorders: A randomized clinical trial. *JAMA Psychiatry, 71*(5), 547–556.

Brown, L.A., Gaudiano, B.A., & Miller, I.W. (2011). Investigating the similarities and differences between practitioners of second and third wave cognitive-behavioral therapies. *Behavior Modification, 35*(2), 187–200.

Bryant, F.B., & Veroff, J. (2007). *Savoring: A new model of positive experience.* Mahwah, NJ: Lawrence Erlbaum Associates, Publishers.

Carroll, K.M., Ball, S.A., Martino, S., Nich, C., Babuscio, T.A., Nuro, K.F., Gordon, M.A., Portnoy, G.A., & Rounsaville, B.J. (2008). Computer-assisted delivery of cognitive-behavioral therapy for addiction: A randomized trial of CBT4CBT. *American Journal of Psychiatry, 165*(7), 881–888.

Carroll, K.M., & Onken, L.S. (2005). Behavioral therapies for drug abuse. *The American Journal of Psychiatry, 162*(8), 1452–1460.

Carroll, K.M., Rounsaville, B.J., Nich, C., Gordon, L.T., Wirtz, P.W., Gawin, F.H. (1994). One year follow-up of psychotherapy and pharmacotherapy for cocaine dependence: Delayed emergence of psychotherapy effects. *Archives of General Psychiatry, 51*, 989–997.

Center for Substance Abuse Treatment (2005). *Medication-assisted treatment for opioid addiction in opioid treatment programs.* Treatment Improvement Protocol (TIP) Series 43. HHS Publication No. (SMA) 08–4214. Rockville, MD: Substance Abuse and Mental Health Services Administration.

Center for Substance Abuse Treatment (2006). *Detoxification and substance abuse treatment.* Treatment Improvement Protocol (TIP) Series 45. HHS Publication No. (SMA) 06–4131. Rockville, MD: Substance Abuse and Mental Health Services Administration.

Chiesa, A., & Serretti, A. (2014). Are mindfulness-based interventions effective for substance use disorders? A systematic review of the evidence. *Substance Use & Misuse, 49*(5), 492–512.

Chiesa, A., Serretti, A., & Jakobsen, J.C. (2013). Mindfulness: Top-down or bottom-up emotion regulation strategy? *Clinical Psychology Review, 33*, 82–96.

Conklin, C.A., Salkeld, R.P., Perkins, K.A., & Robin, N. (2013). Do people serve as cues to smoke? *Nicotine & Tobacco Research, 15*(12), 2081–2087.

Creswell, J.D. (2017). Mindfulness interventions. *Annual Review of Psychology, 68*, 491–516.

De Souza, I.C., de Barros, V.V., Gomide, H.P., Miranda, T.C., Menezes, V.P., Kozasa, E.H., & Noto, A.R. (2015). Mindfulness-based interventions for the treatment of smoking: A systematic literature review. *Journal of Alternative and Complementary Medicine, 21*(3), 129–140.

Delfabbro, P., & King, D. (2015). On finding the C in CBT: The challenges of applying gambling-related cognitive approaches to video-gaming. *Journal of Gambling Studies, 31*, 315–329.

Ducharme, L.J., Knudsen, H.K., Abraham, A.J., & Roman, P.M. (2010). Counselor attitudes toward the use of motivational incentives in addiction treatment. *American Journal of Addictive, 19*(6), 496–503.

Dunn, R., Callahan, J.L., & Swift, J.K. (2013). Mindfulness as a transtheoretical clinical process. *Psychotherapy, 50*(3), 312–315.

Dutra, L., Stathopoulou, G., Basden, S.L., Leyro, T.M., Powers, M.B., & Otto, M.W. (2008). A meta-analytic review of psychosocial interventions for substance use disorders. *American Journal of Psychiatry, 165*, 179–187.

Esposito-Smythers, C., Brown, L.K., Wolff, J., Xu, J., Thornton, S., Tiday, J., & The Adolescent Medicine Trials Network for HIV/AIDS Interventions (ATN 069) (2014). Substance abuse treatment for HIV infected young people: An open pilot trial. *Journal of Substance Abuse Treatment, 46*, 244–250.

Farrell, J.M., Reiss, N., & Shaw, I.A. (2014). *The schema therapy clinician's guide*. New York: John Wiley & Sons, Ltd.

Ford, L.K., & Zarate, P. (2010). Closing the gaps: The impact of inpatient detoxification and continuity of care on client outcomes. *Journal of Psychoactive Drugs* (Suppl), 303–314.

Garcia-Fernandez, G., Secades-Villa, R., Garcia-Rodriguez, O., Sanchez-Hervas, E., Fernandez-Hermida, J.R., & Higgins, S.T. (2011). Adding voucher-based incentives to community reinforcement approach improves outcomes during treatment for cocaine dependence. *The American Journal on Addictions, 20*, 456–461.

Garland, E.L. (2013). *Mindfulness-oriented recovery enhancement: For addiction, stress, and pain*. Washington, DC: NASW Press.

Garland, E.L., Fredrickson, B., Kring, A.M., Johnson, D.P., Meyer, P.S., & Penn, D.L. (2010). Upward spirals of positive emotions counter downward spirals of negativity: Insights from the broaden-and-build theory and affective neuroscience on the treatment of emotion dysfunctions and deficits in psychopathology. *Clinical Psychology Review, 30*(7), 849–864.

Garland, E.L., Manusov, E.G., Froeliger, B., Kelly, A., Williams, J.M., & Howard, M.O. (2014). Mindfulness-oriented recovery enhancement for chronic pain and prescription opioid misuse: Results from an early stage randomized controlled trial. *Journal of Consulting and Clinical Psychology, 82*(3), 448–459.

Glasner-Edwards, S., Mooney, L.J., Ang, A., Garneau, H.C., Hartwell, E., Brecht, M., & Rawson, R.A. (2017). Mindfulness based relapse prevention for stimulant dependent adults: A pilot randomized clinical trial. *Mindfulness (NY), 8*(1), 126–135.

Gupta, S. (2015, December 22). Vietnam, heroin and the lesson of disrupting any addiction. *CNN Chief Medical Correspondent*. Updated 8:12 PM ET, Tue.

Harden, T., & Walton, L. (2012). Hoops and healing: The use of athletics for youth involved in recovery. *Alcoholism Treatment Quarterly, 30*, 353–359.

Harris, R. (2009). *ACT made simple: An easy-to-read primer on acceptance and commitment therapy*. Oakland, CA: New Harbinger Publications, Inc.

Hayes, S.C. (2004). Acceptance and commitment therapy, relational frame theory, and the third wave of behavioral and cognitive therapies. *Behavior Therapy, 35*, 639–665.

Hayes, S.C., Pitorello, J., & Levin, M.E. (2012). Acceptance and commitment therapy as a unified model of behavior change. *The Counseling Psychologist, 40*(7), 976–1002.

Henkel, D. (2011). Unemployment and substance use: A review of the literature (1990–2010). *Current Drug Abuse Reviews, 4*, 4–27.

Higgins, S.T., Budney, A.J., Bickel, W.K., Hughes, J.R., Foerg, F., & Badger, G. (1993). Achieving cocaine abstinence with a behavioral approach. *American Journal of Psychiatry, 150*(5), 763–769.

Higgins, S.T., & Rogers, R.E. (2009). Contingency management and the community reinforcement approach. In P. Miller (Ed.) *Evidence-based addiction treatment* (pp. 249–266). New York: Academic Press.

Hoffmann, H., Goodrich, D., Wilson, M., & Janssen, E. (2014). The role of classical conditioning in sexual compulsivity: A pilot study. *Sexual Addiction & Compulsivity, 21*(2), 75–91.

Hoppes, K. (2006). The application of mindfulness-based cognitive interventions in the treatment of co-occurring addictive and mood disorders. *CNS Spectrums, 11*(11), 829–851.

Kabat-Zinn, J. (1994). *Wherever you go, there you are: Mindfulness meditation in everyday life.* New York: Hyperion.

Kadden, R., Carroll, K., Donovan, D., Cooney, N., Monti, P., Abrams, D., Litt, M., & Hester, R. (2003). *Cognitive behavioral coping skills therapy manual: A clinical research guide for therapists treating individuals with alcohol abuse and dependence.* Project MATCH Monograph Series, Volume 3. Rockville, MD: National Institute on Alcohol Abuse and Alcoholism.

Kelly, T.M., Daley, D.C., & Douaihy, A.B. (2014). Contingency management for patients with dual disorders in intensive outpatient treatment for addiction. *Journal of Dual Diagnosis, 10*(3), 108–117.

Kuhn, S., & Gallinat, J. (2011). Common biology of craving across legal and illegal drugs—A quantitative meta-analysis of cue-reactivity brain response. *European Journal of Neuroscience, 33*, 1318–1326. doi: 10.1111/j.1460–9568.2010.07590.x.

Lee, M.T., Horgan, C.M., Garnick, D.W., Acevedo, A., Panas, L., Ritter, G.A., Dunigan, R., Babakhanlou-Chase, H., Bidorii, A., Campbell, K. . . . et al. (2014). A performance measure for continuity of car after detoxification: Relationship with outcomes. *Journal of Substance Abuse Treatment, 47*, 130–139.

Linehan, M.M. (2015). Rationale for dialectical behavior therapy skills training. In *DBT skills training manual*, Second Edition. New York: Guilford.

Ludwig, D.S., & Kabat-Zinn, J. (2008). Mindfulness in medicine. *JAMA, 300*(11), 1350–1352.

Magill, M., & Ray, L.A. (2009). Cognitive-behavioral treatment with adult alcohol and illicit drug users: A meta-analysis of randomized controlled trials. *Journal of Studies on Alcohol and Drugs*, 516–527.

Mark, T.L., Vandivort-Warren, R., & Montejano, L.B. (2006). Factors affecting detoxification readmission: Analysis of public sector data from three states. *Journal of Substance Abuse Treatment, 31*(4), 439–445.

Marlatt, G.A., & Gordon, J.R. (Eds). (1985). *Relapse prevention: Maintenance strategies in the treatment of addictive behaviors*. New York: Guilford Press.

McHugh, R.K., Hearon, B.A., & Otto, M.W. (2010). Cognitive-behavioral therapy for substance use disorders. *Psychiatric Clinic of North America, 33*(3), 511–525.

McKay, J.R. (2017). Making the hard work of recovery more attractive for those with substance use disorders. *Addiction, 112*, 751–757.

Meichenbaum, D. (1977). Cognitive restructuring techniques. In *Cognitive-behavior modification*. The Springer Behavior Therapy Series. Boston, MA: Springer.

Meyers, R.J., & Miller, W.R. (Eds.) (2001). *A community reinforcement approach to addiction treatment*. New York: Cambridge University Press.

Meyers, R.J., Roozen, H.G., & Smith, J.E. (2011). The community reinforcement approach: An update of the evidence. *Alcohol Research & Health*, 380–388.

Moos, R.H. (2007). Theory-based processes that promote the remission of substance use disorders. *Clinical Psychology Review, 27*(5), 537–551.

Moskowitz, J.T., Hult, J.R., Bussolari, C., & Acree, M. (2009). What works in coping with HIV? A meta-analysis with implications for coping with serious illness. *Psychological Bulletin, 135*(1), 121–141.

Moskowitz, J.T., Hult, J.R., Duncan, L.G., Cohn, M.A., Maurer, S., Bussolari, C., & Acree, M. (2012). A positive affect intervention for people experiencing health-related stress: Development and non-randomized pilot test. *Journal of Health Psychology, 17*(5), 676–692.

National Collaborating Centre for Mental Health (UK) (2008). *Drug misuse: Opioid detoxification*. National Institute for Health and Clinical Excellence: Guidance. Leicester: British Psychological Society.

National Institute on Drug Abuse (NIDA) (2018). *Principles of drug addiction treatment: A research-based guide* (Third edition). Retrieved on 04/17/2018 from d14rmgtrw-zf5a.cloudfront.net/sites/default/files/675-principles-of-drug-addiction-treatment-a-research-based-guide-third-edition.pdf.

Nowlan, J.S., Wuthrich, V.M., Rapee, R.M., Kinsella, J.M., & Barker, G. (2016). A comparison of single-session positive reappraisal, cognitive restructuring and supportive counselling for older adults with Type 2 diabetes. *Cognitive Therapy and Research, 40*, 216–229.

O'Farrell, T.J., Murphy, M., Alter, J., & Fals-Stewart, W. (2008). Brief family treatment intervention to promote aftercare among substance abusing patients in inpatient detoxification: Transferring a research intervention to clinical practice. *Addictive Behaviors, 33*, 464–471.

Petry, N.M. (2011). Contingency management: What it is and why psychiatrists should want to use. *The Psychiatrist, 35*(5), 161–163.

Petry, N.M. (2012). *Contingency management for substance abuse treatment: A guide to implementing this evidence-based practice*. New York: Routledge.

Raylu, N., & Oei, T.P.S. (2004). The gambling related cognitions scale (GRCS): Development, confirmatory factor validation and psychometric properties. *Addiction, 99*, 757–769.

Raylu, N., & Oei, T.P.S (2010). *A cognitive behavioural therapy programme for problem gambling*. East Sussex: Routledge.

Rizeanu, S. (2012). Proposal for a cognitive model to the treatment of pathological gambling. *Procedia-Social and Behavioral Sciences, 33*, 742–746.

Roll, J.M. (2007). Contingency management: An evidence-based component of methamphetamine use disorder treatments. *Addiction, 102*(Suppl. 1), 114–120.

Roozen, H.G. (2013). Managing relapses: Encouraging the engagement of alternative rewarding activities: Commentaries. *Addiction, 108*, 1197–1199.

Satel, S., & Lilienfeld, S.O. (2014). Addiction and the brain-disease fallacy. *Frontiers in Psychiatry, 4*(141).

Schacht, J.P., Anton, R.F., & Myrick, H. (2013). Functional neuroimaging studies of alcohol cue reactivity: A quantitative meta-analysis and systematic review. *Addictive Biology, 18*(1), 121–133. doi: 10.1111/j.1369-1600.2012.00464.x.

Scherbaum, N., & Specka, M. (2008). Factors influencing the course of opiate addiction. *International Journal of Methods in Psychiatric Research, 17*(S1), S39–S44.

Segal, Z.V., Williams, J.M.G., & Teasdale, J.D. (2002). *Mindfulness-based cognitive therapy for depression: A new apaproach to preventing relapse.* New York: Guilford Press.

Shorey, R.C., Elmquist, J., Anderson, S., & Stuart, G.L. (2015). The relation between early maladaptive schemas, depression, and generalized anxiety among adults seeking residential treatment for substance use disorders. *Journal of Psychoactive Drugs, 47*(3), 230–238.

Smith, J.E., & Meyers, R.J. (2001). The treatment. In R.J. Meyers & W.R. Miller (Eds.) *A community reinforcement approach to addiction treatment* (pp. 28–61). New York: Cambridge University Press.

Spear, S.E. (2014). Reducing readmissions to detoxification: An interorganizational network perspective. *Drug and Alcohol Dependence, 137*, 76–82.

Solinas, M., Chauvet, C., Thiriet, N., el Rawas, R., & Jaber, M. (2008). Reversal of cocaine addiction by environmental enrichment. *Proceedings of the National Academy of Sciences of the United States of America, 105*(44), 17145–17150.

Srebnik, D., Sugar, A., Coblentz, P., McDonell, M.G., Angelo, F., Lowe, J.M., Ries, R.K., & Roll, J. (2013). Acceptability of contingency management among clinicians and clients within a co-occurring mental health and substance use treatment program. *The American Journal on Addictions, 22*, 432–436.

Stevenson, J.G., Oliver, J.A., Hallyburton, M.B., Sweitzer, M.M., Conklin, C.A., & McClernon, F.J. (2017). Smoking environment cues reduce ability to resist smoking as measured by a delay to smoking task. *Addictive Behaviors, 67*, 49–52.

Sun, A.P. (2006, May). The initial unequal footing to begin with: A challenge to the "free will" theory. Paper presented at the 14th Annual meeting of the Society for Prevention Research. San Antonio, Texas.

Timko, C., Schultz, N.R., Britt, J., & Cucciare, M.A. (2016). Transitioning from detoxification to substance use disorder treatment: Facilitators and barriers. *Journal of Substance Abuse Treatment, 70*, 64–72.

Treadway, M.T., & Lazar, S.W. (2009). The neurobiology of mindfulness. In F. Didonna (Ed.) *Clinical handbook of mindfulness* (pp. 45–58). New York: Springer.

Troy, A.S., Wilhelm, F.H., Shallcross, A.J., & Mauss, I.B. (2010). Seeing the silver lining: Cognitive reappraisal ability moderates the relationship between stress and depressive symptoms. *Emotion, 10*(6), 783–795.

Tuten, L.M., Jones, H.E., Schaeffer, C.M., & Stitzer, M.L. (2012). Essential goals for competing with drug use. In *Reinforcement-based treatment for substance use disorders: A comprehensive behavioral approach* (pp. 69–92). Washington, DC: American Psychological Association.

Valyear, M.D., Villaruel, F.R., & Chaudhri, N. (2017). Alcohol-seeking and relapse: A focus on incentive salience and contextual conditioning. *Behavioural Processes, 141*, 26–32.

Vederhus, J.K., Timko, C., Kristensen, O., Hjemdahl, B., & Clausen, T. (2014). Motivational intervention to enhance post-detoxification 12-Step group affiliation: A randomized controlled trial. *Addiction, 109*(5), 766–773.

Volkow, N.D., Fowler, J.S., & Wang, G.J. (2003). The addicted human brain: Insights from imaging studies. *The Journal of Clinical Investigation, 111*(10), 1444–1451.

Walton, M.T., & Hall, M.T. (2016). The effects of employment interventions on addiction treatment outcomes: A review of the literature. *Journal of Social Work Practice in the Addictions, 16*(4), 358–384.

Winkler, M.H., Weyers, P., Mucha, R.F., Stippekohl, B., Stark, R., & Pauli, P. (2011). Conditioned cues for smoking elicit preparatory responses in healthy smokers. *Psychopharmacology, 213*, 781–789. doi: 10.1007/s00213-010-2033-2.

Witkiewitz, K., Warner, K., Sully, B., Barricks, A., Stauffer, C., Thompson, B.L., & Luoma, J.B. (2014). Randomized trial comparing mindfulness-based relapse prevention with relapse prevention for women offenders at a residential addiction treatment center. *Substance Use & Misuse, 49*(5), 536–546.

Young, J.E., Klosko, J.S., & Weishaar, M.E. (2003). *Schema therapy: A practitioner's guide.* New York: Guilford.

APPENDIX A1

THE CRAFFT QUESTIONNAIRE—SELF ADMINISTERED

The CRAFFT Questionnaire (version 2.1)
To be completed by patient

Please answer all questions **honestly**; your answers will be kept **confidential**.

During the PAST 12 MONTHS, on how many days did you:

1. Drink more than a few sips of beer, wine, or any drink containing **alcohol**? Put "0" if none.
   # of days

2. Use any **marijuana** (weed, oil, or hash by smoking, vaping, or in food) or "**synthetic marijuana**" (like "K2," "Spice")? Put "0" if none.
   # of days

3. Use **anything else to get high** (like other illegal drugs, prescription or over-the-counter medications, and things that you sniff, huff, or vape)? Put "0" if none.
   # of days

READ THESE INSTRUCTIONS BEFORE CONTINUING:
- If you put "0" in ALL of the boxes above, ANSWER QUESTION 4, THEN STOP.
- If you put "1" or higher in ANY of the boxes above, ANSWER QUESTIONS 4-9.

	No	Yes
4. Have you ever ridden in a **CAR** driven by someone (including yourself) who was "high" or had been using alcohol or drugs?	☐	☐
5. Do you ever use alcohol or drugs to **RELAX**, feel better about yourself, or fit in?	☐	☐
6. Do you ever use alcohol or drugs while you are by yourself, or **ALONE**?	☐	☐
7. Do you ever **FORGET** things you did while using alcohol or drugs?	☐	☐
8. Do your **FAMILY** or **FRIENDS** ever tell you that you should cut down on your drinking or drug use?	☐	☐
9. Have you ever gotten into **TROUBLE** while you were using alcohol or drugs?	☐	☐

NOTICE TO CLINIC STAFF AND MEDICAL RECORDS:
The information on this page is protected by special federal confidentiality rules (42 CFR Part 2), which prohibit disclosure of this information unless authorized by specific written consent. A general authorization for release of medical information is NOT sufficient.

© John R. Knight, MD, Boston Children's Hospital, 2016.
Reproduced with permission from the Center for Adolescent Substance Abuse Research (CeASAR), Boston Children's Hospital.
For more information and versions in other languages, see **www.ceasar.org**

APPENDIX A2

THE CRAFFT QUESTIONNAIRE—CLINICIAN INTERVIEW

The CRAFFT Interview (version 2.1)
To be orally administered by the clinician

Begin: "*I'm going to ask you a few questions that I ask all my patients. Please be honest. I will keep your answers confidential.*"

Part A
During the PAST 12 MONTHS, on how many days did you:

1. Drink more than a few sips of beer, wine, or any drink containing **alcohol**? Say "0" if none.

   # of days

2. Use any **marijuana** (weed, oil, or hash by smoking, vaping, or in food) or "**synthetic marijuana**" (like "K2," "Spice")? Put "0" if none.

   # of days

3. Use **anything else to get high** (like other illegal drugs, prescription or over-the-counter medications, and things that you sniff, huff, or vape)? Say "0" if none.

   # of days

Did the patient answer "0" for all questions in Part A?

Yes ☐   No ☐

↓   ↓

Ask CAR question only, then stop   **Ask all six CRAFFT* questions below**

Part B

		No	Yes
C	Have you ever ridden in a **CAR** driven by someone (including yourself) who was "high" or had been using alcohol or drugs?	☐	☐
R	Do you ever use alcohol or drugs to **RELAX**, feel better about yourself, or fit in?	☐	☐
A	Do you ever use alcohol or drugs while you are by yourself, or **ALONE**?	☐	☐
F	Do you ever **FORGET** things you did while using alcohol or drugs?	☐	☐
F	Do your **FAMILY** or **FRIENDS** ever tell you that you should cut down on your drinking or drug use?	☐	☐
T	Have you ever gotten into **TROUBLE** while you were using alcohol or drugs?	☐	☐

*Two or more YES answers suggest a serious problem and need for further assessment. See back for further instructions ➡

NOTICE TO CLINIC STAFF AND MEDICAL RECORDS:
The information on this page is protected by special federal confidentiality rules (42 CFR Part 2), which prohibit disclosure of this information unless authorized by specific written consent. A general authorization for release of medical information is NOT sufficient.

THE CRAFFT QUESTIONNAIRE

1. **Show your patient his/her score on this graph and discuss level of risk for a substance use disorder.**

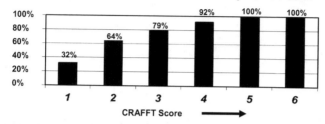

Percent with a DSM-5 Substance Use Disorder by CRAFFT score*

CRAFFT Score	1	2	3	4	5	6
%	32%	64%	79%	92%	100%	100%

*Data source: Mitchell SG, Kelly SM, Gryczynski J, Myers CP, O'Grady KE, Kirk AS, & Schwartz RP. (2014). The CRAFFT cut-points and DSM-5 criteria for alcohol and other drugs: a reevaluation and reexamination. Substance Abuse, 35(4), 376–80.

2. **Use these talking points for brief counseling.**

   1. **REVIEW** screening results
      For each "yes" response: *"Can you tell me more about that?"*

   2. **RECOMMEND** not to use
      "As your doctor (nurse/health care provider), my recommendation is not to use any alcohol, marijuana or other drug because they can: 1) Harm your developing brain; 2) Interfere with learning and memory, and 3) Put you in embarrassing or dangerous situations."

   3. **RIDING/DRIVING** risk counseling
      "Motor vehicle crashes are the leading cause of death for young people. I give all my patients the Contract for Life. Please take it home and discuss it with your parents/guardians to create a plan for safe rides home."

   4. **RESPONSE** elicit self-motivational statements
      Non-users: *"If someone asked you why you don't drink or use drugs, what would you say?"* Users: *"What would be some of the benefits of not using?"*

   5. **REINFORCE** self-efficacy
      "I believe you have what it takes to keep alcohol and drugs from getting in the way of achieving your goals."

3. **Give patient Contract for Life.** Available at www.crafft.org/contract

---

© John R. Knight, MD, Boston Children's Hospital, 2016.
Reproduced with permission from the Center for Adolescent Substance Abuse Research (CeASAR),
Boston Children's Hospital.

(617) 355-5433 www.ceasar.org

For more information and versions in other languages, see www.ceasar.org.

APPENDIX B

THE ALCOHOL USE DISORDERS IDENTIFICATION TEST (AUDIT)—(INTERVIEW VERSION)

Read questions as written. Record answers carefully. Begin the AUDIT by saying "Now I am going to ask you some questions about your use of alcoholic beverages during this past year." Explain what is meant by "alcoholic beverages" by using local examples of beer, wine, vodka, etc. Code answers in terms of "standard drinks." Place the correct answer number in the box at the right.

1. How often do you have a drink containing alcohol? (0) Never [Skip to Qs 9–10] (1) Monthly or less (2) 2 to 4 times a month (3) 2 to 3 times a week (4) 4 or more times a week	3. How often do you have six or more drinks on one occasion? (0) Never (1) Less than monthly (2) Monthly (3) Weekly (4) Daily or almost daily *Skip to Questions 9 and 10 if Total Score for Questions 2 and 3 = 0*
2. How many drinks containing alcohol do you have on a typical day when you are drinking? (0) 1 or 2 (1) 3 or 4 (2) 5 or 6 (3) 7, 8, or 9 (4) 10 or more	4. How often during the last year have you found that you were not able to stop drinking once you had started? (0) Never (1) Less than monthly (2) Monthly (3) Weekly (4) Daily or almost daily

5. How often during the last year have you failed to do what was normally expected from you because of drinking? (0) Never (1) Less than monthly (2) Monthly (3) Weekly (4) Daily or almost daily ☐	8. How often during the last year have you been unable to remember what happened the night before because you had been drinking? (0) Never (1) Less than monthly (2) Monthly (3) Weekly (4) Daily or almost daily ☐
6. How often during the last year have you needed a first drink in the morning to get yourself going after a heavy drinking session? (0) Never (1) Less than monthly (2) Monthly (3) Weekly (4) Daily or almost daily ☐	9. Have you or someone else been injured as a result of your drinking? (0) No (2) Yes, but not in the last year (4) Yes, during the last year ☐
7. How often during the last year have you had a feeling of guilt or remorse after drinking? (0) Never (1) Less than monthly (2) Monthly (3) Weekly (4) Daily or almost daily ☐	10. Has a relative or friend or a doctor or another health worker been concerned about your drinking or suggested you cut down? (0) No (2) Yes, but not in the last year (4) Yes, during the last year ☐

Record total of specific items here:_____

If total is greater than recommended cut-off, consult User's Manual.

Scoring: A score $\geq$ 8: Hazardous or harmful alcohol use

Note: AUDIT questions should be answered using standard drinks (i.e., one 12 oz beer [about 5% alcohol], one 5 oz table wine [about 12% alcohol], or 1.5 oz hard liquor [about 40% alcohol])

Babor, T.F., Higgins-Biddle, J.C., Saunders, J.B., & Monteiro, M.G. (2001). *AUDIT: The Alcohol Use Disorders Identification Test, Guidelines for use in primary care.* World Health Organization

Reproduced, with the permission of the publisher, from *The Alcohol Use Disorders Identification Test: guidelines for use in primary care, AUDIT, second edition.* Geneva, World Health Organization, 2000 (The AUDIT test: interview version Page 17 http://whqlibdoc.who.int/hq/2001/WHO_MSD_MSB_01.6a.pdf, accessed 21 February, 2018).

APPENDIX C

THE CANNABIS USE DISORDERS IDENTIFICATION TEST—REVISED (CUDIT-R) (SELF ADMINISTRATION)

Have you used any cannabis over the past six months? YES/NO

If **YES**, please answer the following questions about your cannabis use. Circle the response that is most correct for you in relation to your cannabis use over the past six months

1. How often do you use cannabis? (0) Never (1) Monthly or less (2) 2 – 4 times a month (3) 2-3 times a week (4) 4 or more times a week	3. How often during the past 6 months did you find that you were not able to stop using cannabis once you had started? (0) Never (1) Less than monthly (2) Monthly (3) Weekly (4) Daily or almost daily
2. How many hours were you "stoned" on a typical day when you had been using cannabis? (0) Less than 1 (1) 1 or 2 (2) 3 or 4 (3) 5 or 6 (4) 7 or more	4. How often during the past 6 months did you fail to do what was normally expected from you because of using cannabis? (0) Never (1) Less than monthly (2) Monthly (3) Weekly (4) Daily or almost daily

5. How often in the past 6 months have you devoted a great deal of your time to getting, using, or recovering from cannabis? (0) Never (1) Less than monthly (2) Monthly (3) Weekly (4) Daily or almost daily	7. How often do you use cannabis in situations that could be physically hazardous, such as driving, operating machinery, or caring for children: (0) Never (1) Less than monthly (2) Monthly (3) Weekly (4) Daily or almost daily
6. How often in the past 6 months have you had a problem with your memory or concentration after using cannabis? (0) Never (1) Less than monthly (2) Monthly (3) Weekly (4) Daily or almost daily	8. Have you ever thought about cutting down, or stopping, your use of cannabis? (0) Never (2) Yes, but not in the past 6 months (4) Yes, during the past 6 months

Scores of 8 points or more: hazardous cannabis use

Scores of 12 points or more: a possible cannabis use disorder (further intervention may be required).

Source: Adamson, S.J., Kay-Lambkin, F.J., Baker, A.L., Lewin, T.J., Thornton, L., Kelly, B.J., & Sellman, J.D. (2010). An improved brief measure of cannabis misuse: The Cannabis Use Disorders Identification Test—Revised (CUDIT-R). *Drug and Alcohol Dependence, 110*, 137–143.

APPENDIX D

CLINICAL INSTITUTE WITHDRAWAL ASSESSMENT FOR ALCOHOL, REVISED (CIWA-AR)

Patient:_____ Date: _____

Time: _____:_____

     (24 hour clock, midnight=00:00)

Pulse or heart rate, taken for one minute:_____

Blood pressure:_____/_____

NAUSEA AND VOMITING—Ask "Do you feel sick to your stomach? Have you vomited?" Observation.	TACTILE DISTURBANCES— Ask "Have you any itching, pins and needles sensations, any burning, any numbness, or do you feel bugs crawling on or under your skin?" Observation.
0 no nausea and no vomiting 1 mild nausea with no vomiting 2 3 4 intermittent nausea with dry heaves 5 6 7 constant nausea, frequent dry heaves and vomiting	0 none 1 very mild itching, pins and needles, burning or numbness 2 mild itching, pins and needles, burning or numbness 3 moderate itching, pins and needles, burning or numbness 4 moderately severe hallucinations 5 severe hallucinations 6 extremely severe hallucinations 7 continuous hallucinations

TREMOR—Arms extended and fingers spread apart. Observation. 0 no tremor 1 not visible, but can be felt fingertip to fingertip 2 3 4 moderate, with patient's arms extended 5 6 7 severe, even with arms not extended	AUDITORY DISTURBANCES—Ask "Are you more aware of sounds around you? Are they harsh? Do they frighten you? Are you hearing anything that is disturbing to you? Are you hearing things you know are not there?" Observation. 0 not present 1 very mild harshness or ability to frighten 2 mild harshness or ability to frighten 3 moderate harshness or ability to frighten 4 moderately severe hallucinations 5 severe hallucinations 6 extremely severe hallucinations 7 continuous hallucinations
PAROXYSMAL SWEATS—Observation. 0 no sweat visible 1 barely perceptible sweating, palms moist 2 3 4 beads of sweat obvious on forehead 5 6 7 drenching sweats	VISUAL DISTURBANCES—Ask "Does the light appear to be too bright? Is its color different? Does it hurt your eyes? Are you seeing anything that is disturbing to you? Are you seeing things you know are not there?" Observation. 0 not present 1 very mild sensitivity 2 mild sensitivity 3 moderate sensitivity 4 moderately severe hallucinations 5 severe hallucinations 6 extremely severe hallucinations 7 continuous hallucinations
ANXIETY—Ask "Do you feel nervous?" Observation. 0 no anxiety, at ease 1 mild anxious 2 3 4 moderately anxious, or guarded, so anxiety is inferred 5 6 7 equivalent to acute panic states as seen in severe delirium or acute schizophrenic reactions	HEADACHE, FULLNESS IN HEAD—Ask "Does your head feel different? Does it feel like there is a band around your head?" Do not rate for dizziness or lightheadedness. Otherwise, rate severity. 0 not present 1 very mild 2 mild 3 moderate 4 moderately severe 5 severe 6 very severe 7 extremely severe

AGITATION—Observation.	ORIENTATION AND CLOUDING OF SENSORIUM— Ask "What day is this? Where are you? Who am I?" Observation.
0 normal activity 1 somewhat more than normal activity 2 3 4 moderately fidgety and restless 5 6 7 paces back and forth during most of the interview, or constantly thrashes about	0 oriented and can do serial additions 1 cannot do serial additions or is uncertain about date 2 disoriented for date by no more than 2 calendar days 3 disoriented for date by more than 2 calendar days 4 disoriented for place and/or person

Total CIWA-Ar Score _____

Rater's Initials _____

Maximum Possible Score 67

"Patients scoring less than 10 do not usually need additional medication for withdrawal" (Mee-Lee et al., 2013, p. 395).

Source: Sullivan, J.T., Sykora, K., Schneiderman, J., Naranjo, C.A., & Sellers, E.M. (1989) Assessment of alcohol withdrawal: The Revised Clinical Institute Withdrawal Assessment for Alcohol Scale (CIWA-Ar). *British Journal of the Addictions, 84*(11), 1353–1357.

CIWA-Ar is not copyrighted.

INDEX

Page numbers in *italic* indicate a figure and page numbers in **bold** indicate a table on the corresponding page.

A-B-C framework 291–292, *293*, 297
abstinence: acamprosate and 257; in behavioral couples therapy (BCT) 227; disulfiram (Antabuse) and 260; opioid addiction and 155; quality of life and 104–106; reinforcement/reward 323; rewards of 311–312; sobriety sampling and 322; substance abuse and 104
Abulseoud, O.A. 163
acamprosate: alcohol use disorder (AUD) and 256–257; guidelines for 257; physician prescribing of 255; withdrawal syndrome reduction and 257, 260
acceptance and commitment therapy (ACT): empowerment and 239; goals and aspirations in 239; hope and 239; processes of 239–240; recovery and 48; relapse prevention and 305, 320; sense of purpose and 136
Acevedo, A. 290
Achterberg, T. van 86–87
ACQS model: co-occurring disorders (COD) and 7; defining 3; fundamentals of addiction and 3; quality of life and 10; social factors and 12, 144; treatment strategies for **15–20**
Acree, M. 200
Adan, A. 72
addiction: adverse childhood experiences (ACE) and 126–127; attentional bias and 297; barriers to rewards 311–312; behavioral treatments 47–48; as a brain disease 4, 6, 34, 45; as a chronic disease xi, xii, 6–7, 10, 31–34, 45–47, 103, 170–171, 289; clinician alliances and 218–220; compulsivity and 34–35, 42–45, 306; cultural factors and 13; defining 27, 32, 171; as a disorder of choice 32–33, 47; etiology of 35; everyday life and 48; family support for 220–227; fear of withdrawal symptoms 210; fundamentals of 3; genetic factors of 29–30; habilitation for 312; habituation and 35, 42–43; historical explanations of 1; impulsivity and 6, 35, 42, 44; impulsivity and 306; internal resources and 210–211; material poverty and 11–12, 106–111; mindfulness and 306; moral model of 4–5; neurobiological processes of 30–32; pharmacological treatments 47; phenomenological/clinical features of 27–29; as a primary disease 6–7; relapsing nature of 6; reward deficiency syndrome 312; self-help groups for 220; self-medication theory 4–5; self-recovery from 3; social factors and 12–14, 144–146; social networks and 217–218; spectrum of 31–35; spiritual poverty and 12, 106; stigma of 47; strategies to combat 38–39; trauma and 121

347

addiction heritability 29

addiction liability 29

Addictions and Trauma Recovery Integrated Model (ATRIUM) 76

addiction treatment: case management and 10; characteristics of individuals in 3; classical conditioning and 295–297; co-occurring disorders (COD) and 8–10; employment and 315–316; established/evidence-based 317–322; feminist-based model 124; functional analysis and 292–294; gender-informed 161–162; hope and 245–246; interpersonal relationships and 113–117, 119–120; intimate partner violence (IPV) and 123; involuntary 2; marital distress and 114; mindful savoring in 316–317; motivational interviewing approach 313; nonjudgmental relationships 118; OARS approach 187; patient aftercare and 287, 290–291; pharmacotherapy for 246, 254–256, 313; philosophies of 153, 155–156, 194, 313; prevention and 3; psychiatric disorders and 8; psychosocial integration and 10; quality of life and 11, 102–104, 106, 311–313; recreational activities and 314–315; social factors and 145, 188–189; social networks and 220–227; spirituality and 47, 236; therapeutic alliances in 219–220, 281; voluntary 2; well-being and 111–112; *see also* cognitive behavioral therapy (CBT); medication-assisted treatment (MAT); Twelve Step programs

Adler, Alfred 298

Adolescent Brain Cognitive Development (ABCD) Study 181–182

adolescent community reinforcement approach (A-CRA) 187–188, 322

Adolescent Community Reinforcement Approach for Adolescent Cannabis Users, The (Godley) 188

adolescent marijuana use: addiction and 177–178, 181; adverse consequences of 176–181, 184; cannabis dependence syndromes 178; cognitive impairment and 180–182; as a gateway drug 184; health impacts and 183–184; increase in use 175–176; legalization impacts 174–175; mental health issues and 182; motor-vehicle accidents and 179–180; parent use and 186; prevention strategies 186; reduced school performance and 180–182; schizophrenia development and 61, 182; screening for 185; treatment strategies for 187–188; withdrawal syndromes 178

adolescents: attention deficit/hyperactivity disorder (ADHD) and 68, 80–81, 85; attention deficit/hyperactivity disorder-SUD comorbidity 80, 88; CRAFFT (Appendix A1 and Appendix A2); family structure and 118; internet gaming disorder and 117–118; interpersonal relationships and 117; parent-child relationship and 117–118; patience and 88; self-medication and 81

adoption studies 30

adverse childhood experiences (ACE): addiction and 126–127; categories of 126–127; chronic disease and 126, 130; cognitive behavioral therapy (CBT) and 131; emotional processing and 129; executive function (EF) and 129; expressive writing and 131; health-risk behaviors/psychopathology and 126–129, 131; intergenerational 127, 129–130; learning and 126, 128; mindfulness-based intervention (MBI) 131; prevention strategies 128–130; school and community in 130; screening for 128–129; stress and 110; tertiary care for 130–131; unemployment and 126

Affect Regulation Training (Berking and Whitley) 233

affirmation xii, 216, 219, 237

African Americans: drug arrests of 190; drug court treatment and 145, 190–191; recreational marijuana use by 160, 175–176

Agar, M.H. 270

Aghakhani, N. 222

Agrawal, A. 181

AIDS epidemic *see* HIV-AIDS patients

INDEX

Al-Anon 323
Albert, M.A. 109
alcohol and other drugs (AOD): addictive power of 5; craving for 5–6; self-medication theory 4–5; treatment strategies for 63; *see also* alcohol use disorder (AUD); substance use disorder (SUD)
Alcoholics Anonymous (AA): definition of addiction in 33; God and 213–214, 229; higher power approach and 212–214; influences on 213; long-term recovery and 45; non-using relationships 118–119; on pathological narcissism 213; self-help groups in 228; Twelve Steps of 213–214
alcohol use disorder (AUD): acamprosate and 257–258, 260; adopted people and 30; antisocial personality disorder (ASPD) and 56; defining 33; diagnostic criteria for 33, 46; disulfiram (Antabuse) and 256, 260–262; expressed emotion and 114; gambling disorder and 30; gender convergence in 159; gender differences in 163; genetic factors of 29–30; health insurance and poverty status 107–108, **108**; major depressive disorder and 69; material poverty and 11; naltrexone and 258–260; pathological narcissism and 213; pharmacological treatments and 79, 247, 252–253, 255–262; relapse prevention and 256–260, 262; schizophrenia comorbidity and 60, 67; space/geographical factor 158; withdrawal management 250–252; withdrawal syndromes 247–249, 252–253, 259
Alcohol Use Disorders Identification Test (AUDIT) 339–341
Alexander, B.K. 217
Alexander, Bruce 4, 12, 102, 134
Alfonso, J.P. 41
Almqvist, C. 82
Alzheimer's disease 43
American Society of Addiction Medicine (ASAM) 27, 53, 171
Ammerman, S.D. 176, 186
An, R. 160

Anda, R.F. 127–128
Anderson, B.J. 127
Anderson, S. 70, 303
Andrade, R. 127
Ang, A. 39
Angelo, F. 325
Angermeyer, M.C. 159
Antabuse *see* disulfiram (Antabuse)
Anthenelli, R.M. 163
antidepressants 72–73, 79
antipsychotic medications 61, 65–67, 73
antisocial personality disorder (ASPD): drug use disorder comorbidity and 54; genetic factors of 29; impulsivity and 92; rates of 89; substance abuse comorbidity and 56, 88–92
Antunez, J.M. 72
Arkes, J. 190
Arroyo, K. 124
ASAM Patient Placement Criteria 53
ASAM Treatment Criteria for Addictive, Substance-Related, and Co- Occurring Conditions 53, 250–252
ASPD *see* antisocial personality disorder (ASPD)
atomoxetine 41, 83
attentional bias 297
attentional deployment 234
attention deficit/hyperactivity disorder (ADHD): adolescents and 68, 80–81, 85; behavioral addiction and 84; co-occurring disorders (COD) and 57; impulsivity and 81; substance use disorder comorbidity and 68; treatment strategies for 44, 57
attention deficit/hyperactivity disorder-SUD comorbidity: adolescents and 80, 88; cognitive behavioral therapy (CBT) 85–86; common factor theory 81; coping strategies 86–87; executive function (EF) impairment 85–86; integrated cognitive behavioral therapy (ICBT) and 85–86; patience and 88; pharmacological treatments 83–85; psychoeducation and 84; rates of 80–81; self-medication theory and 81; social skills training 87; treatment strategies for 83–88

autism spectrum disorder (ASD): behavioral addiction and 82–83; self-medication theory and 82–83

autism spectrum-SUD comorbidity: cognitive behavioral therapy (CBT) 85–86; common factor theory 83; coping strategies 86–87; electronics and 88; executive function (EF) impairment 85–86; genetic factors of 82; internet gaming disorder and 88; pharmacological treatments 83–85; self-medication theory and 82–83; social skills training 87; treatment strategies for 83–88

automatic pilot 306–307

autonomy 217, 237, 302

avoidance coping strategy 117

Ayanian, J.Z. 109

Babakhanlou-Chase, H. 290

Babuscio, T.A. 319

Bachrach, K. 155

Back, S.E. 75–76

Bae, H. 175

Bailey, G.L. 127, 155

Baker, A.L. 75

Baler, R. 36, 38, 40

Baler, R.D. 181, 183

Ball, S.A. 319

Barrett, E.L. 75

Barry, C.L. 270

Barry, K.L. 185

Beaty, B. 115

Beaver, K.M. 30

Beck, A.T. 298

Becker, B.D. 128

Beckwith, M. 119

behavioral addiction: attention deficit/hyperactivity disorder and 84; autism spectrum disorder and 82–83; continuum of 170–171; Cooper's Triple-A Engine 167; digital dope 166; disagreement over 2, 166, 168–171; emergence of 165; food addiction 167; Gamblers Anonymous 33, 172; gambling disorder 169; habitual use of pornography 173; internet addiction 2, 172; internet gaming disorder 166, 171; internet porn 167; Love and Sex Addiction Anonymous 172; over-prescribing and 169; pharmacotherapy for 166, 172–173, 255; process addiction 166; research in 171–172; self-help groups 172; society's views on 168–169; technological change and 165–168; Technology Addiction Anonymous 172; treatment strategies for 172

behavioral choice theory 311

behavioral couples therapy (BCT) 225–227

Behavioral Treatment for Substance Abuse in Serious and Persistent Mental Illness (BTSAS) 63

behavioral treatments: acceptance and commitment therapy 48; addiction and 47–48; antisocial personality disorder-SUD patients and 90; cognitive behavioral therapy 42, 48; community reinforcement approach (CRA) 48; contingency management (CM) 48; dialectical behavioral therapy 48; mindfulness-based intervention (MBI) 42, 48, 304–305; mindfulness-oriented recovery enhancement (MORE) 42; motivational interviewing approach 42, 48; pharmacological treatments and 246; prefrontal cortex deficits and 41–42; response-cost procedure 42; self-help groups 48; spirituality and 48; withdrawal management and 287, 289–325

Behavior Rating Inventory of Executive Functions—Adult Version (BRIEF-A) 41

Bellack, A.S. 63

Bennett, M. 63

Bennett, M.E. 63, 67

benzodiazepines: alcohol detox and 252, 255; bipolar disorder and 73; buprenorphine and 267, 273; cautions against 149, 151

Berglund, M. 263, 278

Berglund, P. 159

Bergman, B.G. 228

Bergman, H. 115

Berking, Matthias 233

INDEX

Best, D. 119
Betters, R. 124
Bevans, K.B. 128
Bhatt, S. 155
Bidorii, A. 290
Biernacka, J.M. 163
Billieux, J. 169
Binswanger, I.A. 115
biosocial theory 232
bipolar disorder: alcohol use disorder
(AUD) and 55; pharmacotherapy for
73; substance abuse and 57–58, 68;
suicide and 10
Bisaga, A. 280
Blanco, C. 89
Blom, T.J. 163
Blow, F.C. 185
Booth, B.M. 185
borderline personality disorder (BPD):
impulsivity and 92; rates of 89; self-
destructive behavior and 92; sense of
purpose in life and 135; substance abuse
comorbidity and 88–89; support groups
and 93; treatment strategies for 92–93;
Twelve Step programs and 93; *see also*
mood disorders
Bornovalova, M.A. 90–91
Borowsky, I.W. 130
Boscarino, J.A. 7, 54
bottom-up regulation 307
Bowen, S. 70
Bowen, S. 319–320
Boyd, S.M. 114
Boyne, H. 221
Bradshaw, K.R. 63, 67
Brady, K.T. 72, 75–76
brain disease model of addiction (BDMA):
acceptance of 4; chronic exposure
in 36–38; compulsivity and 34–36;
controversy in 31; defining 30–31;
impulsivity and 35–36; neuroadaptation
and 36–37; self-medication theory and
35–36; spectrum of addiction 31–35;
transition to levels of addition in 34
"Brain Disease Model of Addiction"
(Volkow and Koob) 1
brain imaging 5–6; *see also* functional
magnetic resonance imaging (fMRI)

Brandon-Friedman, R.A. 136
Breen, C. 266
Brief Intervention (BI) 185–186
Briggs, R.D. 129
Brink, W. van den 43, 86–87
Britt, J 290
Bromet, E.J. 159
Brooks, E. 176
Brooks-Russell, A. 176
Brown, B.S. 270
Brown, L.K. 324
Brown, Q.L. 157
Brown, S. 116
Brown, Stephanie 231
Brown, V.B. 120
Browne, K.C. 77
Brugha, T.S. 159
Brunner, M.D. 163
Bryant, F.B. 316–317
Buchheimer, N. 103
Budman, S.H. 116
Bull, S. 176
buprenorphine: access/barriers to 276–277;
effectiveness of 263, 265, 272–273;
guidelines for 273–276; implanted
262, 273, 275–276; methadone and
274; office-based 275, 277; opioid
addiction and 153, 253, 262–263, 265,
271–277; physician prescribing of
277; psychosocial interventions and
275–276; relapse prevention and 262;
side effects of 272–273
buprenorphine-naloxone 155, 267, 273
bupropion 72–73, 83
Burge, S.K. 117
Burke, N.J. 128
Busschbach, J. van 86–87
Bussolari, C. 200
Butler, S.F. 116
Butwicka, A. 82
Bux, D.A. 79–80

Cadoret, R.J. 29
Calcaterra, S. 115
Callahan, J.L. 309
Campbell, K. 290
Canan, F. 80
cannabidiol (CBD) 178

cannabis use disorder (CUD): development of 177–178; pharmacotherapy for 186–187; treatment strategies for 184, 186–188; *see also* marijuana use

Cannon, M. 56, 183

Capstick, C. 76

Caracuel, A. 40–41

Carliner, H. 157

Carpenter, R.W. 92

Carrington, P.J. 108, 119

Carrion, V.G. 128

Carroll, K. 79

Carroll, K.M. 319

Carter, A. 1, 254

Caspi, A. 56, 183

CAT (commitment, activation, and taking steps) 238

Catalano, L.T. 63, 67

Centers for Disease Control and Prevention (CDC) 58, 149

Cerdá, M. 175–176

Chamberlain, S.R. 44

change talk 238

Chapman, C. 157

Chapman, D.P. 127

Chauhan, M. 163

Chawla, N. 319–320

Chen, C.S. 46

Chermack, S.T. 185

Chiesa, A. 39, 307–308

child welfare system (CWS) 194

China: alcohol use disorder (AUD) in 158; economic reforms in 147; gender differences in addiction 163; heroin use in 58, 147–148; internet-related addiction in 166; methadone use in 191–192, 264, 270

Chinitz, S. 129

Choi, K.W. 130

Chou, S.P. 68

chronic disease: addiction as i, xii, 6–7, 10, 31–34, 45–47, 103, 170–171, 289; adverse childhood experiences (ACE) and 126, 130; opioid addiction as 152

chronic pain: alternative treatments for 60; comorbid addiction strategies and 59–60; opioid addiction and 7–8, 54, 58–59, 247; opioid prescriptions for

60, 148; self-medication and 58–59; substance use disorder (SUD) and 7

Chudzynski, J. 39

Chung, M.C. 215

Cicero, T.J. 147

cigarette smoking *see* tobacco smoking

Ciraulo, D.A. 252, 254, 257, 260, 270

CIWA-Ar *see* Clinical Institute Withdrawal Assessment for Alcohol, Revised (CIWA-Ar)

classical conditioning theory: cue-induced craving and 46; relapse prevention and 295–297

Clausen, T. 289

Cleary, M. 222

Cleaveland, C.L. 111

Cleland, C. 54

Cleveland, I.N. 117

Clinical Institute Withdrawal Assessment for Alcohol, Revised (CIWA-Ar) 250

Clinical Opiate Withdrawal Scale (COWS) 250–251, 274

clinician-patient therapeutic alliance: addiction treatment and 218–220; family therapy and 226; hope and 220; withdrawal management and 287–288

clonidine 253

Coblentz, P. 325

Cochrane, Archie 211

cognitive behavioral therapy (CBT): adverse childhood experiences (ACE) and 131; attention deficit/hyperactivity disorder-SUD comorbidity 85–86; autism spectrum-SUD comorbidity 85–86; cannabis use disorder (CUD) and 187–188; cognitive reappraisal and 297–301, 308; cognitive restructuring and 298–301, 305; contingency management (CM) and 323–324; distorted thinking and 301; functional analysis and 187; intimate partner violence perpetrators and 124; long-term effects of 319; mindfulness-based 69–70, 305; motivational interviewing (MI) and 64; motivation enhancement therapy and 69; neural system and 42; personality disorder-SUD comorbidity

INDEX

91; pharmacological treatments and 73; relapse prevention and 48, 229, 318–319; schema-focused 301–304, 318–319; schizophrenia-SUD comorbid patients 64–65; treatment outcomes of 64

cognitive change 234

cognitive reappraisal: cognitive restructuring and 298–300; positive reappraisal and 298, 300–301; relapse prevention and 297–298; top-down emotional regulation and 308

cognitive restructuring: psychoeducation and 299; relapse prevention and 297–300, 305, 320; thinking patterns in 298–301

Cohen, A.N. 67

Cohen, L. 79–80

Cohen, L.R. 76

Coin, M. 40

cold executive function 40

Cole, B. 54

collaborative opioid prescribing model (CoOP) 276–277

Collard, C.S. 105

Colozzi, I. 108, 119

common factor theory 74–75, 81, 83, 89

communication: autism spectrum-SUD comorbidity patients and 87; family members and 224–225, 227; family/social relationships and 113–114; patient/treatment teams 129, 133, 246, 291; skills training and 294, 297, 322

community: adverse childhood experiences (ACE) and 130; connection and 217; integration into 110, 193; social networks and 115, 119, 217; spirituality and 47, 211

community reinforcement and family training (CRAFT) 225, 289, 322–323

community reinforcement approach (CRA): behavioral skills training in 322; contingency management (CM) and 323; employment and 322; functional analysis and 321; Happiness Scale 322; naturalistic rewards in 323; recovery and 11, 38–39, 48, 314, 321–323; recreational/social counseling in 322; relationship counseling in 322;

sense of purpose and 136; sobriety sampling in 322

Community Reinforcement Approach to Addiction Treatment, A (Meyers and Miller) 323

community trauma 121

Compton, W.M. 181, 183

compulsivity: addiction and 34–35, 42–45, 306; defining 42–43; explanations for 44–45; negative reinforcement and 6, 45; neuroadaptation and 44; recovery and 35

concerned significant other (CSO) 322–323

concurrent treatment of PTSD and substance use disorders using prolonged exposure (COPE) 75–76

conduct disorder 29, 54, 56, 188

Conklin, C.A. 295

connection: addiction and 136, 212; community and 217; family 220–221, 225–226; higher power approach and 212, 214; human instinct for 112; self-help groups and 228; social networks and 217–218; spirituality and 212, 214

Conti, M.T. 127

contingency management (CM): antisocial personality disorder-SUD patients and 90; cannabis use disorder (CUD) and 187; cognitive behavioral therapy (CBT) and 323–324; community reinforcement approach (CRA) and 323; contrived rewards in 323–324; effectiveness of 323, 325; principles of 324–325; reinforcers in 324–325; relapse prevention and 48, 323; rewarding recovery and 38–39, 314, 321

Contingency Management for Substance Abuse Treatment (Petry) 325

co-occurring disorders (COD): categories of 7; detection of risk factors in 55; genetic factors and 56; identification of 54–55; integrated treatment and 55, 57–58; major depressive disorder-SUD comorbidity 69; neurobiology and 53; quality of life and 11; rates of 53–54; self-medication theory and 8–9, 54; substance use disorder (SUD) and

53–57; suicide and 10; treatment of 8–10, 53–55
Cook, C. 212
Cooper, A.L. 167
Cooper, C.B. 39
Copeland, Mary Ellen 93
COPE treatment 75–76
coping strategies 72, 86–87
Cowan, B.W. 160, 175
COWS *see* Clinical Opiate Withdrawal Scale (COWS)
CRAFFT Interview 336–337
CRAFFT Questionnaire 334
cravings: addiction and 34, 38; cue-induced 46–47; relapse and 47, 253–254; remission and 46; stress-induced 46; withdrawal-induced 46
Creating Change therapy 77
Creswell, J.D. 306, 310
criminal justice system: antisocial personality disorder-SUD patients and 90; community integration and 193; family relationships and 114; marijuana legalization and 174, 185; pharmacotherapy resistance in 153; posttraumatic stress disorder-SUD comorbidity rates 74
Crocq, M. 1
Cuberos, G. 40
Cucciare, M.A. 290
cue-induced craving 46–47
Czerny, A.B. 221

Daily Recovery Contract 227
Dalley, J.W. 44
Dancel, R. 250, 252
DARN (desire, ability, reason, and need) 238
Daughters, S.B. 90–91
Davis, K.E. 109
Davoli, M. 266
DBT Skills Training Manual (Linehan) 233
De Civita, M. 221
DeFulio, A. 105
Degenhardt, L. 183
Delgado-Pastor, L.C. 41
delirium tremens 249, 252
DeLisi, L.E. 183

DeLisi, M. 30
Demyttenaere, K. 159
Deng, Xiaoping 147
Dennis, K. 13
Dennis, M.L. 47
Denys, D. 43
depression *see* major depressive disorder (MDD)
Deris, F. 215
Derrick, J. 114
Derrick, J.L. 113
Desai, N. 79
detoxification *see* withdrawal management
detoxification facilities 289
Devitt, T.S. 109
DeWalt, D.A. 250, 252
Diagnostic Statistical Manual, 5th edition (DSM-5): alcohol use disorder (AUD) 33; behavioral addiction 2; cannabis use disorder (CUD) 178; gambling disorder 169, 171; phenomenological/ clinical features of addiction in 27–28; on remission 46; substance use disorder (SUD) 31–32, 34
dialectical behavioral therapy (DBT) 48, 305, 320
Dibley, A.R. 191
Dickerson, F. 63
Dickinson, A. 45
Dickinson, D. 63
Dickman, S.L. 153
Di Forti, M. 183
digital addiction *see* internet-related addiction
disadvantaged communities 111; *see also* material poverty
distress tolerance 235–236
disulfiram (Antabuse): efficacies of 260–261, 264; guidelines for 261–262; physician prescribing of 255; posttraumatic stress disorder-SUD clients and 79; relapse prevention and 256
Dixon, L.B. 63
Dobkin, P.L. 221
Dolezal, B.A. 39
Dong, M. 127
Donovan, Shaun 193

dopamine system: drug addiction and 40; mesolimbic 37–38, 61; neuroadaptation and 36–37; non-drug activities and reinforcers 38–39; reinforcement of drug effects 38; schizophrenia symptoms and 62; treatment and 44

dorsolateral prefrontal cortex 40

Double Trouble in Recovery 65

Drug Addiction Treatment Act (DATA) 271

drug court approach: African Americans and 145, 190–191; criticism of 190; development of 189–190; drug treatment referrals 190; low completion rates and 190–191; medication coverage in 155; pharmacotherapy resistance by 153–154, 190, 192; racial bias in 145, 190; recidivism reduction and 145, 153, 190; treatment approach of 189; types of 189

drug use disorder: co-occurring disorders (COD) and 54; dopamine (DA) and 37–38, 40; genetic factors of 29; health insurance and poverty status 107–108, **108**; material poverty and 11; mood disorder comorbidity and 68; schizophrenia comorbidity and 60; stigma of 122; strategies to combat 38–39; tolerance of 38; trauma and 121; withdrawal from 38; see also opioid use disorders (OUD); substance use disorder (SUD)

DSM-IV-TR 33

Dube, S.R. 127

Dubreuil, M.E. 212

Dumont, D.M. 153

Dundon, W.D. 73

Dunigan, R. 290

Dunn, R. 309

early maladaptive schemas (EMS) 69–71, 302–304

Edwards, A.C. 30

Edwards, V. 128

Ehrenkaufer, R.L. 103

Ehrenreich, H. 260

Eisenberger, N.I. 112

Ekleberry, S.C. 90–91, 93

el-Guebaly, N. 163

Ellerbe, L. 256

Ellis, M.S. 147

Elmquist, J. 70, 303

Emery, G. 298

emotional pain 59

emotional processing 129

emotion regulation skills: attentional deployment and 234; biosocial theory and 232; bottom-up 307–308; cognitive change and 234; cognitive reappraisal and 308; development of 235–236; distress tolerance and 235–236; families and 233; four domains of 233; inner strengths and 232; interpersonal effectiveness skills and 235; mindfulness and 234–235, 307–308; problem-solving 235; response modulation and 234; situation modification and 234; situation selection 233–234; strategies for 233–236; top-down 308

empathy 62

employment: quality of life and 36, 103, 316; recovery and 315–316; relapse prevention and 108–109, 322; sobriety and 109; social networks and 316; see also unemployment

empowerment 239

engagement coping skills 72

Epidemiologic Catchment Area Study (ECA) 32–33

Epstein, S. 270

Erdogan, M. 121

Erga, A.H. 41, 104

Erlich, P.M. 7, 54

Esposito-Smythers, C. 324

established/evidence-based treatment 317–322

Evans, S.W. 88

Evins, E. 183

Ewer, P.L. 75

executive function (EF) 40–41, 85–86, 129

exercise 38–39

existential purpose in life 111

expressed emotion 114

expressive writing 131

extended release naltrexone (XR-NTX): development of 264; effectiveness of

155, 264–265, 280; opioid addiction and 155, 264; patient compliance and 258; side effects of 259; *see also* naltrexone

Fairman, B. 157
Falcone, M.A. 183
Fallot, R. 120
family support: barriers to 222–224; blame/conflict in 222–223; clinician facilitation of 225–226; communication and 224; coping skills/self care 224–225; emotion dysregulation and 233; family abuse/mental health issues and 223–224; gambling disorder and 221; isolation/resistance to 223; recovery and 220–223; therapies for 226–227
Fang, X.Y. 117
Farrell, J.M. 318
Fathers for Change 125
Faure, S.C. 130
Felitti, V.J., 127–128, 130
feminist-based treatment model 124
Feng, T. 176
fentanyl 149, 152
Fenton, M.C. 89
Fink, B.C. 135
Fishbain, D.A. 54
"five clocks" concept 194
Flori, J.N. 127
Flynn, E. 176
Foa, E.B. 79–80
Fong, C. 54, 153
food addiction 167–168
Ford, D.C. 126, 128
Forlini, C. 1, 254
Formal Mindfulness meditations 309
Forrest, C.B. 128
Forster, M. 130
Foss, M.A. 47
foster care 127, 132
"four clocks" concept 194
Fowler, J.S. 36, 38, 40
Frances, Allen 169
Franken, I.H.A. 168
Frankl, Victor 137, 230–231
Friedland, D. 211
Frisen, L. 82
Frontal Systems Behavioral Scale 40

functional analysis: A-B-C framework *293*, 297; addiction treatment and 292–293; cognitive behavioral therapy (CBT) and 187; negative consequence assessment and 294; relapse prevention and 292, 294; skills training and 292–294
functional magnetic resonance imaging (fMRI) 2, 5, 41
Furr-Holden, C.D.M. 157

Gaag, R.J. van der 83
Gage, H.D. 103
Galea, S. 175
Gallagher, J.R. 191
Gallis, T.L. 73
Gallupe, O. 108, 119
Gamblers Anonymous (GA) 33, 228
gambling disorder: alcohol use disorder (AUD) and 30; as behavioral addiction 2, 169–170; as a brain disease 7; diagnostic criteria for 33; distorted thinking patterns in 299–300; family involvement in treatment for 221; levels of 31–32; personality disorder-SUD comorbidity 89; twin research in 30; women and 163
Gardner, S.L. 13, 194
Garland, E. 39
Garland, E.L. 306, 308, 312, 316, 320–321
Garnick, D.W. 290
Geerts, L. 130
Geier, T. 89
gender: addiction treatment and 161–162; genetic factors and 30; marijuana use and 156–157, 160; in substance use 156–160; tobacco smoking and 158–159; *see also* women
Generalized Anxiety Disorder 56
genetics: addiction heritability and 29; addiction liability and 29; alcohol use disorder (AUD) and 29–30; co-occurring disorders (COD) and 56; drug dependence and 29; gambling disorder and 30; gender and 30; impacts of 29–30; impulsivity and 30
Gerhard, G.S. 7, 54
Geske, J.R. 163
Gilchrist, M. 250, 252

Giles, W.H. 127
Gill, K. 221
Gilreath, T. 157
Glasser, William 102
Globalization of Addiction, The
  (Alexander) 4
Goal Management Training (GMT) 41
God: Alcoholics Anonymous (AA) and
  213–214; attachment to 211, 215–216;
  higher power approach and 212–213;
  individual beliefs and 229
Godley, H. 188
Goldberg, R. W. 63
Goldstein, R.B. 68
Gonzales, R. 39
Gonzalez, R. 183
Goodrich, D. 295
Goossens, P. 86–87
Gordon, A. 256
Gordon, M.A. 319
Gower, A.L. 130
Grant, B. 89
Grant, B.F. 68, 147
Grant, J.E. 44
Grant, K.A. 103
Gratz, K.L. 232
Green, R.S. 121
Green, T.C. 116
Greene, M.C. 228
Greenstein, E. 89
Gressard, C.F. 231
Grimes Serrano, J.M. 116
Gross, J.J. 233
Gueorguieva, R. 79
Gundersen, D.C. 176

Haan, L. de 168
habituation: addiction and 35, 42–43;
  conditioning and 45; defining 43;
  mindfulness and 306–307; motor habits
  and 43
Hagedorn, H. 256
Hagen, E. 41, 104
Hagen, K.P. 41, 104
Haglund, M. 39
Hall, M.T. 105, 109–110
Hall, W. 1, 181, 183, 254
Hallyburton, M.B. 295

Han, B. 69
Han, J.J. 7, 54
Happiness Scale 322
Harden, T. 315
Hardin, C. 153
Hari, Johann 212
Harrington, H. 183
Harris, A.H.S. 256
Harris, M. 120
Hasin, D. 89
Hasin, D.S. 68, 147, 175, 178
Haslam, C. 119
Haslam, S.A. 119
Hasson, A. 272
Hayes, S.C. 239, 305
Hazle, Barry, Jr. 229
Healthy Steps for Young Children
  program 128
Heeren, A. 169
Heffner, J.L. 163
Hellman, J.L. 128
Helminiak, D.A. 211, 228, 232
Henderson, C.E. 188
Hendriks, V. 188
Henkel, D. 105, 109
Herman, Judith 77, 131
heroin addiction: nonmedical pain relievers
  (NMPR) and 8; prescription opioid
  transition to 145; *see also* opioid and
  heroin epidemic; opioid use disorders
  (OUD)
Herron, A. 79–80
Hester, R. 168
Heyman, G.M. 32–33
Hien, D. 79–80
Hien, D.A. 76
hierarchy of human needs 103, 107, 120,
  134
Higgins, S.T. 323
higher power approach: belief in 229;
  connection and 212, 214; defining
  212; hope and 210, 212; recovery and
  212–216; Twelve Step philosophy in
  212–215; units in 212
high risk theory 74
high susceptibility theory 74
Hillhouse, M. 272
historical trauma 121

HIV-AIDS patients: CBT/CM treatment for 324; drug use and 122, 154, 192; methadone and 191, 264; positive reappraisal and 300; spiritual well-being and 215

Hjemdahl, B. 289

Hodgins, D.C. 163, 170

Hoffman, S.N. 7, 54

Hoffman, T. 30

Hoffmann, H. 295

Hogue, A. 88

Holtyn, A.F. 105

homeless persons: posttraumatic stress disorder and 74; substance abuse and 105

Homish, G.G. 113

hope instillation: acceptance and commitment therapy and 239; clinician facilitation of 220, 245; higher power approach and 210, 212; motivational interviewing and 239; recovery and 210, 212, 220, 245–246; Twelve Step programs and 245

Hopfer, C. 180

Hoppes, K. 307

Hopwood, S. 75

Horgan, C.M. 290

Horton, E.G. 135

hot executive function 40

housing instability: addiction and 103; discharged inmates and 193; quality of life and 103; relapse prevention and 108–109; substance abuse and 105; *see also* subsidized housing

Hser, Y. 272

Hsiao, S. 46

Hu, M. C. 79–80

Huang, B. 68

Huang, D. 272

Huang, W. 67

Huang, Y. 180

Hubicka, B. 115

Huizink, A.C. 181

Hult, J.R. 200

hyperalgesia 59

Imms, P. 79–80

impaired control 28

impulsivity: addictive behavior and 6, 35, 42, 44, 306; attention deficit/

hyperactivity disorder (ADHD) and 81; dimensions of 43–44; genetics and 30, 44; limbic reward pathway and 43; neuroadaptation and 37, 44; personality disorder-SUD comorbidity and 92; prefrontal cortex and 43; substance use disorder (SUD) and 43

Informal Mindfulness 309

Ingle, P.J. 221

inner strengths approach: acceptance and commitment therapy (ACT) and 239–240; developmental model of recovery in 231–232; emotion regulation skills and 232–236; meaning in life 230–231; motivational interviewing in 237–239; strategies for 230

integrated cognitive behavioral therapy (ICBT) 76, 85–86

International ADHD in Substance Use Disorders Prevalence Study 80–81

internet gaming disorder: attention deficit/hyperactivity disorder (ADHD) and 173; autism spectrum disorder (ASD) and 88; as behavioral addiction 2; as a brain disease 7; cravings and 46; interpersonal relationships and 117–118; parental modeling and 118; parenting quality and 117

internet-related addiction: autism spectrum disorder (ASD) and 82, 173; global reach of 166; impact on brain 168; personality disorder and 89–90; pornography and 167, 173; rates of 167; research in 172

interpersonal effectiveness skills 235

interpersonal psychotherapy (IPT) 71–72

interpersonal relationships: addiction treatment and 113–120; expressed emotion and 114; nonjudgmental 118; non-using 118–119; parent-child/family/social 117–118; reciprocal 118–120; recovery and 118; social pain and 112–113; spouse/family/social 113–116; well-being and 111–112

interpersonal violence: trauma and 120–121; women victims of 156, 160

Intervention (Johnson) 236

intimate partner violence (IPV): addiction treatment and 123–124; contexts of

122–123; motivational interviewing and 125; perpetrators of 124–125; rates of 122; self-medication and 123; stress and 110; trauma and 122–126; women and 122–124
Ishibashi, K. 39
Iyegbe, C. 183

Jakobsen, J.C. 39, 307–308
Janssen, E. 295
Jetten, J. 119
Johansson, B.A. 263, 278
Johnson, J. 135
Johnson, J.E. 71, 109, 118
Johnson, K.M. 77–78
Johnson, R.M. 157–158
Johnson, Vernon 236
Johnson Intervention approach 323
Johnston, L.D. 176
Jones, H.E. 314, 316
Jones, L. 107
Jørgensen, C.H. 260
Joseph, H. 54
Jun, M. 116
Jung, J. 68

Kahan, M. 273
Kampman, K.M. 73
Kaplan, J.R. 103
Karaca, S. 80
Karpyak, V.M. 163
Kelly, J.F. 228
Kelly, S.M. 270
Kendler, K.S. 29–30
Kenney, S. 127
Kern, A.C. 175
Kerr, D.C.R. 175
Keyes, K. 89, 157
Keyes, K.M. 175–176
Khazaal, Y. 169
Killeen, T.K. 76
Kimber, J. 266
Kipnis, S. 54
Kirouac, M. 135
Kirsch, J. 250, 252
Kissin, W. 276
Kivlahan, D. 256
Klevens, J. 126
Klingemann, H. 33

Klosko, J.S. 301, 318
Knapp, C.M. 252, 254, 257, 260, 270
Ko, C.H. 46
Ko, H.-C. 89
Kolliakou, A. 183
Kontos, E.Z. 109
Koob, G. 1, 4, 34, 44
Korchmaros, J. 127
Koss, M.P. 128
Kosten, T. 280
Kourgiantakis, T. 223–224
Krampe, H. 260
Kranzler, H.R. 112, 252, 254–255, 257, 260
Krausz, M. 74, 124, 131
Kristensen, O. 289
Kronenberg, L.M. 85–87
Krueger, R. 89
Krug, L.M. 129
Kuo, C.C. 109, 118
Kurtz, S.P. 147

Lan, J. 117
Lane, H.-Y. 89
Lane, S.P. 92
Langedijk, Mark 33
Langman, L. 215
Langstrom, N. 82
Larsson, H. 82
Lassiter, P.S. 221
Latino students 160, 176
Laudet, A.B. 10, 103–105
Laurell, H. 115
Lauritzen, G. 89, 109
Leach, D. 112
Leary, M.R. 112
Lee, J.D. 155
Lee, M.T. 290
Lehavot, K. 78
Lejuez, C.W. 90–91
Lembke, A. 256
Lenzi, M. 160
Leonard, K.E. 113
Levin, F.R. 79–80, 88
Levin, M.E. 239
Levinson, C. 79
Lewinson, T. 105
Lewis, B. 164–165
Lewis, J. 54

Li, K. 74
Licari, A. 116
Lichtenstein, P. 30, 82
Liddle, H.A. 188
Lieberman, M.D. 112
Liles, E.A. 250, 252
Lilienfeld, S.O. 34–35, 297
limbic reward pathway: compulsivity and 44–45; impulsivity and 43; neuroadaptation and 37–38, 40
limited reparenting 304
Lin, W.C. 46
Linden, I.A. 74, 124, 131
Lindgren, A. 263, 278
Linehan, Martha 233–235
Linehan, M.M. 232
Ling, W. 271
Lipkus, I.M. 114
Litt, L.C. 76
Liu, C. 180
Liu, G.C. 46
Liu, Q.X. 117
Lonn, S. 30
Lopez, V. 222
Lopez-Castro, T. 79–80
Loveland Cook, C.A. 117
Lowe, J.M. 325
Luigjes, J. 43
Luijten, M. 168
Luna, N. 135
Lundahl, B. 124
Lundervold, A.J. 41, 104
Lundstrom, S. 82
Lynskey, M. 181, 183
Lynskey, M.T. 181

MacDonald, G. 112
MacDonald, J.M. 190
Mach, R.H. 103
Machielsen, M.W.J. 168
MacKillop, J. 114
MacKinnon, S. 135
macro factors: addiction and 144–145, 147, 188; drug courts as 189–191; five clocks as 195; methadone clinics as 191–192; social policies as 188; subsidized housing as 193–194
Maes, H.H. 30

major depressive disorder (MDD): alcohol use disorder (AUD) and 69; cognitive behavioral therapy (CBT) and 69; suicide attempts and 55
major depressive disorder-SUD comorbidity: cognitive behavioral therapy (CBT) and 69–70; engagement coping skills and 72; integrated treatment and 69; interpersonal psychotherapy and 71–72; modification of early maladaptive schemas and 69–70; pharmacological treatments 72–73; self-medication theory and 68; strategies for 68–72; theories for 55–56; treatment outcomes of 68–72
Malloy, T. 135
marijuana legalization: cost effectiveness of 174; criminal justice system and 174, 185; impact on adolescents 174–175, 185; increase in use 160, 174–175; medicinal 173–175, 184; perceptions of 174, 176, 184; recreational 160, 173, 175, 184
marijuana use: abnormal brain development and 181; addiction and 177–181; adolescent-onset 61, 174, 176–181; adverse consequences of 174, 176–181; alcohol and 180; antisocial personality disorder (ASPD) and 56; cannabis dependence syndromes 177–178; cognitive impairment and 180; as a gateway drug 184; gender convergence in 156–158, 160; health impacts and 183–184; liberalization of policy and 160; low-income men and 157; motor-vehicle accidents and 179–180; negative achievements and 181; schizophrenia development and 61, 182–183; screening for 185–186; THC levels 178–180; underage 174–176, 184; women and 156–157, 160, 175; see also cannabis use disorder (CUD)
marijuana withdrawal syndrome 178
marital therapy 114
Mark, T.L. 255
Marks, Isaac 171
Marks, J.S. 128
Marlatt, G.A. 319–320

Marotta, J. 221
Marrari, E.A. 270
Marte, Coss 216
Martin, N.G. 181
Martin, R.A. 135
Martino, S. 319
Martins, S.S. 147
Maslow, A. 103, 106–107, 111, 120, 134
Mason, Z.S. 129
material poverty: addiction and 11–12, 106–111; disadvantaged communities 111; relapse risk and 108–109; social causation hypothesis and 107; social drift hypothesis and 107; stress and 110; *see also* poverty-addiction linkage
Mattick, R.P. 266
Matto, H.C. 111
Matusow, H. 153
Maurage, P. 169
Mauro, P.M. 157
Mauss, I.B. 300
Mawson, E. 119
McClay, J. 56, 183
McClernon, F.J. 295
McDonell, M.G. 325
McKay, J.R. 41, 104, 312
McLaughlin, K.A. 129
McLean, C.P. 79–80
McLellan, A.T. 59
McLeod, C 276
McMillan, G. 221
McMorris, B.J. 130
McPherson, C. 221
meaning in life: attitude and 231; creativity in 230; experience in 230–231; future-oriented 230; present-oriented 230
meaning therapy 137
medical marijuana legalization (MML): adolescent and young adult impact 174–175; factors for 173–174; perceptions of 174, 184
medication-assisted treatment (MAT): access to 152–153; agonists and 153–154, 253, 262–264; antagonists and 154–155, 258–259, 262–263; cost barriers and 155; drug court resistance to 153–154, 190; opposition to 154; stigma of 269; treatment philosophies

155–156; *see also* pharmacological treatments
medication noncompliance: decreasing 66–67; schizophrenia patients and 65–67
meditation practice 308–310
Meichenbaum, D. 298
Meier, M.H. 183
mental illness: adverse childhood experiences (ACE) and 127; health insurance and poverty status 107–108, **108**; material poverty and 11
Merrick, M.T. 126
Merz, S. 75
mesolimbic dopamine system 37–38, 61
methadone: advantages of 266; barriers to 269–270; benefits of 191–192; buprenorphine and 274; clinics for 191–192; controls on 270–271; drug court resistance to 153–154, 190, 192; effectiveness of 263, 265–266; guidelines for 267–269; intimate partner violence survivors and 123; legalization of 191, 264; macro factors and 192; opioid addiction and 134, 151, 153–154, 188, 191, 253, 262–271; opposition to 154–155, 191; side effects of 268–269; social factors and 188–189; stigma of 264–265, 269
methylphenidate 41
Metzler, M. 126
Meyers, R.J. 294, 323
Miele, G.M. 76
Mikulich-Gilbertson, S.K. 68
Miller, A.M. 160, 175
Miller, W.R. 323
Mills, K.L. 75
Min, M. 116
Min, S. 68
Min, S.J. 115, 180
mindfulness-based cognitive therapy (MBCT) 70, 305
mindfulness-based intervention (MBI): addiction treatment and 38–39; adverse childhood experiences (ACE) and 131; emotion regulation skills and 234–235; neural system and 42; relapse prevention and 48, 69–70

mindfulness-based relapse prevention (MBRP) 305, 319–320

Mindfulness-Based Relapse Prevention for Addictive Behaviors (Bowen et al.) 320

mindfulness-oriented recovery enhancement (MORE): cognitive function and 42; cognitive restructuring and 320; mindfulness savoring and 320–321; positive emotions and 320; positive reappraisal and 320–321; rewarding recovery and 38–39, 305, 314

Mindfulness-Oriented Recovery Enhancement for Addiction, Stress, and Pain (Garland) 321

mindfulness therapies: brain pattern alteration through 308; clinician practice of 310; components of 309–310; consciousness and 307; defining 305–306; effectiveness of 306–307; emotion regulation skills and 234–235, 307–308; ending automatic pilot with 306–307; ending habituation with 306–307; Formal/Informal 309; meditation practice 308–310; neuropsychology and 41; practice in 310; psychoeducation and 309; relapse prevention and 304–305, 319–320; risks of 310; types of 305

mindful savoring 316–317, 320–321

Miotto, K. 271

Miranda, R. 212

Mitchell, S.G. 270

Moffitt, T.E. 56, 183

Mojtabai, R. 69

mood disorders: cognitive behavioral therapy (CBT) and 69; early maladaptive schemas (EMS) and 70; interpersonal psychotherapy and 71–72; mindfulness therapies and 69–70; pharmacotherapy for 72–73; substance abuse and 68–69; treatment strategies for 68–73

Mooney, L. 39

Mooney, L.J. 39, 271

Moos, B.S. 104, 109

Moos, R.H. 104, 109

moral development 231

moral model of addiction 4–5

Morgan, B.D. 59

Morgan, D. 103

Moskowitz, J.T. 300

motivational enhancement therapy (MET) 187

motivational intervention 289

motivational interviewing (MI): change talk in 238; client-centeredness of 237–238; cognitive function and 42; facilitating change through 236–237; goals and aspirations in 239; intimate partner violence (IPV) and 125; personality disorder-SUD comorbidity 90; quality of life and 11; relapse prevention and 48; relational component of 237–238; schizophrenia-SUD comorbid patients 64; sense of purpose and 136; technical component of 238; withdrawal management and 289

motivation enhancement therapy 64, 69

motor habits 43

Mucha, R.F. 295

Mueller, S.R. 115

Multidimensional Family Therapy for Adolescent Cannabis Users (Liddle) 188

multiple dimensional family therapy (MDFT): adolescent marijuana use and 187–188; clinician-patient therapeutic alliance 226; goals of 226; parent-adolescent bond in 226; substance abuse and 225

Munzing, T. 148

Murray, R. 56, 183

Murthy, Vivek 149

Mustain, J.R. 211, 228, 232

Myers, U.S. 77

Nader, M. 273

Nader, M.A. 103

Nader, S.H. 103

Najavits, L.M. 77–78

naloxone 151–152, 263

naltrexone: advantages of 278; alcohol use disorder (AUD) and 67, 79, 256, 258; craving reduction and 260; disagreement over use of 155–156; guidelines for 258–259, 278–280; implanted 264; major depressive disorder-SUD comorbidity 73; opioid use disorders (OUD) and 262–263, 277–280; overdose and 280; physician prescribing of 255; posttraumatic stress disorder-SUD clients and 79–80; relapse prevention and 155, 191; side effects of 259, 278–280; treatment noncompliance and 278, 280; withdrawal syndromes and 272; *see also* extended release naltrexone (XR-NTX)

narcissistic personality disorder (NPD) 89

Narcotics Anonymous (NA) 213

Nargiso, J.E. 109, 118

National Association of Drug Court Professionals (NADCP) 154

National Institute for Health and Care Excellence (NICE) 260

National Institute on Drug Abuse (NIDA) 34, 264

National Pain Strategy 148

National Prescription Audit (NPA) 255

Navarro, J.F. 72

Neale, M.C. 29

negative consequence assessment 294

negative emotions 163–164

negative reinforcement 6, 45, 91

Neilson, E.K. 124, 131

Nesvag, S.M. 41, 104

neuroadaptation: addiction and 36–39; chronic exposure and 38; compulsivity and 44; dopamine system in 36–39; impulsivity and 37, 44; non-drug activities and reinforcers 38–39; prefrontal cortex and 36–37, 40–42

neurobiological processes: addiction and 30–32; co-occurring disorders (COD) and 53

neurocentrism 31

Newman, R.G. 10, 103

Nich, C. 79, 319

Nicosia, N. 190

Nielsen, S. 271

Nikfarjam, M. 215

Nixon, S.J. 164–165

Noel, F. 74

nonjudgmental relationships 118

nonmedical pain relievers (NMPR) 8

non-using relationships 118–119

Noormohammadi, M.R. 215

Nordberg, A. 191

Nordenberg, D. 128

Nordfjarn, T. 89, 109

Norman, S.B. 77

Novo, P. 155

Nunes, E.V. 155

Nunes, E.V. 280

Nunn, J. 121

Nuro, K.F. 319

OARS approach 187

O'Brien, C.P. 79–80

obsessive compulsive disorder (OCD) 42

O'Connor, P.G. 280

Oei, T.P.S. 299

O'Farrell, T.J. 114, 227

office-based buprenorphine (OBB) 275, 277

O'Grady, K.E. 270

Olesek, K. 136

Olfson, M. 69

Oliva, E. 256

Oliver, J.A. 295

O'Neill, S.J. 109

One Man's Medicine (Cochrane) 211

opioid agonist treatment 154, 253, 262–264

opioid and heroin epidemic: China 147–148; chronic pain and 7–8, 54, 58–59, 148–149, 247; increase in 146–147; drug court approach 153; emotional pain and 59; hyperalgesia and 59; as informal therapy 58; initiatives targeting 148–151; macro factors and 144; medication-assisted treatment (MAT) and 152–155; overdoses and 151–152; overprescribing by physicians and 148–149; pharmacological treatments and 247; prescription opioids use and 147–149; rates of heroin use 147; United States 146–148; *see also* prescription opioids

opioid antagonist treatment 154–155, 258–259, 262–263

Opioid Initiative 148

opioid overdoses: naloxone and 151–152; naltrexone and 280

opioid treatment programs (OTP) 275, 277

opioid use disorders (OUD): abstinence and 155–156; buprenorphine and 271–277; as a chronic disease 152; methadone and 134, 151, 153–154, 188, 190–192, 253, 262–271; naltrexone and 277–278; opioid agonist treatment and 154, 253, 262–264; opioid antagonist treatment and 154–155, 258–259, 262–263; overprescribing by physicians and 8, 58–59, 144–145; pharmacological treatments and 247, 253, 262–280; relapse prevention and 262–280; schizophrenia comorbidity and 67; screening for 161; withdrawal management 250–251; withdrawal syndromes 248, 250–251, 253; *see also* prescription opioids

orbitofrontal cortex 40

Oslin, D. 79–80

Oslin, D.W. 73

overdoses *see* opioid overdoses

Oxford Group 213

pain management: prescription opioids and 58–59, 144, 150; treatment strategies for 151–152

Panas, L. 290

Panebianco, D. 108, 119

Paparelli, A. 183

Papini, S. 79–80

Paraherakis, A. 221

parental modeling 118

parent-child/family/social relationships: addiction treatment and 117–118; adolescents and 117–118; family structure and 118; parental modeling and 118; parenting quality and 117

Park, H. 116

Parkinson's disease 43–44

Parnham, T. 157

Parvin, N. 215

Patel, J.R. 222–225

pathological narcissism 213

patience 88

Pauli, P. 295

Pearson, M.R. 135

Pedersen, B. 260

Pedersen, E.R. 67

Pelc, I. 188

Perez-Garcia, M. 40

personality disorder-SUD comorbidity: cognitive behavioral therapy (CBT) and 91; common factor theory and 89; contingency management (CM) and 90; gambling disorder and 89; impulsivity and 92; internet addiction and 89–90; motivational interviewing and 90; negative reinforcement and 91; rates of 88–89; recovery as freedom in 90–91; self-medication theory and 89; treatment strategies for 90–93; Twelve Step programs and 91–92

Peselow, E. 56

Peterson, J.A. 270

Petrakis, I. 78

Petrakis, I.L. 79

Petry, N.M. 324–325

Pettinati, H.M. 73

Phan, O. 188

pharmacological criteria 28

pharmacological treatments: alcohol use disorder (AUD) and 79, 247, 252–253, 255–262; attention deficit/hyperactivity disorder-SUD comorbidity 83–85; autism spectrum-SUD comorbidity 83–85; barriers to 255–256; behavioral addiction and 166; behavioral therapy and 246; cognitive behavioral therapy (CBT) and 73; major depressive disorder-SUD comorbidity 72–73; opioid use disorders (OUD) and 247, 253, 262–280; physician prescribing of 255–256; posttraumatic stress disorder-SUD comorbidity 79–80; prefrontal cortex deficits and 41; psychosocial therapy and 80, 246; relapse prevention and 254–280; schizophrenia-SUD comorbid patients 65–66; substance addiction and 47, 247; *see also* medication-assisted treatment (MAT)

Phibbs, S. 175

Pickering, R.P. 68

PirouziFard, M. 30

Pitorello, J. 239

Poh, E. 175
Pohl, M. 59
Poling, J. 79
political war trauma 121
pornography 167, 173
Portenoy, R.K. 54
Portnoy, G.A. 319
Ports, K.A. 126
Positive Addiction (Glasser) 102
positive emotions 163, 320
positive reappraisal: interventions for 300–301; mindfulness and 320–321; recovery and 320; relapse prevention and 298, 300–301, 321
positron emission tomography (PET) 5
post-detox programs 254
posttraumatic stress disorder (PTSD): addiction and 120; antidepressants and 79; prolonged exposure therapy (PE) and 75–76; treatment outcomes of 55
posttraumatic stress disorder-SUD comorbidity: addiction-focused interventions 78; common factor theory and 74–75; COPE treatment 75–76; exposure therapy and 75–76; high risk theory and 74; high susceptibility theory and 74; homeless persons and 74; non-exposure-based treatments 76–77; pharmacological treatments 79–80; psychoeducation and 76; psychosocial interventions 80; rates of 73–74; self-medication theory and 74; skills training 76; stage-based framework 77–78; theories for 74; treatment outcomes of 76–78; treatment strategies for 75–78; Twelve Step programs and 77; veterans and 73
Potenza, M. 169
Potenza, M.N. 80
poverty *see* material poverty; spiritual poverty
poverty-addiction linkage: alcohol-attributable disease and 108; cigarette smoking and 107–108; disadvantaged neighborhoods and 111; employment assistance 110; health insurance and 107, **108**; housing instability and 109; psychosocial interventions 106; recovery

and 106; relapse risk and 108; social causation hypothesis and 107; social drift hypothesis and 107; socioeconomic status-related resources and 108–109; stress reduction 110; treatment strategies for 110–111; unemployment and 109
prefrontal cortex: addiction and 40–41; behavioral treatments and 41–42; executive function (EF) and 40–41; functions of 40; impulsivity and 43; neuroadaptation and 36–38, 40–42; pharmacological treatments and 41
prescription drug monitoring program (PDMP) data 150–151
prescription opioids: addictive qualities of 148; extensive prescribing of 58–59, 146–148; guidelines for 145, 149–151; hyperalgesia and 59; improvements to practice of 149; pain management and 58–59, 144, 150
Pressley, J.C. 180
Prioleau, O. 103
problematic internet use 117
probuphine 272–273
prolonged exposure therapy (PE) 75–76
psychiatric disorders: gender and 162–163; self-medication and 56–57; substance abuse and 8, 56–57
Psychodynamic/Attachment Therapy 125
psychoeducation: attention deficit/hyperactivity disorder-SUD comorbidity and 84; distorted thinking patterns and 299; intimate partner violence survivors and 124; mindfulness therapies and 309; posttraumatic stress disorder-SUD clients and 76; schizophrenia-SUD comorbid patients and 64, 67
psychological well-being: interpersonal relationships and 111–112; purpose in life and 111; trauma and 111
psychosocial dislocation theory 102, 112
psychosocial integration: addiction and 4–5, 103; addiction treatment and 10
psychosocial interventions: antisocial personality disorder-SUD patients and 90; pharmacological treatments and

80, 246, 275–276; schizophrenia-SUD comorbid patients and 63, 75
Public Health Model 166
public housing authorities (PHA) 193
Puente, A. 40

quality of life (QoL): abstinence and 104–106; addiction and 4–5; addiction treatment and 10–11, 102–104, 106, 311–313; co-occurring disorders (COD) and 11; defining 103; employment and 316; hierarchy of human needs and 103, 107; interpersonal relationships and 112–120; material poverty and 107–111; recovery and 36; remission and 104–105; resource levels and 104–106; self-medication and 106; sense of purpose and 134–137; spiritual poverty and 111–112; substance abuse and 104–105; trauma and 120–134
Quello, S.B. 72

racial bias 145, 190
Racine, A.D. 129
Rahim-Juwel, R. 157
Ralevski, E. 79
Ranby, K.W. 114
randomized controlled trials (RCT) 77
Rawson, R.A. 39
Raylu, N. 299
reciprocal relationships 118–120
recovery: abstinence and 106; affirmation and xii; developmental model of 231–232; elements of long-term 11; emotion regulation skills and 232–233; employment and 315–316; family participation in 220–227; higher power and 210, 212–216; hope and 210, 212, 220; inner strengths approach 230–240; interpersonal relationships and 115–119; interventions for xii, xiii; long-term 227; mindful savoring in 316–317; moral development and 231; quality of life and 36, 106, 313; recreational activities and 314–315; relapse prevention and 45, 47, 54; rewarding 311–325; self-help groups and 227–230; self-monitoring 45; sober

periods and xii; social identity model of 119; social networks and 210, 217–222; spirituality and 209–213, 215–216; stages of 231–232; women and 116
recreational activities: counseling and 322; recovery and 314–315
recreational marijuana legalization (RML): adolescent and young adult impact 175–176; African American students and 160, 175; factors for 173; increase in use 160, 175–176, 184; Latino students and 160, 176; perceptions of 176, 184; social acceptance of 184; women and 160, 175
reinforcement-based treatment (RBT) 321
Reisinger, H.S. 270
Reiss, N. 318
relapse: cravings and 47, 253–254; influence of family on 164; material poverty and 108–109; negative emotions and 163–164; positive emotions and 163; rewards of 311; triggers for 47; women and 163–164
relapse prevention: A-B-C framework and 291–292; acamprosate and 256–258; alcohol use disorder (AUD) and 256–262; buprenorphine and 262; classical conditioning and 295–297; cognitive behavioral therapy (CBT) and 318–319; cognitive reappraisal and 297–301; community reinforcement approach (CRA) 321–323; contingency management (CM) and 48, 323; established/evidence-based treatment 317–322; functional analysis and 292–294; methadone and 262; mindfulness and 69–70, 304–305, 319–320; mindful savoring in 320; naltrexone and 258, 262; opioid use disorders (OUD) and 262–280; pharmacotherapy for 254–280; post-detox aftercare and 254; recovery and 45, 47, 54; schema healing and 297, 301–304; schema therapy and 318–319; skills training and 292–294, 297; treatment retention 263–264, 267, 272, 278, 280; treatment strategies for 254; triggers for 295–297; withdrawal management and 253–254

Relapse Prevention and Relationship Safety (RPRS) 123
relationship counseling 322
remission: addiction as choice/disease and 32–33; cravings and 34; defining 46; employment and 109; long-term recovery and 104–105
Renner, J.A., Jr. 270
Resko, S. 185
response-cost procedure 42
response modulation 234
reward deficiency syndrome 312
rewards: of abstinence 311; barriers to 311–313; employment and 315–316; mindful savoring in 316–317; quality of life enhancement and 311–313; in recovery 311–325; recreational activities and 314–315; treatment philosophies and 313
Rich, J.D. 153
Ries, R.K. 325
Riggs, D.S. 79–80
Riggs, P.D. 68
Rigter, H. 188
Risi, M.M. 127
Risk Evaluation and Mitigation Strategy (REMS) program 276
risky use 28, 177, 249
Ritter, G.A. 290
Robertson, C. 39
Robins, Lee 296–297
Rodriguez, L.M. 114
Rogers, Carl 238
Rogers, R.E. 323
Rohsenow, D.J. 135
Roiser, J.P. 44
Roll, J. 325
Rollins, A.L. 109
Roos, A. 130
Roos, C.R. 135
Roozen, H.G. 313
Rosenblum, A. 54
Rosenfeld, J. 75
Rosenman, R. 160, 175
Rosomoff, H. L. 54
Rosomoff, R.S. 54
Ross, S. 56
Rothman, E.F. 157
Rounsaville, B. 79

Rounsaville, B.J. 319
Rowe, C. 188
Ruan, W.J. 68
Ruglass, L. 79–80
Rukstalis, M. 7, 54
Rush, A.J. 298
Rush, Benjamin 1
Russia: methadone prohibition in 154, 188, 191, 264; naltrexone use in 191, 264
Ryan, S.A. 176, 186
Ryff, C.D. 109

Saha, T. 147
Saha, T.D. 68
Saint-Jacques, M. 223–224
Sakai, J.T. 180
Salas, J. 117
Saleh, A. 80
Salinas, I. 40
Sallis, H. 183
Salomonsen-Sautel, S. 180
Saloner, B. 270
Sannibale, C. 75
Santaella-Tenorio, J. 147
Santiago-Ramajo, S. 40
Sargeant, M.N. 90–91
Sarvet, A. 147, 176
Sarvet, A.L. 157
Satel, S. 34–35, 297
Saxon, A.J. 272
Schaeffer, C.M. 314, 316
Schaub, M.P. 188
Schein, A.Z. 227
schema healing: relapse prevention and 297, 301; therapy for 301–304
schema modes 303–304
schemas: changing 301; early maladaptive 69–70, 302–304; formation of 301
schema therapy: cognitive techniques in 304; dysfunctional schema modes and 303–304; early maladaptive schemas and 301–303; experiential techniques in 304; limited reparenting in 304; techniques of 304
Schema Therapy (Young et al.) 318
Schema Therapy Clinician's Guide, The (Farrell et al.) 318
Scherrer, J. 117
Schimmenti, A. 169

schizophrenia: genetic factors of 182–183; marijuana use and 61, 182–183; opioid use disorders (OUD) and 67

Schizophrenia PORT Psychosocial Treatment Recommendations and Summary Statements 63, 66

schizophrenia-SUD comorbid patients: alcohol use disorder (AUD) and 60; antipsychotic medications 61, 65–67; cognitive behavioral therapy (CBT) and 64–65; drug use disorder and 60; empathy and 62; integrated treatment and 62–64; medication noncompliance and 65–67; motivational interviewing (MI) and 64; motivation enhancement therapy and 64; pharmacological treatments 65–66; psychoeducation and 64, 67; psychosocial interventions 63; resources and services for 67; self-medication and 61; treatment compliance and 61; treatment outcomes of 64–65; Twelve Step programs and 65

Schneider, F.D. 117

Schoevers, R.A. 86

Schonbrun, Y.C. 109, 118

Schorr, A. 277

Schrag, R.D.A. 129

Schuckit, M.A. 269

Schulenberg, J. 176

Schultz, N.R. 290

Schuster, R. 90–91

Schwabe, L. 45

Schwartz, R.P. 270

Scott, B.G. 128

Scott, C.K. 47

Scott, K.M. 159

Screening, Brief Intervention, and Referral to Treatment (SBIRT) 161, 184–186

Secular Organizations for Sobriety/Save Our Selves (SOS) 229

Seedat, S. 159

Seeking Safety (SS) 76–77

selective serotonin reuptake inhibitors (SSRIs) 72

self-change 32–33

self-help groups: abstinence and 155; antisocial personality disorder-SUD patients and 92; behavioral addiction and 48, 172; borderline personality disorder (BPD) and 93; connection and 228; ex-inmates and 115; functions of 228; long-term recovery and 227–229; schizophrenia-SUD comorbid patients and 63; secular 229; social networks and 218, 220; Twelve Step programs and 212–213, 228–229

Self-Management and Recovery Training (SMART) 229–230, 245

self-medication theory: attention deficit/hyperactivity disorder-SUD comorbidity 81; autism spectrum disorder (ASD) and 82–83; chronic pain and 58; co-occurring disorders (COD) and 8–9, 54, 57; defining 4; identification and treatment of root problems in 35–36; intimate partner violence (IPV) and 123; major depressive disorder (MDD) and 68; personality disorder-SUD comorbidity 89; posttraumatic stress disorder-SUD comorbidity 74; psychiatric disorders and 57; quality of life and 5, 106; schizophrenia patients and 61

self-recovery 3, 33

sense of purpose in life: addiction recovery and 134–135; borderline personality disorder (BPD) and 135; depression and 135; facilitating 136–137; quality of life and 134

Serlachius, E. 82

serotonergic reuptake inhibitor (SRI) 79

Serretti, A. 39, 307–308

sertraline 79

Shallcross, A.J. 300

Sharron, K. 127

Shaw, B.F. 298

Shaw, I.A. 318

Shefner, R.T. 109, 118

Sher, K.J. 92

Shi, Y. 160

Shields, R.T. 30

Shmulewitz, D. 157

Shorey, R.C. 70, 303

Sigmon, S.C. 280

Sikkema, K.J. 130

Silver, E.J. 129

Silverman, K. 105

Simpson, T.L. 78

situation modification 234
situation selection 233–234
Sjoerds, Z. 43
skills training: behavioral 322; functional analysis and 292–294; relapse prevention and 297, 322; substance abuse and 76
Skodol, A. 89
Slade, T. 157
Slopen, N. 109
Smith, J.E. 294
Smith, L. 59
Smith, S.M. 68
Sobell, L.C. 33
Sobell, M.B. 33
sobriety sampling 322
social causation hypothesis 107
social detoxification 251–252
social drift hypothesis 107
social factors: addiction and 12–14, 146; treatment service delivery and 145
social identity model of recovery 119
social impairment 28
social learning theory 124
social network approach: addicted people and 217–218; connection and 217–218; emotional support in 218; family participation in 220–227; patient-clinician alliances in 218–220; recovery and 210, 217–220
social pain 112–113
social skills training 87
Song, X. 255
Sonne, S.C. 72
Sonnefeld, J. 276
Spear, S.E. 290
Spies, C.D. 260
spirituality: addiction and 47, 209–213, 215, 236; attachment to God in 211, 215–216; connection and 212; defining 211–212; emotion regulation in 232; loss of faith in 216; recovery and 215–216; religion and 211–212, 215–216; well-being and 211–212, 215–216
spiritual poverty 12, 106
Spitz, A.M. 128
spouse/family/social relationships: addiction treatment and 113–116;

criminal justice system involvement and 114–115; expressed emotion and 114; recovery and 115–116; women and 116
Srebnik, D. 325
Srivastava, A. 273
Stanton, A. 276
Stark, R. 295
Stein, D.J. 130
Stein, M.D. 127
Stephens, J.R. 250, 252
Stephens, M.A.C. 277
Stevens, S. 127
Stevenson, J.G. 295
Stewart, M.A. 29
Stewart, W.F. 7, 54
Stipelman, B.A. 90–91
Stippekohl, B. 295
Stitzer, M.L. 314, 316
Stoller, K.B. 270, 277
Strehlau, V. 74, 124, 131
Strength at Home Men's Program 125
stress-induced craving 46
stress reduction 110
structural violence 131
Stuart, G.L. 70, 303
subsidized housing: bans on drug convictions 193; macro factors and 193–194
Substance Abuse and Mental Health Services Administration (SAMHSA) 120–121, 133
Substance Abuse-Domestic Violence Behavioral Therapy (SADV) 125
substance addiction: as a brain disease 6; Public Health Model of 166; society's views on 168; subsidized housing and 193–194; withdrawal syndromes 247–248
substance use disorder (SUD): abstinence and 104; attention deficit/hyperactivity disorder comorbidity and 80–88; autism spectrum disorder comorbidity and 81–83, 87–88; as behavioral addiction 2; as a brain disease 7; chronic pain and 7; continuum of 170; co-occurring disorders (COD) and 53–57; cravings and 34, 46; diagnostic criteria for 34; distorted thinking patterns in 299; emotion dysregulation

and 232; family-based treatments for 225; gender convergence in 156–165; impaired control in 28; impulsivity and 43; integrated treatment and 62–64; levels of 31–32, 34; major depressive disorder comorbidity and 55–56, 68–73; mood disorder comorbidity and 68; personality disorder comorbidity and 88–93; pharmacological criteria in 28; pharmacological treatments and 247; posttraumatic stress disorder comorbidity and 73–80; psychiatric disorders and 8, 56–57; psychosocial interventions 63; quality of life and 104–105; risky use in 28; schizophrenia-as-secondary-to 61; schizophrenia comorbidity and 60–67; screening for 161; assessment of 28–29; social impairment in 28; social pain and 112; space/geographical factor 158; spectrum of 31–32; time/cohort factor 157–158; trauma and 120–122; treatment of 10–11; Twelve Step programs and 65; withdrawal syndromes 248–249; *see also* schizophrenia-SUD comorbid patients
SUD *see* substance use disorder (SUD)
Sugar, A. 325
suicide: addiction and 33; co-occurring disorders (COD) and 10; health insurance and poverty status **108**
Sumnall, H. 107
Sun, A.P. 62, 104, 110, 116, 132, 168
Sundquist, J. 30
Sundquist, K. 30
Surratt, H.L. 147
Suvak, M. K. 79–80
Swanson, J.M. 183
Sweitzer, M.M. 295
Swift, J.K. 309
Swift, W. 157
system-oriented trauma: causes of 133; re-traumatization and 121, 131–133; structural violence and 131

Taiwan: heroin use in 58; internet-related addiction in 166; methadone use in 192, 264, 270
Tamm, L. 68

Teesson, M. 75, 157
Telang, G. 36, 38, 40
telescoping 164–165
Temporary Assistance for the Needy Families (TANF) system 13, 194
Teresa, Mother, Saint 12
tetrahydrocannabinol (THC) 174, 178–180, 182
Thege, B.K. 170
therapeutic alliances 218–220
Thomas, C. 272
Thompson, G.R. 134, 137
Thornton, S. 324
Thurstone, C. 180
Tiday, J. 324
Timko, C. 289–290
tobacco smoking: antisocial personality disorder (ASPD) and 56; education and 109; gender and 158–159; health insurance and poverty status 107–108; interpersonal relationships and 113–114; material poverty and 11, 109
Tonks, Z. 157
Tønnesen, H. 260
Torchalla, I. 74, 124, 131
Torrington, M. 271
Tossmann, P. 188
Tracy, E.M. 116
trauma: addiction and 121; clinician 133; drug use disorder and 121; effects of 120; group level 121; individual level 120–121; interpersonal violence and 120–121; intimate partner violence (IPV) and 122–126; safety needs and 111, 120; substance abuse and 120–122; system-oriented 121, 131–133; treatment outcomes and 111; treatment strategies for 120–126; well-being and 111
Trauma Affect Regulation: Guide for Education and Therapy (TARGET) 76
trauma recovery 77–78
Trauma Recovery and Empowerment Model (TREM) 76
Treatment Improvement Protocol (TIP) 262
Trello-Rishel, K. 68
Treloar, H.R. 212

INDEX

371

Tremblay, J. 223–224
Trevisan, L. 79
trigger relapse 295–297
Triple-A Engine 167
Troughton, E. 29
Troy, A.S. 300
Trull, T.J. 92
Tull, M.T. 232
Tulp, Nicholaes 1
Tuten, L.M. 314, 316
Twelve Step programs: antisocial
    personality disorder-SUD clients and
    91–92; borderline personality disorder
    (BPD) and 93; connection and 228;
    criticism of 229; efficacy of 228; higher
    power approach and 212–215; hope
    and 245; posttraumatic stress disorder-
    SUD clients and 77; professional
    treatment and 229; purpose in life and
    136; recovery and xii; religious nature of
    229; substance use disorder (SUD) and
    65; themes of 213; *see also* Alcoholics
    Anonymous (AA)
twins research: addiction and 29–30;
    early-onset marijuana use 182; gambling
    disorder and 30; gender and 30; shared
    genetic factors in 29–30

unemployment: addiction and 105–107,
    109–110; adverse childhood experiences
    (ACE) and 126; schizophrenia-SUD
    comorbid patients 61
unequal gendered power relationships 123
US Department of Health and Human
    Services (HHS) 148
US Department of Housing and Urban
    Development (HUD) 193
US Food and Drug Administration (FDA)
    255
Utrecht Coping List 87

vanDellen, M.R. 114
Vanderloo, M. 124
Van Emmerik-van Oortmerssen, K. 86
Van Wijngaarden-Cremers, P.J.M. 83
Vaughn, M.G. 30
Vedel, E. 86
Vederhus, J.K. 289

Veltman, D.J. 168
Verdejo-Garcia, A. 40–41
Verhulst, B. 29
Veroff, J. 316–317
Verweij, K.J.H. 181
veterans: heroin addiction and 296;
    posttraumatic stress disorder and 74
video game addiction 82–83
Vigilant, L.G. 134
Vilar-Lopez, R. 40
vocational trauma 121
Volkow, N.D. 1, 4, 34, 36, 38, 40, 44, 56,
    59, 181, 183
Volpicelli, J. 79–80
Vythilingum, B. 130

Wade, R. 128
Walderhaug, E. 41, 104
Wall, M. 176
Wall, M.M. 175
Walton, L. 315
Walton, M.A. 185
Walton, M.T. 105, 109–110
Wang, G.J. 36, 38, 40
Warden, D. 68
Wasmuth, S. 136
Watkins, K. 105
Watt, M.H. 130
Weems, C.F. 128
Weishaar, M.E. 301, 318
Weiss, S.R.B. 181, 183
Wellness Recovery Action Plan (WRAP)
    93, 245
Weyers, P. 295
White, D.M. 59
Whitley, Brian 233
Wiklund, L. 211
Wilhelm, F.H. 300
Williams, A.E. 231
Williams, C.A. 109, 118
Williams, D.R. 109
Williams, K.S. 221
Williams, R.J. 170
Williamson, D.F. 128
Willis, R. 221
Wilson, M. 295
Winhusen, T. 68
Winkler, M.H. 295

INDEX

Wisdom, J.P. 221

withdrawal management: behavioral/
psychosocial therapy and 287, 289–325;
clinician facilitation of 288–290;
cravings and 46; defining 247–248;
family participation in 289–290;
inpatient/outpatient procedures for
250, 254; motivation and 289; patient
aftercare and 287, 289–291; patient
retention and 287; pharmacological
treatments and 252–253, 256–257,
272; relapse prevention and 253–254,
291–293; strategies for 288–289;
symptom assessment for 250–252

withdrawal syndromes: acamprosate and
257; assessment of 250–251; defining
247–248; fear of severe 248; individuals
likely to develop 249; marijuana use
178; medication for 252; naltrexone and
272; risk factors for 249

Witkiewitz, K. 70, 135

Wolf, O.T. 45

Wolff, J. 324

women: alcohol use and 156–157,
159–160, 163–164; childhood trauma
and 130; habilitation for 312; health
impact of substance use on 160;
influence of family on 164; influence
of menstrual cycle on 164; intimate
partner violence (IPV) and 122–124;
marijuana use and 156–157, 160,
175; positive reappraisal and 300;
psychiatric/psychological problems
162–163; recovery and 116; relapse
and 163–164; risk factors 161–162;
screening for 161; self-medication and
162; spouse/family/social relationships
and 116; stress and 124; telescoping

and 164–165; tobacco smoking and
158–159; treatment strategies for 161;
unequal gendered power relationships
123; *see also* gender

Women for Sobriety (WFS) 229, 245

Wood, D.S. 124

Wood, E. 180

Wood, H. 167

Woodin, E.M. 170

Woody, G. 280

World Health Organization (WHO) 12,
108, 158

Wright, J.P. 30

Wu, J.Y.-W. 89

Xie, H. 73

Xu, J. 324

Xuan, Z. 157

Yan, N. 117

Yang, M.J. 46

Yates, W.R. 29

Yen, C.F. 46

Yen, J.Y. 46

Young, A.S. 67

Young, J.E. 301, 318

Young, N.K. 13, 194

Yuan, X.J. 117

Yucel, M. 43

Yusko, D.A. 79–80

Zhang, H. 68

Zhao, M. 271

Zhou, Z.K. 117

Zimmerman, M. 185

Zinn, Jon Kabat 309

Zlotnick, C. 71, 109, 118

Zucker, R.A. 185